Lecture Notes in Computer Science 2989

Edited by G. Goos, J. Hartmanis, and J. van Leeuwen

Springer
Berlin
Heidelberg
New York
Hong Kong
London
Milan
Paris
Tokyo

Susanne Graf Laurent Mounier (Eds.)

Model Checking Software

11th International SPIN Workshop
Barcelona, Spain, April 1-3, 2004
Proceedings

 Springer

Series Editors

Gerhard Goos, Karlsruhe University, Germany
Juris Hartmanis, Cornell University, NY, USA
Jan van Leeuwen, Utrecht University, The Netherlands

Volume Editors

Susanne Graf
Laurent Mounier
VERIMAG
2, avenue de Vignate, 38610 Grenoble-Gières, France
E-mail: {Susanne.Graf, Laurent.Mounier}@imag.fr

Library of Congress Control Number: 2004102408

CR Subject Classification (1998): F.3, D.2.4, D.3.1, D.2

ISSN 0302-9743
ISBN 3-540-21314-7 Springer-Verlag Berlin Heidelberg New York

Springer-Verlag is a part of Springer Science+Business Media

springeronline.com

© Springer-Verlag Berlin Heidelberg 2004
Printed in Germany

Typesetting: Camera-ready by author, data conversion by PTP-Berlin, Protago-TeX-Production GmbH
Printed on acid-free paper   SPIN: 10994757   06/3142   5 4 3 2 1 0

Preface

Since 1995, when the SPIN workshop series was instigated, SPIN workshops have been held on an annual basis in Montréal (1995), New Brunswick (1996), Enschede (1997), Paris (1998), Trento (1999), Toulouse (1999), Stanford (2000), Toronto (2001), Grenoble (2002) and Portland (2003). All but the first SPIN workshop were organized as satellite events of larger conferences, in particular of CAV (1996), TACAS (1997), FORTE/PSTV (1998), FLOC (1999), the World Congress on Formal Methods (1999), FMOODS (2000), ICSE (2001, 2003) and ETAPS (2002). This year again, SPIN was held as a satellite event of ETAPS 2004. The co-location of SPIN workshops with conferences has proven to be very successful and has helped to disseminate SPIN model checking technology to wider audiences. Since 1999, the proceedings of the SPIN workshops have appeared in Springer-Verlag's Lecture Notes in Computer Science series.

The history of successful SPIN workshops is evidence for the maturing of model checking technology, not only in the hardware domain, but increasingly also in the software area. While in earlier years algorithms and tool development around the SPIN model checker were the focus of this workshop series, for several years now the scope has been widened to include more general approaches to software model checking techniques and tools as well as applications.

The SPIN workshop has become a forum for all practitioners and researchers interested in model checking based techniques for the validation and analysis of communication protocols and software systems. Techniques based on explicit representations of state spaces, as implemented for example in the SPIN model checker or other tools, or techniques based on combinations of explicit representations with symbolic representations, are the focus of this workshop. It has proven to be particularly suitable for analyzing concurrent asynchronous systems. The workshop topics include theoretical and algorithmic foundations and tools, model derivation from code and code derivation from models, techniques for dealing with large and infinite state spaces, timing and applications. The workshop aims to encourage interactions and exchanges of ideas with all related areas in software engineering.

Papers went through a rigorous reviewing process. Each submitted paper was reviewed by three program committee members. Of 48 submissions, 19 research papers and 3 tool presentations were selected. Papers for which one of the editors was a co-author were handled by a sub-committee chaired by Gerard Holzmann.

In addition to the refereed papers, four invited talks were given; of these three were ETAPS invited speakers: Antti Valmari (Tampere, Finland) on the Rubik's Cube and what it can tell us about data structures, information theory and randomization, Mary-Lou Soffa (Pittsburgh, USA) on the foundations of code optimization, and Robin Milner (Cambridge, UK) on the grand challenge of building a theory for global ubiquitous computing. Finally, the SPIN invited speaker Reinhard Wilhelm (Saarbrücken, Germany) gave a talk on the analysis of timing models by means of abstract interpretation.

This year we took up an initiative started in 2002 and solicited tutorials that provided opportunities to get detailed insights into some validation tools and the methodologies of their use. Out of 3 submissions, the program committee selected 2 tutorials.

- An "advanced SPIN tutorial" giving an overview of recent extensions of the SPIN model checker as well as some methodological advice for its use. It was mainly addressed to users who want to use SPIN as a modelling and validation environment.
- A tutorial on the IF validation environment providing an overview of the IF modelling language and the main functionalities of the validation toolbox. It was addressed to users who want to use IF as a validation environment by feeding it with models in the IF language, or in SDL or UML, but also to tool developers who would like to interface their tools with the IF environment.

Acknowledgements. The volume editors wish to thank all members of the program committee as well as the external reviewers for their tremendous effort that led to the selection of this year's program. We furthermore wish to thank the organizers of ETAPS 2004 for inviting us to hold SPIN 2004 as a satellite event and for their support and flexibility in accommodating the particular needs of the SPIN workshop. We wish to thank in particular Fernando Orejas and Jordi Cortadella. Finally, we wish to thank Springer-Verlag for providing us with the possibility to use a conference online service free of charge, and the METAFrame team, in particular Martin Karusseit, for their very valuable and reactive support.

January 2004   Susanne Graf
                                                                       Laurent Mounier

Organization

SPIN 2004 was the 11th instance of the SPIN workshop on Model Checking of Software. It was held in cooperation with ACM SIGPLAN as a satellite event of ETAPS 2004, the European Joint Conferences on Theory and Practice of Software, which was organized by the Technical University of Catalonia in Barcelona, Spain.

Advisory Committee

Gerard Holzmann
Amir Pnueli

Steering Committee

Thomas Ball
Susanne Graf
Stefan Leue

Moshe Vardi
Pierre Wolper (chair)

Program Committee

Chairs: Susanne Graf (VERIMAG, Grenoble)
Laurent Mounier (VERIMAG, Grenoble)

Bernard Boigelot (Liège, Belgium)
Dragan Bošnački (Eindhoven, Netherlands)
David Dill (Stanford, USA)
Javier Esparza (Stuttgart, Germany)
Patrice Godefroid (Bell Labs, USA)
Susanne Graf (Grenoble, France)
John Hatcliff (Kansas State, USA)

Gerard Holzmann (NASA/JPL, USA)
Stefan Leue (Freiburg, Germany)
Pedro Merino (Malaga, Spain)
Laurent Mounier (Grenoble, France)
Mooly Sagiv (Tel Aviv, Israel)
Scott Stoller (Stony Brook, USA)
Antti Valmari (Tampere, Finland)

Reviewers

Robby
Suzana Andova
Gerd Behrmann
Saddek Bensalem
Marius Bozga
Cas Cremers
Maria del Mar Gallardo
Manuel Diaz
Jürgen Dingel
Jean-Claude Fernandez
Jaco Geldenhuys
Keijo Heljanko

Radu Iosif
Natalia Ioustinova
Rajeev Joshi
Tommi Junttila
Antero Kangas
Timo Karvi
Barbara König
Yassine Lakhnech
Johan Lilius
Jesus Martinez
Richard Mayr
Iulian Ober

Shaham Ohad
Michael Périn
Ilya Shlyakhter
Stavros Tripakis
Jaco van de Pol
Kimmo Varpaaniemi
Wei Wei
Tim Willemse
Eran Yahav
Ping Yang
Greta Yorsh

Table of Contents

Abstraction and Symbolic Methods

Applications

Tutorials

Formal Analysis of Processor Timing Models

Reinhard Wilhelm*

Informatik
Universität des Saarlandes
Saarbrücken

Abstract. Hard real-time systems need methods to determine upper bounds for their execution times, usually called worst-case execution times. This talk gives an introduction into state-of-art Timing-Analysis methods. These use Abstract Interpretation to predict the system's behavior on the underlying processor's components and Integer Linear Programming to determine a worst-case path through the program. The abstract interpretation is based on an abstract processor model that is conservative with respect to the timing behavior of the concrete processor. Ongoing work is reported to analyze abstract processor models for properties that have a strong influence on the expected precision of timing prediction and also on the architecture of the timing-analysis tool. Some of the properties we are interested in can be model checked.

1 WCET Determination

Hard real-time systems need methods to determine upper bounds for their execution times, usually called worst-case execution times, (WCET). Based on these bounds, a schedulability analysis can check whether the underlying hardware is fast enough to execute the system's task such that they all finish before their deadlines. This problem is nontrivial because performance-enhancing architectural features such as caches, pipelines, and branch prediction introduce "local non-determinism" into the processor behavior; local inspection of the program can not determine what the contribution of an instruction to the program's overall execution time is. The execution history determines whether the instruction's memory accesses hit or miss the cache, whether the pipeline units needed by the instruction are occupied or not, and whether branch prediction is correct or not.

2 Tool Architecture

State-of-art Timing-Analysis methods split the task into (at least) two subtasks, the prediction of the task's behavior on the processor components such as caches and pipelines, formerly called "micro-architecture modeling" [HBW94], and the determination of a worst-case path. They use Abstract Interpretation to predict

---

* Work reported herein is supported by the Transregional Collaborative Research Center AVACS of the Deutsche Forschungsgemeinschaft.

S. Graf and L. Mounier (Eds.): SPIN 2004, LNCS 2989, pp. 1–4, 2004.

the system's behavior on the underlying processor's components and Integer Linear Programming to determine a worst-case path through the program [LMW99]. A typical tool architecture is the one of aiT, the tool developed and marketed by AbsInt Angewandte Informatik in Saarbrücken, cf. Fig. 1.

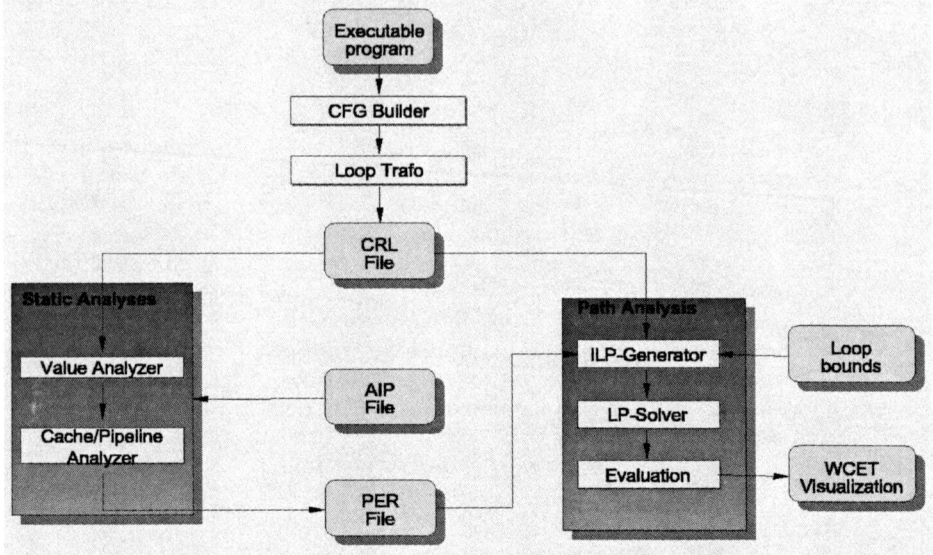

Fig. 1. Architecture of the aiT WCET analysis tool

The articles [FHL+01,LTH02] report on WCET tool developments for complex processor architectures, namely the Motorola ColdFire 5307 and the Motorola PowerPC 755. These were the first fully covered complex processors.

3   Timing Anomalies

The architecture of WCET–tools and the precision of the results of WCET analyses strongly depend on the architecture of the employed processor [HLTW03]. Out-of-order execution and control speculation introduce interferences between processor components, e.g. caches, pipelines, and branch prediction units. These interferences forbid modular designs of WCET tools, which would execute the subtasks of WCET analysis consecutively. Instead, complex integrated designs are needed resulting in high demand for space and analysis time.

In the following, several such properties of processor architectures are described. They cause the processor to display what is called *Timing Anomalies* [Lun02]. Timing anomalies are contra-intuitive influences of the (local) execution time of one instruction on the (global) execution time of the whole program. The interaction of several processor features can interact in such a way that a locally faster execution of an instruction can lead to a globally longer execution time of the whole program. This is only the first case of a timing anomaly. The general case is the following. Different assumption about the processor's execution state, e.g. the fact that the instruction is or is not in the instruction cache, will result in a difference ΔT_1 of the execution time of the instruction between these two cases. Either assumption may lead to a difference ΔT of the global execution time compared to the other one. We say that a timing anomaly occurs if either

$\Delta T_1 < 0$ i.e., the instruction executes faster, and
  $\Delta T < \Delta T_1$, the overall execution is accelerated by more than the acceleration of the instruction, or
  $\Delta T > 0$, the program runs longer than before.
$\Delta T_1 > 0$ i.e., the instruction takes longer to execute, and
  $\Delta T > \Delta T_1$ i.e., the overall execution is extended by more than the delay of the instruction, or
  $\Delta T < 0$ i.e., the overall execution is the program takes less time to execute than before.

The case $\Delta T_1 < 0 \wedge \Delta T > 0$ is a critical case for WCET analysis. It makes it impossible to use local worst case scenarios for WCET computation. This necessitates a conservative, i.e., upper approximation to the damages potentially caused by all cases or forces the analysis to follow all possible scenarios.

Unfortunately, as [LS99,Lun02] have observed, the worst case penalties imposed by a timing anomaly may not be bounded by an architecture-dependent, but program-independent constant, but may depend on the program size. This is the so-called *Domino Effect*. This domino effect was shown to exist for the Motorola PowerPC 755 in [Sch03].

4   Formal Analysis of Processor Timing Models

The abstract-interpretation-based timing analysis is based on abstract processor models that are conservative with respect to the timing behavior of the concrete processors. To prove this is a major endeavor to be undertaken in the Transregional Collaborative Research Center AVACS. Another line of research is the derivation of processor timing models from formal specifications in VHDL or Verilog.

We are currently applying formal analysis of timing models to check for relevant properties, e.g., use model checking to detect timing anomalies and domino effects or their absence, resp. Bounded model checking can be used to check for the existence of upper bounds on the damage done by one processor component onto the state of another one, e.g. the damage of a branch misprediction to the instruction cache by loading superfluous instructions. The bound can be computed from architectural parameters, such as the depth of the pipeline and the length of prefetch queues.

Acknowledgements. Thanks go to Stephan Thesing for clarifications about timing anomalies.

References

[FHL⁺01]   C. Ferdinand, R. Heckmann, M. Langenbach, F. Martin, M. Schmidt, H. Theiling, S. Thesing, and R. Wilhelm. WCET Determination for a Real-Life Processor. In T.A. Henzinger and C. Kirsch, editors, *Embedded Software*, volume 2211 of *Lecture Notes in Computer Science*, pages 469 – 485. Springer, 2001.

[HBW94]   Marion G. Harmon, T.P. Baker, and David B. Whalley. A Retargetable Technique for Predicting Execution Time of Code Segments. *Real-Time Systems*, 7:159–182, 1994.

[HLTW03]   Reinhold Heckmann, Marc Langenbach, Stephan Thesing, and Reinhard Wilhelm. The influence of processor architecture an the design and the results of WCET tools. *IEEE Proceedings on Real-Time Systems*, 91(7):1038–1054, July 2003.

[LMW99]   Yau-Tsun Steven Li, Sharad Malik, and Andrew Wolfe. Performance estimation of embedded software with instruction cache modeling. *Design Automation of Electronic Systems*, 4(3):257–279, 1999.

[LS99]   Thomas Lundqvist and Per Stenström. Timing anomalies in dynamically scheduled microprocessors. In *Proceedings of the 20th IEEE Real-Time Systems Symposium (RTSS'99)*, pages 12–21, December 1999.

[LTH02]   M. Langenbach, S. Thesing, and R. Heckmann. Pipeline Modelling for Timing Analysis. In *Static Analysis Symposium*, volume 2274 of *LNCS*, pages 294–309. Springer Verlag, 2002.

[Lun02]   Thomas Lundqvist. *A WCET Analysis Method for Pipelined Microprocessors with Cache Memories*. PhD thesis, Chalmers University of Technology, Göteborg, Sweden, 2002.

[Sch03]   Joern Schneider. *Combined Schedulability and WCET Analysis for Real-Time Operating Systems*. PhD thesis, Saarland University, 2003.

Typical Structural Properties of State Spaces

Radek Pelánek[*]

Department of Computer Science, Faculty of Informatics
Masaryk University Brno, Czech Republic
xpelanek@fi.muni.cz

Abstract. Explicit model checking algorithms explore the full state space of a system. We have gathered a large collection of state spaces and performed an extensive study of their structural properties. The results show that state spaces have several typical properties and that they differ significantly from both random graphs and regular graphs. We point out how to exploit these typical properties in practical model checking algorithms.

1 Introduction

Model checking is an automatic method for formal verification of systems. In this paper we focus on explicit model checking which is the state-of-the-art approach to verification of asynchronous models (particularly protocols). This approach explicitly builds the full *state space* of the model (also called Kripke structure, occurrence or reachability graph). The state space represents all (reachable) states of the system and transitions among them. The state space is used to check specifications expressed in a suitable temporal logic. The main obstacle of model checking is *state explosion* — the size of the state space grows exponentially with the size of the model description. Hence, model checking has to deal with extremely large graphs.

The classical model for large unstructured graphs is the *random graph* model of Erdős and Renyi [11]. In this model every pair of nodes is connected with an edge with a given probability p. Large graphs are studied in many diverse areas, such as social sciences (networks of acquaintances), biology (food webs, protein interaction networks), geography (river networks), and computer science (Internet traffic, world wide web). Recent extensive studies of these graphs revealed that they share many common structural properties and that these properties differ significantly from properties of random graphs. This observation led to the development of more accurate models for large graphs occurring in practice (e.g., 'small worlds' and 'scale-free networks' models) and to a better understanding of processes in these networks. For example, it improved the understanding of the spread of diseases and vulnerability of computer networks to attacks; see Barabasi [2] and Watts [32] for a high-level overview of this research and further references.

[*] Supported by GA ČR grant no. 201/03/0509

S. Graf and L. Mounier (Eds.): SPIN 2004, LNCS 2989, pp. 5–22, 2004.
© Springer-Verlag Berlin Heidelberg 2004

In model checking, we usually treat state spaces as arbitrary graphs. However, since state spaces are generated from short descriptions, it is clear that they have some special properties. This line of thought leads to the following questions:

1. What do state spaces have in common? What are their typical properties?
2. Can state spaces be modeled by random graphs or by some class of regular graphs in a satisfactory manner?
3. Can we exploit these typical properties to traverse or model check a state space more efficiently? Or at least to better analyze complexity of algorithms? Can some information about a state space be of any use to the user or to the developer of a model checker?
4. Is there any significant difference between toy academical models and real life case studies? Are state spaces similar to such an extent that it does not matter which models we choose for benchmarking our algorithms?

Methodology. The basic approach is the following: we measure many graph parameters of a large collection of state spaces and try to draw answers from the results. We restrict ourselves to asynchronous models, because these are typically investigated by explicit model checkers. We consider neither labels on edges nor atomic propositions in states and thus we focus only on structural properties of graphs. For generating state spaces we have used four well-known model checkers (SPIN [22], CADP [14], Murphi [10], μCR [16]L) and two experimental model checkers. In all, we have used 55 different models including many large case studies (see Appendix A). In this report we summarize our observations, point out possible applications, and try to outline some answers. The project's web page [1] contains more details about investigated state spaces and the way in which they were generated. Moreover, interested reader can find on the web page all state spaces in a simple textual format together with a detailed report for each of them, summary tables for each measured parameter, and more summary statistics and figures.

Related work. Many authors point out the importance of the study of models occurring in practice (e.g., [13]). But to the best of our knowledge, there has been no systematic work in this direction. In many articles one can find remarks and observation concerning typical values of individual parameters, e.g., diameter [5, 28], back level edges [31,3], degree, stack depth [20]. Some authors make implicit assumptions about the structure of state spaces [7,23] or claim that the usefulness of their approach is based on characteristics of state spaces without actually identifying these characteristics [30]. Groote and van Ham [17] try to visualize large state spaces with the goal of providing the user with better insight into a model.

Organization of the paper. Section 2 describes studied parameters, results of measurements, their analysis, and possible application. Section 3 compares different classes of state spaces. An impatient reader can jump directly to Section 4 where our observations are summarized and where we provide some answers. Finally, the last section outlines several new questions for future research.

2   Parameters of State Spaces

A *state space* is a relational structure which represents the behavior of a system
(program, protocol, chip, ...). It represents all possible states of the system and
transitions between them. Thus we can view a state space as a simple directed
graph[1] $G = (V, E, v_0)$ with a set of vertices V, a set of directed edges $E \subseteq V \times V$,
and a distinguished initial vertex v_0. Moreover, we suppose that all vertices are
reachable from the initial one. In the following we use *graph* when talking about
generic notions and *state space* when talking about notions which are specific to
state spaces of asynchronous models.

2.1   Degrees

Out-degree (*in-degree*) of a vertex is the number of edges leading from (to) this
vertex. *Average degree* is just $|E|/|V|$. The basic observation is that the average
degree is very small – typically around 3 (Fig. 1). Maximal in-(out-)degree is
often several times higher than the average degree but with respect to the size of
the state space it is small as well. Hence state spaces do not contain any 'hubs'.
In this respect state spaces are similar to random graphs, which have Poisson
distribution of degrees. On the other hand, scale free networks discussed in the
introduction are characterized by the power-law distribution of degrees and the
existence of hubs is a typical feature of such networks [2].

   The fact that state spaces are sparse is not surprising and was observed long
ago[2]. It can be quite easily explained: the degree corresponds to a 'branching
factor' of a state; the branching is due to parallel components of the model
and due to the inner nondeterminism of components; and both of these are
usually very small. In fact, it seems reasonable to claim that in practice $|E| \in
O(|V|)$. Nevertheless, the sparseness is usually not taken into account either
in the construction of model checking algorithms or in the analysis of their
complexity.

   In many cases the average degree is even smaller than two, since there are
many vertices with degree one. This observation can be used for saving some
memory during the state space traversal [4].

2.2   Strongly Connected Components

A *strongly connected component* (SCC) of G is a maximal set of states $C \subseteq V$
such that for each $u, v \in C$, the vertex v is reachable from u and vice versa. The
quotient graph of G is a graph (W, H) such that W is the set of the SCCs of G
and $(C_1, C_2) \in H$ if and only if $C_1 \neq C_2$ and there exist $r \in C_1, s \in C_2$ such that
$(r, s) \in E$. The *SCC quotient height* of the graph G is the length of the longest

---

[1] We consider state spaces as simple graphs, i.e., we do not consider self-loops and
    multiedges. Although these may be significant for model checking temporal logics,
    they are not that important for the structural properties we consider here.
[2] Holzman [20] gives an estimate 2 for average degree.

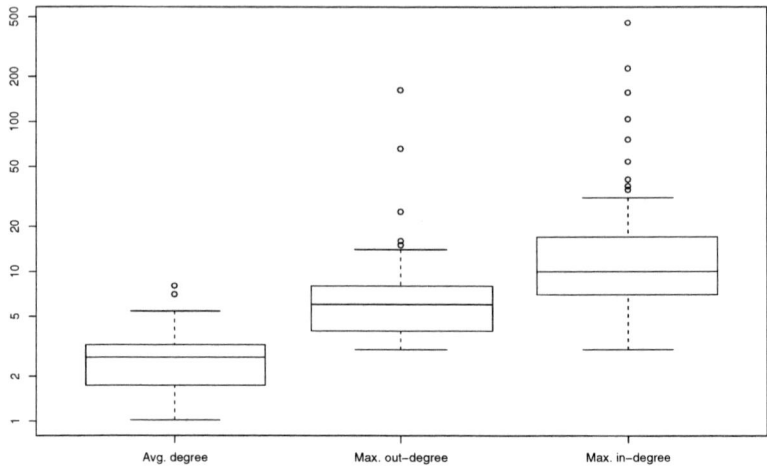

Fig. 1. Degree statistics. Values are displayed with the boxplot method. The upper and lower lines are maximum and minimum values, the middle line is a median, the other two are quartiles. Circles mark outliers. Note the logarithmic y-axis.

path in the quotient graph of G. A component is *trivial* if it contains only one vertex. Finally, a component is *terminal* if it has no successor in the quotient graph.

For state spaces, the height of the SCC quotient graph is small. In all but one case it is smaller than 200, in 70% of cases it is smaller than 50. The structure of quotient graph has one of the following types:

- there is only one SCC component (18% of cases),
- there are only trivial components (the graph is acyclic) (14% of cases),
- there is one large component which contains most states; the largest component is usually terminal and often it is even the only terminal.

The number of SCCs can be very high, but this is mainly due to trivial components. The conclusion is that most states lie either in the largest component or in some trivial component and that the largest component tends to be 'at the bottom' of the SCC quotient graph.

SCCs play an important role in many model checking algorithms and the above stated observation can be quite significant with respect to practical applicability of some approaches, for example:

- The runtime of symbolic SCC decomposition algorithms [12,25] depends very much on the structure of the SCC quotient graph. The thorough analysis [27] shows that the complexity of these algorithms depends on the SCC quotient height, the number of SCC, and the number of nontrivial SCC. We note that symbolic algorithms are usually used for synchronous models (whereas our

2   Parameters of State Spaces

A *state space* is a relational structure which represents the behavior of a system (program, protocol, chip, ...). It represents all possible states of the system and transitions between them. Thus we can view a state space as a simple directed graph[1] $G = (V, E, v_0)$ with a set of vertices V, a set of directed edges $E \subseteq V \times V$, and a distinguished initial vertex v_0. Moreover, we suppose that all vertices are reachable from the initial one. In the following we use *graph* when talking about generic notions and *state space* when talking about notions which are specific to state spaces of asynchronous models.

2.1   Degrees

Out-degree (*in-degree*) of a vertex is the number of edges leading from (to) this vertex. *Average degree* is just $|E|/|V|$. The basic observation is that the average degree is very small – typically around 3 (Fig. 1). Maximal in-(out-)degree is often several times higher than the average but with respect to the size of the state space it is small as well. Hence state spaces do not contain any 'hubs'. In this respect state spaces are similar to random graphs, which have Poisson distribution of degrees. On the other hand, scale free networks discussed in the introduction are characterized by the power-law distribution of degrees and the existence of hubs is a typical feature of such networks [2].

The fact that state spaces are sparse is not surprising and was observed long ago[2]. It can be quite easily explained: the degree corresponds to a 'branching factor' of a state; the branching is due to parallel components of the model and due to the inner nondeterminism of components; and both of these are usually very small. In fact, it seems reasonable to claim that in practice $|E| \in O(|V|)$. Nevertheless, the sparseness is usually not taken into account either in the construction of model checking algorithms or in the analysis of their complexity.

In many cases the average degree is even smaller than two, since there are many vertices with degree one. This observation can be used for saving some memory during the state space traversal [4].

2.2   Strongly Connected Components

A *strongly connected component* (SCC) of G is a maximal set of states $C \subseteq V$ such that for each $u, v \in C$, the vertex v is reachable from u and vice versa. The *quotient graph* of G is a graph (W, H) such that W is the set of the SCCs of G and $(C_1, C_2) \in H$ if and only if $C_1 \neq C_2$ and there exist $r \in C_1, s \in C_2$ such that $(r, s) \in E$. The *SCC quotient height* of the graph G is the length of the longest

---

[1] We consider state spaces as simple graphs, i.e., we do not consider self-loops and multiedges. Although these may be significant for model checking temporal logics, they are not that important for the structural properties we consider here.

[2] Holzman [20] gives an estimate 2 for average degree.

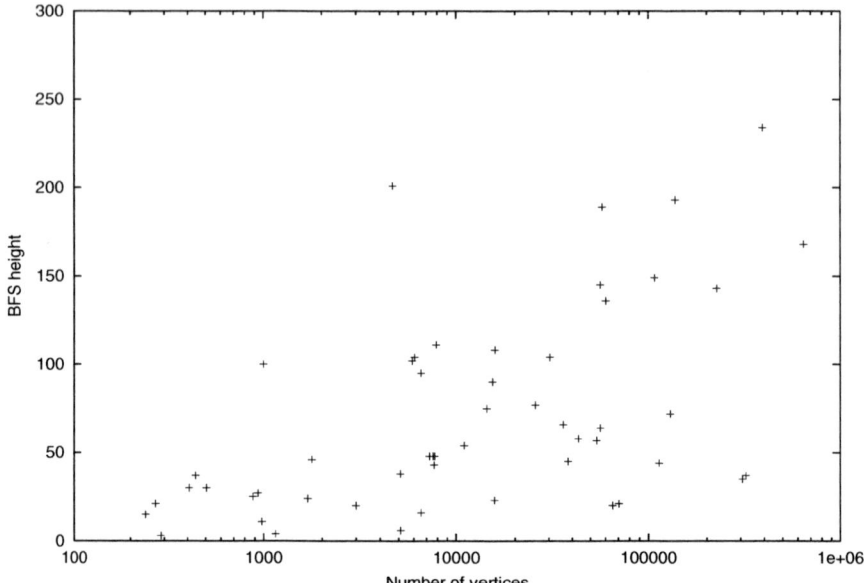

Fig. 2. The BFS height plotted against the size of the state space. Note the logarithmic x-axis. Three examples have height larger than 300.

- Tronci et al. [31,24] exploit locality of edges for state space caching. Their technique stores only recently visited states. The efficiency (and termination) of their algorithm rely on the fact that most edges are local and hence target states of edges are usually in the cache. In a similar way, one could exploit typical lengths of back level edges or try to estimate the maximal length of a back level edge and use this estimate as a key for removing states from the cache.
- The algorithm for distributed cycle detection by Barnat et al. [3] has complexity proportional to the number of back level edges.
- The typical shape of the BFS level graph can be exploited for a prediction of the size of a state space. Particularly, when a model checker runs out of memory it may be useful to see the BFS level graph — it can help the user to decide, whether it will be sufficient just to use a more powerful computer (or a distributed computation on several computers) or whether the model is hopelessly big and it is necessary to use some reduction and/or abstraction. This is easy to implement (and add to existing model checkers) and in our experience it can be very useful to the user.

Depth-First Search (DFS). Next we consider the depth-first search from the initial vertex. The behavior of DFS (but not the completeness) depends on the

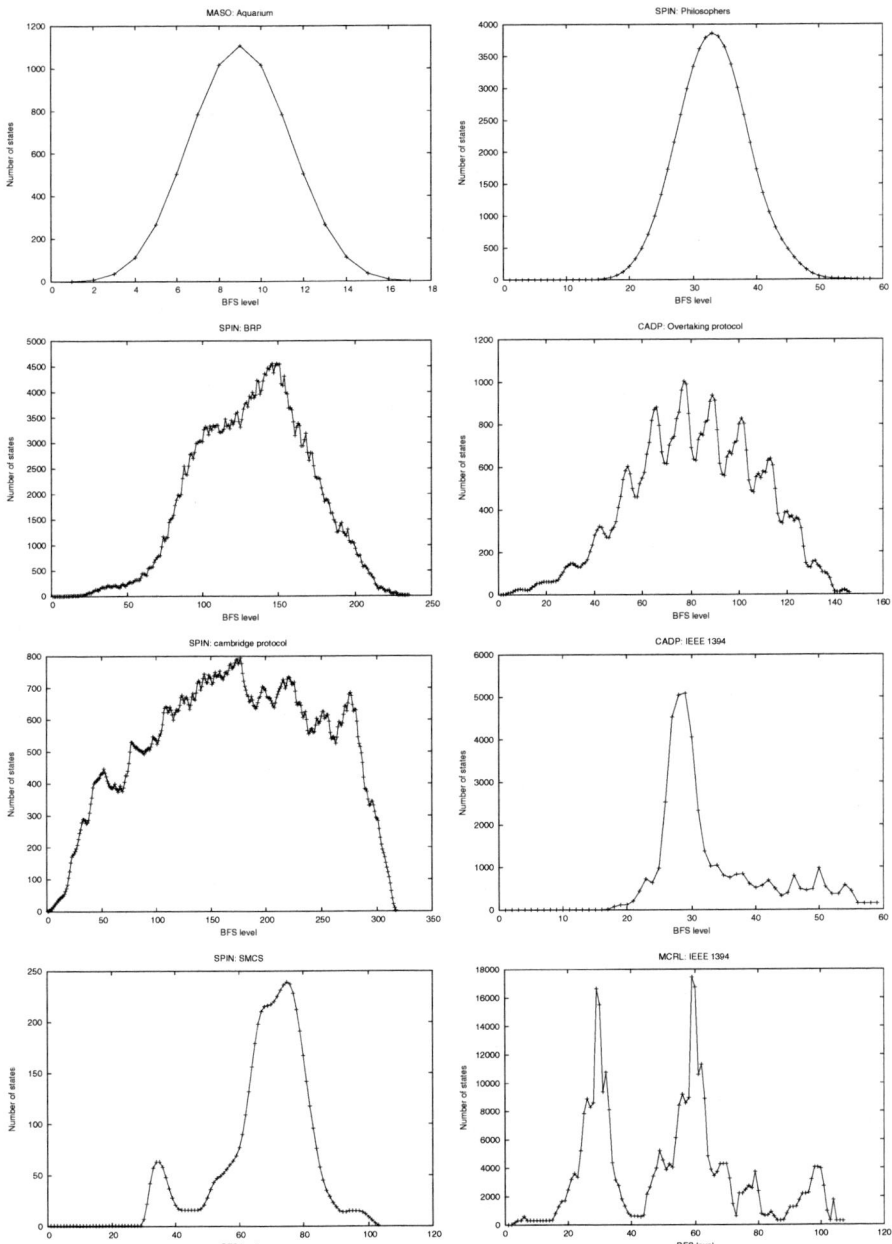

Fig. 3. BFS level graphs. For simple models the curve is really smooth and bell-like. For more complex models it can be a bit ragged. The last two graphs show that there are exceptions which have more 'peaks' (but these are rare exceptions).

order in which successors of each vertex are visited. Therefore we have considered several runs of DFS with different orderings of successors.

If we plot the size of the stack during DFS we get a *stack graph*. Fig. 4 shows several stack graphs (for more graphs see [1]). The interesting observation is that the shape of the graph does not depend much on the ordering of successors. The stack graph changes a bit of course, but the overall appearance remains the same. Moreover, each state space has its own typical graph. In contrast, all random graphs have rather the same, smooth stack graph.

When we count the length of cycles encountered during DFS we find out that there are several typical lengths of cycles which occur very often; after the observation of the typical lengths of back level edges this does not come as a great surprise.

These observations point out interesting structural properties of state spaces (and their differences from random graphs) but do not seem to have many direct applications. The only one is the stack cycling technique [21] which exploits the fact that the size of the stack does not change too quickly and stores part of the stack on the magnetic disc. Stack graphs could provide better insight into how to manage this process.

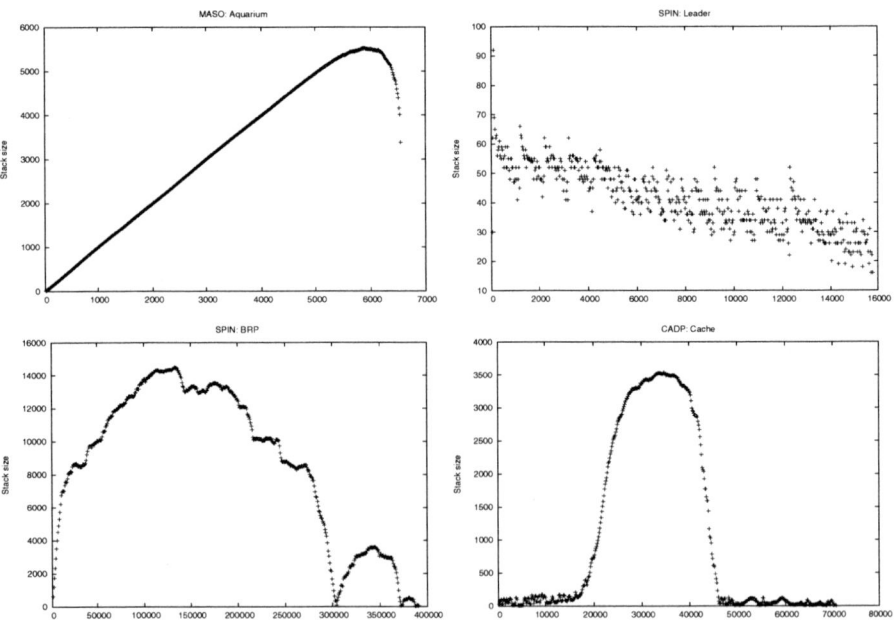

Fig. 4. Stack graphs. The first one is the stack graph of a very simple model. Stack graphs of random graphs are similar to this one. The other three stack graphs correspond to more complex models.

Queue and Stack Size. For implementations of the breadth- and depth-first search one uses queue and stack data structures. These data structures are in most model checkers treated differently from a set of already visited states. This set (usually implemented as a hash table) is considered to be the main memory consumer. Therefore its size is reduced using sophisticated techniques: states are compressed with lossless compression [19] or bit-state hashing [18], stored on magnetic disc [29], or only some states are stored [4,15]. On the other hand, the whole queue/stack is typically kept in memory without any compression. Our measurements show that the sizes of these structures are often as much as 10% of the size of a state space; see Fig. 5 for results and comparison of queue and stack sizes. Thus it may happen that the applicability of a model checker becomes limited by the size of a queue/stack data structure. Therefore it is important to pay attention to these structures when engineering a model checker. We note that this is already done is some model checkers – SPIN can store part of a stack on disc [21], UPPAAL stores all states in the hash table and maintains only references in a queue/stack [9].

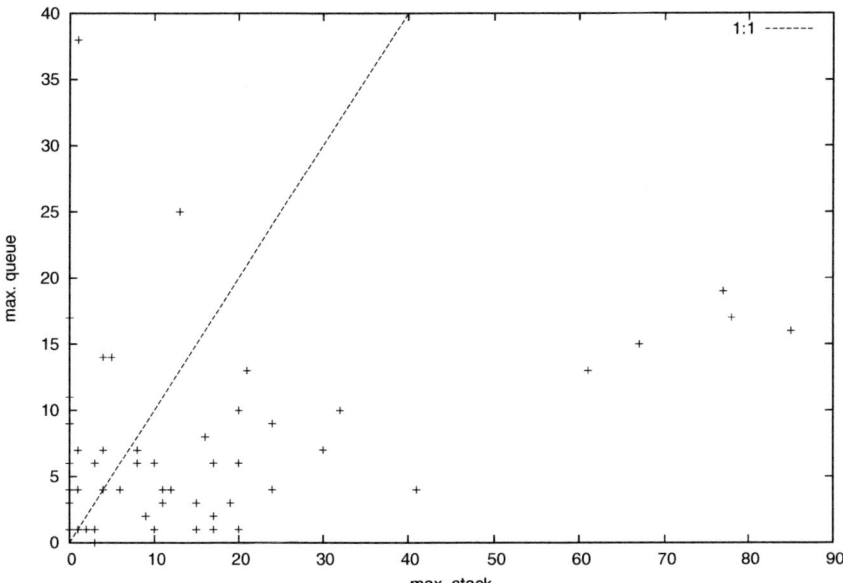

Fig. 5. A comparison of maximal queue and stack sizes expressed as percentages of the state space size. Note that the relative size of a queue is always smaller than 40% of the state space size whereas the relative size of a stack can go up to 90% of the state space size.

2.4   Distances

The *diameter* of a graph is the length of the largest shortest path between two vertices. The *girth* of a graph is the length of the shortest cycle. Since diameter and girth are expensive to compute[4] we can determine them only for small state spaces.

However, experiments for small graphs reveal that we can compute good estimates of these parameters with the use of the breadth- and depth-first search. The BFS height can be used to estimate the diameter. For most state spaces the diameter is smaller than 1.5 times the BFS height. Note that for general graphs the diameter can be much larger than the BFS height. DFS can be used to estimate the girth – it is not guaranteed to find the shortest cycle but our experience shows that in practice it does.

It is a 'common belief' (only partially supported in some papers) that the diameter is small. Our experiments confirm this belief. In most cases the diameter is smaller than 200, often much smaller[5]. The girth is in most cases smaller than 8.

The fact that the diameter is small is practically very important. Several algorithms (e.g., [28,12,25]) and the bounded model checking approach [5] directly exploit this fact. Moreover, the fact that the diameter is small suggests that many of the very long counterexamples (as produced by some model checkers) are caused by a poor search and not by the inherent complexity of the bug.

2.5   Local Structure

As the next step we try to analyze the local structure of state spaces. In order to do so, we employ some ideas from the analysis of social networks. A typical characteristics of social networks is *clustering* — two friends of one person are friends together with much higher probability than two randomly picked persons. Thus vertices have a tendency to form clusters. This is a significant feature which distinguishes social networks from random graphs.

In state spaces we can expect some form of clustering as well — two successors of a state are more probable to have some close common successor than two randomly picked states. Specifically, state spaces are well-known to contain many 'diamonds'. We try to formalize these ideas and provide some experimental base for them.

- A *diamond* rooted at v_1 is a quadruple (v_1, v_2, v_3, v_4) such that $\{(v_1, v_2), (v_1, v_3), (v_2, v_4), (v_3, v_4)\} \subseteq E$.
- The *k-neighborhood* of v is the set of vertices with distance from v smaller or equal to k.

---

[4] In the context of large state spaces even quadratic algorithms are expensive.

[5] Diameters of state spaces are very small with respect to their size and to the theoretical worst case. But compared to random graphs or 'small world' networks it is still rather large (the diameter of these graphs is proportional to the logarithm of their size).

– The *k-clustering coefficient* of a vertex v is the ratio of the number of edges to the number of vertices in the k-neighborhood (not counting the v itself). If the clustering coefficient is equal to 1, no vertex in the neighborhood has two incoming edges within this neighborhood. A higher coefficient implies that there are several paths to some vertices within the neighborhood. Random graphs have clustering coefficients close to 1.

The measurements confirm that the local structure of state spaces significantly differ from random graphs (see [1] for more details):

– The size of neighborhood grows much more slowly for state spaces than for random graphs (Fig. 6). This is because the clustering coefficient of state spaces increases (rather linearly) with average degree.
– Diamonds display an interesting dependence on the average degree. For a state space with average degree less than two there are a small number of diamonds. For state spaces with average degree larger than two there are a lot of them.
– Although girth is small for all state spaces, short cycles are abundant only in some graphs — only one third of state spaces have many short cycles.
– The local structure is similar in all parts of a state space.

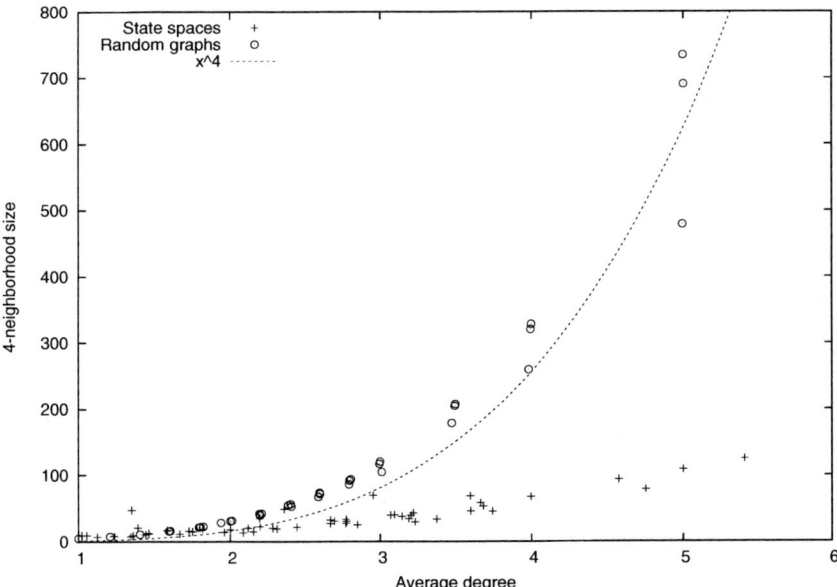

Fig. 6. Relationship between the size of 4-neighborhood and the average degree, and a comparison with random graphs.

The bottom line of these observations is that the local structure depends very much on the average degree. If the average degree is small then the local structure of the state space is tree-like (without diamonds and short cycles, with many states of degree one). Whereas with the high average degree it has many diamonds and high clustering coefficient. The rather surprising consequence is that the local structure depends on the model only in as much as the average degree does.

This is just the first step in understanding the local structure of state spaces, so it is difficult to give any specific applications. Some of these properties could be exploited by traversal methods which do not store all states [4]. Since the size of a neighborhood grows rather slowly, it might be feasible to do some kind of 'look-ahead' during the exploration of a state space (this is not the case for arbitrary graphs).

3   Comparisons

3.1   Specification Languages and Tools

Most parameters seem to be independent of the specification language used for modeling and the tool used for generating a state space. In fact, the same protocols modeled in different languages yield very similar state spaces. This can be seen as an encouraging result since it says that it is fair to do experimental work with just one model checker.

We have noticed some small differences. For example, Promela models often have sparser state spaces. But because we do not have the same set of examples modeled in all specification languages, we cannot fully support these observations at the moment.

3.2   Toy versus Industrial Examples

We have manually classified examples into three categories: toy (16), simple (25), and complex (14) (see Appendix A). The major criterion for the classification was the length of the model description. The comparison shows differences in most parameters. Here we only briefly summarize the main trends; more detailed figures can be found on the project's web page [1]:

- The average degree is smaller for state spaces of complex models. This is important because the average degree has a strong correlation with the local structure of the state space (see Section 2.5).
- The maximal size of the stack during DFS is significantly shorter for complex models (Fig. 7).
- The BFS height and the diameter are larger for state spaces of complex models.
- The number of back level edges is smaller for state spaces of complex models but they have longer back level edges.

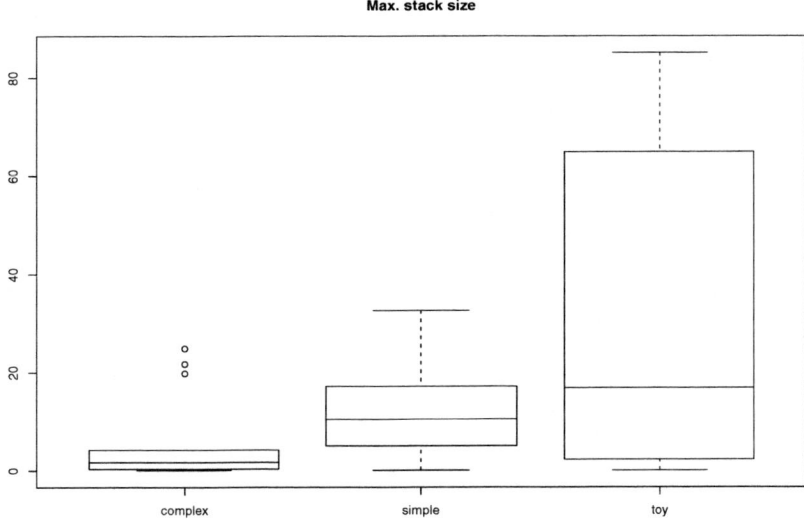

Fig. 7. The maximal stack size (given in percents of the state space size) during DFS. Results are displayed with the boxplot method (see Fig. 1 for explanation).

- Global structure is more regular for state spaces of toy models. This is demonstrated by BFS level graphs and stack graphs which are much smoother for state spaces of toy models.

These results stress the importance of having complex case studies in model checking benchmarks. Particularly experiments comparing explicit and symbolic methods are often done on toy examples. Since toy examples have more regular state spaces, they can be more easily represented symbolically.

3.3   Similar Models

We also compared the state spaces of similar models — parametrized models with different values, abstracted models, models with small syntactic change. Moreover, we have compared full state spaces and state spaces reduced with partial order reduction and strong bisimulation.

The resulting state spaces are very similar — most parameters are (nearly) the same or are appropriately scaled with respect to the change in the size of the state space. The exception is that a small syntactic change in a model can sometimes produce a big change of the state space. This occurs mainly in cases where the small change corresponds to some error (or correction) in the model. This suggests that listing state space's parameters could be useful for users during modeling — the significant change of parameters between two consecutive versions of a model can serve as a warning of a potential error (this can be even done automatically).

4   Conclusions: Answers

Although we have done our measurements on a restricted sample of state spaces, we believe that it is possible to draw general conclusions from the results. We used several different model checkers and models were written by several different users. Results of measurements are consistent — there are no significant exceptions from reported observations.

What are typical properties of state spaces?

State spaces are usually sparse, without hubs, with one large SCC, with small diameter and small SCC quotient height, with many diamond-like structures.

These properties can not be explained theoretically. It is not difficult to construct artificial models without these features. This means that observed properties of state spaces are not the result of the way state spaces are generated nor of some features of specification languages but rather of the way humans design/model systems.

Can state spaces be modeled by random graphs or by some class of regular graphs?

State spaces are neither random nor regular. They have some internal structure, but this structure is not strictly regular. This is illustrated by many of our observations:

– local clustering (including diamonds) is completely absent in random graphs
– stack graphs and BFS level graphs are quite structured and ragged, while for both regular and random graphs they are much smoother
– typical values of lengths of back level edges and cycles
– the diameter is larger than for random graphs but small compared to the size of the state space (definitely much smaller than for common regular graphs)

Can we exploit typical properties during model checking?

Typical properties can be useful in many different ways. Throughout the paper we provide several pointers to work that exploits typical values of parameters and we give some more suggestions about how to exploit them.

Values of parameters are not very useful for non-expert users who are not usually aware of what a state space is, but they may be useful for advanced users of the model checker. Properties of the underlying state space can provide users with feedback on their modeling and sanity checks — users can confront obtained parameters with their intuition (particularly useful for SCCs) and compare parameters of similar models, e.g., original and modified model.

The parameter values can be definitively useful for developers of tools, particularly for researchers developing new algorithms — they can help to explain the behavior of new algorithms.

Are there any differences between toy and complex models?

Although state spaces share some properties in common, some can significantly differ. Behavior of some algorithms can be very dependent on the structure of the state space. We can illustrate it on an experiment with random walk. We have performed series of very simple experiments with random walks on generated state spaces. For some graphs one can quickly cover 90% of the state space by random walk, whereas for other we were not able to get beyond 3%. So it is really important to test algorithms on a large number of models before one draws any conclusions.

Particularly, there is a significant difference between state spaces corresponding to complex and toy models. Moreover, we have pointed out that state spaces of similar models are very similar. We conclude that it is not adequate to perform experiments just on few instancies of some toy example[6] and we support calls for a robust set of benchmark examples for model checking [13].

5   Future Work: New Questions

- What more can we say about state spaces when we consider atomic propositions in states (respectively good/bad states)? What is the typical distribution of good/bad states? How many are there? Where are they? What are the properties of product graphs used in LTL model checking (product with Büchi automaton) and branching time logic model checking (game graphs)? Do they have the same properties or are there any significant differences?
- Can we estimate structural properties of a state space from static analysis of its model?
- In this work we consider mainly 'static' properties of state spaces. We have briefly mentioned only the breadth- and depth-first search, but there are many other possible searches and processes over state spaces (particularly random walk and partial searches). What is the 'dynamics' of state spaces?
- What is the effect of efficient modeling [26] on the resulting state space?
- State spaces are quite structured and regular. But how can we capture this regularity exactly? How can we employ this regularity during model checking? Can the understanding of the local structure help us to devise symbolic methods for asynchronous models?

Acknowledgment. I thank my supervisor, Ivana Černá, for many valuable discussions and suggestions, and for comments on previous drafts of this paper. Pavel Krčál, Tomáš Hanžl, and other members of the ParaDiSe laboratory have provided useful feedback. Finally, I thank anonymous reviewer for detailed comments.

---

[6] Thou shalt not do experiments (only) on Philosophers.

References

1. http://www.fi.muni.cz/~xpelanek/state_spaces.
2. A.L. Barabasi. *Linked: How Everything Is Connected to Everything Else and What It Means*. Plume, 2003.
3. J. Barnat, L. Brim, and J. Chaloupka. Parallel breadth-first search LTL model-checking. In *Proc. Automated Software Engineering (ASE 2003)*, pages 106–115. IEEE Computer Society, 2003.
4. G. Behrmann, K.G. Larsen, and R. Pelánek. To store or not to store. In *Proc. Computer Aided Verification (CAV 2003)*, volume 2725 of *LNCS*, pages 433–445, 2003.
5. A. Biere, A. Cimatti, E. Clarke, and Y. Zhu. Symbolic model checking without BDDs. In *Proc. Tools and Algorithms for the Construction and Analysis of Systems (TACAS 1999)*, volume 1579 of *LNCS*, pages 193–207, 1999.
6. I. Černá and R. Pelánek. Distributed explicit fair cycle detection. In *Proc. SPIN workshop*, volume 2648 of *LNCS*, pages 49–73, 2003.
7. A. Cheng, S. Christensen, and K. H. Mortensen. Model checking coloured petri nets exploiting strongly connected components. In *Proc. International Workshop on Discrete Event Systems*, pages 169–177, 1996.
8. S. Christensen, L.M. Kristensen, and T. Mailund. A Sweep-Line Method for State Space Exploration. In *Proc. Tools and Algorithms for Construction and Analysis of Systems (TACAS 2001)*, volume 2031 of *LNCS*, pages 450–464, 2001.
9. A. David, G. Behrmann, K. G. Larsen, and W. Yi. Unification & sharing in timed automata verification. In *Proc. SPIN Workshop*, volume 2648 of *LNCS*, pages 225–229, 2003.
10. D. L. Dill, A. J. Drexler, A. J. Hu, and C. Han Yang. Protocol verification as a hardware design aid. In *Proc. Computer Design: VLSI in Computers and Processors*, pages 522–525. IEEE Computer Society, 1992.
11. P. Erdős and A. Renyi. On random graphs. *Publ. Math.*, 6:290–297, 1959.
12. K. Fisler, R. Fraer, G. Kamhi Y. Vardi, and Z. Yang. Is there a best symbolic cycle-detection algorithm? In *Proc. Tools and Algorithms for Construction and Analysis of Systems (TACAS 2001)*, volume 2031 of *LNCS*, pages 420–434, 2001.
13. M. B. Dwyer G. S. Avrunin, J. C. Corbett. Benchmarking finite-state verifiers. *International Journal on Software Tools for Technology Transfer (STTT)*, 2(4):317–320, 2000.
14. H. Garavel, F. Lang, and R. Mateescu. An overview of CADP 2001. *European Association for Software Science and Technology (EASST) Newsletter*, 4:13–24, August 2002.
15. P. Godefroid, G.J. Holzmann, and D. Pirottin. State space caching revisited. *Formal Methods in System Design*, 7(3):227–241, 1995.
16. J.F. Groote and A. Ponse. The syntax and semantics of μCRL. In *Algebra of Communicating Processes '94*, Workshops in Computing Series, pages 26–62, 1995.
17. J.F. Groote and F. van Ham. Large state space visualization. In *Proc. of Tools and Algorithms for Construction and Analysis of Systems (TACAS 2003)*, volume 2619 of *LNCS*, pages 585–590, 2003.
18. G. J. Holzmann. An analysis of bitstate hashing. In *Proc. Protocol Specification, Testing, and Verification, INWG/IFIP*, pages 301–314, 1995.
19. G. J. Holzmann. State compression in SPIN: Recursive indexing and compression training runs. In *Proc. SPIN Workshop*. Twente Univ., 1997.

20. G.J. Holzmann. Algorithms for automated protocol verification. *AT&T Technical Journal*, 69(2):32–44, 1990.

21. G.J. Holzmann. The engineering of a model checker: the gnu i-protocol case study revisited. In *Proc. SPIN Workshop*, volume 1680 of *LNCS*, pages 232–244, 1999.

22. G.J. Holzmann. *The Spin Model Checker, Primer and Reference Manual*. Addison-Wesley, 2003.

23. A. L. Lafuente. Simplified distributed LTL model checking by localizing cycles. Technical Report 176, Institut für Informatik, Universität Freiburg, July 2002.

24. G. D. Penna, B. Intrigila, E. Tronci, and M. V. Zilli. Exploiting transition locality in the disk based Murphi verifier. In *Proc. Formal Methods in Computer-Aided Design (FMCAD 2002)*, volume 2517 of *LNCS*, pages 202–219, 2002.

25. K. Ravi, R. Bloem, and F. Somenzi. A comparative study of symbolic algorithms for the computation of fair cycles. In *Proc. Formal Methods in Computer-Aided Design (FMCAD 2000)*, volume 1954 of *LNCS*, pages 143–160, 2000.

26. Theo C. Ruys. Low-fat recipes for SPIN. In *Proc. SPIN Workshop*, volume 1885 of *LNCS*, pages 287–321, 2000.

27. F. Somenzi, K. Ravi, and R. Bloem. Analysis of symbolic SCC hull algorithms. In *Proc. Formal Methods in Computer-Aided Design (FMCAD 2002)*, volume 2517 of *LNCS*, pages 88–105, 2002.

28. U. Stern. *Algorithmic Techniques in Verification by Explicit State Enumeration*. PhD thesis, Technical University of Munich, 1997.

29. U. Stern and D. L. Dill. Using magnatic disk instead of main memory in the Murphi verifier. In *Proc. Computer Aided Verification (CAV 1998)*, volume 1427 of *LNCS*, pages 172–183, 1998.

30. E. Tronci, G. D. Penna, B. Intrigila, and M. Venturini. A probabilistic approach to automatic verification of concurrent systems. In *Proc. Asia-Pacific Software Engineering Conference (APSEC 2001)*, pages 317–324. IEEE Computer Society, 2001.

31. E. Tronci, G. D. Penna, B. Intrigila, and M. V. Zilli. Exploiting transition locality in automatic verification. In *Proc. Correct Hardware Design and Verification Methods (CHARME 2001)*, volume 2144, pages 259–274, 2001.

32. D. J. Watts. *Six Degrees: The Science of a Connected Age*. W.W. Norton & Company, 2003.

A   Models

Tool	Model	Type	Size
Murphi	Peterson's mutual exclusion algorithm	toy	882
Murphi	Parallel sorting	toy	3,000
Murphi	Hardware arbiter	simple	1,778
Murphi	Distributed quering lock	simple	7,597
Murphi	Needham-Schroeder protocol	complex	980
Murphi	Dash protocol	complex	1,694
Murphi	Cache coherence protocol	complex	15,703
Murphi	Scalable coherent interface (SCI)	complex	38,034

Tool	Model	Type	Size
SPIN	Peterson protocol for 3 processes	toy	30,432
SPIN	Dining philosophers	toy	54,049
SPIN	Concurrent sorting	toy	107,728
SPIN	Alternating bit protocol	simple	442
SPIN	Readers, writers	simple	936
SPIN	Token ring	simple	7,744
SPIN	Snooping cache algorithm	simple	14,361
SPIN	Leader election in unidirectional ring	simple	15,791
SPIN	Go-back-N sliding window protocol	simple	35,861
SPIN	Cambridge ring protocol	simple	162,530
SPIN	Model of cell-phone handoff strategy	simple	225,670
SPIN	Bounded retransmition protocol	simple	391,312
SPIN	ITU-T multipoint communication service	complex	5,904
SPIN	Flight guidance system	complex	57,786
SPIN	Flow control layer validation	complex	137,897
SPIN	Needham-Schroeder public key protocol	complex	307,218
CADP	Alternating bit	simple	270
CADP	HAVi leader election protocol	simple	5,107
CADP	INRES protocol	simple	7,887
CADP	Invoicing case study	simple	16,110
CADP	Car overtaking protocol	simple	56,482
CADP	Philips' bounded retransmission protocol	simple	60,381
CADP	Directory-based cache coherency protocol	simple	70,643
CADP	Reliable multicast protocol	simple	113,590
CADP	Cluster file system	complex	11,031
CADP	CO4 protocol for distributed knowledge bases	complex	25,496
CADP	IEEE 1394 high performance serial bus	complex	43,172
μCRL	Chatbox	toy	65,536
μCRL	Onebit sliding window protocol	simple	319,732
μCRL	Modular hef system	complex	15,349
μCRL	Link layer protocol of the IEEE-1394	complex	371,804
μCRL	Distributed lift system	complex	129,849
Divine	Cabbage, goat, wolf puzzle	toy	52
Divine	Dining philosophers	toy	728
Divine	MSMIE protocol	simple	1,241
Divine	Bounded retransmition protocol	simple	6,093
Divine	Alternating bit protocol	simple	11,268
MASO	Aquarium example	toy	6,561
MASO	Token ring	toy	7680
MASO	Alternating bit protocol	toy	11,268
MASO	Adding puzzle	toy	56,561
MASO	Elevator	simple	643,298

State Caching Reconsidered

Jaco Geldenhuys

Tampere University of Technology, Institute of Software Systems
PO Box 553, FIN-33101 Tampere, FINLAND
jaco@cs.tut.fi

Abstract. *State caching* makes the full exploration of large state spaces possible by storing only a subset of the reachable states. While memory requirements are limited, the time consumption can increase dramatically if the subset is too small. It is often claimed that state caching is effective when the cache is larger than between 33% and 50% of the total state space, and that random replacement of cached states is the best strategy. Both these ideas are re-investigated in this paper. In addition, the paper introduces a new technique, *stratified caching*, that reduces time consumption by placing an upper bound on the extra work caused by state caching. This, and a variety of other strategies are evaluated for random graphs and graphs based on actual verification models. Measurements made with SPIN are presented.

1   Introduction

Model checking by explicit state enumeration has become increasingly successful in the last decade, but suffers from the well-known state space explosion problem. Techniques for palliating the problem abound, but once the size of a model crosses a certain line, the only hope is a partial search of the state space. While such probabilistic approaches are valuable in detecting violations of the specification, they cannot guarantee correctness; when possible, a full exploration of the state space is, of course, preferable.

This paper focuses on *state caching*, one of the earliest techniques to deal with state space explosion. During state space exploration the reached states are stored in a hash table or similar data structure. When a previously visited state is reached again, it is found among the stored states and does not have to be re-explored. When a new state is generated and the state store is full (i.e., available memory has been exhausted), an already stored state is selected and discarded to make room for the new state. By replacing an old state, the model checker commits itself to re-investigate the state, should it be reached again. This may entail re-doing previous work, but full exploration of the state space is guaranteed.

While this approach makes effective use of the available memory, the running time may increase dramatically if too few states are cached. The received wisdom is that state caching is effective when the cache is larger than somewhere between 33% and 50% of the total state space, and that random replacement of states

S. Graf and L. Mounier (Eds.): SPIN 2004, LNCS 2989, pp. 23–38, 2004.

is the best strategy. These ideas are re-investigated and found to be somewhat misleading.

We propose a new replacement strategy called *stratified caching*. Broadly speaking, it places an upper limit on the amount of redundant work that is performed when an already visited but replaced state is reached again. It does this by only replacing states at predetermined depths, or *strata*, hence the name.

Section 2 examines how state caching has been presented in the literature, and in Section 3 stratified caching is introduced and discussed. Section 4 evaluates a range of caching strategies for both random and actual state graphs, some initial results for a single model are reported in Section 5, and, finally, conclusions are presented in Section 6.

2   State Space Exploration and State Caching

During state space exploration the reached states are stored in a table. When a previously visited state is reached again, it is found in the table and does not have to be re-explored. When a new state is generated and the table is full (i.e., the available memory has been exhausted), there are three possibilities:

  A. Abandon the search, explaining that the memory has been exhausted.
  B. Discard the new state and pretend that it has been seen before.
  C. Select an old state and replace it with the new state.

It is not immediately clear why possibility A would ever be preferred over B or C. Of course, it is important to notify the user that the memory has been exhausted: she may wish to interrupt the exploration and investigate alternatives. It may be that the model is faulty in some way and that the memory exhaustion is a symptom of this. Or the user may wish to investigate a simplified model, alternative options for state exploration or other reduction strategies. But it seems sensible to always continue the search with either possibility B or C. However, the implementation of possibility B or C may require memory and time overheads which the user wishes to avoid in the "default" operating mode of the state space exploration tool. Memory considerations are usually not critical since, as we shall see, state caching works well even if the cache is slightly smaller than the state space. In other words, the memory overhead may not make any real difference to the user. Time overhead is another issue and it is difficult to say, in general, whether it is wise to use or not use state caching as a default.

Possibility B results in a partial exploration of the state space, and issues such as omission probability and coverage come into play. In this case, the search may yield false positives, claiming that the model satisfies the correctness specification when, in fact, it does not, while all violations of the correctness specification are valid. As indicated in the introduction, this paper looks only at full exploration.

Possibility C is known as *state caching*, the focus of this paper. By replacing the old state, the model checker commits itself to reinvestigate the old state should it be reached again. Although this may redo work that has been done before, it does not lead to incorrect results.

State caching works well when the cache is slightly smaller than the state space. If relatively few states are replaced, the probability of revisiting a replaced state is low and even if it happens, the state's successors will probably be found in the cache. As the cache grows smaller and smaller compared to the state space, the re-exploration of states grows more and more frequent, and when the cache is very small, the problem of redundant work becomes severe. Under these conditions, the probability of revisiting a replaced state, and having to revisit its successors and their successors is high. Furthermore, each state that is revisited is re-inserted in the cache (since the depth-first algorithm cannot tell that it is not a new state) and displaces another state in the cache, in this way making matters even worse.

Depth-first search is guaranteed to terminate when state caching is used as long as states on the depth-first search path are never replaced, and the cache is large enough. Because states on the depth-first search path cannot be replaced, it is possible that too small a cache can eventually "fill up" with such states, in which case the search cannot proceed and must terminate early. (For general graphs, state caching does not work at all for breadth-first search, and offers a limited improvement in performance for mixed depth- and breadth-first search strategies; in the rest of the paper only depth-first search is considered.)

2.1   State Caching in the Literature

The first discussion of state caching for model checking is by Holzmann [10]. As far as we are aware, there have been three sets of papers that report significant results about state caching.

• In [10] — which is an overview of a number of verification techniques and not an in-depth discussion of state caching — the author investigates state caching for a single model of 150000 states. States are replaced using "simple blind round robin selection", but it is not clear what data structure is used to store the states and whether all states are considered equally in the evaluation of this criterion. The conclusion of the paper is that a cache of roughly half the size of the state space can still provide acceptable performance.

In a later paper [11] (published after but written before [10]) Holzmann investigates five different replacement strategies as implemented in the *trace* tool, a forerunner of SPIN [12]. The strategies are based on replacing

H1. most frequently visited states;
H2. least frequently visited states;
H3. states in the currently largest class of states, where the class of a state is defined by the number of times it has been visited;
H4. oldest states (i.e., those states that have been in the cache longest); and
H5. states in the bottom half of the current search tree.

As before [10], no details about how states are stored, are given. This is significant, because the data structure affects the behaviour of the state cache with respect to redundant work, memory and time consumption. The strategies are also not clearly defined: there is no indication of how to choose between possible candidate states in strategies H1 and H2, and the "bottom half" in strategy H5 can be interpreted in a number of different ways.

The strategies are investigated "for a range of medium sized protocols". Two examples are presented, one with 4523 and the other with 8139 unique states. The paper concludes that strategy H4 is consistently the fastest (resulting in a tolerable increase in running time) even though in one of the examples it performs the most unnecessary work by far (59% "double work" compared to a maximum of 0.5% by the other strategies). No conclusions about the minimum size of the state cache are reached. Confusingly, many future references refer to H4 as "random replacement", even though it is clearly not presented as such in the paper. Also, H5 is sometimes described as replacing the state corresponding to the smallest subtree of the depth-first tree; this may be its intention, but it is not how the strategy is defined in the paper.

• Jard and Jéron investigate state caching in [13] and in [14,15]. Like the earlier work [10,11], these papers do not focus on state caching *per se*. In the last two works, the authors generate random graphs that are explored using depth-first search and, based on the earlier findings [11], a state cache with random replacement. They report that, in a typical case, a cache using 40% of the normal memory yields 70% more visited states and a 50% increase in running time. In the best case, the cache size is reduced to 10% of the state space with only a 1% increase in the number of visited states.

• The effect of partial-order methods [8,18,21] on state caching is addressed by Godefroid, Holzmann, and Pirottin in [7]. *Sleep sets* [6] is a partial-order method that eliminates most of the interleaving of independent transitions without reducing the number of states. (The combination of sleep sets and *persistent sets* [8], which also reduces the number of states, is further investigated by Godefroid [9].) In [6] state caching (without sleep sets) is first investigated for four models of real-world protocols using the SPIN verifier [12]. The models have a transition/state ratio of roughly 3, and the authors report that the cache can be reduced to 33% to 50% the size of the state space. These findings confirm the general results of [10,11].

The details of the state caching can be determined fully because the authors have made their software publically available. States are stored in an open hash table with pointers to singly linked lists of states with the same hash value. A state is inserted by appending it to the linked list pointed to by its hash slot. After each insertion, a check is made to see if the state store is full. If so, an old state is selected and discarded to make room for the next insertion. Although the paper claims to use a random replacement strategy, it is clear from the code that this is not entirely accurate. The linked lists are scanned cyclically and within each list the state that has been in the cache longest, and therefore occurs towards the front of the list, is always chosen first.

With sleep sets the performance of state caching improves dramatically. The transition/state ratio of one model decreases from 2.88 to 1.45 and a cache of about 25% the size of the state space suffices. For the other three models, the use of sleeps sets reduces the ratio from 2.80, 3.54, and 2.58 to 1.12, 1.04, and 1.04, respectively. For these, the cache performs spectacularly well: a cache size of only 0.2% to 3% the size of the state space suffices for a complete exploration of the models. Unfortunately, the running time increases by a factor of between 2 and 4, but it is not clear whether this is caused by the implementation of the sleep sets or the state caching.

2.2   Other Work Related to State Caching

The performance of state caching using open addressing — also known as closed hashing — has also been investigated [5,19], but, due to space constraints, this approach is not considered here. Other techniques that may improve the effectiveness of state caching have been suggested, sometimes in more general contexts. This includes the identification of states to replace preferentially [7, 10], heuristic state space exploration [4], probabilistic caching of states [3], and precomputation to enhance replacement strategies [17].

3   Stratified Caching

When a state cache contains only a few replaced states, the probability of revisiting a deleted state is small, the probability that the state has a deleted child is smaller, the probability that the child also has a deleted child is smaller still, and so on. As the number of replacements grows, these probabilities increase to the point where practically every deleted state has at least one deleted child, and most states have several. Revisiting a deleted state in this situation leads to a considerable amount of redundant work; not only do large subtrees require re-exploration, but each revisited state is also re-inserted in the cache, pushing out yet another state, and causing a cascade of revisits.

Stratified caching limits the redundant work by placing an upper bound on how much deeper than usual each branch of the depth-first tree needs to be explored, hereafter referred to as the *extra depth*. It does this by only replacing states at specified levels of the depth-first search tree. All states at a certain level form a "stratum" of states.

It is generally not possible to know how deep the depth-first search will go and how many strata there will be, so strata are classified as "available" or "unavailable" for replacement based on their level *modulo a certain number* m. When a stratified caching strategy specifies that all strata of level k modulo m are available for replacement, this means that the states at levels $k, k+m, k+2m, \ldots$ may be replaced while the states of other strata must remain in the cache. Figure 1 shows available strata boxed in gray for the $k = 1$, $m = 3$ case.

Assuming that the depth-first tree is deep enough, that the states of the state space are uniformly distributed over the different levels modulo m, and that the probability of a revisit is uniformly distributed over the states, the expected extra depth is at most $1/m$ and the maximum extra depth is 1. As the search progresses, an available state can be replaced by either another available state,

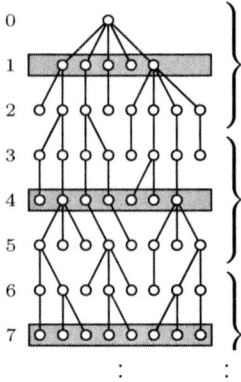

Fig. 1. Stratified caching for the $k = 1$, $m = 3$ case

in which case the expected extra depth remains constant, or by an unavailable state, in which case the expected extra depth decreases slightly. Unfortunately, because at most $1/m$ of the states are available for replacement, the cache is quickly exhausted (i.e., filled only with unreplaceable states) and the search must be aborted. Smaller values of m increase the number of available strata and therefore the fraction of replaceable states, but the minimum value for m is 2, meaning that at most $1/2$ of states can be available for replacement in this setting. Another way to increase the number of replaceable states is to increase the number of available strata within each modulo group. For example, if strata 2 and 3 modulo 5 are available for replacement, the expected extra depth is at most $3/5$ and the maximum extra depth is 2.

In this paper, the following approach is taken: Initially, $k = 1$ and $m = 2$. Once the available states are exhausted, all the states in the odd (available) strata are states currently on the depth-first search stack. (If a state from an odd stratum were not on the stack, it would have been available for replacement, but the cache has been exhausted and there are no more replaceable states.) Instead of aborting the search at this point, the value of m is doubled to 4, and k is changed to $1\ldots3$. This process may be repeated several times, as illustrated in Figure 2. After the nth doubling, $m = 2^{n+1}$, $k = 1\ldots m-1$, the expected extra depth is at most $(m-1)/2$ and the maximum extra depth is $m-1$.

An idea similar to stratified caching has been described in [2]. There the authors investigate several heuristics that indicate whether or not a particular state should be stored at all. In fact, that work focuses on the minimal set of states that need to be stored, in other words, heuristics for selecting a covering set of vertices. Storing all states and replacing selectively replacing some holds the obvious advantage of avoiding a potentially significant amount of work, but it is also true that, for some models, storing only some of the states can improve performance even further.

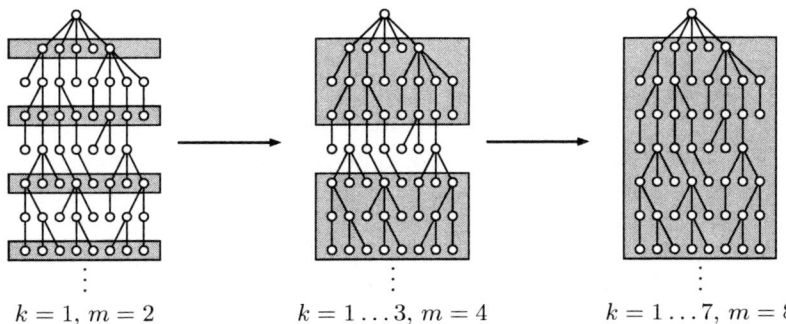

$$k = 1, m = 2 \qquad k = 1 \ldots 3, m = 4 \qquad k = 1 \ldots 7, m = 8$$

Fig. 2. Stratified caching with doubling modulo

4   Experiments with Random and Real Graphs

Our initial goal was to compare stratified caching and a random replacement strategy, but doubts arose about the optimality of random replacement. To resolve the matter, we conducted a set of experiments that explore graphs using state caching and a variety of state replacement strategies.

The replacement strategies are based on the following five state attributes: (E) stack entry time, (X) stack exit time, (D) search depth, (I) current indegree, and (O) current outdegree. A specific replacement strategy is a combination of attributes (denoted by uppercase letters) and negated attributes (denoted by lowercase letters). For example, the specification "DiX" indicates that states are first ordered by their ascending depth, then by their descending indegree, and finally by the ascending time of stack entry. When a state is selected for replacement, the least state according to this ordering is chosen.

Only attributes E and X are unique to each state. Therefore, a specification such as "dE" is unambiguous, as there is only one deepest, least recently entered state, while the specification "Io" is ambiguous, as there can be many states with minimal indegree and maximal outdegree. Note that the order of attributes is important: "OIX" and "IOX" describe two different replacement strategies.

In addition to the five attributes, two pseudo-attributes are used: (R) random selection, and (S) stratified caching. When the R pseudo-attribute is added to an ambiguous specification "s", states for replacement are chosen by randomly selecting one of the eligible states specified by s, and the resulting specification "sR" is unambiguous. The S pseudo-attribute can be combined with any unambiguous specification "s" to yield a strategy that selects a state within the available strata according to s, and employs the doubling-modulo stratified caching strategy discussed in the last section.

It is not easy to compare these strategies to those in [11]. Strategy H1 is clearly something of the form "i...", but in [11] a complete scan of the state store is performed to find the most frequently visited state, and it is therefore influenced by the hash function. Likewise, H2 corresponds to something of the form "I...". In [11] strategy H4 is said to select the oldest state in the cache, which is what "E" does, but H4 is often referred to as random replacement, which corresponds to "R". H3 and H5 have no direct counterparts among the strategies investigated.

In total, 790 unambiguous specifications were investigated. The specifications are not only unambiguous, but also independent of the state storage scheme. (Note that it is not really possible to implement an ambiguous specification — the ambiguity must be resolved in some undisclosed way — and such specifications were not considered.)

The experiments in this section focus on the cache size and the amount of redundant work; memory and time consumption are not at issue here. Experience has shown that, if care is taken with the implementation, redundant work gives a good indication of the time consumption. Apart from empirical observation, there is also an intuitive argument to support this claim: The proportion of extra states explored brings about an equal proportion of extra transitions, and the number of transitions is the dominating factor in the execution time of a state exploration tool. Accurate calculation of the memory consumption of the different specifications is also possible, but, for lack of space, we do not discuss it here. It is important to note, however, that the optimality of the strategies should be judged on their memory consumption and not the amount of redundant work involved.

4.1   Experiments with Random Graphs

In the first set of experiments, random graphs were generated using the same method described in [14], and shown in Figure 3. Each random graph is determined by three parameters: the desired number of states S, the maximum outdegree D of any node, and a seed R for the random number generator. For both random graph generation and random replacement strategies, the $(2^{19937} - 1)$-period Mersenne Twister random number generator [16] is used.

States are generated in a breadth-first fashion; for each new state an outdegree d is chosen uniformly in the range $0 \ldots D$; the probability that an outgoing transition leads to a new state is 0.5 for the first $\lfloor S/2 \rfloor$ states and then decreases linearly until it reaches 0 when the number of states reaches S; destination states of transitions that lead to old states are chosen uniformly from among the already generated states. This algorithm may terminate before enough states have been generated, if, for example, an outdegree $d = 0$ is chosen for the initial state. It is therefore repeated until at least $.9S$ states have been generated.

The graphs generated in this way are called *unweighted* and have a transition/state ratio of $D/2$. However, it is not only the average number but also the distribution of revisits that affect the performance of state caching. The algorithm was therefore adjusted to also generate *weighted* graphs: instead of choosing the revisited states by uniform selection (line 10 of Figure 3), each state was weighted by its number of incoming transitions. (The root state was given an additional incoming edge, since otherwise it would never be selected). Figure 4 shows the distribution of revisits for weighted and unweighted graphs; these match the distributions of many actual models.

```
          GenerateGraph(S, D, R)
 1    random seed := R
 2    repeat
 3        Enqueue(q, 0) ; n := 1
 4        while NotEmpty(q)
 5            s := Dequeue(q)
 6            d := Random(0 ... D)
 7            for i := 1 to d
 8                p := 1 − Max(0.5, n/S)
 9                if Random(0 ... 1) > p  {revisit an old state}
10                    t := Random(0 ... n − 1)
11                else  {generate a new state}
12                    t := n ; n := n + 1
13                    Enqueue(q, t)
14                endif
15                AddTransition(s, t)
16            endfor
17        endwhile
18    until n ≥ .9S
```

Fig. 3. Code for generation of random graphs

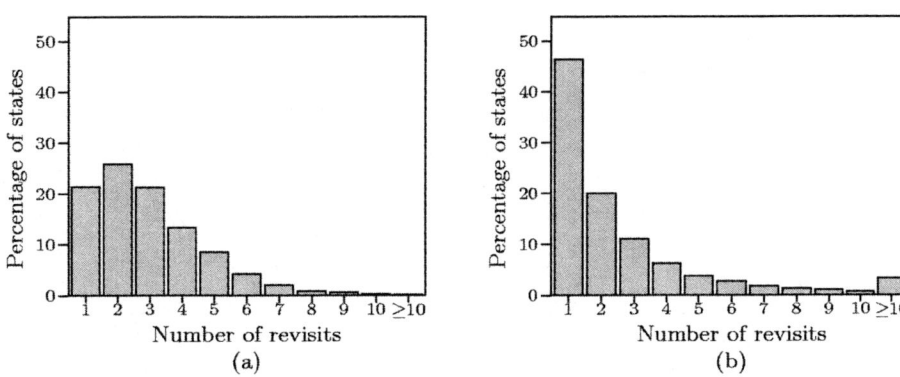

Number of revisits

(a)

Number of revisits

(b)

Fig. 4. The distribution of state revisits for (a) the unweighted random graph $S = 5000$, $D = 6$, $R = 22222222$, and (b) the weighted random graph $S = 5000$, $D = 6$, $R = 55555555$. In (a), for example, roughly 22% of states are visited only once, and roughly 26% of states are visited twice.

Thirty unweighted and thirty weighted random graphs were generated using the parameter values $S = 5000$, $D = 6, 10, 20$, and $R = 11111111n$ for $n = 0, 1, \ldots 9$. Different values of S had no discernible effect on the results, and 5000 was chosen as a representative value. Each random graph was explored using each of the unambiguous specifications as a cache replacement strategy. For the

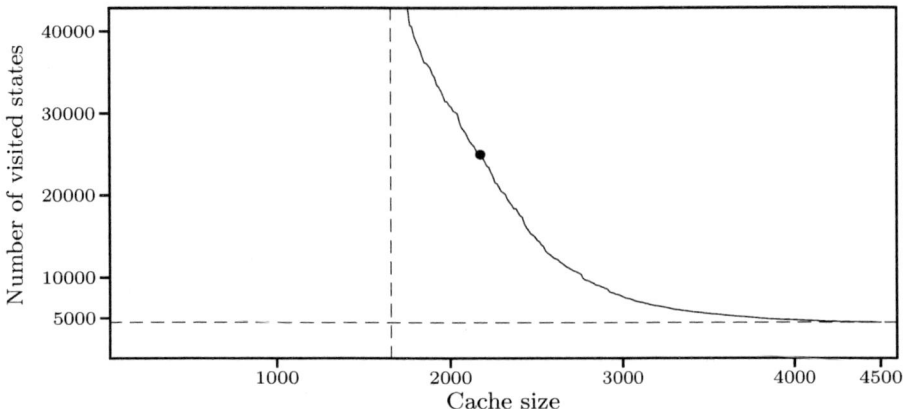

Fig. 5. The behaviour of the replacement strategy "iDx" (among the states with the highest indegree, select the shallowest states and, from these, choose the state that exited the depth-first stack first) on the unweighted random graph $S = 5000$, $D = 6$, $R = 0$. The graph has 4505 states (shown as the horizontal dashed line), 13249 transitions and a maximum search depth of 1658 (shown as the vertical dashed line).

initial run, the cache size was the same as the state space size; during subsequent runs it was decremented in steps of $1 + \lfloor S/400 \rfloor$, roughly 0.25% of the state space size. This process terminated once the number of visited states exceeded 10 times the size of the state space, or once the cache reported that it was full.

A typical result is shown in Figure 5. The dot in the center shows, for example, that a cache of 48.3% the size of the state space produced 24975 reported visited states, while the actual number of states is only 4505. The reported/actual states ratio — which we call the *redundant work factor* — is therefore 5.54. The replacement strategies are difficult to compare: minimum cache size is important, but so is the redundant work factor and the relationship between the two variables. Moreover, the maximum tolerable redundant work factor is a subjective limit.

Table 1 presents the results of the experiments with weighted and unweighted graphs separated. Different limits on the redundant work factor are shown in the first column, labeled f. In each row, the best strategies and their performance are shown for the ten graphs with $D = 6$, the ten graphs with $D = 10$, the ten graphs with $D = 20$, and, in the last major column, the thirty graphs combined. The best strategy was determined by averaging the minimum cache size data points for each strategy and selecting the strategy with the lowest average. In the case of more than one minimum, the strategy with the lowest average redundant work factor is shown. In a few cases two strategies of the form "se" and "sx" (or "sE" and "sX") performed equally well. The minor columns give the averaged minimum cache size as a percentage of the state space size, the redundant work factor, and the strategy specifications selected as the best. Lastly, the value of m in the heading row is the maximum stack depth expressed as a percentage of the state space size; this is minimum possible size of the cache.

Table 1. State caching results for random graphs

	Unweighted random graphs										
	$D = 6$			$D = 10$			$D = 20$			Combined		
f	$m = 37.43$			$m = 52.35$			$m = 70.13$			$m = 53.30$		
2	51.48	1.99	OIx	69.92	1.99	Ox	85.33	1.99	ODIe/x	68.95	1.99	OIx
3	44.22	2.96	OIR	62.43	2.99	OIDE/X	79.71	2.96	ODiR	62.15	2.97	OIDE/X
4	41.32	3.92	OIR	59.05	3.96	OIe	76.88	3.93	ODIe/x	59.12	3.94	OIDe/x
5	39.76	4.91	OIR	57.18	4.93	OIDe/x	75.16	4.90	ODIR	57.42	4.90	OIDe/x
6	38.79	5.78	OIR	56.00	5.85	OIDR	74.03	5.91	ODR	56.30	5.83	OIe
7	38.13	6.27	IOe	55.11	6.86	OIe	73.28	6.84	OIe	55.56	6.75	OIe
8	37.97	7.11	OIe	54.48	7.78	OIe	72.74	7.72	OIDR	55.06	7.54	OIe
9	37.94	7.15	OIe	54.03	8.65	OIe	72.29	8.75	OIDE/X	54.76	8.17	OIe
10	37.89	7.30	OIe	53.74	9.49	OIe	71.98	9.70	OIDR	54.55	8.79	OIe
	Weighted random graphs											
	$D = 6$			$D = 10$			$D = 20$			Combined		
f	$m = 25.71$			$m = 35.51$			$m = 49.67$			$m = 36.96$		
2	37.06	1.98	IOE	51.05	1.98	IOE	66.24	1.99	IOE	51.45	1.98	IOE
3	31.78	2.94	IOR	45.08	2.96	IODR	60.47	2.96	IOE	45.81	2.95	IOR
4	29.20	3.90	IOe	42.20	3.96	IODe/x	57.89	3.90	IODe/x	43.13	3.92	IODe/x
5	27.27	4.87	IOe	39.83	4.94	IODe/x	56.10	4.89	IOR	41.15	4.89	IOe
6	26.61	5.56	IOe	38.20	5.90	IODe/x	54.41	5.92	IOx	39.78	5.80	IOe
7	26.37	5.94	IOe	37.02	6.89	IODR	53.11	6.89	IODe/x	38.89	6.56	IOe
8	26.34	5.99	IOe	36.34	7.66	IOx	52.07	7.85	IOe	38.29	7.28	IOx
9	26.34	5.99	IOe	36.13	8.07	IOx	51.39	8.68	IODe/x	37.96	7.66	IOe
10	26.34	5.99	IOe	36.10	8.16	IODE/X	50.90	9.46	IODR	37.81	8.08	IODR

The first thing to note is that the table gives a very narrow view of the results, since there is no indication of how other strategies fared. For example, for unweighted graphs with $D = 20$ and $f = 4$, there are 14 other strategies that attain the 76.88% minimum cache size; they are not shown because their redundant work factor exceeded that of "ODIe/x". In total, 32 strategies came in below 77%, 65 strategies below 80%, and 230 strategies below 85%. The disadvantage of not showing all these results is, however, balanced by the consistency of the results, not to mention the problem of presenting such a volume of data.

The random replacement and the stratified caching strategies did not fare well enough to appear in the table. For unweighted graphs the average minimum cache size for random replacement ("R") is between 7.41% and 25.73% higher than that of the best strategy. Although stratified caching (specifically "eS") fared consistently better, its figures are still between 4.11% and 16.18% higher.

Instead, the "OI..." and "IO..." strategies dominate. The I attribute selects states with low indegree. Even if, as reported in [11], the number of past visits is not highly correlated with future visits, this approach works since, if many states are visited only once or twice, it is right more often than it is wrong. The

O attribute selects states with low outdegree. If these states are revisited, there are fewer children that may have been replaced and need to be re-investigated.

The D attribute also appears several times among the more highly connected graphs. This suggests that back edges are more likely to lead to closer levels, making it pay off to replace the shallowest states first. This may be due to the generation process: since there are more states at the deeper levels, deeper states have a higher probability of being selected for revisits. As to the occurrence of the e/x and E/X patterns, we believe that the disambiguating attribute (one of E/e/X/x/R) in all of the specifications is somewhat arbitrary, although the e attribute seems to have a slight edge.

For the moment, all these observations are speculative, and warrant further investigation. It is, however, clear that a redundant work limit of $f = 10$ is too generous; even when $f = 5$ the best strategies came within 5% of the absolute minimum cache size.

4.2   Experiments with Real Graphs

In addition to random graphs, several Promela models were converted (after partial order reduction by the SPIN tool) to graphs and explored as above, but with a redundant work factor limit of $f = 5$; the results are shown in Table 2. The columns show the model name, the number of states (in column *states*), the transition/state ratio (column d), the maximum stack depth as a percentage of S (column m), the minimum cache size as a percentage of S (column s), the redundant work factor (column *rwf*), and the number of best strategies and their specifications.

The results fall into roughly three groups: for the first group (dining, erasthostenes, mobile2, schedule, and gobackn2) "OX" (i.e., least outdegree and then least recently removed from stack) strategies work best, for the second group (dbm, X509, mobile1, petersonN, rap, pftp, slide, and gobackn) "RS" (stratified caching with random selection of available states) strategies work best, and for the last group (the other graphs) the best strategies were more varied. At present we are unable to explain this grouping, but hope to investigate it further.

When the performance (defined as $s - m$) of the strategies are averaged over the graphs and sorted, the stratified caching strategies occupy the top half of the list. In other words, the worst strategy with stratified caching outperforms the best strategy without, or to put it another way, of the replacement strategies previously considered in the literature, none achieved a better place than halfway down this list. At the top of the list is the "RS" (stratified caching with a doubling modulo in combination with random selection) strategy: its average minimum cache size is 5.41% higher than m, and its average redundant work factor is 3.12.

5   A SPIN Implementation

To further investigate the viability of some state caching schemes, the SPIN model checker was modified to include state caching. Three alternatives to out-of-the-box SPIN were investigated. The first alternative uses a cache replacement

Table 2. State caching results for graphs based on actual models

Model	states	d	m	s	rwf	Best strategies
mutex	428	2.0	15.42	24.53	3.16	3 IeS ieS eS
abp2	1440	1.3	23.26	23.40	1.02	5 iOe Oie OIe IOe Oe
cabp	2048	4.1	38.13	47.41	4.37	14 OdIeS OdIxS OdieS OdeS ...
dining	2071	3.6	71.32	74.02	3.99	5 OiXS IOXS OIXS OXS iOXS
erathostenes	2092	1.2	10.71	12.24	1.51	5 iOX OiX OIX IOX OX
mobile2	3300	2.0	23.36	23.79	4.94	5 iOX OiX OIX IOX OX
schedule	3328	1.3	16.29	16.77	1.37	5 iOX OiX OIX IOX OX
dbm	5111	4.0	1.96	15.07	4.58	1 iRS
X509	6093	2.0	0.89	13.52	4.68	1 RS
snoopy	9342	1.4	16.73	17.00	1.79	1 OiR
mobile1	9970	2.0	7.16	13.75	3.86	1 RS
gobackn2	14644	1.8	30.47	31.28	4.71	5 iOX OiX OIX IOX OX
petersonN	16719	1.8	29.40	31.17	3.82	1 RS
rap	26887	7.9	0.23	18.16	1.81	1 RS
pftp	47355	1.4	3.18	6.91	3.39	1 RS
riaan	67044	1.1	0.26	1.27	3.32	1 OR
slide	89910	1.5	11.07	12.91	4.48	1 ORS
gobackn	90209	1.5	11.03	12.32	4.65	1 OIdRS

Table 3. SPIN state caching results for a model of leader election in a general graph

Memory limit	SPIN 4.1.0		+ [7]		+ OX		+ XS	
	rwf	time	rwf	time	rwf	time	rwf	time
No limit	1.00	2.16	–	–	–	–	–	–
100	–	–	1.00	2.29	1.00	2.26	1.00	2.26
80	–	–	1.00	5.55	1.06	2.49	1.00	2.36
60	–	–	1.02	17.82	1.13	2.71	1.00	2.78
50	–	–	1.04	29.84	1.16	3.10	1.00	2.50
40	–	–	1.07	47.21	1.19	2.91	1.01	2.55
30	–	–	1.16	76.09	1.22	3.01	1.01	2.64
20	–	–	2.28	231.97	1.25	3.09	1.04	2.70
10	–	–	–	–	26.19	63.89	1.14	3.03

scheme identical to that of [7]. The second new version implements the OX strategy, identified as one of the "winners" in the previous section. It would have been instructive to investigate the RS strategy also, but true random selection is nontrivial to implement, especially in SPIN where state cache entries do not have a uniform length and cannot be determined a priori. It would be possible to ask the user to specify the size of the state vector, and this may not be unreasonable. However, to make the comparison as fair as possible, it was decided to implement the XS strategy as the third alternative SPIN version.

Table 4. Performance of bitstate hashing with respect to partial/full exploration

-w *param.*	*states*	*trans.*	*time*
22	276112	350318	2.51
23	279982	354744	2.57
24	280880	355762	2.59
25	281155	356069	2.61
26	281207	356127	2.63
27	281261	356190	2.66
28	281263	356192	2.72

Table 3 shows the results of running the three new versions on SPIN on a single model of the echo algorithm with extinction for electing leaders in an arbitrary network, as described in [20, Chapter 7]. The memory limit is given in 2^{20} bytes, the redundant work factor is defined as before, and the time is given in seconds. The experiments were performed on a 2.6GHz Pentium 4 machine with 512 megabytes of memory running Linux. These are only preliminary results and further experiments on more models are required to form a better idea of how well stratified caching behaves. From the figures in the table it is however clear that for this particular model this form of stratified caching outperforms the other two implementations.

While the model may be quite small (it has only 281263 states and 356192 transitions), it is interesting to look at the behaviour of bitstate hashing. Table 4 shows the value of the -w parameter which specifies the number of bits to use for bitstate hashing, the number of states and transitions reported by SPIN, and the time in seconds. Only when 2^{28} bits = 32 megabytes are used, does the system investigate the full state space. This does not reflect on bitstate hashing in general: even when it does not explore the full state space, it can find true errors in models. However, the important point is that state caching techniques can extend the limit beyond which we are forced to resort to partial exploration of state spaces.

6   Conclusions

We have shown, for both random graphs and graphs based on actual models, that for a substantial but not unlimited increase in running time, the cache can often be reduced to close to the minimum size imposed by the maximum stack depth. The maximum increase in running time is close to tenfold for the experiments in Table 1, and almost fivefold in Table 2; for the XS strategy in Table 3 the running time is only at most 1.4 times more than normal.

The results of the experiments are not as easy to interpret as we might have hoped. The strategies that worked best with random graphs are very different from those that worked best with actual models. For random graphs the results were more consistent than for actual models, perhaps indicating that the generated graphs represent only one "kind" of model. The experiments did however show that, by itself, random replacement is never the best strategy. Stratified caching in combination with random replacement emerged as the best strategy for almost half of the graphs based on actual models. In other cases, strategies based on the minimal outdegree and indegree of states proved successful.

We believe that stratified caching can be improved even further by selecting available strata based on the average outdegree, average indegree, or simply the number of states in a stratum. Its performance in the experiments makes it a strong candidate for the replacement strategy, whenever state caching is used.

Acknowledgments. This work was funded by the TISE graduate school and by the Academy of Finland.

References

1. G. Ausiello, P. Crescenzi, G. Gambosi, V. Kann, A. Marchetti-Spaccamela, M. Protasi. *Complexity and Approximation.* Springer-Verlag, 1999.
2. G. Berhmann, K. G. Larsen, R. Pelánek. To store or not to store. *Proc. 15th Intl. Conf. on Computer-Aided Verification,* LNCS#2725, pp. 433–445, 2003.
3. L. Brim, I. Černá, M. Nečesal. Randomization helps in LTL model checking. *Proc. Joint Intl. Workshop on Process Algebra and Probabilistic Methods, Performance Modeling and Verification,* LNCS#2165, pp. 105–119, 2001.
4. S. Edelkamp, A. L. Lafuente, S. Leue. Directed explicit model checking with HSF-SPIN. *Proc. 8th Intl. SPIN Workshop on Model Checking of Software,* LNCS#2057, pp. 57–79, 2001.
5. J. Geldenhuys. *Efficiency Issues in the Design of a Model Checker.* Master's thesis, University of Stellenbosch, 1999.
6. P. Godefroid. Using partial orders to improve automatic verification methods. *Proc. 2nd Intl. Conf. on Computer-Aided Verification,* LNCS#531, pp. 176–185, 1990.
7. P. Godefroid, G. J. Holzmann, D. Pirottin. State space caching revisited. *Proc. 4th Intl. Conf. on Computer-Aided Verification,* LNCS#663, pp. 175–186, 1992. Also appeared in *Formal Methods in System Design,* 7(3):227–241, 1995. http://www.montefiore.ulg.ac.be/services/verif/po-pack.html
8. P. Godefroid. *Partial-order Methods for the Verification of Concurrent Systems, An Approach to the State-explosion Problem.* PhD thesis, University of Liège, Dec 1994. Also published as LNCS #1032, Springer-Verlag, 1996.
9. P. Godefroid. On the costs and benefits of using partial-order methods for the verification of concurrent systems. *Proc. Workshop on Partial Order Methods in Verification,* DIMACS Series vol. 29, pp. 289–303, 1996.
10. G. J. Holzmann. Tracing protocols. *AT&T Technical J.,* 64(10):2413–2433, 1985.
11. G. J. Holzmann. Automated protocol validation in *Argos,* assertion proving and scatter searching. *IEEE Trans. on Software Engineering,* 13(6):683–696, 1987.
12. G. J. Holzmann. *Design and Validation of Computer Protocols.* Prentice Hall, 1991.
13. C. Jard, T. Jéron. On-line model checking for finite linear temporal logic specifications. *Proc. Intl. Workshop on Automatic Verification Methods for Finite State Systems,* LNCS#407, pp. 275–285, 1989.

14. C. Jard, T. Jéron. Bounded memory algorithm for verification on-the-fly. *Proc. 3rd Intl. Conf. on Computer-Aided Verification*, LNCS#575, pp. 192–202, 1991.
15. C. Jard, T. Jéron, J.-C. Fernandez, L. Mounier. On-the-fly Verification of Finite Transition Systems. Tech. rep. #701, IRISA, 1993.
16. M. Matsumoto, T. Nishimura. Mersenne Twister: A 623-dimensionally equidistributed uniform pseudorandom number generator. *ACM Trans. on Modeling and Computer Simulation*, 8(1):3–30, 1998.
    `http://www.math.keio.ac.jp/~matumoto/emt.html`
17. A. N. Parashkevov, J. T. Yantchev. Space efficient reachability analysis through use of pseudo-root states. *Proc. 3rd Intl. Conf. on Tools and Algorithms for the Construction and Analysis of Systems*, LNCS#1217, pp. 50–64, 1997.
18. D. Peled. All from one, one for all: On model checking using representatives. In *Proc. 5th Intl. Conf. Computer-Aided Verification*, LNCS #697, pp. 409–423, Jun 1993.
19. U. Stern, D. L. Dill. Combining state space caching and hash compaction. *Methoden des Entwurfs und der Verifikation digitaler Systeme, 4. GI/ITG/GME Workshop*, pp. 81–90, 1996.
20. G. Tel. *Introduction to Distributed Algorithms*. Cambridge University Press, 2nd edition, 2000.
21. A. Valmari. A stubborn attack on state explosion. *Formal Methods in System Design* 1(1), pp. 297–322, 1992.

Directed Error Detection in C++ with the Assembly-Level Model Checker StEAM

Peter Leven[1] and Tilman Mehler[2] and Stefan Edelkamp[2]

[1] Institut für Informatik, Georges-Köhler Allee, Geb. 51,
Albert-Ludwigs-Universität Freiburg, Germany
`leven@informatik.uni-freiburg.de`
[2] Fachbereich Informatik, Universität Dortmund, Baroper Str. 301,
44221 Dortmund, Germany
{`tilman.mehler,stefan.edelkamp`}`@cs.uni-dortmund.de`

Abstract. Most approaches for model checking software are based on the generation of abstract models from source code, which may greatly reduce the search space, but may also introduce errors that are not present in the actual program.

In this paper, we propose a new model checker for the verification of native `c++`-programs. To allow platform independent model checking of the object code for concurrent programs, we have extended an existing virtual machine for `c++` to include multi-threading and different exploration algorithms on a dynamic state description.

The error reporting capabilities and the lengths of counter-examples are improved by using heuristic estimator functions and state space compaction techniques that additionally reduce the exploration efforts.

The evaluation of four scalable simple example problems shows that our system *StEAM*[1] can successfully enhance the detection of deadlocks and assertion violations.

1   Introduction

Model checking [4] refers to exhaustive exploration of a system with the intention to prove that it satisfies one or more formal properties. After successful application in fields like hardware design, process engineering and protocol verification, some recent efforts [3,13,18,23] exploit model checking for the verification of actual programs written in e.g. `Java` or `c`.

Most of these approaches rely on the extraction of a formal model from the source code of the program. Such a model can in turn be converted into the input language of an existing model checker (e.g. Spin [17]). The main advantage of abstract models is the reduction of state space.

Some model checkers - e.g. dSpin [6] - also consider dynamic aspects of computer programs, like memory allocation and dynamic object creation. These aspects must be mapped to the respective description language. If this is not

---

[1] State Exploring Assembly Model Checker

S. Graf and L. Mounier (Eds.): SPIN 2004, LNCS 2989, pp. 39–56, 2004.

carefully addressed, the model may not correctly reflect all aspects of the actual program. Moreover, some of these approaches require manual intervention of the user which means that one has to be familiar with the input language of the model checker.

A different approach is considered in the Java model checker JPF. Instead of extracting a model from the source code, JPF [24] uses a custom-made Java virtual machine to check a program on the byte-code level. This eliminates the problem of an inadequate model of the program - provided that the virtual machine works correctly. The developers of JPF choose Java as the target programming language for several reasons [25]: First, Java features object-orientation and multi-threading in one language. Second, Java is simple. And third, Java is compiled to byte-code and hence the analysis can be done on byte-code level (as opposed to a platform-specific machine code). Also it was decided to keep JPF as modular and understandable to others as possible, sacrificing speed.

StEAM, the model checker presented in this paper, addresses a more general approach to such low-level program model checking. Based on a virtual processor, called the *Internet Virtual Machine* (IVM), the tool performs a search on machine-code compiled from a c++ source. On one hand, this provides the option to model-check programs written in the industrial standard programming language, while, on the other hand, the generic approach is extendible to any compiler-based programming language with reasonable effort. Our method of reduction keeps state spaces small to compete with memory efficiency of other model checkers that apply model abstraction.

The architecture of *StEAM* is inspired by JPF. However the developers faced some additional challenges. First, there is no support for multi threading in standard c++. The language as well as the virtual machine had to be extended. Second, since the virtual machine is written in plain c, so is *StEAM*. Although this increases development time, we believe that the model checker will in the long term benefit from the increased speed of c compared to Java. Memory-efficiency is one of the most important issues of program model checking. There are various options for a time-space trade-off to save memory and explore larger state spaces. However, such techniques require that the underlying tool is fast. Moreover *StEAM* successfully ties the model checking algorithm with an existing virtual machine. A task thought impossible by the developers of JPF [25].

The paper is structured as follows. First, it introduces the architecture of the system. Next, it shows which extensions were necessary to enable program model checking, namely the storage of system states, the introduction of non-determinism through threads, and different exploration algorithms to traverse the state space in order to validate the design or to report errors. We illustrate the approach with a small example. The complex system state representation in *StEAM* is studied in detail. We introduce an apparent option for state space reduction and explain, why heuristics estimates accelerate the detection of errors and the quality of counter-examples. Experiments show that *StEAM* effectively applies model checking of concurrent c++-programs. Finally we relate *StEAM* to other work in model checking, and conclude.

2   Architecture of the Internet C Virtual Machine

The *Internet C Virtual Machine* (ICVM) by Bob Daley aims at creating a programming language that provides platform-independence without the need of
rewriting applications into proprietary languages like c♯ or Java. The main purpose of the project was to be able to receive precompiled programs through the
Internet and run them on an arbitrary platform without re-compilation. Furthermore, the virtual machine was designed to run games, so simulation speed
was crucial.

The Virtual Machine. The virtual machine simulates a 32-bit CISC CPU with a
set of approximately 64,000 instructions. The current version is already capable
of running complex programs at descend speed, including the commercial game
Doom[2]. This is a strong empirical evidence that the virtual machine works correctly. Thus, dynamic aspects are carefully addressed. IVM is publicly available
as open source[3].

The Compiler. The compiler takes conventional c/c++ code and translates it
into the machine code of the virtual machine. ICVM uses a modified version of
the GNU C-compiler gcc to compile its programs. The compiled code is stored in
ELF (Executable and Linking format), the common object file format for Linux
binaries. The three types of file representable are object files, shared libraries
and executables, but we will consider mostly executables.

ELF Binaries. An ELF-binary is partitioned in sections describing different
aspects of the object's properties. The number of sections varies depending on
the respective file. Important are the DATA and BSS sections. Together, the two
sections represent the set of global variables of the program.

The BSS section describes the set of non-initialized variables while the DATA
section represents the set of variables that have an initial value assigned to them.
When the program is executed, the system first loads the ELF file into memory.
For the BSS section additional memory must be allocated, since non-initialized
variables do not occupy space in the ELF file.

Space for initialized variables, however, is reserved in the DATA section of
the object file, so accesses to variables directly affect the memory image of the
ELF binary. Other sections represent executable code, symbol table etc., not to
be considered for memorizing the state description.

3   Multi-threading

In the course of our project, the virtual machine was extended with multi-
threading capabilities, a description of the search space of a program, as well
as some special-purpose program statements which enable the user to describe

---

[2] www.doomworld.com/classicdoom/ports
[3] ivm.sourceforge.net

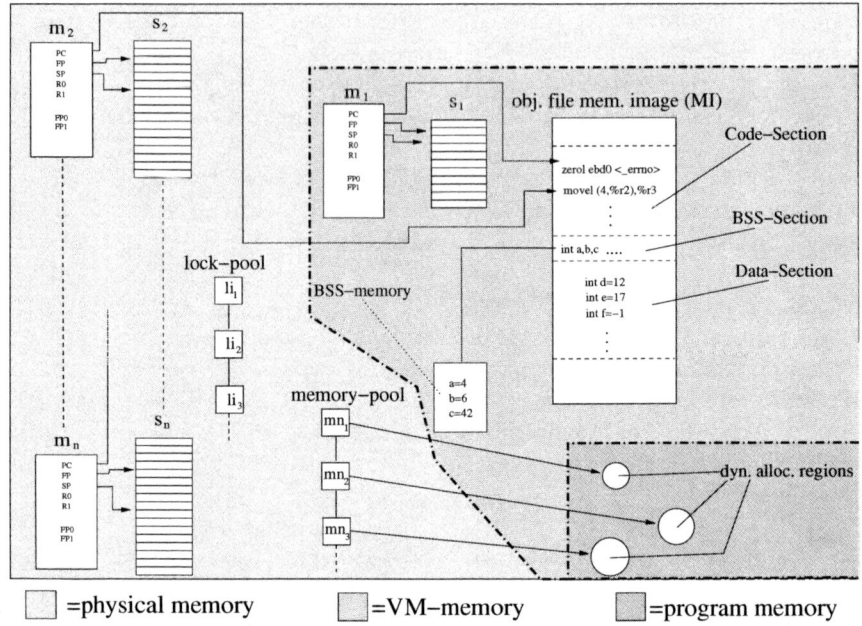

Fig. 1. System state of a *StEAM* program.

and guide the search. Figure 1 shows the components that form the state of a concurrent program for *StEAM*.

System Memory Hierarchy. Memory is organized in three layers: Out-most is the physical memory which is only visible to the model checker. The subset *VM-memory* is also visible to the virtual machine and contains information about the main thread, i.e., the thread containing the main method of the program to check. The program memory forms a subset of the VM-memory and contains regions that are dynamically allocated by the program.

Stacks and Machines. For n threads, we have *stacks* $s_1, \ldots, s_n$ and *machines* $m_1, \ldots, m_n$, where s_1 and m_1 correspond to the *main* thread that is created when the verification process starts. Therefore, they reside in VM-memory. The machines contain the hardware registers of the virtual machine, such as the program counter (PC) and the *stack* and *frame pointers* (SP, FP). Before the next step of a thread can be executed, the content of machine registers and stack must refer to the state immediately after the last execution of the same thread, or, if it is new, directly after initialization.

Dynamic Process Creation. From the running threads, new threads can be created dynamically. Such a creation is recognized by *StEAM* through a specific pattern of machine instructions. *Program counters* (PCs) indicate the byte offset of the next machine instruction to be executed by the respective thread, i.e., they point to some position within the code-section of the object file's *memory image* (MI). MI also contains the information about the DATA and BSS sections. Note that (in contrast to the DATA section) the space for storing the contents of the variables declared in the BSS section lies outside the MI and is allocated separately.

Memory- and Lock-Pool. The *memory-pool* is used by *StEAM* to manage dynamically allocated memory. It consists of an AVL-tree of entries (memory nodes), one for each memory region. They contain a pointer to address space which is also the search key, as well as some additional information such as the identity of the thread, from which it was allocated.

The *lock-pool* stores information about locked resources. Again an AVL-tree stores lock information.

4 Exploration

There is a core difference between the *execution* of a multi-threaded program and the *exploration* of its state space. In the first case, it suffices to restore machine registers and stack content of the executed thread.

To explore a program state space, the model checker must restore the state of DATA and BSS, as well as the memory and lock pool. Although *StEAM* does support program simulation, we consider only exploration.

Special Command Patterns. On the programming level, multi-threading is realized through a base class `ICVMThread`, from which all thread classes must be derived. A class derived from `ICVMThread` must implement the methods `start`, `run` and `die`. After creating an instance of the derived thread-class, a call to *start* will initiate the thread execution.

The *run*-method is called from the *start*-method and must contain the actual thread code. New commands e.g. `VLOCK` and `VUNLOCK` for locking have been integrated using macros. The compiler translates them to usual `c++`-code which does not influence the user-defined program variables. During program verification code patterns are detected in the virtual machine where special commands, like locking, are executed. This way of integration avoids manipulation of the compiler.

Example. Figure 1 shows a simple program `glob` which generates two threads from a derived thread class `MyThread`, that access a shared variable *glob*.

The `main` program calls an atomic block of code to create the threads. Such a block is defined by a pair of `BEGINATOMIC` and `ENDATOMIC` statements. Upon creation, each thread is assigned a unique identifier `ID` by the constructor of the super class. An instance of `MyThread` uses `ID` to apply the statement `glob=(glob+1)*ID`.

Table 1. The source of the program `glob`.

```
01. #include "IVMThread.h"
02. #include "MyThread.h"
04. extern int glob;
05.
06. class IVMThread;
07. MyThread::MyThread()
08.   :IVMThread::IVMThread(){
09. }
10. void MyThread::start() {
11.  run();
12.    die();
13. }
14.
15. void MyThread::run() {
16.    glob=(glob+1)*ID;
17. }
18.
19. void MyThread::die() {
20. }
21.
22. int MyThread::id_counter;
```

```
01. #include <assert.h>
02. #include "MyThread.h"
03. #define N 2
04.
05. class MyThread;
06. MyThread * t[N];
07. int i,glob=0;
08.
09. void initThreads () {
10.   BEGINATOMIC
11.     for(i=0;i<N;i++) {
12.       t[i]=new MyThread();
13.       t[i]->start();
14.     }
15.   ENDATOMIC
16. }
17.
18. void main() {
19.   initThreads();
20.   VASSERT(glob!=8);
21. }
```

The `main` method contains a `VASSERT` statement. This statement takes a boolean expression as its parameter and acts like an assertion in established model checkers like e.g. SPIN [17]. If *StEAM* finds a sequence of program instructions (the *trail*) which leads to the line of the `VASSERT` statement, and the corresponding system state violates the boolean expression, the model checker prints the trail and terminates.

In the example, we check the program against the expression `glob!=8`. Figure 2 shows the error trail of *StEAM*, when applied to `glob`. Thread 1 denotes the main thread, Thread 2 and Thread 3 are two instances of `MyThread`. The returned error trail is easy to trace. First, instances of `MyThread` are generated and started in one atomic step. Then the one-line `run`-method of Thread 3 is executed, followed by the `run`-method of Thread 2. We can easily calculate why the assertion is violated. After Step 3, we have `glob=(0+1)*3=3` and after step 5 we have `glob=(3+1)*2=8`. After this, the line containing the `VASSERT`-statement is reached.

The assertion is only violated, if the `main` method of Thread 3 is executed before the one of Thread 2. Otherwise, `glob` would take the values 0, 2, and 9. By default, *StEAM* uses depth first search (DFS) for a program exploration. In general, DFS finds an error quickly while having low memory requirements. As a drawback, an error trails found with DFS can become very long, in some cases even too long to be traceable by the user. In the current version, *StEAM* supports

```
Step 1: Thread 1 - Line 10 src-file: glob.c -  initThreads
Step 2: Thread 1 - Line 16 src-file: glob.c -  main
Step 3: Thread 3 - Line 15 src-file: MyThread.cc - MyThread::run
Step 4: Thread 3 - Line 16 src-file: MyThread.cc - MyThread::run
Step 5: Thread 2 - Line 15 src-file: MyThread.cc - MyThread::run
Step 6: Thread 2 - Line 16 src-file: MyThread.cc - MyThread::run
Step 7: Thread 1 - Line 20 src-file: glob.c -  main
Step 8: Thread 1 - Line <unknown> src-file: glob.c -  main
```

Fig. 2. The error-trail for the 'glob'-program.

DFS, breadth-first search (BFS) and the heuristic search methods best-first (BF) and A* (see e.g. [9]).

Detecting Deadlocks. StEAM automatically checks for deadlocks during a program exploration. A thread can gain and release exclusive access to a resource using the statements VLOCK and VUNLOCK which take as their parameter a pointer to a base type or structure. When a thread attempts to lock an already locked resource, it must wait until the lock is released. A deadlock describes a state where all running threads wait for a lock to be released. A detailed example is given in [21].

Hashing. StEAM uses a hash table to store already visited states. When expanding a state, only those successor states not in the hash table are added to the search tree. If the expansion of a state S yields no new states, then S forms a leaf in the search tree. To improve memory efficiency, we fully store only those components of a state which differ from that of the predecessor state. If a transition leaves a certain component unchanged - which is often the case for e.g. the lock pool - only the reference to that component is copied to the new state. This has proven to significantly reduce the memory requirements of a model checking run. The method is similar to the *Collapse Mode* used in Spin [16]. However, instead of component indices, *StEAM* directly stores the pointers to the structures describing respective state components. Also, only components of the immediate predecessor state are compared to those of the successor state. A redundant storing of two identical components is therefore possible. Additional savings may be gained through reduction techniques like heap symmetry [19], which are subject to further development of *StEAM*.

5   Accelerating Error Detection

Our approaches to accelerate error detection are twofold. First, we reduce the state space of assembly-level program state exploration. Second, we invent heuristics, which accelerate error detection, especially the search for deadlocks.

Although *StEAM* can model check real c++ programs, it is limited in the size of problems it can handle. Unmodified c++ programs have more instructions than abstract models other model checker take as their input. The state space usually grows exponential in the number of threads including the number of executed machine instruction in each thread as a factor. For each instruction, all permutations of thread orders can occur and have to be explored.

Lock and Global Compaction. The occurrence of an error does not depend on every execution order. An exploration of a single thread has to be interrupted only after lock/unlock or access to shared variables. Each access to local memory cells cannot influence the behaviour of other threads. Therefore, we realized two kinds of state reduction techniques.

The first one, called *lock* and *global compaction, lgc* for short, executes each thread until the next access to shared memory cells. Technically, this is performed by looking at the memory regions, that each assembly level instruction accesses and at lock instructions.

Source Line Compaction. The second kind of exploration, *nolgc* for short, requires each source line to be atomic. No thread switch is allowed during execution of a single source line. This is not immediate, since each line of code correspond to a sequence of object code instruction.

The implication for the programmer is that infinite loops that e.g wait for change of a shared variable, are not allowed in a single source line. We expect the body of the loop to be unfolded in forthcoming source. The source line compaction is only sound with respect to deadlock detection, if read and write access as well as lock and unlock access to the same variable are not included in one line.

Both techniques reduce thread interleaving and link to the automated process of partial order reduction, which has been implemented in many explicit state model checking systems [20,7]. The difference is that we decide, whether or not a thread interleaving has to be considered by looking at current assembler instruction and the lock pool.

6   Directed Program Model Checking

Heuristics have been successfully used to improve error detection in concurrent programs, see e.g. [12,8]. States are evaluated by an estimator function, measuring the distance to an error state, so that states closer to the faulty behavior have a higher priority and are considered earlier in the exploration process. If the system contains no error, there is no gain, the whole search space is enumerated. Compared to blind search, the only loss is due to additional computational resources for the heuristics.

Most-Block and Interleaving. An appropriate example for the detection of deadlocks is the *most-block* heuristic. It favors states, where more threads are blocked. Another established estimate used for error detection in concurrent programs is the *interleaving* heuristic. It relies on maximizing the interleaving of thread executions [12].

In the following we consider new aspects to improve the design of estimator functions. In *StEAM* heuristics either realize single ideas or mixed ones, so we first start with three basic primitives: lock, shared variables and thread-id, followed by a treatment on how to combine them to higher-order functions.

Lock. In the *lock* heuristic, we prefer states with more variables locks and more threads alive. Locks are obvious preconditions for threads to become blocked. Only threads that are still alive can get blocked in the future.

Shared Variable. Finally, we considered the access to shared variables. We prefer a change of the active thread after a global read or write access. The objective is that after accessing a global variable, other threads are likely to be affected.

Thread-Id. Threads are of equal class in many cases. If threads have equal program code and differ only in their *thread-id*, their internal behaviour is only slightly different. If the threads are ordered linear ascending according to their id, we may prefer the last one.

The *thread-id* heuristics can be seen as kind of a *symmetry reduction* rule, because we impose a preference ordering on similar threads, which sets a penalty to the generation of equivalent state generation. Symmetric reduction based on ordered thread-IDs and their PC values is e.g. analyzed in [2] and integrated into *dSpin*. One advantage compared to other approaches in symmetry reduction is, that we encoded the similarity measure into the estimator function. Therefore, the approach is more flexible and can be combined easily with other heuristics. Moreover, no explicit computation of canonical states takes place and the approach is not specialized to a certain problem domain.

Favoring Patterns. Each thread has internal values and properties that we can use to define which thread execution we favor in an exploration step, e.g. thread-id (ID), PC, number of locked variables, number of executed instructions so far, and flags like *blocked* and *alive*. If *blocked* is set, the thread is waiting for a variable to be unlocked. If *alive* is unset, the thread will not be executed anymore: it is dead.

We select a subset of all possible components to define heuristics. The pattern for some relevant components for an example system state is shown in Figure 3. We call those patterns *favoring*, as they favor states in the exploration. In the following we explain one of the heuristics in use, namely the *pbb* heuristic.

If we add simply the number of all blocked threads in an heuristic, we obtain the mentioned most blocked heuristic. But many states have the same number of blocked threads. The number of equal states, that can be obtained from a given state by permuting thread-ids and reordering the threads can be exponential in the number of threads.

To favor only a few of equivalent states, one concept of favoring patterns we use are *neighbor groups*, maximal groups of consecutive threads having a

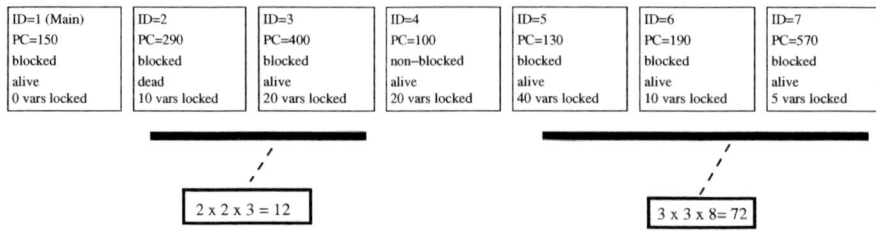

Fig. 3. Favoring patterns.

certain property, in our example flag *blocked*. Additionally, we prefer systems states, where the *neighbor groups* are rightmost. We abbreviate *neighbor group* by *group*.

For a combined estimate for the entire state, we first square the size of each group. To express the preference for rightmost group, we multiply the obtained value with the largest thread-id in the group. Then the values for each *group* are added. In the example of Figure 3, we have value 12 for the first group and value 72 for the second group yielding the sum 94.

To prefer states with more threads blocked, we additionally add the cubed number of the total of all blocked threads. For the maximum possible number of blocked threads this value is compatible with the previous sum. In our example five threads are blocked, so that the final preference value is $94 + 625 = 721$.

Table 2 summarizes the applied heuristics together with a brief description. Newly contributed heuristic start with *pba*, known ones refer to [12].

7   Experimental Results

An evaluation of *StEAM* has been performed on a Linux based PC (AMD Athlon XP 2200+ processor, 1 GB RAM, 1,800 MHz clock speed). The memory has been limited to 900 MB and the search time to 20 minutes.

Models. We conducted experiments with four scalable programs, e.g. simple communication protocols. Even though the selection is small and contains not very elaborated case studies, the state space complexity of the programs can compare with the code fragments that are often considered for program model checking.

The first model is the implementation of a deadlock solution to the dining philosophers problem (*philo*) as described in [10,21].

The second model implements an algorithm for the leader election protocol (*leader*). Here an error was seeded, which can cause more than one process to be elected as the leader. Both of the above models are scalable to an arbitrary number of processes.

Table 2. Known (*mb,int*) and newly introduced heuristics.

Heuristic	Abb.	Description
most blocked	mb	Counts the number of blocked threads
interleaving	int	The history of executed thread numbers is considered to prefer least recently executed threads
preferred alive & blocked	pba	Adds the cubed number of all blocked threads, the squared number of all alive threads and for each *group* of alive threads the squared number of threads weighted with the rightmost thread-id.
preferred blocked	pbb	Add the cubed number of all blocked threads, the squared number of all blocked threads and for each *group* of blocked threads the squared number of threads weighted with the rightmost thread-id.
read & write	rw	Prefers write access to shared variables and punishes read accesses without intermediate write access on each thread.
lock n' block	lnb	Count the number of locks in all threads and the number of blocked threads.
preferred locked 1	pl1	Counts the squared number of locks in all threads and the squared number of blocked threads.
preferred locked 2	pl2	Counts the squared number of locks in all threads and the squared number of *groups* of blocked and alive threads, where rightmost *groups* are preferred by weighting each *group* with the largest thread-id.
alternating read & write	aa	Prefers alternating read and write access.

The third model, is a C++ implementation of the optical telegraph protocol (*opttel*), which is described in [15]. The model is scalable in the number of telegraph stations and contains a deadlock.

The fourth model is an implementation of a bank automata scenario (*cashit*). Several bank automata perform transaction on a global database (withdraw, request, transfer). The model is scalable in the number of automata. A wrong lock causes an access violation.

Undirected Search. The undirected search algorithms considered are BFS and DFS. Table 3 shows the results. For the sake of brevity we only show the result for the maximum scale (*s*) that could be applied to a model with a specific combination of a search algorithm with or without state space compaction (*c*), for which an error could be found. We measure trail length (*l*), the search time (*t* in 0.1s) and the required memory (*m* in KByte). In the following *n* denotes the scale factor of a model and *msc* the maximal scale.

In all models BFS already fails for small instances. For example in the dining philosophers, BFS can only find a deadlock up to $n = 6$, while heuristic search can go up to $n = 190$ with only insignificant longer trails. DFS only has an

Table 3. Results with Undirected Search.

		cashit				leader				opttel				philo			
	c	s	l	t	m	s	l	t	m	s	l	t	m	s	l	t	m
DFS	y	1	97	151	134	80	1,197	247	739	9	8,264	214	618	90	1,706	166	835
DFS	n	1	1,824	17	96	12	18,106	109	390	6	10,455	221	470	20	14,799	463	824
BFS	y	-	-	-		5	56	365	787	2	21	24	97	6	13	160	453
BFS	n	-	-	-		3	66	30	146	-	-	-		4	26	57	164

advantage in *leader*, since higher instances can be handled, but the produced trails are longer than those of heuristic search.

Heuristic Search. Table 4 and Table 5 depict the obtained results for directed program model checking.

The *int* heuristic, used with BF, shows some advantages compared to the undirected search methods, but is clearly outperformed by the heuristics which are specifically tailored to deadlocks and assertion violations. The *rw* heuristic performs very strong in both, *cashit* and *leader*, since the error in both protocols is based on process communication. In fact *rw* produces shorter error trails than any other method (except BFS).

In contrast to our expectation, *aa* performs poorly at the model *leader* and is even outperformed by BFS with respect to scale and trail length. For *cashit*, however, *aa*, leading to the shortest trail and *rw* are the only heuristic that find an error for $n = 2$, but only if the *lgc* reduction is turned off. Both of these phenomena of *aa* are subject to further investigation.

The lock heuristics are especially good in *opttel* and *philo*. With BF and *lgc* they can be used to a *msc* of 190 (*philo*) and 60 (*opttel*). They outperform other heuristics with *nolgc* and the combination of A* and *lgc*. In case of A* and *nolgc* the results are also good for *philo* (n=6 and n=5; msc is 7).

According to the experimental results, the sum of locked variables in continuous block of threads with locked variable is a good heuristic measure to find deadlocks. Only the *lnb* heuristic can compare with *pl1* and *pl2* leading to a similar trail length. In case of *cashit pl2* and *rw* outperform most heuristics with BF and A*: with *lgc* they obtain an error trail of equal length, but *rw* needs less time. In the case of A* and *nolgc pl2* is the only heuristic which leads to a result for *cashit*. In most cases both *pl* heuristics are among the fastest.

The heuristic *pba* is in general moderate but sometimes, e.g. with A* and *nolgc* and *opttel* (*msc* of 2) and *philo* (*msc* of 7) outperforming. The heuristic *pbb* is often among the best, e.g. *leader* with BF and *lgc* ($n = 6$, $msc = 80$), *philo* with BF and *lgc* (n=150; *msc* is 190) and *philo* with A* and *nolgc* ($n = 6$, $msc = 7$). Overall the heuristics *pba* and *pbb* are better suited to A*.

Experimental Summary. Figure 4 summarizes our results. We measure the performance by extracting the fourth root of the product of trail length, processed

Table 4. Results with Best-First Search.

SA	C	s	cashit			leader				opttel				philo			
			l	t	m	s	l	t	m	s	l	t	m	s	l	t	m
pl1	y	1	97	150	134	5	73	89	285	60	602	210	770	190	386	166	622
pl2	y	1	97	59	120	5	73	94	312	60	601	210	680	190	385	487	859
mb	y	1	97	150	134	80	1,197	247	737	9	6,596	160	518	150	750	213	862
lnb	y	1	97	150	134	5	73	86	263	60	602	211	763	190	386	168	639
int	y	1	98	91	128	5	57	395	789	2	22	12	98	8	18	193	807
aa	y	1	84	03	97	5	72	278	637	-	-	-		6	14	208	449
rw	y	1	61	02	97	60	661	195	671	2	309	07	98	90	1,706	178	854
pba	y	1	97	90	121	80	1,197	244	740	9	6,596	161	513	90	450	43	234
pbb	y	1	97	150	134	80	1,197	244	741	9	6,596	160	510	150	750	210	860
pl1	n	1	1,824	17	97	4	245	94	284	40	1,203	200	705	150	909	340	859
pl2	n	1	792	09	97	4	245	168	376	40	1,202	193	751	150	908	327	857
mb	n	1	1,824	17	97	12	18,106	107	428	6	10,775	235	489	60	1,425	102	548
lnb	n	1	1824	17	97	4	245	92	284	40	1,203	197	719	150	909	344	856
int	n	1	1,824	17	97	3	68	37	139	-	-	-		5	33	234	663
aa	n	2	328	86	146	3	132	28	139	-	-	-		4	27	73	197
rw	n	2	663	147	463	40	1,447	104	470	2	494	68	206	20	14,799	469	822
pba	n	1	792	14	97	12	18,106	109	411	6	10,775	235	470	40	945	33	239
pbb	n	1	1,824	17	97	12	18,106	109	407	6	10,775	236	471	60	1,425	102	571

states, time and memory (geometric mean of the arguments). We use a log-scale on both axes.

In the case of the leader election protocol, the advantage of compaction is apparent. The maximum possible scale almost doubles, if the compaction is used. The graphic shows that *rw* and DFS perform similar, finally DFS is a little bit better with lgc, but *rw* is much better with *nolgc*. BFS, *int*, and *aa* behave similar in both cases.

In *opttel*, the heuristics *lnb*, *pl1* and *pl2* are performing best. The *pl2* heuristic only starts to perform well with $n = 15$, before the curve has a high peak. It seems, that the preference of continuous blocks of alive or blocked thread has only a value, after increasing a certain scale, here 10. The *pab* and *pbb* heuristic perform similar up to an *msc* of 9.

In *philo*, the heuristics *pl1*, *pl2*, *pba*, *pbb* are performing best. If only BF is considered, the heuristic *lnb* behaves similar than *pl1* and *pl2*. Again, *pl2* has an initial peak. DFS is performing well to *msc* of 90.

In the experiments the new heuristics show an improvement in many cases. In the case of deadlock search the new lock and block heuristics are superior to *most blocked*. The *lgc* compaction often more than doubles the maximum possible model scale.

Table 5. Results for A*.

	c		cashit				leader				opttel				philo		
		s	l	t	m	s	l	t	m	s	l	t	m	s	l	t	m
pl1	y	-	-	-		5	56	345	711	3	32	39	215	190	386	166	631
pl2	y	1	61	2,781	387	5	56	358	760	2	21	03	98	190	385	482	860
mb	y	-	-	-		5	56	397	769	2	22	19	98	7	16	111	371
lnb	y	-	-	-		5	56	342	719	2	22	15	98	8	18	82	286
int	y	-	-	-		5	57	406	785	2	22	13	98	7	16	177	629
aa	y	-	-	-		5	61	385	744	2	22	41	171	6	14	208	449
rw	y	1	61	1958	310	7	78	163	589	2	22	24	98	6	14	208	449
pba	y	-	-	-		5	56	378	648	3	32	130	424	60	122	191	628
pbb	y	-	-	-		5	56	396	777	3	32	195	573	60	122	193	634
pl2	n	1	136	10,568	614	3	66	32	141	-	-	-		5	38	172	485
mb	n	-	-	-		3	66	32	151	-	-	-		4	27	39	155
rw	n	-	-	-		3	66	21	97	-	-	-		4	27	71	199
pba	n	-	-	-		3	66	29	138	2	63	547	845	7	51	424	872
pbb	n	-	-	-		3	66	32	139	-	-	-		6	45	187	431

8 Related Work

We discuss other projects, that deal with model checking or software testing.

CMC [22], the c Model Checker, checks c and c++ implementations directly by generating the state space of the analyzed system during execution. *CMC* has mainly been used to check correctness properties of network protocols The checked correctness properties are assertion violations, a global invariant check avoiding routing loops, sanity checks on table entries and messages and memory errors. CMC is specialized to event based systems supporting process communication through shared memory. The successor states are generated by calling all possible event handlers from the given state. CMC is capable to detect an error between two events and to state the kind of violation. The only witness of an error is the sequence of processed events. A sequence of events does not lead straight forward to the executed source lines, while a *StEAM* error trail states every executed source line. To control the behaviour of the dynamic memory allocation, `malloc` is overloaded, such that processes with the same sequence of calls to `malloc` have the same memory map for all allocated variables. *StEAM* identifies memory allocation and access by directly interpreting the machine code.

Verisoft [11] uses the same approach as *CMC*. A scheduler emulates the process environment and calls event handlers to generate all possible sequences of events. In contrast to *CMC*, *Verisoft* does not store all processed states in a hash table. It combines persistent sets and sleep sets, that refer to a notion of independency of transitions to restrict search. This is advantageously, if the search graph is

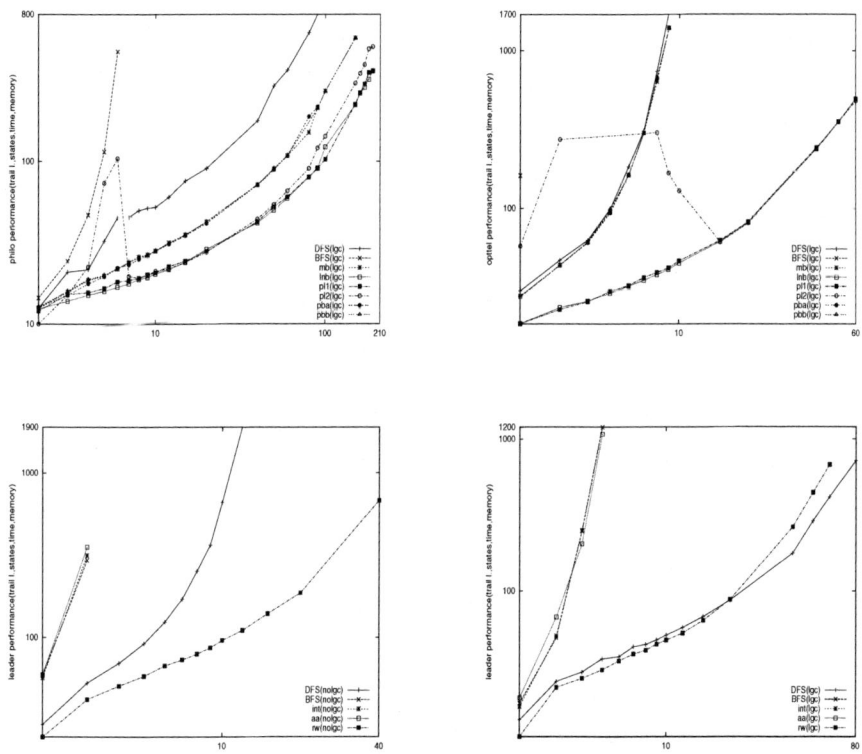

Fig. 4. Performance for philo/lgc, opttel/lgc, leader/nolgc, leader/lgc. x-axes denote scale, y-axes denote the geometric mean of trail length, states, time and memory.

finite and acyclic. To avoid infinite search for arbitrary search graphs, the search is depth-bounded. This approach minimizes memory usage, but may lead to repeated computation of identical states that are not identified as such. The limitation of the search-depth can miss the detection of errors.

sC++ and AX. In [3], semantics are described to translate sC++ source code into Promela - the input language of the model checker Spin [17]. The language sC++ is an extension of `c++` with concurrency. Many simplifying assumptions are made for the modeling process: only basic types are considered, no structures, no type definitions, no pointers. A similar approach is made by the tool *AX* (Automaton eXtractor) [18]. Here, Promela models can be extracted from `c` source code at a user defined level of abstraction.

BLAST [14], the *Berkeley Abstraction Software Toolkit* is a model checker for c programs, which is based on the property-driven construction and model checking of software abstractions. The tools takes as its input a c program and a safety monitor written in c. The verification process is based upon counterexample driven refinement: Starting from an abstract model of the program as a pushdown automaton, the tool checks, if the model fulfills the desired property. If an error state is found, BLAST automatically checks, if the abstract counterexample corresponds to a concrete counterexample in the actual program. If this is not the case, an additional set of predicates is chosen to build a more concrete model and the property is checked anew.

SLAM [1] also uses counter-example driven refinement. Here a boolean abstraction of the program is constructed. Then a reachability analysis is performed on the boolean program. Afterwards, additional predicates are discovered to define the boolean program - if necessary.

Bandera [5] constitutes a multi-functional tool for Java program verification. Bandera is capable of extracting models from Java source code and converting them to the input language of several well known model checkers such as Spin or SMV. As one very important option to state space reduction, Bandera allows to *slice* source code.

Bogor [23] is a model checking framework with an extendible input language for defining domain-specific state space encodings, reductions and search algorithms. It allows domain experts to build a model checker optimized for their specific domain without in-depth knowledge about the implementation of a specific model checker. The targeted domains include code, designs and abstractions of software layers. Bogor checks systems specified in a revised version of the BIR format, which is also used in Bandera [5,13].

9   Conclusion

This paper introduces *StEAM*, an assembly-level c++ model checker. We give insight into the structure and working of our tool. The purpose of the tool is to show that the verification of actual c++ programs is possible without generating an abstract model of the source code.

Our approach of directed program model checking outperforms undirected search with respect to trail length and maximum scale. We further extended the set of heuristics in model checking that are specifically tailored to find deadlocks and assertion violations. Many of the newly invented heuristics perform better than known heuristics. One option are *favoring pattern*, heuristics that relate to *symmetry reduction*. Another contribution are *lgcs*, that relate to *partial order reduction*. Both approaches encode pruning options in form of state preference rules and significantly improves the performance with respect to most search methods.

StEAM currently supports assertions for the definition of properties. This already allows testing for safety properties and invariants, which may be sufficient in many cases. However, for the verification of more complex properties, support for temporal logics like LTL is desirable. Subsequent work will focus on how the functionality of such logics can be implemented in a straightforward manner, that is accessible for practitioners. Also, we will add automatic detection of illegal memory access.

In the future we will also consider new models, heuristics and search methods, e.g. we will integrate variations of DFS such as iterative deepening and related search methods to reduce the memory requirements.

Acknowledgements. Tilman Mehler is supported by DFG, in the project *Directed Model Checking with Exploration Algorithms of Artificial Intelligence*. Stefan Edelkamp is supported by DFG, in the project *Heuristic Search*. We thank Bob Daley for his friendly support concerning ICVM.

References

1. T. Ball and S. K. Rajamani. The SLAM Project: Debugging System Software via Static Analysis. In *ACM SIGPLAN-SIGACT symposium on Principles of programming languages*, pages 1–3, 2002.
2. D. Bosnacki, D. Dams, and L. Holenderski. A Heuristic for Symmetry Reductions with Scalarsets. In *International Symposium on FME: Formal Methods for Increasing Software Productivity*, pages 518–533, 2001.
3. T. Cattel. Modeling and Verification of sC++ Applications. In *Tools and Algorithms for the Construction and Analysis of Systems (TACAS)*, pages 232–248, 1998.
4. E. M. Clarke, O. Grumberg, and D. A. Peled. *Model checking*. MIT Press, 1999.
5. J. Corbett, M. Dwyer, J. Hatcliff, C. Pasareanu, Robby, S. Laubachand, and H. Zheng. Extracting Finite-state Models from Java Source Code. In *International Conference on Software Engineering (ICSE)*, pages 439–448, 2000.
6. C. Demartini, R. Iosif, and R. Sisto. dSPIN: A dynamic extension of SPIN. In *Model Checking Software (SPIN)*, pages 261–276, 1999.
7. M. Dwyer, J. Hatcliff, V. Prasad, and Robby. Exploiting Object Escape and Locking Information in Partial Order Reduction for Concurrent Object-Oriented Programs. *To appear in Formal Methods in System Design Journal (FMSD)*, 2004.
8. S. Edelkamp, A. L. Lafuente, and S. Leue. Trail-directed Model Checking. In Scott D. Stoller and Willem Visser, editors, *Electronic Notes in Theoretical Computer Science*, volume 55. Elsevier Science Publishers, 2001.
9. S. Edelkamp and P. Leven. Directed Automated Theorem Proving. In *Logic for Programming Artificial Intelligence and Reasoning (LPAR)*, pages 145–159, 2002.
10. S. Edelkamp and T. Mehler. Byte Code Distance Heuristics and Trail Direction for Model Checking Java Programs. In *2nd Workshop on Model Checking and Artificial Intelligence (MoChArt)*, pages 69–76, 2003.
11. P. Godefroid. Model Checking for Programming Languages using Verisoft. In *Symposium on Principles of Programming Languages*, pages 174–186, 1997.

12. A. Groce and W. Visser. Model Checking Java Programs using Structural Heuristics. In *International Symposium on Software Testing and Analysis (ISSTA)*, pages 12–21, 2002.

13. J. Hatcliff and O. Tkachuck. The Bandera Tools for Model-checking Java Source Code: A User's Manual. Technical report, Kansas State University, 1999.

14. A. Henzinger, R. Jhala, R. Majumdar, and G. Sutre. Software Verification with BLAST. In *Model Checking Software (SPIN)*, pages 235–239, 2003.

15. G. J. Holzmann. *Design and Validation of Computer Protocols*. Prentice-Hall, Englewood Cliffs, New Jersey, 1991.

16. G. J. Holzmann. State Compression in SPIN. In *Third Spin Workshop*, Twente University, The Netherlands, 1997.

17. G. J. Holzmann. The Model Checker SPIN. *Software Engineering*, 23(5):279–295, 1997.

18. G. J. Holzmann. Logic Verification of ANSI-C code with SPIN. In *Model Checking Software (SPIN)*, pages 131–147, 2000.

19. R. Iosif. Exploiting Heap Symmetries in Explicit-State Model Checking of Software. In *International Conference on Automated Software Engineering (ICSE)*, pages 26–29, 2001.

20. A. Lluch-Lafuente, S. Leue, and S. Edelkamp. Partial Order Reduction in Directed Model Checking. In *Model Checking Software (SPIN)*, pages 112–127, 2002.

21. T. Mehler and P. Leven. *Introduction to StEAM - An Assembly-Level Software Model Checker*. Technical report, University of Freiburg, 2003.

22. M. Musuvathi, D. Park, A. Chou, D. Engler, and D. Dill. CMC: A Pragmatic Approach to Model Checking Real Code. In *Symposium on Operating Systems Design and Implementation (OSDI)*, 2002.

23. Robby, M. B. Dwyer, and J. Hatcliff. Bogor: An Extensible and Highly-Modular Software Model Checking Framework. In *European Software Engineering Conference (ESEC)*, pages 267–276, 2003.

24. W. Visser, K. Havelund, G. Brat, and S. Park. Java PathFinder - second generation of a Java model checker. Post-CAV Workshop on Advances in Verification, (WAVe), 2000.

25. W. Visser, K. Havelund, G. Brat, and S. Park. Model Checking Programs. In *International Conference on Automated Software Engineering (ICSE)*, pages 3–12, 2000.

Fast and Accurate Bitstate Verification for SPIN

Peter C. Dillinger and Panagiotis Manolios

Georgia Institute of Technology
College of Computing, CERCS Lab
801 Atlantic Drive
Atlanta, GA 30332-0280
{peterd,manolios}@cc.gatech.edu

Abstract. Bitstate hashing in SPIN has proved invaluable in probabilistically detecting errors in large models, but in many cases, the number of omitted states is much higher than it would be if SPIN allowed more than two hash functions to be used. For example, adding just one more hash function can reduce the probability of omitting states at all from 99% to under 3%. Because hash computation accounts for an overwhelming portion of the total execution cost of bitstate verification with SPIN, adding additional independent hash functions would slow down the process tremendously. We present efficient ways of computing multiple hash values that, despite sacrificing independence, give virtually the same accuracy and even yield a speed improvement in the two hash function case when compared to the current SPIN implementation.

Another key to accurate bitstate hashing is utilizing as much memory as is available. The current SPIN implementation is limited to only 512MB and allows only power-of-two granularity (256MB, 128MB, etc). However, using 768MB instead of 512MB could reduce the probability of a single omission from 20% to less than one chance in 10,000, which demonstrates the magnitude of both the maximum and the granularity limitation. We have modified SPIN to utilize any addressable amount of memory and use any number of efficiently-computed hash functions, and we present empirical results from extensive experimentation comparing various configurations of our modified version to the original SPIN.

1   Introduction

"Bitstate verification" [10] is a term that has been used by the model checking community to refer to explicit-state model checking with Bloom filters. Explicit-state model checkers, such as Holzmann's SPIN, have been used with great success in a variety of domains, including verification of finite-state, concurrent systems, such as cache coherence and network protocols.

Much of the research in model checking is focused on tackling the *state explosion problem*: a linear increase in the number of components leads to an exponential increase in the size of the resulting models. State explosion is a particularly acute problem in the context of explicit model checking, as memory requirements depend linearly on the size of the state space. Because the most efficient explicit-state techniques call for storing the set of all visited states in core memory, making the representation of the visited set more compact means larger models can be explored more quickly. By resorting to probabilistic

S. Graf and L. Mounier (Eds.): SPIN 2004, LNCS 2989, pp. 57–75, 2004.
© Springer-Verlag Berlin Heidelberg 2004

methods of storing the visited set, the representation can be made exceptionally compact, enabling much larger state spaces to be tackled efficiently. The drawback of probabilistic methods, of course, is that there is a possibility of omitting states with errors.

The Bloom filter is a popular choice of data structure for compactly storing sets [2]. The main parameter for tuning a Bloom filter is the number of hash functions used, and the bitstate mode of SPIN utilizes a Bloom filter with 2 hash functions. In [17], Wolper and Leroy promote using 20 hash functions instead of Holzmann's choice of just 2, for in many cases, SPIN would be more accurate if more hash functions were used. However, Holzmann notes that the choice of 2 "was adopted in SPIN as a compromise between runtime expense and coverage," and explains why using more hash functions is impractical [11]:

> In a well-tuned model checker, the run-time requirements of the search depend linearly on k[, the number of hash functions used]: computing hash values is the single most expensive operation that the model checker must perform. The larger the value of k, therefore, the longer the search for errors will take. In the model checker SPIN, for instance, a run with $k = 90$ would take approximately 45 times longer than a run with $k = 2$.

We have discovered a Bloom filter enhancement that gives virtually the same effect as using more independent hash functions, but at a fraction of the runtime cost. For example, this technique alone can produce the effect of 20 hash functions with only 2.3 times the cost of using 2 hash functions—far from Holzmann's factor of 10. In the process of incorporating our technique into SPIN, we discovered other ways of improving the speed and accuracy of bitstate verification in SPIN. More specifically, we show that making more intelligent use of the Jenkins hash function [13] can significantly speed up verification. We tackle issues associated with accommodating an arbitrary amount of memory, and show how this simple issue can easily make orders of magnitude of difference in the possibility of incomplete coverage.

This paper is oriented toward describing and evaluating implementation considerations we made when implementing our modified version of SPIN. The analysis of our techniques in this paper is mostly experimental; a more formal, mathematical analysis of our techniques will appear elsewhere. We refer to our system as "Triple SPIN," or 3SPIN, which is available on the Web for download [5].

Many experimental results are presented throughout. All timings were taken on a 2.53Ghz Pentium 4 with 512MB of RDRAM running Red Hat Linux 7.3. We used version 3.1.1 of the GNU C compiler with third-level general optimizations and all Pentium 4-specific optimizations enabled.

To combat the state explosion problem, in addition to hashing—the main topic of this paper—explicit state model checkers use techniques such as partial order reductions [6, 8] and symmetry reductions [3]. The improvements to bitstate verification discussed in this paper do not affect its compatibility with these techniques, but we have disabled reductions in all of our tests in order to easily measure accuracy.

This paper is organized as follows. In Section 2 we give an overview of Bloom filters and show that they are quite sensitive to the number of hash functions used, *e.g.*, the expected number of omissions when using two hash functions can be several orders of magnitude greater than the number of expected omissions when using the optimal number of hash functions. Bloom filters employing more than two hash functions were thought to be impractical because of the running time overhead they incur, but in Sections 3 and 4 we present new techniques to address this issue. In Section 5 we address the memory limitations imposed by the current implementation of bitstate verification in SPIN, version 4.0.7. We wrap up with experimental results incorporating all the techniques from the paper in Section 6, and give conclusions and future directions for the research in Section 7.

2   Bloom Filters in Verification

In this section we overview Bloom filters and consider in more detail the trade-offs involved in a Bloom filter and how these apply in the realm of verification. We also present some analysis that sets up a framework for evaluating our results.

For the basics, we turn to Bloom himself [1]:

> [A Bloom filter] completely gets away from the conventional concept of organizing the hash area into cells. The hash area is considered as N individual addressable bits, with addresses 0 through $N - 1$. It is assumed that all bits in the hash area are first set to 0. Next, each message in the set to be stored is hash coded into a number of distinct bit addresses, say $a_1, a_2, \ldots, a_d$. Finally, all d bits addressed by a_1 through a_d are set to 1.
>
> To test a new message a sequence of d bit addresses, say $a'_1, a'_2, \ldots, a'_d$, is generated in the same manner as for storing a message. If all d bits are 1, the new message is accepted. If any of these bits is zero, the message is rejected.

In this paper, we refer to the d functions that produce the indices into the bit vector as the "index functions" and use m, k, and n to represent the size, in bits, of the Bloom filter, the number of index functions used, and the number of objects added to the Bloom filter, respectively.

Although Bloom filters can be very compact, the downside is that when a membership query indicates that an element is in the Bloom filter, there is a certain probability of an error—that is, of a *false positive*. If we assume that the index functions are independent and uniform, then the probability that an index function does not select a specific bit is $p = 1 - \frac{1}{m}$. After inserting i elements into the Bloom filter, the probability that a specific bit is still 0 is p^{ki}. Therefore, the probability of a false positive, after i elements have been added to the Bloom filter, is $\left(1 - p^{ki}\right)^k$.

While the false positive rate is the primary metric for evaluation and optimization in many applications of Bloom filters [2], the way we use Bloom filters in verification gives rise to two more meaningful metrics: the expected number of omissions and the probability of having no omissions.

We compute the expected number of omissions when attempting to add n distinct states by adding the probability of a false positive when i states have already been added to the Bloom filter, as i ranges from 0 to $n - 1$.

$$\sum_{i=0}^{n-1} \left(1 - p^{ki}\right)^k$$

To compute the probability of no omissions at all, we start by noting that in a Bloom filter containing i elements, the probability that adding a new element does *not* lead to an omission is just 1 minus the probability of a false positive, $1 - \left(1 - p^{ki}\right)^k$ The probability of there not being an omission at all is just the product of there not being an omission as i ranges from 0 to $n - 1$:

$$\prod_{i=0}^{n-1} \left(1 - \left(1 - p^{ki}\right)^k\right)$$

Both verification metrics, the number of expected omissions and the probability of no omissions, depend on m, n, and k. We have very little control over the values of m and n, as m is bound by the amount of memory we have available (the more the better) and n is the size of the transition system under consideration. Therefore, to obtain the best results for a fixed m and n, we have to choose the appropriate value of k. Figure 1 shows that the expected number of omissions is quite sensitive to the number of index functions used (note that we use a log scale on the y-axis). We ran 3SPIN, calling the Jenkins hash function k times, and using a 1MB Bloom filter on an instance of the PFTP problem consisting of 606,211 states. We varied k from 1 to 32 and we report the actual number of omissions, averaged over 100 runs. Notice that the number of omissions when using two index functions is about two orders of magnitude greater than the number of omissions when using eleven index functions.

The second curve in Figure 1 shows the number of expected omissions as given by the formula above for n equal to 606,211. There is a sizable gap between the two curves which at first one may think is due to less-than-ideal index functions, but the disparity is actually caused by a shortcoming of the theoretical analysis, which only considers one of two types of omissions. "Hash omissions" are those states that are omitted because of false positive Bloom filter queries. "Transitive omissions" are those states that are never reached because they are made unreachable by other omissions and, thus, are never queried against the Bloom filter. The gap in Figure 1 is mostly due to transitive omissions; *i.e.*, in our implementation there is an observable number of states (out of the 606,211 in total) that are never even considered. The theoretical analysis is far from useless, however, for as the figure shows, minimizing the number of hash omissions tends to also minimize all omissions.

More significantly, if the number of hash omissions is zero, the number of transitive omissions is also zero; consequently, the probability of no hash omissions is also the probability of no omissions altogether. Unlike expected omissions, the probability of no omissions matches almost exactly experimental results (see Table 1), justifying our "transitive omission" argument for the disparity in Figure 1.

We have seen that using the optimum number of index functions is very important in getting the most accuracy out of Bloom filters. While an analysis showing how to choose k is beyond the scope of this paper, a useful formula for estimating the best k given m and n is

$$\left\lceil 3.8^{\frac{1}{\frac{m}{n} + 4.2}} \cdot \frac{m}{n} \cdot ln\, 2 \right\rceil$$

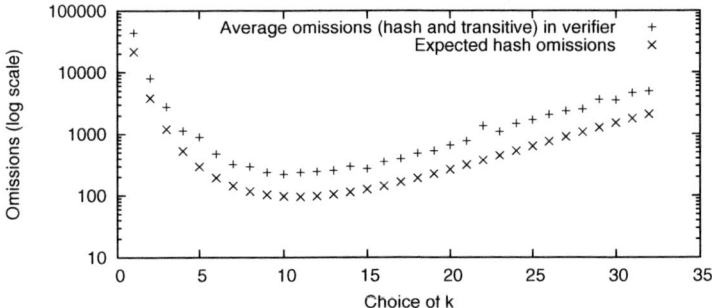

Fig. 1. We show the expected and observed omissions out of 606,211 states using 1MB for the Bloom filter, as k is varied. The theoretical optimum value for k is 11.

This closed estimate for the best k in verification was derived by refining a formula from [2], $\frac{m}{n} \cdot \ln 2$, which estimates the k that minimizes the false positive rate. Validation of our formula's accuracy will appear in future work.

3 Double and Triple Hashing

While Bloom filters employing more than two index functions can improve accuracy, they were thought to be impractical because of the running time overhead they incur. In this section we describe techniques for efficiently computing index values from just two or three hash values. Our techniques are similar to the "double hashing" scheme for collision resolution in open-addressed hash tables. While we give a short overview of double hashing below, a good reference is Chapter 11 of [4], and for a more complete account see [14,7].

3.1 Double Hashing Description

Open addressing refers to a type of hashing where elements are stored directly in a hash table. To insert an element the hash table is probed until an empty location is found, and a query consists of probing the table until either the element is found or it is clear that the element is not in the table. The probing sequence is obtained by applying a sequence of hash functions to an element. Just as with Bloom filters, applying multiple hash functions can incur a significant performance penalty. Double hashing is an efficient way of implementing open addressing which only uses two hash functions to generate a probing sequence. The first value (call it x) is the starting index of the probing sequence. Given some index in the probing sequence, the next is obtained by adding the second value (call it y). The addition is done modulo the number of indices to ensure that the sum is also a valid index.

Our double hashing scheme for Bloom filters is based on this idea: instead of using a sequence of index functions that are computed independently, use two functions, a and b, to compute values x and y, and use simple arithmetic on those values to generate all the required indices for each Bloom filter operation:

```
x := a(d) MOD m
y := b(d) MOD m
f[0] := x
i := 1
while i < k
        x := (x + y) MOD m
        f[i] := x
        i := i + 1
```

Note that $f[i] = x + iy\ MOD\ m$. Although in this pseudocode we store the index values into an array f, in actual code we would use the values as soon as they are computed, and, likewise, only compute as many values as are needed.

We MOD $a(d)$ and $b(d)$ because we are assuming that a and b are stock hash functions that have not been tailored to output values in our index space. SPIN requires similar MOD operations to get index values from hash functions, but the designers chose to only allow Bloom filter sizes that are powers of 2 so that efficient bit masking can be used for the MOD operations. Implementation of the MOD operations are discussed in Section 5.2, in which we describe how to efficiently loosen the power-of-two restriction.

As presented, the algorithm has a complication with respect to values of y. For example, if $y = 0$, only one unique index is probed. One way to fix this problem is to ensure that y is relatively non-zero and relatively prime to m. The way 3SPIN deals with this issues is discussed in Section 5.3.

3.2 Double Hashing Example

It may not be clear to those who are not intimately familiar with Bloom filters that our double hashing scheme can actually give higher accuracy than using just two index functions. Figures 2, 3, and 4 demonstrate that boosting k with double hashing can lead to better accuracy.

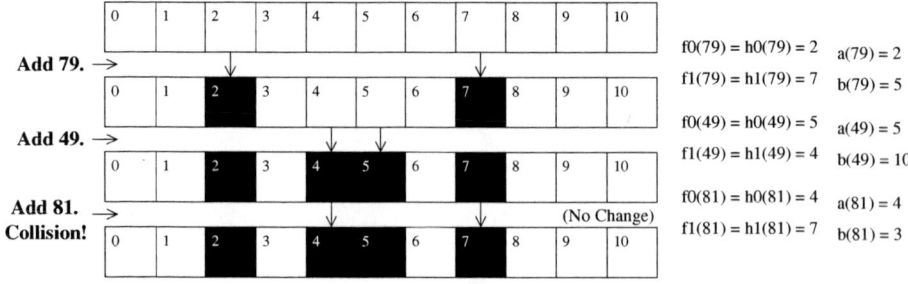

Fig. 2. We add data 79, 49, and 81 to a Bloom filter where $k = 2$ and $m = 11$. A collision occurs when 81 is queried/added. (We have set up the index functions to operates identically with or without double hashing when $k = 2$.)

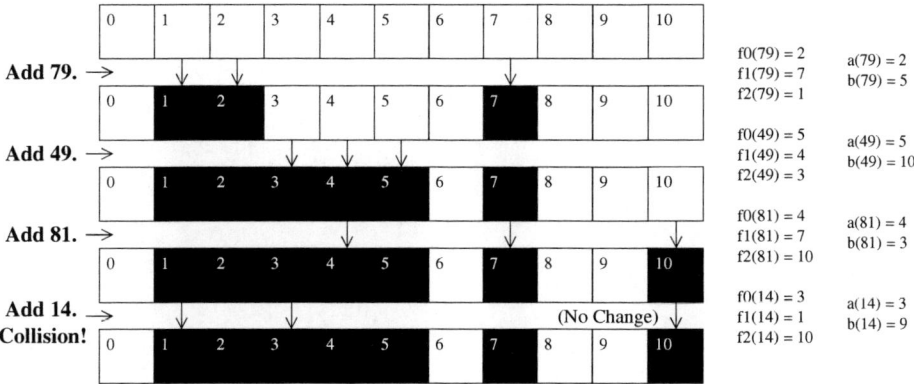

Fig. 3. We add data 79, 49, 81, and 14 to the same Bloom filter as in Figure 2 except $k = 3$ and double hashing is used. A collision occurs when 14 is queried/added.

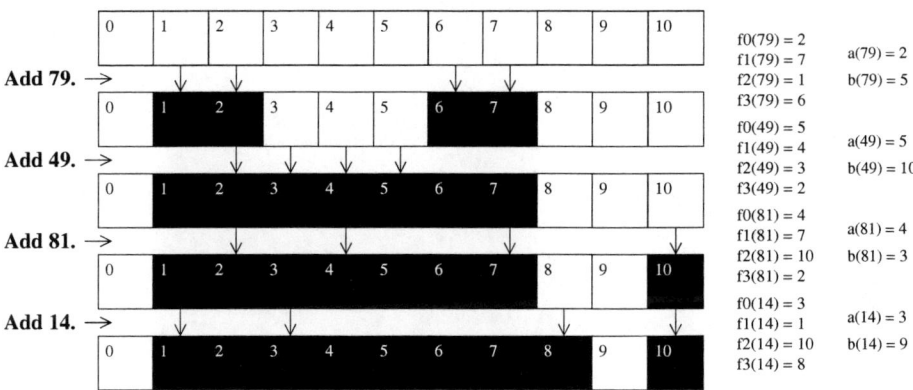

Fig. 4. This is the same example as in Figure 3 except $k = 4$. No collisions occur.

Figure 2 shows a Bloom filter to which elements 79, 49, and 81 are added. For this Bloom filter $k = 2$; that is, as many as two bits are set for each added element. If we interpret the figure as not using double hashing, the hash functions h_0 and h_1 serve as the index functions, and are defined as $h0(d) = d\ MOD\ 11$ and $h1(d) = (d\ DIV\ 11)\ MOD\ 11$. We can make the $k = 2$ case of double hashing yield the same pair of indices for all inputs by making $a(d) = h0(d)$ and $b(d) = (h1(d) - h0(d))\ MOD\ 11$. Recall from the double hashing algorithm that we compute the index functions for double hashing with $f_i(d) = (a(d) + i \cdot b(d))\ MOD\ m$, and in our example $m = 11$.

Adding 82 in Figure 2 does not change any bits in the Bloom filter and, thus, would have caused a hash omission if we were exploring a state space. If we boost k to 3 with double hashing, however, the collision is avoided and state 81 would not be omitted, as illustrated in Figure 3.

Likewise, adding 14 in Figure 3 would lead to an omission. Figure 4 shows that if 4 double-hashed index functions had been used instead, there would have been no omissions.

We have shown that using double hashing to implement more index functions can yield better accuracy than just using two hash values as indices, but more important is the degree of double hashing's accuracy and how that accuracy compares to using independent hash functions.

3.3   Double Hashing Accuracy

To test the accuracy of double hashing with respect to the expected number of omissions, we ran 3SPIN on a 606,211-state instance of PFTP using both double hashing and independent hash functions, while varying k. Figure 5 contains the results, where each data point is obtained by averaging over 100 runs. Notice that the number of omissions that occur with double hashing is very similar to the number of omissions we get when using independent hash functions. Also, the best choice of k for the independent case seems to be the best for the double hashing case as well.

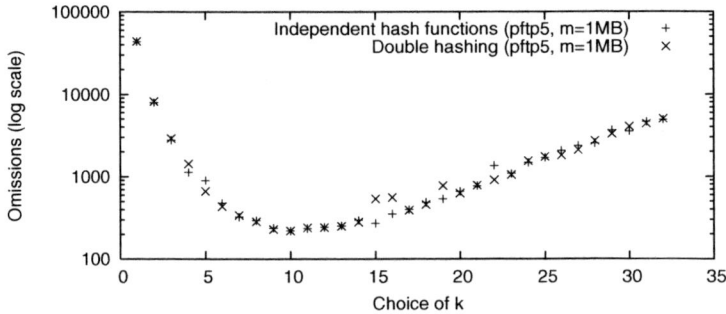

Fig. 5. The above shows the number of omissions from a 606,211-state instance of PFTP when varying the number of index functions and the specified index function implementation. Each data point is the average of 100 iterations. The curve with +'s is the same as in Figure 1.

To test the accuracy of double hashing with respect to the probability of no omissions at all, we ran 3SPIN on the same 606,211-state instance of PFTP with a 2MB Bloom filter using both double hashing and independent hash functions, with k set to 21. A theoretical analysis reveals that verification will be exhaustive 93.4% of the time, and as Table 1 demonstrates, double hashing performs very close to the theoretical expectation, though $4\frac{1}{2}$ times faster than the independent hash function implementation.

The competitive accuracy of double hashing breaks down, however, if one uses enough memory that using independent hash functions would have an almost unde-tectable probability of omissions, such as 1/16,000. Under such a setup, double hashing still has omissions about 2.5% of the time (see Table 3). This observation motivates something stronger than double hashing that has virtually the same speed.

Table 1. We show the results of verifying a 606,211-state instance of PFTP using 2MB for the Bloom filter, 21 index functions, and the specified implementation of those index functions. Each data point is the average of 20,000 iterations.

Implementation	Full coverage runs	Average running time
Independent	93.281%	19.88 seconds
Double Hashing	92.793%	4.43 seconds
Theoretical	93.383%	N/A

3.4   Triple Hashing

In order to achieve very low probabilities of omission, we have extended the idea of double hashing to what we call triple hashing. The idea is to use a function c to compute a value z which modifies y at each step, which is initially b(d). The implementation of triple hashing is an obvious extension to that of double hashing:

```
x, y, z := a(d) MOD m, b(d) MOD m, c(d) MOD m
f[0] := x
i := 1
while i < k
        x := (x + y) MOD m
        f[i] := x
        y := (y + z) MOD m
        i := i + 1
```

Note that $f[i] = x + iy + \frac{i(i-1)}{2}z \; MOD \; m$. The first of two intuitions that can explain the superiority of triple hashing is that we utilize more hash values, and thus collisions in the Bloom filter are less likely to occur. The second intuition is that because the function is more complicated, there is a smaller chance of several indices overlapping with several indices from a single previous addition.

This pseudocode for triple hashing suggests triple hashing would have significantly more per-k overhead than double hashing would, but most of the per-k overhead in double and triple hashing comes from main memory latency. Table 2 demonstrates this. The overhead of triple hashing vs. double hashing at $k = 20$ is not nearly enough to make (Double, $k = 21$) faster than (Triple, $k = 20$), assuming we do not have to compute any more hash values–an assumption that is addressed in Section 4.

Finally, in Table 3 we show that triple hashing can achieve much higher accuracy than double hashing. Triple seems to come much closer to what we expect from independent hash functions, but triple hashing is, of course, much faster than using independent hash functions, as Table 2 confirms.

4   The Jenkins Hash Function

The previous section gave an efficient way to reduce the problem of computing k index values from a state to the problem of computing just two or three. In this section we

Table 2. We present the running times of verifying a 606,211-state instance of PFTP using 2MB for the Bloom filter, the specified number of index functions, and the specified implementation of those index functions, although all implementations did the same amount of hash computation whether needed or not.

Implementation	Index functions	Average running time
Double	21	3.78 seconds
Triple	21	3.84 seconds
Double	20	3.61 seconds
Triple	20	3.73 seconds
Independent	21	9.36 to 19.88s (see Table 4)

Table 3. We show the results of verifying a 606,211-state instance of PFTP using 3MB for the Bloom filter, 30 index functions, and the specified implementation of those index functions. We use 100,000 iterations for each implementation, which is insufficient for quantifying the accuracies with any precision, but does give strong indication of the magnitudes.

Implementation	Proportion of runs with any omissions
Double Hashing	1 in 40
Triple Hashing	1 in 10,000
Theoretical	1 in 16,352

show how to get the most data out of a popular hash function and compute these two or three values in much less time than the default configuration of SPIN 4.0.7 computed the two hash values for $k = 2$ bitstate hashing.

4.1 Getting the Most from Jenkins

Because of its high quality and fast speed, Bob Jenkins' LOOKUP2 hash function [13, 12] is a popular choice among implementers of hash tables and Bloom filters; after all, the function is the default hash function in SPIN 4.0.7. Even though it only produces a 32-bit value, the function is often used to produce larger values or sequences of values by calling the function multiple times with different seed values.

If we take a look at the LOOKUP2 function, however, we see that it propagates a full 96 bits of data as it iterates over the input. What the function returns is just a 32-bit fragment of the propagated 96 bits. Although the word returned is the only one that satisfies certain properties that can be tested in Jenkins' lookup2.c [12], we have found that for our purposes, extracting all three words from a single run of Jenkins is about as good as calling the function three times.

4.2   Accuracy Validation

First we ran tests on Jenkins to make sure that each of the three output words are uniform on their own. If this were not the case, two sufficiently large[1], unique, randomly-chosen inputs would have better than a 1 in 2^{32} chance of producing the same 32-bit word of output. Equivalently, a 32-bit output is not uniform if inputs have better than a 1 in 2^8 chance of their output matching one of 2^{24} unique outputs. Running exactly this test repeatedly for each output word yielded probabilities that quickly converged at 1 in 2^8, as desired.

Next we sought to evaluate pairwise independence among the three pairings of output words. We followed a similar procedure to that above, except we were attempting to establish the uniformity of a 64-bit output. Observing only one repeated 64-bit output, we were unable to put an upper bound on the entropy in the output, but our results indicate the entropy is likely greater than 60 bits for each pair of words, leaving no doubt that extracting more than one word from Jenkins gives us access to substantially more hash information, if not a full 96 bits.

From a more practical standpoint, we ran tests to validate that using all three words from each call to Jenkins gives about the same accuracy in a Bloom filter as calling Jenkins three times. Table 4 shows the results of 20,000 executions each for two versions of SPIN, both of which use 21 index functions. The "Slow Jenkins" version uses separate calls to Jenkins for each index function—up to 21 calls for each Bloom filter operation. The "Fast Jenkins" version uses three words from each call to Jenkins and, thus, incurs a maximum cost of seven Jenkins calls per operation. We actually observed slightly higher accuracy with "Fast Jenkins," but the results are not statistically significant enough to establish that relationship. The results do establish that both implementations yield accuracy exceptionally close to what is expected in theory.

NOTE: These tests do not utilize double or triple hashing; the combination of all techniques is tested and validated in Section 6.

Table 4. We show the results of verifying a 606,211-state instance of PFTP using 2MB for the Bloom filter, 21 index functions, and the specified implementation of those index functions. We ran 20,000 iterations of each implementation.

Implementation	Full coverage runs	Average running time
Slow Jenkins	93.281%	19.88 seconds
Fast Jenkins	93.339%	9.36 seconds
Theoretical	93.383%	N/A

---

[1] We tested using seven words of input.

4.3 Speed Boost

Table 4 also includes execution times for the "Slow Jenkins" version and the "Fast Jenkins" versions. Hash computation clearly dominates the total execution cost, because a 67% reduction in hash computation time resulted in a 53% reduction in overall required execution time.

The "Fast Jenkins" version utilizing three index functions runs more quickly than the Jenkins configuration of SPIN 4.0.7, which uses two index functions, because "Fast Jenkins" can generate about three index functions with a single call to Jenkins. The results of these tests are in Table 5. The Jenkins configuration of SPIN 4.0.7 is the $k = 2$ case of what we have been calling "Slow Jenkins".

Table 5. We show the execution times for verifying a 606,211-state instance of PFTP using 2MB for the Bloom filter. The number and implementation of the index functions is indicated in the table.

Implementation	Index functions	Average running time
SPIN Jenkins	2	2.57 seconds
Fast Jenkins	2	1.86 seconds
Fast Jenkins	3	2.09 seconds

5   Arbitrary Memory Utilization

Two restrictions on the amount of memory that can be utilized by a Bloom filter in SPIN can have profound effects on the accuracy of bitstate verification. The first and most clearly debilitating limitation is the upper limit on the amount of memory that can be dedicated to a Bloom filter, 512 Megabytes[2]. The second limitation is that the Bloom filter in SPIN can only be sized to be a power of two. The impact of both limitations is great: theoretical analysis shows that a user of accurate bitstate verification who dedicates 768MB of memory to the Bloom filter instead of 512MB could have a 1 in 10,000 chance of any omissions instead of 1 in 5.

5.1   Increasing the Maximum

The reason for SPIN's maximum of 512 Megabytes dedicated to the Bloom filter is that 512 Megabytes is equal to 2^{32} Mega*bits*, and 32-bit values are used to index into the bit vector. The problem is that as byte- or word-addressed memories get close to the size of their address space, single words become insufficient for addressing individual bits across most of memory. The computer market is currently experiencing this problem, in which many 32-bit machines are sold with more than 512 Megabytes of memory.

---

[2] SPIN 4.0.7 would actually only work with up to 256MB for us, but analysis suggests that this is an implementation bug and not a design flaw.

Any solution to this problem would almost certainly involve more computation, so the best solution is likely to be one that eliminates the need for some existing computation. An example of such existing computation is the process of dividing a bit vector index into a word or byte index and an index of the bit within that word or byte. These operations boil down to dividing by some small power of two and taking the modulus with that same power of two, which can be implemented with bit shifting and bit masking, respectively.

Our solution, which we call "parallel indexing," accommodates any addressable amount of memory and eliminates a little bit of previously required per-k computation by computing word indexes and bit-within-word indexes independently. Consider having two sets of index functions: $F_0, F_1, \ldots, F_{k-1}$ give the addresses of the words to retrieve and $f_0, f_1, \ldots, f_{k-1}$ tell which bit to extract from each word. We can apply triple hashing on an A, B, and C to get the F_i values and the same on a, b, and c to get the f_i values. Because none of these functions is ever required to return more bits than can be stored in a word, the computation is simple.

5.2   Precise Granularity

Modifying SPIN to use any specified amount of memory for the Bloom filter is simple, but ensuring that accuracy is maintained and that the implementation is efficient is not as easy. The simple answer to using any amount of memory is to allocate that much, and then MOD hash function results by the appropriate value whenever indexes are computed.

Accuracy. The first problem with the simple answer is that MOD-ing by any value can affect the accuracy of the data structure. Consider a case in which one is *not* using "parallel indexing" and allocates about $\frac{2}{3}$rds of 2^{32} bits, about 341MB, for the Bloom filter. If we MOD the result of a 32-bit hash function to get an index, the first half of the indexes are twice as likely to be chosen as the second half. We can think of the MOD operation as putting the input values into m equivalence classes. No matter how hard we try to make the distribution among classes more uniform than what MOD gives us, if we have 50% more elements than equivalence classes, half of the classes are going to contain two elements and half are going to contain one element.

Our choice of indexing words as opposed to bytes in the parallel indexing scheme lessens the impact of the uniformity problem by a factor of four (in the 32-bit case), making the problem unlikely to ever have an observable impact. Whereas byte indexing gave a worst case of some indexes being twice as likely to be chosen as others, word indexing yields a worst case of some being 25% more likely. So even if m is a few Gigabytes, the difference is not significant, as Table 6 reveals.

Speed. The simple solution's second problem is that MOD operations on arbitrary values are much more costly than, for example, taking a modulus with respect to a power of two, which can be implemented with bit masking. In fact, outside of SPIN we have observed C's unsigned modulus operator to be ten times as slow as bit masking on a Pentium 4. Which MOD operations can we optimize away if using double or triple hashing and the parallel indexing scheme?

Table 6. We show the result of verifying a 723,035-state instance of LEADER using 2MB for the Bloom filter and 17 independent index functions, while varying the ratio of the probability of an index landing in the first half of the bit space over the second. Each data point is the average of 420 iterations.

Case	Ratio	% of full coverage runs
Byte indexing	2 : 1	16.16%
Word indexing	5 : 4	39.29%
Uniform	1 : 1	41.19%

The first observation is that the range on the bit-within-word indexes are always powers of two and, thus, can be optimized with bit masking.

While it is important for the a values in computing word indexes to have a fairly uniform distribution over all possible indexes, cheating on b and c does not sacrifice as much. In fact, we can MOD with respect to the greatest power of 2 less than m to compute values for b and c, enabling us to use bit masking for these.

Although we have reduced the number of unoptimized MOD operations for the initialization phase of each Bloom filter operation to just one (computing a), the most important MOD operations to optimize are those that happen within the iteration part of each Bloom filter operation, executing as many as k times for each Bloom filter operation.

In the triple hashing case, we can cheat even further on the ranges of values for b and c and eliminate the MOD for y := y + z altogether. More specifically, if $b + c \cdot k < m$ then y (initialized to b) will never overflow with respect to m, because y only needs to be incremented by z (whose value is c) $k - 1$ times.

The following observation allows us to speed up the MOD for x := (x + y): on each iteration of the loop we are guaranteed that $0 \le x < m$ and $0 \le y < m$. Thus, $0 \le x + y < 2m$, leaving only two cases to handle: $(x + y)\ MOD\ m = x + y$ (if $x + y < m$) and $(x + y)\ MOD\ m = x + y - m$ (otherwise; $m \le (x + y) < 2m$). We update this line from the pseudocode to reflect the optimization:

```
x := (x + y) MOD m
```

to be these lines:

```
x := x + y
if (x >= m) then x := x - m
```

The new code is much more efficient, as the graph in Figure 6 shows. The faster version in the graph implements triple hashing and all the optimizations discussed in this section, requiring just one unoptimized modulus per Bloom filter operation. The slower version does not use the optimization just described, requiring up to k unoptimized modulus operations per Bloom operation.

One thing to notice about the times reflected in the graph is that whenever the memory space is a power of two, both implementations run at the same slightly faster speed. Our modified version of SPIN dynamically picks the implementation best suited for the

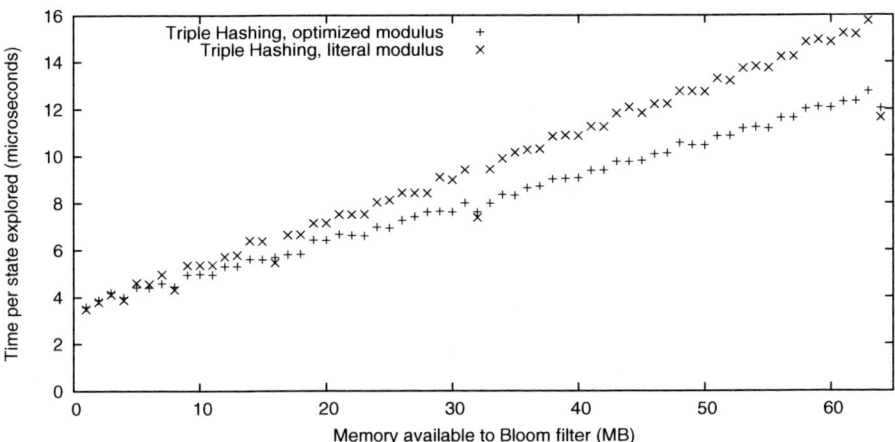

Fig. 6. This graph plots verification times for PFTP5 ($n = 606,211$) and depicts the difference in execution times resulting from optimizing $k - 1$ modulus operations per Bloom operation. k is varied from 1 to 27 to be optimal with respect to m/n.

choices of m and k. There are implementations optimized for when m is a power of two and, orthogonally, for when $k \leq 2$.

From the observation that the power of two cases are optimized in the graph, we see that even after our optimizations for utilizing arbitrary memory, we can still incur an execution speed cost of up to a few percent. Such an overhead is likely to be well worth the cost if it enables someone to use nearly twice as much memory.

5.3 With Our 96-Bit Jenkins

In this short section we reveal the synergy between the various approaches to improving the speed and accuracy of bitstate verification in SPIN.

With the 96 bits we get from a single call to Jenkins, we have enough hash information to effectively utilize triple hashing, parallel indexing, and precise memory utilization. We call our version incorporating all of these enhancements "Triple SPIN," or 3SPIN for short. Figure 7 has the precise breakdown of hash information used in 3SPIN.

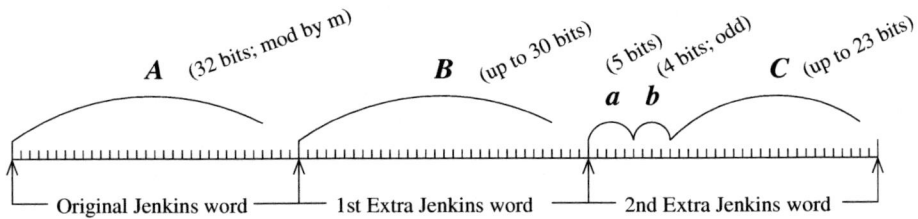

Fig. 7. The above diagram shows how we utilize the 96 bits of output from Jenkins.

A, B, and C give 3SPIN triple hashing on the word indexes, and a and b give double hashing on the bit-within-word indexes. Notice that we only use 4 bits for b even though it could be a 5-bit value; the reason is that making b odd (by multiplying by two and adding one) ensures that every bit-within-word index is unique up to $k = 32$. This guarantee ensures that each Bloom filter operation addresses k *unique* bit positions in the bit vector.

6   Overall Evaluation

In this section we evaluate 3SPIN, the system incorporating all the techniques described in this paper. Figure 8 shows that the observed average omissions for the various implementations is so close that it is hard to detect any differences. As previous tests have shown, we would need many high-accuracy runs to have a chance of distinguishing the implementations based on accuracy.

Figure 8 also shows the execution times for the tests. Unlike the number of omissions, the execution times are *profoundly* different, with our techniques taking about 1/4 the time of the implementation not taking advantage of our improvements when $k = 14$. Notice also that our $k = 14$ takes less than twice as much time as our $k = 2$—a far cry from Holzmann's experience with independent hash functions [11,10], which suggests $k = 14$ to be seven times as slow.

Figures 9 and 10 show the results when various amounts of memory are available for allocation to the Bloom filter. Notice that the versions that do not incorporate any of our enhancements for arbitrary memory allocation to the Bloom filter can only utilize an amount of memory equal to the greatest power of two not greater than m. For example, when 48MB is available, the unenhanced versions act as if only 32MBs are available, because that is the most the user can specify without requiring more than 48MB. If only 32MB is available, all versions using the best k (14 in this case) expect around 100 omissions, but when 48MB is available, 3SPIN expects about 1/100th as many omissions. Even though 3SPIN is using $k = 21$ to make best use of the 48MB, it runs in about 2/3rds the time. If, once again, only 32MB were available, 3SPIN would run in about half the time of the version with independent hash functions.

The version using two independent index functions was included in Figures 9 and 10 to reflect what is available in the latest version of SPIN, 4.0.7. According to these results, 3SPIN can utilize about 7 index functions ($m = 14$MB in this case) as fast as SPIN 4.0.7 can utilize two, and at that point 3SPIN expects about 1/13th as many omissions, partially because it is utilizing more memory and partially because it is using a more suitable k.

Our last set of experimental results (Table 7) just confirm that our results generalize to models other than those we have used in the rest of the paper.

7   Conclusions and Future Work

Early work by Holzmann and others has shown the utility of the Bloom filter data structure for probabilistically verifying systems with explicit state model checkers [9]. The main parameter for tuning a Bloom filter is the number of hash functions used, k, but there is a tension between accuracy and efficiency, as small values of k lead to fast

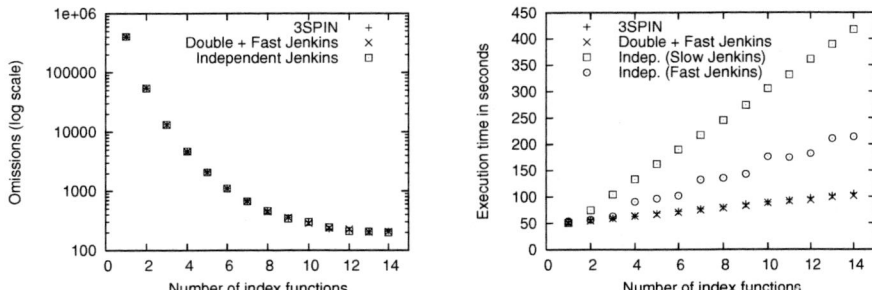

Fig. 8. On the left we have plotted the number of omissions from a 14,536,469-state instance of PFTP(D=1,Q=2) using 32MB for the Bloom filter and k values up to 14, the optimal for this m and n. The right shows the execution times for the same tests. Each data point represents about 5 iterations.

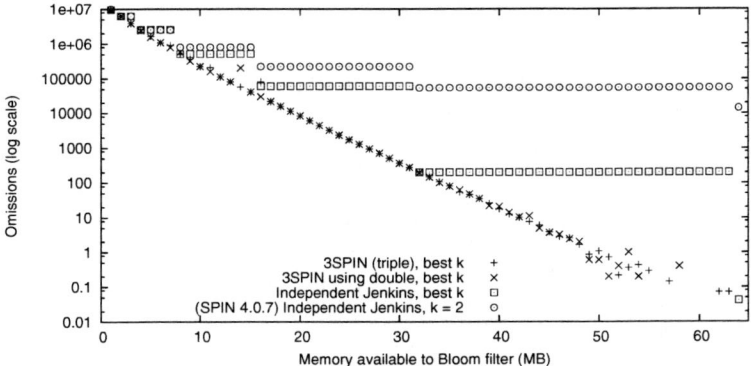

Fig. 9. Here we have plotted the number of omissions from PFTP(D=1,Q=2) for various implementations and various amounts of memory available to the Bloom filter. Notice that implementations only supporting power-of-two granularity will only utilize the greatest power of two less than or equal to the amount available. Each data point is the average over about 20 iterations.

Table 7. Validation of our approaches using models other than PFTP. In each case, all our techniques and optimizations are used. The k values are annotated with either "(opt)", indicating that the choice was optimal for m and n, or "(sub)" indicating we chose a k different from the optimal. All these models are included in the SPIN distribution.

Model	States	m	k	% runs full	Expected	Iterations
Peterson4	7,308,888	32MB	25 (opt)	99.11%	99.15%	336
Leader7	723,035	3MB	8 (sub)	77.34%	75.69%	331
Sort9	2,509,313	8MB	20 (opt)	59.88%	63.38%	329

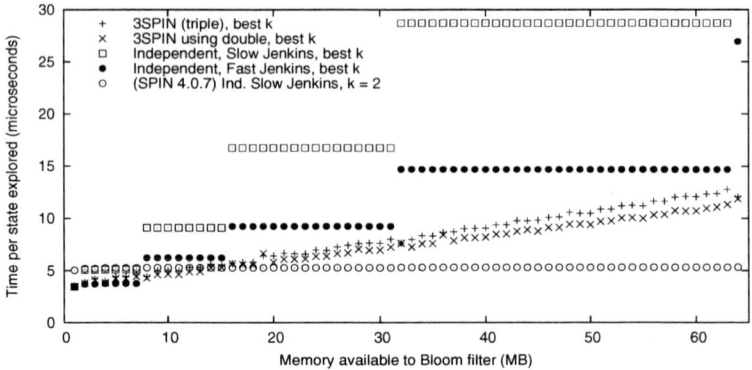

Fig. 10. This graph shows times for the executions in Figure 9. Note that four implementations use the optimal values for k, which range from 1 to 27 depending on m. The other implementation, SPIN 4.0.7, always uses $k = 2$, which explains why it becomes the fastest at $m = 14$MB.

running times, but the value of k that yields the best accuracy may be quite large. SPIN is optimized for speed, and, thus, it only allows k to be 1 or 2. Holzmann justified this choice by pointing out that running a well-tuned model checker with 2 hash functions can be $\frac{j}{2}$ times faster than using j hash functions. The belief was that one could get accuracy or efficiency, but not both.

We show that you can have your cake and eat it too. We have entitled this paper "Fast *and* Accurate Bitstate Verification for SPIN," because that is exactly what we provide with 3SPIN, a system we developed by modifying SPIN 4.0.7. Key components of 3SPIN include our double and triple hashing techniques for Bloom filters, which greatly reduce the execution time of highly-accurate bitstate verification. In fact, 3SPIN can use about 7 hash functions while running as fast as SPIN (using 2 hash functions).

3SPIN also has the ability to use as much main memory for the Bloom filter as is available, whereas SPIN only allows the size of the Bloom filter to be a power of 2, up to 512MB. The motivation behind this improvement is simple: using more available main memory for the Bloom filter *always* improves the expected accuracy of a bitstate search. For example, by using just 50% more memory than SPIN allows, we can be 2,000 times less likely to have an omission.

For future work, we plan to explore the use of Bloom filters in verification from a more analytical standpoint and to examine the impact of this work on techniques such as sequential multihashing [10]. We also plan to compare our techniques to other probabilistic verification techniques such as hash compaction [15,16].

References

1. B. H. Bloom. Space/time trade-offs in hash coding with allowable errors. *Communications of the ACM*, 13(7):422–426, July 1970.
2. A. Broder and M. Mitzenmacher. Network applications of Bloom filters: A survey. In *Proc. of the 40th Annual Allerton Conference on Communication, Control, and Computing*, pages 636–646, 2002.

3. C.N. Ip and D.L. Dill. Better verification through symmetry. In D. Agnew, L. Claesen, and R. Camposano, editors, *Computer Hardware Description Languages and their Applications*, pages 87–100, Ottawa, Canada, 1993. Elsevier Science Publishers B.V., Amsterdam, Netherland.

4. T. H. Cormen, C. Stein, R. L. Rivest, and C. E. Leiserson. *Introduction to Algorithms*. McGraw-Hill Higher Education, 2001.

5. P. C. Dillinger. 3SPIN Home Page. http://www.cc.gatech.edu/~peterd/3spin/.

6. P. Godefroid and P. Wolper. A partial approach to model checking. In *Logic in Computer Science*, pages 406–415, 1991.

7. G. H. Gonnet. *Handbook of Algorithms and Data Structures*. Addison-Wesley, 1984.

8. G. Holzmann and D. Peled. Partial order reduction of the state space. In *First SPIN Workshop*, Montrèal, Quebec, 1995.

9. G. J. Holzmann. Algorithms for automated protocol validation. Technical Report 69:32-44, AT&T Technical Journal, 1990.

10. G. J. Holzmann. An analysis of bitstate hashing. In *Proc. 15th Int. Conf on Protocol Specification, Testing, and Verification, INWG/IFIP*, pages 301–314, Warsaw, Poland, 1995. Chapman & Hall.

11. G. J. Holzmann. *The Spin Model Checker: Primer and Reference Manual*. Addison-Wesley, Boston, Massachusetts, 2003.

12. B. Jenkins. http://burtleburtle.net/bob/c/lookup2.c, 1996.

13. B. Jenkins. Algorithm alley: Hash functions. *Dr. Dobb's Journal*, September 1997.

14. D. E. Knuth. *The Art of Computer Programming*, volume 3: Sorting and Searching. Addison Wesley Longman Publishing Co., Inc., 2nd edition, 1997.

15. U. Stern and D. L. Dill. Improved probilistic verification by hash compaction. In *Correct Hardware Design and Verification Methods*. Volume 987 of Lecture Notes in Computer Science, 1995.

16. U. Stern and D. L. Dill. A new scheme for memory-efficient probabilistic verification. In *Joint Int. Conf. on Formal Description Techn. for Distr. Systems and Comm. Protocols, and Protocol Spec., Testing, and Verification*, pages 333–348, 1996.

17. P. Wolper and D. Leroy. Reliable hashing without collision detection. In *5th International Conference on Computer Aided Verification*, pages 59–70, 1993.

Model-Driven Software Verification

Gerard J. Holzmann
Rajeev Joshi

JPL Laboratory for Reliable Software
California Institute of Technology
4800 Oak Grove Drive
Pasadena, CA 91006
gerard.j.holzmann@jpl.nasa.gov
rajeev.joshi@jpl.nasa.gov

Abstract. In the classic approach to logic model checking, software verification requires a manually constructed artifact (the model) to be written in the language that is accepted by the model checker. The construction of such a model
typically requires good knowledge of both the application being verified and of
the capabilities of the model checker that is used for the verification. Inadequate knowledge of the model checker can limit the scope of verification that
can be performed; inadequate knowledge of the application can undermine the
validity of the verification experiment itself.
In this paper we explore a different approach to software verification. With this
approach, a software application can be included, without substantial change,
into a verification test-harness and then verified directly, *while preserving the
ability to apply data abstraction techniques.* Only the test-harness is written in
the language of the model checker. The test-harness is used to drive the application through all its relevant states, while logical properties on its execution are
checked by the model checker. To allow the model checker to track state, and
avoid duplicate work, the test-harness includes definitions of all data objects in
the application that contain state information.
The main objective of this paper is to introduce a powerful extension of the
SPIN model checker that allows the user to directly define data abstractions in
the logic verification of application level programs.

1. Introduction

In the classic approach to software verification based on logic model checking techniques, the verification process begins with the manual construction of a high-level
model of a source program. The advantage of this approach is that the model can
exploit a broad range of abstraction techniques, which can significantly lower the verification complexity. The disadvantage is that the construction of the model requires
not only skill in model building, but also a fairly deep understanding of the functioning of the implementation level code that is the target of the verification. Any misun-
derstanding translates into a loss of accuracy of the model and thereby into a loss of
accuracy of the verification. If errors are found in the model checking process, these
misunderstandings can often be removed, but if no errors are found the user could
erroneously conclude that the application was error free.

In this paper we describe a new verification method that in many cases of practical
interest can avoid the need to manually construct a verification model, while still
retaining the capability to define powerful abstractions that can be used to reduce

S. Graf and L. Mounier (Eds.): SPIN 2004, LNCS 2989, pp. 76–91, 2004.
© Springer-Verlag Berlin Heidelberg 2004

verification complexity. We call this method "model-driven software verification."

In Section 2 we discuss the basic method of using embedded C or C++ code within SPIN verification models, and we discuss a relatively small extension that was introduced in SPIN version 4.1 to support data abstraction on embedded C code. Section 3 contains a discussion of two example applications, Section 4 reviews related work, and Section 5 presents our conclusions.

2. Model Checking with Embedded C Code

SPIN versions 4.0 and later support the inclusion of embedded C or C++ code within verification models [8,9]. A total of five different primitives can be used to connect a verification model to implementation level C code. Some of these primitives serve to define what the *state* of the model is, with optionally some of the state information residing in the application. Other primitives serve to define either conditional or unconditional *state transitions*.

One of the primitives that can be used to define *state* is c_decl, which is normally used to introduce the types and names of externally declared C data objects that are referred to in the model. Another primitive of this type is c_track, which is used to define which of the data objects that appear in the embedded C code should be considered to hold state information that is relevant to the verification process.

Two other primitives define state *transitions* with the help of C code. The first of these is c_code, which can be used to enclose an arbitrary fragment of C code that is used to effect the desired state transition. The last primitive we discuss here is c_expr, which can be used to evaluate an arbitrary side-effect free expression in C to compute a Boolean truth value that is then used to determine the executability of the statement itself.

Figure 1 illustrates the use of these four primitives with a small example.

```
c_decl {
        extern float x;
        extern void fiddle(void);
};

c_track "&x" "sizeof(float)";

init {
        do
        :: c_expr { x < 10.0 } -> c_code { fiddle(); }
        :: else -> break
        od
}
```

Fig. 1. Embedded C Code Primitives.

The first statement in this example introduces definitions of an externally declared floating point variable named x and an externally declared function named fid-dle(). Presumably, the variable holds state information we are interested in, and the function defines a state transition. To record the fact that the external variable holds state information that must be tracked by the model checker, the c_track primitive is used to provide the model checker with two salient facts: the address of the variable and its size in bytes. The model checker will now instrument the verification engine to copy the current value of variable x into the state descriptor after any transition in which its value could have changed (i.e., after every execution of a c_code statement). Similarly, whenever the verifier performs a backtracking step for any statement that could have changed the value of the variable, the code of the verifier is again instrumented to reset the value of x to the copy of its previous value that was stored in the state descriptor for the earlier state.

The init process in this example model will now repeatedly call the external function fiddle() until it sees that the value of floating point variable x is less than 10.0, after which it will stop.

Effectively, these extensions allow us to introduce new datatypes in verification models, well beyond what PROMELA supports, and it allows us to define new types of transitions, with SPIN performing the normal model checking process.

It is important to note here that the c_track primitive, as used here, supports two separate goals: state tracking and state matching.

☐   State *tracking* allows us to accurately restore the value of data objects to their previous states when reversing the execution of statements during the depth-first search process.

☐   State *matching* allows us to recognize when a state is revisited during the search. When a state is revisited, the model checker can immediately backtrack to a previous state to avoid repeating part of the search that cannot yield new results.

We will see shortly that if we modify the way in which state information can be matched, while retaining accurate tracking, we can define powerful abstractions that can significantly reduce the complexity of verifications.

2.1. Tracking without Matching

There are cases where the value of an external data object should be tracked, to allow the model checker to restore the value of these data objects when *backtracking*, but where the data object does not actually hold relevant state information. It could also be that the data object does hold state information, but contains too much detail. In these cases we would benefit from defining abstractions on the data that are used in state *matching* operations, while retaining all details that are necessary to restore state in the application in *tracking* operations.

A relatively small extension that makes it possible to do this was included in SPIN, starting with version 4.1. The extension is to support an additional, and optional, argument to the c_track primitive that specifies whether the data object that is referred to should be matched in the statespace. There are two versions:

```
c_track "&x" "sizeof(float)" "Matched";
```

and

```
c_track "&x" "sizeof(float)" "UnMatched";
```

with the first of these two being the default if no third argument is provided (and backward compatible with the original definition of the c_track primitive in [9]).

The value of *unmatched* data objects is saved on the search stack, but not in the state descriptor.

The resulting SPIN nested-depth first search algorithm is identical to the one

```
 1 proc dfs1(s)
 2         add s to Stack1
 3         add {f(s),0} to States
 4         for each transition (s,a,s') do
 5                 if {f(s'),0} not in States then dfs1(s') fi
 6         od
 7         if accepting(f(s)) then seed := {f(s),1}; dfs2(s,1) fi
 8         delete s from Stack1
 9 end

10 proc dfs2(s)    /* nested search */
11         add s to Stack2
12         add {f(s),1} to States
13         for each transition (s,a,s') do
14                 if {f(s'),1} == seed then report cycle
15                 else if {f(s'),1} not in States then dfs2(s') fi
16         od
17         delete s from Stack2
18 end
```

Fig. 2. Nested Depth-First Search with Abstraction (cf. Fig. 8 in [1]).

discussed in [1] in the context of a discussion on symmetry reduction. For convenience, Figure 2 reproduces the algorithm as it was discussed in [1] (see [9] for a more basic description of the standard nested depth-first search algorithm). The abstract representation of a state is computed here by abstraction function f(s).

2.2. Validity of Abstractions

The extension of the c_track primitive allows us to include data in a model that has relevance to the accurate execution of implementation level code, but no relevance to the verification of that code.

The simplest use of this new option is to use it to track data without storing it in the model checker's state-vector, where before the only way to track it would have been to do just that. When used in this way, the use of unmatched c_track primitives equates to *data hiding*.

Another use is to use unmatched c_track statements to hide the values of selected data objects from the state-vector, and then to add abstraction functions (implemented in C) to compute abstract representations of the data that will now be matched in the state-vector, using additional *matched* c_track primitives. We can now achieve true abstractions, though of course only of the value of data objects.

As a simple example of the latter type of use, consider two implementation level integer variables x and y that appear in an application program. Suppose further that the absolute value of these two variables can be shown to be irrelevant to the verification attempt, but the fact that the sum of these two variables is odd or even is relevant. We can now setup the required data abstraction for this application by defining the following c_track primitives:

```
/* data hiding */
        c_track "&x" "sizeof(int)" "UnMatched";
        c_track "&y" "sizeof(int)" "UnMatched";
/* abstraction: */
        c_track "&sumxy" "sizeof(unsigned char)" "Matched";
```

and we add the abstraction function:

```
c_code {
        void abstraction(void) { sumxy = (x+y)%2; }
}
```

which should now be called after each state transition that is made through calls on the application level code.

The abstractions have to be chosen carefully, to make sure that they preserve the logical soundness and completeness of the verification. This is clearly not true for all possible abstractions one could define with the mechanism we have discussed. Consider, for instance, the abstraction above in the context of the following model:

```
init {
        c_code { x = y = 0; abstraction(); };
        do
        :: c_code { x = (x+1)%M ; y = (y+1)%N ; abstraction(); }
        od
}
```

Suppose we are checking the invariant that $x + y$ is even. This invariant holds for the model above if both M and N are even, but not in general. For instance, it does not hold for the case $M = 3$, $N = 4$. In this case, the model checker would stop the search after exploring the first transition, and erroneously declare that the invariant holds. In the next subsection, we describe a sufficient condition for ensuring that the verification is sound with respect to the abstraction, for a given model.

2.3. Sufficient Conditions for Soundness

The model-checker checks properties by exploring the set of reachable states, starting from a predetermined initial state. Exploring a state consists of enumerating its successors, determining which of these states are potentially *relevant*, and recording the newly encountered states in some data-structure. This data-structure is, for instance, a stack in a depth-first search, and it is a queue in a breadth-first search.

Given a symmetric relation ~ on concrete states, a state s is considered *relevant* if the search has not seen any state t such that $s{\sim}t$. In the following discussion, we will refer to states that have been visited in the search at least once as *encountered* states, and to those encountered states whose complete set of successors has been computed as *explored* states. (Note that the use of no abstraction corresponds to the situation in which ~ is the identity relation. In this case a state is considered relevant if it has not been encountered before.)

The search algorithm we have outlined explores states in the concrete model, and in effect maintains a concrete path to each state on the depth-first search stack. Thus any abstraction relation is necessarily logically complete. To ensure that the abstraction relation ~ is also logically sound, we need to ensure that its use does not cause the search algorithm to miss any error states. Below, we present a condition for ensuring this. We use the following notation: w, x, y, z denote states, and σ, τ denote paths. We write σ_i to denote the i-th state in σ. We use $\rightarrow$ to denote the transition relation, so $x \rightarrow y$ denotes that there is a transition from state x to state y.

A symmetric relation on concrete states is a *bisimulation* [13] when it satisfies the following condition:

$$\forall w, y, z: \; w{\sim}y \wedge y \rightarrow z => (\exists x: \; w \rightarrow x \wedge x{\sim}z) \qquad (1)$$

Thus states w and y are bisimilar if, whenever there is a transition from y to z, there is a successor x of w such that x and y are also bisimilar. Given a bisimulation ~, we say paths σ and τ *correspond* when $\forall i$: $\sigma_i \sim \tau_i$.

The importance of bisimulation is given by the following theorem [1,2].

Theorem. Let ~ be a bisimulation, and let AP be a set of atomic propositions such that every proposition P in AP satisfies

$$\forall x, y: \quad P(x) \wedge x \sim y \Rightarrow P(y) \tag{2}$$

Then, any two bisimilar states satisfy the same set of CTL* state formulas over propositions in AP. Furthermore, any two corresponding paths satisfy the same set of CTL* path formulas over propositions in AP. □

This means that when conditions (1) and (2) are both satisfied, the abstraction will preserve logical soundness.

3. Two Sample Applications

3.1. Tic Tac Toe

We will illustrate the use of the new verification option, and the types of data abstraction it supports, with a small example. For this example we will use a model of the game of tic tac toe. First, we will write the model in basic PROMELA, as a pure SPIN model and show its complexity. Then we will rewrite the model to include some operations in embedded C code, and we will show how abstractions can now be used to lower the verification complexity well below what was possible with the pure SPIN model, without sacrificing accuracy.

The pure PROMELA version of the model is shown in Figure 3.

We represented the 3x3 board in a two-dimensional array b, constructed with the help of PROMELA `typedef` declarations. Because the players in this game strictly alternate on moves, we can use a single process and record in a `bit` variable z which player will make the next move. Player 0 will always make the first move here. A square has value 0 when empty, and is set to either 1 or 2 when it is marked by one of the two players. In the first `if` statement, a player picks any empty square to place a mark. When no empty squares are left, a draw is reached and the game stops. When a move could be made, the player checks for a win, and if one is found it prints the board configuration for the winning position and forces a deadlock (to allow us to distinguish these states from normal termination where the process exits). We have enclosed the computation in an `atomic` sequence, to achieve that no intermediary states are stored during the model checking process, only the final board positions that are computed.

The verification of this model explores 5,510 states. Clearly, we are not exploiting the fact that the game board has many symmetries. There are, for instance, both rotational symmetries and mirror symmetries (left/right and top/bottom) that could be taken into account to reduce verification complexity. In principle, the SPIN model could be rewritten to account for these symmetries, but this is surprisingly hard to do, and risks the introduction of inaccuracy in the verification process.

With careful reasoning, we can see that there are only 765 unique board positions in the game, and 135 of these positions are winning for one of the two players, e.g. [14]. The maximum number of moves that can be made is further trivially 9. In our first verification attempt we therefore did considerably more work than is necessary.

```
#define SQ(x,y)   !b.r[x].s[y] -> b.r[x].s[y] = z+1
#define H(v,w)    b.r[v].s[0]==w && b.r[v].s[1]==w && b.r[v].s[2]==w
#define V(v,w)    b.r[0].s[v]==w && b.r[1].s[v]==w && b.r[2].s[v]==w
#define UD(w)     b.r[0].s[0]==w && b.r[1].s[1]==w && b.r[2].s[2]==w
#define DD(w)     b.r[2].s[0]==w && b.r[1].s[1]==w && b.r[0].s[2]==w

typedef Row   { byte s[3]; };
typedef Board { Row  r[3]; };

Board b;
bit z, won;

init {
        do
        :: atomic { /* do not store intermediate states */
           !won ->
           if       /* all valid moves */
           :: SQ(0,0)  :: SQ(0,1)  :: SQ(0,2)
           :: SQ(1,0)  :: SQ(1,1)  :: SQ(1,2)
           :: SQ(2,0)  :: SQ(2,1)  :: SQ(2,2)
           :: else -> break /* a draw: game over */
           fi;

           if    /* winning positions */
           :: H(0,z+1) || H(1,z+1) || H(2,z+1)
           || V(0,z+1) || V(1,z+1) || V(2,z+1)
           || UD(z+1)  || DD(z+1) ->
                /* print winning position */
                printf("%d %d %d\n%d %d %d\n%d %d %d\n",
                       b.r[0].s[0], b.r[0].s[1], b.r[0].s[2],
                       b.r[1].s[0], b.r[1].s[1], b.r[1].s[2],
                       b.r[2].s[0], b.r[2].s[1], b.r[2].s[2]);
                won = true /* and force a stop */
           :: else -> z = 1 - z                    /* continue */
           fi;

           } /* end of atomic */
        od
}
```

Fig. 3. Tic Tac Toe, Pure PROMELA Model.

We will now revise the model to make use of a C function to store the board configuration in a C data structure, and to perform the moves that are non-deterministically selected with a SPIN model (which now starts to perform the function of a test-harness around a C application).

We will retain the same basic structure of the algorithm. Again, a win will result in a deadlock, and a draw will lead to normal process termination. In the first version of the model with embedded C code, shown in Figure 4, we track and match all relevant external data, which in this case includes just the the board configuration.

We have introduced variables x and y to record the square that is selected in the first part of the algorithm. The location of the square is passed to the C function that will now place the mark in that square and check for a win. The C function play() returns either a 2 if the last move made produced a win, or a 1 if it did not and the turn should go to the next player, as before.

```
#define SQ(a,b)    c_expr { (!board[a][b]) } -> x=a; y=b

c_decl {
        extern short board[3][3];
        extern short play(int, int, int);
};

c_track "&board[0][0]" "sizeof(board)";        /* matched */

byte x, y, z, won;

init {
    do
    :: atomic { !won ->
        if    /* all valid moves */
        :: SQ(0,0) :: SQ(0,1) :: SQ(0,2)
        :: SQ(1,0) :: SQ(1,1) :: SQ(1,2)
        :: SQ(2,0) :: SQ(2,1) :: SQ(2,2)
        :: else -> break    /* a draw */
        fi;
        c_code {
            switch (play(now.x, now.y, now.z+1)) {
            default: printf("cannot happen\n"); break;
            case 1: now.z = 1 - now.z; break;
            case 2: now.won = 1; break; /* force a stop */
            }
            now.x = now.y = 0; /* reset */
        }
      }
    od
}
```

Fig. 4. Tic Tac Toe, Version with Embedded C Code.

The external C function is shown in Figure 5. Perhaps not surprisingly, this model explores the same number of states as the pure SPIN model, and declares the same number of winning positions, though it does not have to search as deeply into the depth-first search tree (31 steps instead of 40 for the earlier model).

We will now change the last model into one that uses data abstraction. The new model is shown in Figure 6.

We have turned off state matching on the board configuration, while retaining the tracking capability that allows us to perform an accurate depth-first search. We have also introduced a new integer variable named abstract that we will use to record an abstract value of the board configuration, taking into account all symmetries that exist on the game board. This value is both tracked and matched. The rest of the test harness specification is unchanged.

We must now extend the C function a little, to provide the computation of the abstract board value. We do so by calling an extra function board_value() that is called in function play() immediately after the new mark is placed.

The details of this computation, shown in the Appendix, are not too important. Suffice it to say that each board configuration is assigned a unique value between 0 and 19682, by assigning a numeric place value to each square. The board value is computed for each rotation and mirror reflection of the board, and the minimum of the 8 resulting numbers is selected as a canonical representation of the set. That number is

```
#define H(a,b)  (board[a][0]==b && board[a][1]==b && board[a][2]==b)
#define V(a,b)  (board[0][a]==b && board[1][a]==b && board[2][a]==b)
#define UD(b)   (board[0][0]==b && board[1][1]==b && board[2][2]==b)
#define DD(b)   (board[2][0]==b && board[1][1]==b && board[0][2]==b)

short board[3][3];

short
play(int x, int y, int z)
{
    board[x][y] = z;         /*place mark */

    /* check for win: */
    if ((H(0,z) || H(1,z) || H(2,z)
    ||   V(0,z) || V(1,z) || V(2,z)
    ||   DD(z) || UD(z))
    {    Printf("%d %d %d\n%d %d %d\n%d %d %d\n",
         board[0][0], board[0][1], board[0][2],
         board[1][0], board[1][1], board[1][2],
         board[2][0], board[2][1], board[2][2]);
         return 2;            /* last move wins */
    }
    return 1;                 /* game continues */
}
```

Fig. 5. C Source Code for Play().

stored in the state descriptor, and used in state matching operations. A state will now match if a board configuration is encountered that is equivalent to one previously seen, taking all rotational and mirror symmetries into account. Yet the execution of the actual code always works with the full detail on the actual board configuration.

Table 1. TicTacToe Verification.

Version	States	Depth	Wins
Pure SPIN Model	5510	40	942
Model with Embedded C Code	5510	31	942
Model with Embedded C Code and Data Abstraction	771	31	135
Minimum Required for Solution	765	9	135

The number of reachable states is with this data abstraction reduced to 771 states, with 135 of these state declared as winning positions, as shown in Table 1. Since the actual number of uniquely different board configurations is 765, SPIN encounters just six cases here where it revisits an old configuration with different values for the additional state variables x, y, or z.

It should be noted that we could also have used the c_track mechanism to introduce a new state variable that captures the non-abstracted board value (i.e., without taking into account the equivalence of rotations and mirror reflections of the game board). By storing and tracking the board value as a single 4-byte integer, rather than as the original 9-byte array of marks, we then define an application specific data compression on part of the state information, and similarly benefit by achieving a reduction of the memory requirements. This means that our new c_track mechanism can not just exploit user-defined abstractions, but also user-defined lossless or lossy data compression methods. Of course, for verification accuracy we will normally want to restrict

```
c_decl {
        extern short board[3][3];
        extern short play(int, int, int);
        extern short abstract;        /* board value */
};

c_track "&board[0][0]" "sizeof(board)" "UnMatched";
c_track "&abstract"    "sizeof(short)"; /* matched */

byte x, y, z, won;

init {
     do
     :: atomic { !won ->
        if    /* all valid moves */
        :: c_expr { (!board[0][0]) } -> x = 0; y = 0
        :: c_expr { (!board[0][1]) } -> x = 0; y = 1
        :: c_expr { (!board[0][2]) } -> x = 0; y = 2
        :: c_expr { (!board[1][0]) } -> x = 1; y = 0
        :: c_expr { (!board[1][1]) } -> x = 1; y = 1
        :: c_expr { (!board[1][2]) } -> x = 1; y = 2
        :: c_expr { (!board[2][0]) } -> x = 2; y = 0
        :: c_expr { (!board[2][1]) } -> x = 2; y = 1
        :: c_expr { (!board[2][2]) } -> x = 2; y = 2
        :: else -> break    /* a draw */
        fi;
        c_code {
            switch (play(now.x, now.y, now.z+1)) {
            default: printf("cannot happen0); break;
            case 1: now.z = 1 - now.z; break;
            case 2: now.won = 1; break; /* force a stop */
            }
            now.x = now.y = 0; /* reset */
        }
        }
     od
}
```

Fig. 6. Tic Tac Toe, With Data Abstraction.

the use to sound abstractions and lossless data compression.

3.2. Soundness

To see that the abstractions we have used in this example are logically sound, we show that they satisfies the conditions (1) and (2) from Section 2.3, as required by the theorem.

For given board configurations $b0$ and $b1$, the relation $b0 \sim b1$ is defined to hold when $b0$ and $b1$ evaluate to the same abstract board value (i.e., the configurations are equivalent upto rotations and reflections). It is easy to check that the state predicate P, where $P(b)$ denotes that b is a winning configuration, satisfies condition (2), since a win is invariant under rotations and reflections.

To see that the abstraction relation $\sim$ satisfies condition (1), note that each transition in the model is either (i) a move by player 1, (ii) a move by player 2, or (iii) a win. We must then show that, for any two equivalent board configurations $b0$ and $c0$, if there is a transition from $b0$ to $b1$, then there is also a transition from $c0$ to $c1$ such that

$c1 \sim b1$.

Consider first a transition of type (i), in which player 1 places a mark at position (i, j). Suppose that $c0$ is a reflection of $b0$ across the vertical axis. Then, it is easy to see that the transition that places the same mark at position $(i, 2 - j)$ must be enabled in $c0$, and results in a state $c1$ that is equivalent to $b1$. A similar argument holds for the other ways in which $c0$ and $b0$ may be equivalent, and for transitions of type (ii).

For transitions of type (iii), it suffices to note that function `play` returns the same value for all equivalent board configurations.

3.3. A Larger Application

For a larger application we will discuss the verification of one of the modules from the flight software for JPL's Mars Exploration Rovers (MER).

The MER software contains 11 threads of execution. Each thread serves one specific application, such as imaging, controlling the robot arm, communicating with earth, and driving. There are 15 shared resources on the rover, to which access must be controlled by an arbiter, which is the target of our verification. The arbiter module prevents potential conflicts between resource requests, and enforces priorities. For instance, it would not make sense to start a communication session with earth while the rover is driving. The policy in this case is that communication is more important than driving, so when a request for communication is received while the rover is driving, the arbiter will make sure that the permission to use the drive motors is rescinded in favor of a new permission to use the rover's antennas.

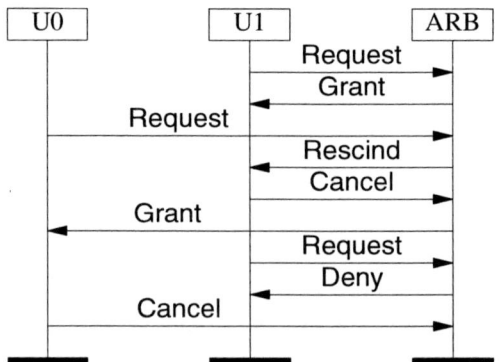

Fig. 7. Sample Communication Scenario.

Figure 7 shows a generic scenario for communication between user threads and the arbiter. In the scenario shown, user U0 requests access to a resource, which is granted by the arbiter. Next, a different user U1 makes a resource request that conflicts with the first one, but has precedence. The arbiter now sends a `Rescind` message to the first user, and waits for the confirmation that the resource is no longer used. Then the arbiter sends a `Grant` message to user U1. A new request from the first user while the second user still retains possession of the resource is now summarily denied by the arbiter. Eventually, the use of every resource must be completed by sending a `Cancel` message to the arbiter, which notifies the arbiter that the resource is now available for other users.

The arbiter module consists of about 3,000 lines of source code, written in ANSI standard C. The arbiter also makes use of a lookup table that records which combinations of resource requests conflict, and what the various priorities are.

With 11 users competing for 15 resources, the complexity of a full-scale exhaustive verification quickly becomes intractable. With the bitstate (supertrace) search mode, SPIN can randomly prune these large search spaces, within limits set by the size of available physical memory on the machine that is used. For exhaustive coverage a different strategy must be followed. One such strategy is divide and conquer. By breaking the problem down into smaller subproblems that can be checked exhaustively we can build confidence that the larger problem has the desired properties (although in this case we cannot conclusively prove it).

As an example, we will look at a subproblem with 3 user processes, competing for access to just 3 of the available resources, cyclically, and in random order. Without the use of abstraction, a problem of this size is at the edge of what can be verified exhaustively with roughly 1 Gbyte of available memory. An experiment like this can be repeated for different subproblems by making different selections of the 3 resources competed for, slowly increasing the confidence in the correctness of the complete solution.

Table 2. MER Arbiter Verification.

Version	States	Time(s)	Mem(Mb)
Pure SPIN Model	272,068	2.2	41.8
Model with Embedded Code	11,453,800	1458.0	701.7
Model with Embedded Code and Abstraction	261,543	5.1	55.2

Table 2 records the number of reachable states for three different versions of a verification model for the arbiter. The first version is a hand-built pure SPIN model of the arbiter algorithm, including only the lookup table from the original code as embedded C code. This model counts 245 lines of PROMELA code, plus 77 lines for the arbiter lookup table.

The second version uses the original arbiter C code, stubbed to isolate it from the rest of the flight code, with all relevant data objects that contain state information tracked and matched, using c_track statements, without abstraction. There is approximately 4,400 bytes of state information that is tracked in this way. This information includes, for instance, a linked list of current and pending reservations, and a freelist of reservation slots. A hand-built test-harness of just 110 lines of PROMELA surrounds the arbiter code (as it did for the much simpler tictactoe example we discussed before), simulating the actions of the 3 selected user processes. The verification for this version of the model could only be completed with the hashcompact state compression option enabled, which effectively reduced memory use to about 127 bytes per state. More effective than this compression option, though, is to use the data abstraction method we discussed. In the third version of the verification model we added these abstractions, restricting the state information that is recorded to its bare essence. In this version we exclude, for instance, the values of pointers that are used to build the linked lists.

Each of the three versions can find counter-examples to logic properties that have known violations (including both safety and liveness properties). The first model, though efficient, can leave doubt about the accuracy of the modeling effort. The second model incurs the penalty of an implementation level verification, carrying along much more data than is necessary to prove the required properties. The third version of the model restores the relatively low complexity of a hand-built model, but has the benefit of precision and strict adherence to the implementation level code.

4. Related Work

There have been several different approaches to the direct verification of implementation level C code, following the early work on automated extraction of verification models from implementation level code as detailed in for instance [3,7,8].

Perhaps best known is the work on Verisoft [6], which is based on the use of partial order reduction theory in what is otherwise a state-less search. In this approach, application level code is instrumented in such a way that its execution can be controlled at specific points in the code, e.g., at points where message passing operations occur or where scheduling decisions are made. The search along a given path of execution is stopped when a user-defined depth is reached, and then restarted from the predefined initial system state to explore alternative paths. The advantage of this approach is that can consume considerably less memory than the traditional state space exploration methods used in logic model checking. It can therefore handle large applications. A relatively small disadvantage is that the method requires code instrumentation. A more significant disadvantage, compared to the method we have introduced in this paper, is that since no state space is maintained, none of the advantages from state space storage are available, such as systematic depth-first search, the verification of not only safety but also liveness properties, and the opportunity to define systematic abstractions. Abstraction in particular can provide significant performance gains. We believe that the methodology introduced in this paper is the first to successfully combine data abstraction techniques and *unrestricted* logic model checking capabilities with the verification of implementation level code.

A second approach that is comparable to our own is the work on the CMC tool [12]. In this tool, an attempt is made to capture as much state information as possible and to store it in a state space using agressive compression techniques, similar to the hash-compact and bistate hashing methods used in Spin [9]. Detailed state information is kept on the depth-first search stack, but no methodology available to distinguish between state information that should be matched, and state information that is only required to maintain data integrity. Potentially this method, though, could be extended with the type of data abstraction techniques we have described in this paper. We believe that effective use of data abstraction techniques will prove to be the key to the successful application of logic model checking techniques in practice.

5. Conclusions

The method we have described for verifying reactive software applications combines data abstraction with implementation level verification. The user provides a test-harness, written in the language of the model checker, that non-deterministically selects inputs for the application that can drive it through all its relevant states. Correctness properties can be verified in the usual way: by making logical statements about reachable and unreachable states, or about feasible or infeasible executions. The state tracking capability allows us to perform full temporal logic verification on implementation level code.

The basic method of maintaining both concrete and abstract representations of states in the search procedure is very similar to algorithms that have been proposed earlier for using (predefined) symmetry reductions in model checkers, e.g. in [1,4].

The method is the easiest to apply in the verification of single-threaded code, with well-defined input and output streams. The two examples we discussed in this paper are both of that type. The method is not restricted to such applications though. Multi-threaded code can be handled, but requires more care. Each thread in the application will need to be prepared to run as standalone threads, with clearly defined inputs and outputs. The user must now identify the portions of program code that can be run as atomic blocks, setting the appropriate level of interleaving for the model checking runs. The test-harness that the user prepares now drives the thread executions directly, selecting the proper level of granularity of execution. The application we studied in [5] is of this type, and could be adapted to use the new method of data abstraction we have discussed here.

The capability to redefine how state information is to be represented, or abstracted, is also similar to the `view` function in TLC [11]. In our case, the abstraction can be defined in any way that C or C++ allows, but it is restricted to the representation of external data objects. Most of the data in a SPIN model could be treated as such (e.g., by declaring them to be `hidden` within the SPIN model itself), with the exception only of the program counters of active processes.

In the setup we have described, each call on the application level code is assumed to execute to completion without interleaving of other actions (i.e., atomically). This is the most convenient way to proceed, but we are not restricted to it. By using a model extractor, such as FeaVer or MODEX [10,15], we can convert selected functions in the application into PROMELA models with embedded C code, optionally using additional source level abstraction functions, and generate a finer-grained model of execution. The instrumentation required for model extraction can, however, complicate the verification process, and require deeper knowledge of the application.

Acknowledgements

The research described in this paper was carried out at the Jet Propulsion Laboratory, California Institute of Technology, under a contract with the National Aeronautics and Space Administration.
The idea to distinguish state information that is tracked on the stack from that stored in the state space was suggested by Murali Rangarajan. The authors also thank Dragan Bosnacki for inspiring discussions on the subject of this paper.

References

[1] D. Bosnacki, *Enhancing state space reduction techniques for model checking.* Ph.D Thesis, 2001. Eindhoven Univ. of Technology, The Netherlands.

[2] E.M. Clarke, O. Grumberg, and D. Peled, *Model Checking*, MIT Press, 1999.

[3] J.C. Corbett, M.B. Dwyer, J.C. Hatcliff, et al., Bandera: Extracting finite state models from Java source code, *Proc. 22nd Int. Conf. on Softw. Eng.*, June 2000, Limerick, Ireland, ACM Press, pp. 439-448.

[4] E.A. Emerson, C.S. Jutla, A.P. Sistla, On Model-Checking for Fragments of mu-Calculus. *Proc. CAV93*, LNCS 697, pp. 385-396.

[5]   P.R. Gluck and G.J. Holzmann, Using Spin Model Checking for Flight Software Verification, *Proc. 2002 Aerospace Conference*, IEEE, Big Sky, MT, USA, March 2002.

[6]   P. Godefroid, S. Chandra, C. Palm, Software model checking in practice: an industrial case study, *Proc. 22nd Int. Conf. on Softw. Eng.*, Orlando, Fl., May 2002, ACM Press, pp. 431-441.

[7]   K. Havelund, T. Pressburger, Model checking Java programs using Java Pathfinder, *Int. Journal on Software Tools for Technology Transfer*, Apr. 2000, Vol. 2, No. 4, pp. 366-381.

[8]   G.J. Holzmann, Logic Verification of ANSI-C Code with Spin, *SPIN Model Checking and Software Verification*, Springer Verlag, LNCS Vol. 1885, pp. 131-147, Sep. 2000.

[9]   G.J. Holzmann, *The SPIN Model Checker: Primer and Reference Manual*, Addison-Wesley, 2003.

[10] G.J.Holzmann and M.H. Smith, An automated verification method for distributed systems software based on model extraction, *IEEE Trans. on Software Engineering*, Vol. 28, 4, pp. 364-377, April 2002.

[11] L. Lamport, *Specifying Systems: the TLA+ language and tools for hardware and software engineers*, Addison-Wesley, 2002.

[12] M. Musuvathi, D.Y.W. Park, A. Chou, D.R. Engler, D.L. Dill, CMC: A pragmatic approach to model checking real code, *Proc. Fifth Symposium on Operating Systems Design and Implementation*, Dec. 2002.

[13] D. Park, Concurrency and automata on infinite sequences. In *5th GI-Conference on Theoretical Computer Science*, pp. 167-183. Springer, 1981.

[14] http://f2.org/maths/ttt.html

[15] http://cm.bell-labs.com/cm/cs/what/modex/

APPENDIX

```c
#define MAXVAL   19682    /* 3 x 3^8 - 1 */
#define B(a,b,c,d)        board[a][b]*r[c][d]

int abstract;

int r0[3][3] = {
        {   1,    3,     9, },
        {  27,   81,   243, },
        { 729, 2187, 6561, },
};

int r1[3][3] = {
        {  729,  27,  1, },
        { 2187,  81,  3, },
        { 6561, 243,  9, },
};

int r2[3][3] = {
        { 6561, 2187, 729, },
        {  243,   81,  27, },
        {    9,    3,   1, },
};

int r3[3][3] = {
        { 9, 243, 6561, },
        { 3,  81, 2187, },
        { 1,  27,  729, },
};

int
comp_row(int r[3][3], int L, int R, int T, int B)
{
        return  B(T,L,0,0) + B(T,1,0,1) + B(T,R,0,2) +
                B(1,L,1,0) + B(1,1,1,1) + B(1,R,1,2) +
                B(B,L,2,0) + B(B,1,2,1) + B(B,R,2,2);
}

void
min_row(int r[3][3])
{       int v;

        v = comp_row(r,0,2,0,2); if (v < abstract) abstract = v;
        v = comp_row(r,2,0,0,2); if (v < abstract) abstract = v;
        v = comp_row(r,0,2,2,0); if (v < abstract) abstract = v;
        v = comp_row(r,2,0,2,0); if (v < abstract) abstract = v;
}

void
board_value(void)
{
        abstract = 2*MAXVAL;
        min_row(r0);
        min_row(r1);
        min_row(r2);
        min_row(r3);
}
```

Minimization of Counterexamples in SPIN

Paul Gastin, Pierre Moro, and Marc Zeitoun

LIAFA, Univ. of Paris 7, Case 7014,
2 place Jussieu, F-75251 Paris Cedex 05, France
{gastin,moro,mz}@liafa.jussieu.fr

Abstract. We propose an algorithm to find a counterexample to some
property in a finite state program. This algorithm is derived from SPIN's
one, but it finds a counterexample faster than SPIN does. In particular it
still works in linear time. Compared with SPIN's algorithm, it requires
only one additional bit per state stored. We further propose another
algorithm to compute a counterexample of minimal size. Again, this algorithm does not use more memory than SPIN does to approximate a
minimal counterexample. The cost to find a counterexample of minimal
size is that one has to revisit more states than SPIN. We provide an
implementation and discuss experimental results.

1 Introduction

Model-checking is used to prove the correctness of properties of hardware and
software systems. When the model is incorrect, locating errors is important to
provide hints on how to correct either the system or the property to be checked.
Model checkers usually exhibit counterexamples, that is, faulty execution traces
of the system. The simpler the counterexample is, the easier it will be to locate,
understand and fix the error. A counterexample can mean that the abstraction
of the system (formalized as the model) is too coarse; several techniques can be
used to refine the model, guided by the counterexample found by the model-
checker [3,1,7]. The refinement stage is done manually or automatically. In any
case, it is important to compute *small* counterexamples (ideally of minimal size)
in case the property is not satisfied: they are easier to understand, they can be
processed more rapidly by automatic tools, and thus they make it possible to
correct underlying errors more easily.

It is well-known that verifying whether a finite state system $\mathcal{M}$ satisfies
an LTL property φ is equivalent to testing whether a Büchi automaton $\mathcal{A} =
\mathcal{A}_\mathcal{M} \cap \mathcal{A}_{\neg\varphi}$ has no accepting run [11], where $\mathcal{A}_\mathcal{M}$ is a Kripke structure describing
the system and $\mathcal{A}_{\neg\varphi}$ is a Büchi automaton describing executions that violate
φ. It is easy, in theory, to determine whether a Büchi automaton has at least
one accepting run. Since there is only a finite number of accepting states, this
problem is equivalent to finding a reachable accepting state and a loop around
it. A counterexample to φ in $\mathcal{M}$ can then be given as a path $\rho = \rho_1\rho_2$ in the
Büchi automaton, where ρ_1 is a simple (loop-free) path from the initial state
to an accepting state, and ρ_2 is a simple loop around this accepting state (see
Figure 1). The model-checker SPIN[9,8] can find counterexamples by exploring

S. Graf and L. Mounier (Eds.): SPIN 2004, LNCS 2989, pp. 92–108, 2004.

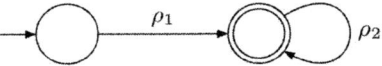

Fig. 1. An accepting path in a Büchi automaton

on the fly the synchronized product of the system and the property. Our goal is to find short counterexamples while sparing memory. The first trivial remark is that we can reduce the length of a counterexample if we do not insist on the fact that the loop starts from an accepting state. Hence, we consider counterexamples of the form $\rho = \rho_1\rho_2\rho_3$ where $\rho_1\rho_2$ is a path from the initial state to an accepting state, and $\rho_3\rho_2$ is a simple loop around this accepting state (see Figure 2). A minimal counterexample can then be defined as a path of this form, such that the length of ρ is minimal.

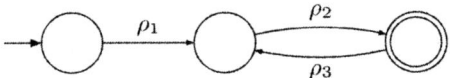

Fig. 2. An accepting path in a Büchi automaton

Finding a counterexample, even of minimal size, can of course be done in polynomial time using minimal paths algorithms based on breadth-first traversals. However, breadth-first traversals are not well-suited to detect loops. Moreover, the model of the system frequently comes from several components working concurrently, and the resulting Büchi automaton can be huge. Therefore, memory is a *critical resource* and, for instance, we cannot afford to store the minimal distance between all pairs of states. Therefore, we retain SPIN's approach and we use a depth-first search-like algorithm [10,5]. Depth-first traversals are well suited to detect loops, but they are not adapted for computing distances between states, which makes the problem more difficult than it first appears.

With this approach, there are actually two difficulties: the first one is to find *one* counterexample, the second one is to find a *small* counterexample, and ideally a *minimal one*.

SPIN has an option to reduce the size of counterexamples it finds. Yet, it does *not* provide the smallest one and results frequently remain too large and difficult to read, even when considering simple systems. For instance, on a natural liveness property on Dekker's mutual exclusion algorithm, SPIN provides a counterexample with 173 transitions. In this case, it is not difficult to see that an error occurs after 23 steps. The reason is that SPIN's algorithm for reducing the size of counterexamples misses lots of them and therefore fails to find the shortest one. Our contribution is the following:

– We propose an algorithm to find a counterexample of a Promela model in linear time. This algorithm is derived from SPIN's, but finds a counterexample faster than SPIN does. Moreover, compared with SPIN's algorithm, it only requires one additional bit per state stored.

- We propose another algorithm to compute a counterexample of minimal size, once a first counterexample has been found. This algorithm does not use more memory than SPIN does with option -i when trying to reduce the size of counterexamples. The cost of finding the shortest counterexample is to revisit more states than SPIN does. However, the algorithm can actually output a sequence of counterexamples of decreasing length found during its execution and can be stopped at any time. The algorithm is also well suited for bounded-model checking: given a maximal size of the counterexamples to be found, it returns one of the smallest such counterexamples, if any.
- We have implemented a version of the last algorithm whose results are indeed much smaller than those given by SPIN. For instance, for Dekker's algorithm, it actually finds the 23 states counterexample.
- We finally propose other improvements to SPIN's algorithm.

The paper is organized as follows. In Section 2, we describe the algorithm to find a first counterexample and we prove its correctness. However, there is no guarantee that this counterexample is of minimal size. In Section 3, we present an algorithm finding a minimal counterexample. While explaining these algorithms, we exhibit various problems that may arise when computing a counterexample with the current SPIN algorithm. An implementation and experimental results are described in Section 4.

2 Finding the First Counterexample

Let $\mathcal{A} = (S, E, s_1, F)$ be a Büchi automaton where S is a finite set of states, $E \subseteq S \times S$ is the transition relation, $s_1 \in S$ is the initial state and $F \subseteq S$ is the set of accepting states. Usually transitions are labeled with actions but since these labels are irrelevant for the emptiness problem, they are ignored in this paper. In pictures, the initial state is marked with an ingoing edge and accepting states are doubly circled. If a state has k outgoing transitions, we number them from 1 to k. Transitions from a state will be considered by the algorithms in the order given by their labels.

A *path* in an automaton is a sequence of states $\gamma = t_1 t_2 \cdots t_k$ (also denoted $t_1, t_2, \ldots, t_k$) such that for all $i < k$ there is a transition from t_i to t_{i+1}. We call k the *length* of γ, and we denote it by $|\gamma|$. The empty path, with no state, is denoted by ε and it has length 0. We say that γ is *simple* if $t_i \neq t_j$ for all $i \neq j$.

A *loop* is a path $t_1 t_2 \cdots t_k$ with $t_k = t_1$. A loop is *accepting* if it contains an accepting state. A loop $t_1 t_2 \cdots t_k$ is a *cycle* if $t_1 t_2 \cdots t_{k-1}$ is a simple path.

An *accepting path*, or *counterexample*, is of the form $\gamma = s_1 \cdots s_k \cdots s_{k+\ell}$ where $s_1 \cdots s_k$ is a path starting from the initial state and $s_k \cdots s_{k+\ell}$ is an accepting loop. Abusing the language, we say that γ is a *simple accepting path* if in addition $s_1 \cdots s_k \cdots s_{k+\ell-1}$ is simple.

In this section, we describe an algorithm finding the first counterexample. It is similar to the nested DFS described in [9,5,2,10], with an improvement that avoids revisiting some states unnecessarily. This improvement is also useful when minimizing the size of the counterexample.

Algorithm 1 uses 4 colors to mark states: *white* < *blue* < *red* < *black*. (We also mark states in grey, but this is just for simplifying the proof.) The color of a state can *only increase*. At the beginning, all states are white and the algorithm DFS_blue is called on the initial state s_1.

Two DFSs alternate, the *blue* and *red* ones. The blue DFS is used to locate reachable accepting states and to start red DFSs from these accepting states in postfix order with respect to the covering tree defined by the blue DFS. A red DFS starts (and interrupts the blue one) whenever one pops an accepting state in the blue DFS. A red DFS only visits blue states, that is states already visited by the blue DFS. We will show that if a red DFS initiated from an accepting state r terminates without finding a counterexample then no state reachable from r may be part of an accepting path. Hence, the color of all states reachable from r may be set to black. This is the purpose of the black DFS.

The DFSs used define, at any time, a current path from the initial state to the current state. For convenience, this current path is stored in a global variable cp. Actually, this is not necessary with our recursive presentation, since it may be obtained as a by-product of the execution stack when the counterexample is found. (For efficiency, SPIN uses an iterative implementation of the DFS, and stores the current path in a global variable.)

Each state $s \in S$ is represented by a structure and the algorithm requires the following additional fields. The extra cost of these data is only 3 bits for each state, while the nested DFS implemented in SPIN only needs 2 bits per state.

- Color color initially white.
- Boolean is_in_cp initially false. This flag is used to test in constant time whether a state belongs to the current path.

When we write **for all** $t \in E(s)$ in the algorithms (see *e.g.* Algorithm 1), we assume that the successors $\{t \in S \mid (s, t) \in E\}$ of s are returned in a fixed order, which is in particular the same in DFS_blue and DFS_red. This fact is important for the correctness of Algorithm 1. We establish simultaneously the following invariants.

Lemma 1. *(1) Invariant for DFS_blue: no black state is part of a simple accepting path and all states reachable from a black state are also black.*
(2) Invariant for DFS_red initiated from DFS_red(r) with $r \in F$: either no state reachable from r is part of a simple accepting path, or there is a simple accepting path going through r and using no black or grey state.

Proof. (1) During DFS_blue(s), if we execute line 8 then all successors of s are black and the result is clear by induction. Now, assume that we execute line 11. Then DFS_red(s) was executed completely and the color of s is grey. Using (2) (with $r = s$) we deduce that no state reachable from s is part of a simple accepting path. Hence, after executing DFS_black(s), the invariant is still satisfied.

Algorithm 1 A version of the nested DFS algorithm: the color-DFS

```
void DFS_blue (State s )
1: push(cp, s); s→is_in_cp := true; s→color := blue
2: for all t ∈ E(s) do
3:    if (t→is_in_cp and t ∈ F) then exit with cp·t as counterexample
4:    else if (t→color = white) then DFS_blue(t) end if
5: end for
6: pop(cp); s→is_in_cp := false
7: if (∀t ∈ E(s), t→color = black) then
8:    s→color := black
9: else if (s ∈ F) then
10:    DFS_red(s)
11:    DFS_black(s)
12: end if

void DFS_red (State s )
1: push(cp, s); s→is_in_cp := true; s→color := red
2: for all t ∈ E(s) do
3:    if (t→is_in_cp and (t ∈ F or t→color = blue)) then
4:        exit with cp·t as counterexample
5:    else if (t→color = blue) then
6:        DFS_red(t)
7:    end if
8: end for
9: pop(cp); s→is_in_cp := false
10: s→color := grey
    /*
     * Note that line 10 of DFS_red is not part of the actual algorithm.
     * Its purpose is simply to clarify the correctness proof.
     * Therefore there are actually only four colors as stated in the
     * description above.
     */

void DFS_black (State s )
1: s→color := black
2: for all t ∈ E(s) do
3:    if (t→color ≠ black) then DFS_black(t) end if
4: end for
```

---

(2) This is the difficult part. First, note that when entering DFS_red(r) there are no grey states and we get property (2) directly from (1). Now, this invariant may only be affected by the execution of line 10 inside some DFS_red(s). When executing this statement, all successors of s are either black, grey, or red. Note that a red successor of s is necessarily on the current path between r and s since the states on cp(r) are still blue, where cp(r) is the current path when DFS_red(r) was called.

Assume that there exists a simple accepting path α going through r and using no black or grey state. Note that all paths using no black state and going from r to an accepting state must cross cp(r)·r. This is due to the postfix order of the calls DFS_red(t) for $t \in F$. Since we can reach an accepting state, following

α from r, unwinding α once if necessary, we get a path β from r to $cp(r) \cdot r$ using no black or grey state. The path $cp(r) \cdot \beta$ is a simple accepting path using no black or grey state.

If $s \notin \beta$ then the invariant still holds after setting the color of s to grey in line 10. Assume now that $s \in \beta$ and let t be the successor of s on the path β. The color of t must be red. Let v be the last state of β whose color is red and write $\beta = \beta_1 v \beta_2$. Since the color of v is red, it is on the current path between r and s and $cp(r) \cdot r$ is a prefix of $cp(v) \cdot v$. Therefore, $cp(v) \cdot v \beta_2$ is a simple accepting path using no grey or black states and does not contain s. Hence, the invariant still holds after setting the color of s to grey at line 10. $\qquad \square$

Remark 1. One can prove that if a call DFS_red(r) with $r \in F$ terminates without finding a counterexample, then all states reachable from r are black or grey. Therefore, at line 10 of DFS_red(s), we could set the color of s to black directly and remove line 11 (the call to DFS_black) in DFS_blue. This modification is fine if we are only interested in finding the first counterexample. But when the color of some state s is set to grey, then we do not know whether s is part of a counterexample or not. In other words, one can deduce that a grey state cannot be part of a counterexample only when the initial call DFS_red(r), with $r \in F$, terminates. In order to avoid revisiting unnecessarily some states, the minimization algorithm presented in Section 3 can use the fact that a black state cannot be part of a counterexample. This is why we do not use this modification.

Since the algorithm visits a state at most 3 times, Algorithm 1 terminates. Moreover, one gets as a corollary of Lemma 1 the following statement.

Proposition 1. *If a Büchi automaton $\mathcal{A}$ admits a counterexample, then Algorithm 1 finds a counterexample on input $\mathcal{A}$.*

2.1   Comparison with SPIN's Algorithm

The difference between our algorithm and SPIN's is that SPIN does not paint states in black to avoid unnecessary revisits of states. More precisely, in SPIN's algorithm, lines 7 to 12 of DFS_blue are replaced with

if $s \in F$ **then** $r := s$; DFS_red(s) **endif**

where r is a global variable used to memorize the origin of the red DFS. To illustrate the benefit of black states, consider the automaton below. Recall that the transition labels indicate in which order successors are considered by the DFSs. With SPIN's algorithm, the large tree is visited twice. The first visit is started with DFS_blue(2) and the second one with DFS_red(3). With our algorithm, when DFS_blue(2) terminates, state 2 is black. Indeed, DFS_blue is called recursively on each state of the tree accessible from state 2. All leaves of this tree, which have no successor, are marked black at lines 7–8, and this propagates back to state 2. Therefore the tree will not be revisited by DFS_red(3).

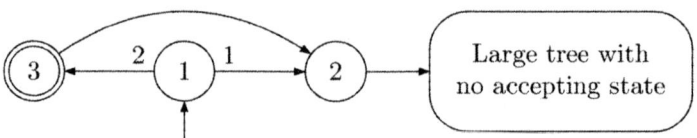

3 Finding a Minimal Counterexample

To find a minimal counterexample, we use a depth-first search [4] which does not necessarily stop when it reaches a state already visited. Indeed, reaching a state s with a distance to the initial state s_1 smaller than for the previous visit of s may lead to a shorter counterexample.

Therefore, in addition to the fields used in Algorithm 1, each state has an integer field depth, storing the smallest length of current paths on which that state occurred. This field remains infinite as long as the state has not been visited, and it can only decrease during the algorithm. We also use an additional variable mce, a stack of states containing the minimal counterexample found so far. It is initially empty. At the end of the algorithm, it will contain a minimal counterexample of the whole automaton.

3.1 SPIN's Algorithm

The current algorithm implemented in SPIN to find a small counterexample is a variation of the nested DFS algorithm [10]. It carries on the visit below a state either if the state is new or if it is found more quickly than during the previous visits. (And, before popping an accepting state, it looks for a loop from that state.) This algorithm cannot guarantee to find a minimal counterexample. The reason is that, after finding the first counterexample, SPIN backtracks whenever it reaches a state with a path longer than the stored distance to the initial state. This is due to the false intuition that using a longer path will never yield a shorter counterexample. There are two cases where this is not appropriate and the minimal counterexample is missed. The following examples illustrate these two cases. As before, transition labels indicate in which order they are visited.

In the automaton of Fig. 3, the first counterexample found is $s_1 s_2 s_3 s_4 s_5 s_6 s_3$.

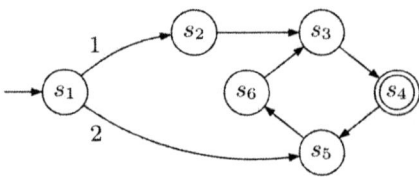

Fig. 3. Missing the minimal counterexample: case 1

After this visit, the state depths are set as follows: $(s_1, 1)$, $(s_2, 2)$, $(s_3, 3)$, $(s_4, 4)$, $(s_5, 5)$, $(s_6, 6)$. SPIN's algorithm then backtracks and s_5 is reached from s_1 with depth 2. Since this is smaller than the previous depth of s_5 the visit proceeds to s_6 which is reached now at depth 3, and then to s_3, reached at depth 4. But 4 is greater than the previous depth of s_3 and SPIN's algorithm would backtrack missing the shortest counterexample which is $s_1 s_5 s_6 s_3 s_4 s_5$.

The second case is when an accepting state is on the current path. Then, even if no depth was reduced after finding the first counterexample, one should revisit already visited states. An example is shown in Fig. 4.

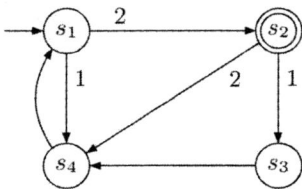

Fig. 4. Missing the minimal counterexample: case 2

The first counterexample found (during the second depth-first search from s_2) is $s_1 s_2 s_3 s_4 s_1$ and the state depths are $(s_1, 1)$, $(s_2, 2)$, $(s_3, 3)$, $(s_4, 2)$. Now, when we reach s_4 from s_2 with the current path $s_1 s_2 s_4$, no depth has been reduced and again SPIN's algorithm would backtrack missing the shortest counterexample which is $s_1 s_2 s_4 s_1$. In this case, the relevant length that was reduced is the length from the accepting state s_2 to s_4 (from 2 to 1). Because memory is the most critical resource, it is not possible to store the length from all accepting states to each state. Therefore, we have to revisit states already visited.

To cope with these cases, Algorithm 2 has two operating modes: a normal one where several criteria can make the algorithm backtrack, and a more careful one, where the visit can only stop when either the current path loops, or becomes longer than the size of the minimal counterexample found so far. In this mode, states may be revisited several times. If the algorithm enters in careful mode while pushing a state s on the current path, it remains in this mode until that occurrence of s is popped off the current path.

In the example of Fig. 3, we would switch to `careful` mode at lines 11–12 of Algorithm 2 when visiting s_5 for the second time, because the field $s_5 \rightarrow$depth gets reduced. In the example of Fig. 4, we would switch to `careful` mode at lines 7–8 when visiting s_2, an accepting state.

The important fact is that being careful only in these two situations is sufficient to catch a minimal counterexample.

3.2   An Algorithm Finding the Minimal Counterexample

Algorithm 2 is again presented by a recursive procedure which tags states while visiting them. Its first argument is the state to be visited. Its second argument is the mode, initially `normal`, used for the visit. When we detect that some counterexample might be missed in that mode, we switch to the careful mode by calling the procedure with `careful` as the second argument. The mode could be implemented as a global variable, which saves memory. Making it an argument of the procedure yields a simpler presentation of the algorithm.

Algorithm 2 Finding a minimal counterexample

```
void DFS_MIN (State s, Boolean mode)
```
1: $\text{push}(\text{cp}, s)$
2: $s{\rightarrow}\text{depth} := \min(\text{length}(\text{cp}), s{\rightarrow}\text{depth})$
3: **for all** $t \in E(s)$ **do**
4: **if** $\text{mce} = \varepsilon$ **or** $(\text{length}(\text{cp}) + 1 < \text{length}(\text{mce})))$ **then**
5:   **if** $t \in \text{cp}$ **then**
6:    **if** closes_accepting(t) **then** $\text{mce} := \text{cp}.t$ **end if**
7:   **else if** $(\text{mode} = \text{careful}$ **or** $t \in F)$ **then**
8:    DFS_MIN$(t, \text{careful})$
9:   **else if** $t{\rightarrow}\text{depth} = \infty$ **then**
10:    DFS_MIN(t, mode)
11:   **else if** $(t{\rightarrow}\text{depth} > \text{length}(\text{cp}) + 1)$ **and** $\text{mce} \neq \varepsilon)$ **then**
12:    DFS_MIN$(t, \text{careful})$
13:   **end if**
14: **end if**
15: **end for**
16: $\text{pop}(\text{cp})$

In the description of Algorithm 2, we use the following functions:

- `int length(p)` returns the length of the path `p` (*i.e.*, its number of states). Since we only use it with `cp` and `mce` as arguments, one can maintain their lengths in two global variables, hence we may assume that this call requires $O(1)$-time.
- `Boolean closes_accepting(t)` returns `true` iff `cp · t` is an accepting path (assuming that `cp` itself is not accepting). To implement this function, one can use another stack of states recording, for each state s of the current path `cp` the depth in `cp` of the last accepting state of `cp` located before s. For instance, if the current path is $[s_1, s_2, s_3, s_4, s_5, s_6]$ and only s_2, s_5 are accepting, then this stack contains $[0, 2, 2, 2, 5, 5]$ (where 0 means that there is no accepting state). The function `closes_accepting` can then be implemented:
  - in $O(1)$-time if we accept to store the depth of each state on the current path. To check that a state closing a cycle creates an accepting cycle, one checks that the depth of its occurrence on the current path is smaller than the depth of the last accepting state on the current path.
  - in $O(n)$-time otherwise, where n is the length of the current path. Nevertheless, the additional stack still gives useful information to avoid visiting the current path. For instance, if $s{\rightarrow}\text{depth}$ (which will be smaller than the depth of s in `cp`) is larger than the depth of the last accepting state on the current path, or if there is no accepting state on it, we know that s does not close an accepting path.

3.3   Correctness of the Algorithm

To prove that Algorithm 2 is correct, we introduce the lexicographic ordering on paths starting from the initial state of the automaton. Recall that if a state has k outgoing transitions, they are labeled from 1 to k according to the order in which they will be processed by the algorithm. Let $\lambda : S \times S \to \mathbb{N}$ assigning to each edge its labeling. We extend λ to paths starting at s_1 by letting $\lambda(s_1) = \varepsilon$ and $\lambda(s_1, s_2, \dots, s_n) = \lambda(s_1, s_2)\lambda(s_2, s_3) \cdots \lambda(s_{n-1}, s_n)$. If γ and γ' are two paths starting at s_1, we say that γ is lexicographically smaller than γ', denoted $\gamma \prec_{\text{lex}} \gamma'$, if $\lambda(\gamma)$ is lexicographically smaller than $\lambda(\gamma')$ (with the usual order over $\mathbb{N}$). We let $\gamma \preceq_{\text{lex}} \gamma'$ iff $\gamma \prec_{\text{lex}} \gamma'$ or $\gamma = \gamma'$.

The first observation is that the algorithm discovers paths in increasing lexicographic order. In other words, each call to DFS_MIN makes the current path greater in the lexicographic ordering.

Lemma 2. *Let α and β be the values of* cp *after two consecutive executions of line 1 of Algorithm 2. Then, $\alpha \prec_{lex} \beta$.*

Proof. First observe that the test at line 5 guarantees that the current path cp remains simple: DFS_MIN will not be called on a state that would close the current path. Let $\alpha = s_1 s_2 \cdots s_\ell$. Then either no state is popped before the next execution of line 1, and β is of the form $\alpha s_{\ell+1}$, hence $\alpha \prec_{\text{lex}} \beta$. Or $1 \le k < \ell$ states are first popped, and the algorithm then pushes t on the current path. By definition of the transition labeling λ, t is a successor of $s_{\ell-k}$ such that $\lambda(s_{\ell-k}, s_{\ell-k+1}) < \lambda(s_{\ell-k}, t)$. Hence, the new value of cp is $\beta = s_1 s_2 \cdots s_{\ell-k} t$ and $\alpha \prec_{\text{lex}} \beta$. □

Corollary 1. *Algorithm 2 halts on any input.*

Proof. There is a finite number of simple paths in a finite graph, cp takes its values in this finite set and each recursive call makes it greater. □

Since Algorithm 2 discovers an increasing sequence of paths in the lexicographic ordering, it is natural to introduce the following sequence $(\gamma_i)_{0 \le i \le p}$. Let $\mathcal{S}$ be the finite set of simple accepting paths. Recall that a simple accepting path is of the form $\alpha s \beta s$ with $\alpha s \beta$ simple and $s\beta \cap F \neq \emptyset$. Since the lexicographic ordering is total, we can define a sequence $(\gamma_i)_{0 \le i \le p}$ as follows:

$$\begin{cases} \gamma_0 = \min_{\preceq_{\text{lex}}} \mathcal{S} & \text{if } \mathcal{S} \neq \emptyset \\ \gamma_{i+1} = \min_{\preceq_{\text{lex}}} \{\gamma \in \mathcal{S} \mid |\gamma| < |\gamma_i|\} & \text{if } \{\gamma \in \mathcal{S} \mid |\gamma| < |\gamma_i|\} \neq \emptyset \end{cases}$$

where $|\gamma|$ denotes the length of γ. By construction, the last element γ_p of this sequence is an accepting path of minimal length. Note that the sequence $\gamma_0, \dots, \gamma_p$ is increasing in the lexicographic ordering and decreasing in length. For $\alpha, \beta \in \mathcal{S}$, we let $\alpha \sqsubseteq \beta$ if $\alpha \preceq_{\text{lex}} \beta$ and $|\alpha| \le |\beta|$. We shall use the following simple fact.

Fact 1 *Each γ_i is $\sqsubseteq$-minimal in $\mathcal{S}$.*

Given a path α, we let $\min(\alpha) = \min\{i \mid \alpha \text{ is a prefix of } \gamma_i\}$ and $\max(\alpha) = \max\{i \mid \alpha \text{ is a prefix of } \gamma_i\}$. By convention, $\min(\alpha) = \infty$ and $\max(\alpha) = -\infty$ if α is not a prefix of some γ_i.

The next proposition implies in particular that Algorithm 2 is correct, since the last value taken by mce is precisely γ_p. It also shows what would be the behavior of a variant of our algorithm which outputs the successive values of mce. Although the time consumption of the algorithm is high, the algorithm can output all counterexamples of the sequence γ_i when they are discovered, and the user can stop the search at any time. For instance, Dekker's algorithm produces about 80 counterexamples.

Proposition 2. *The successive values taken by the variable* mce *during the execution of Algorithm 2 are* $\gamma_{-1} = \varepsilon, \gamma_0, \dots, \gamma_p$.

Proposition 2 is a direct consequence of Proposition 3 below. Indeed, DFS_MIN is initially called with the parameters $(s_1, \texttt{normal})$ if $s_1 \notin F$ and $(s_1, \texttt{careful})$ if $s_1 \in F$. If there exists a counterexample, the hypotheses of Proposition 3 are fulfilled at the beginning of the algorithm, with $s = s_1$, $\delta = \varepsilon$ and $k = 0$. Hence, at the end of the initial call of DFS_MIN on s_1, the value of mce is $\gamma_{\max(s_1)} = \gamma_p$.

Proposition 3. *Let* δs *be a strict prefix of* γ_k *with* $k = \min(\delta s) < \infty$. *Assume that at the beginning of a call* DFS_MIN(s,mode), *we have* cp $= \delta$ *and that for all prefixes* $\delta_1 r$ *of* δs *we had* mce $= \gamma_{\min(\delta_1 r)-1}$ *at the beginning of the call* DFS_MIN(r,_). *Then, at the end of the call* DFS_MIN(s,mode), *we have* mce $= \gamma_{\max(\delta s)}$. *Moreover, whenever the variable* mce *is updated, it is switched from some* $\gamma_{\ell-1}$ *to* γ_ℓ *with* $\ell \geq 0$.

The proof of this proposition in turn uses Lemma 3.

Proof. Let $T = \{t \in E(s) \mid \min(\delta s t) < \infty\}$. Since δs is a strict prefix of $\gamma_{\min(\delta s)}$, we have $T \neq \emptyset$. Write $T = \{t_1, \dots, t_n\}$ with $\lambda(s, t_i) < \lambda(s, t_{i+1})$ for all $1 \leq i < n$. We use an induction on $|\gamma_k| - |\delta s| \geq 1$.

Claim. If before line 4 when considering $t_i \in E(s)$ we have mce $= \gamma_{\min(\delta s t_i)-1}$ then after line 14 of this iteration we have mce $= \gamma_{\max(\delta s t_i)}$.

Let $t = t_i$ and $\ell = \min(\delta s t)$. Either $\ell = 0$ and mce $= \varepsilon$ or $|\texttt{cp}| + 1 = |\delta s t| \leq |\gamma_\ell| < |\texttt{mce}|$ and the test line 4 succeeds.

The first case is when $t \in \texttt{cp} = \delta s$. Then, we have $\gamma_\ell = \delta s t$ and t closes an accepting path. Therefore, mce is updated to γ_ℓ. For any other successor v of s with $\lambda(s, v) > \lambda(s, t)$, we have $|\delta s v| = |\gamma_\ell| = |\texttt{mce}|$, hence the test line 4 fails. Therefore, the value of mce remains γ_ℓ until the end of the call DFS_MIN(s,_). Moreover, from $\gamma_\ell = \delta s t$ we deduce that $i = n$ and $\gamma_\ell = \max(\delta s t_n) = \max(\delta s)$ which proves the claim.

The second case is when $t \notin \texttt{cp} = \delta s$. All hypotheses of Lemma 3 are fulfilled, hence DFS_MIN(t,_) is called. When DFS_MIN(t,_) is called, $\delta s t$ is a strict prefix of γ_ℓ, cp $= \delta s$, mce $= \gamma_{\ell-1} = \gamma_{\min(\delta s t)-1}$ and for all prefixes $\delta_1 r$ of δs we had mce $= \gamma_{\min(\delta_1 r)-1}$ at the beginning of the call DFS_MIN(r,_). Therefore, the hypotheses of Proposition 3 are fulfilled and since $|\gamma_\ell| - |\delta s t| < |\gamma_k| - |\delta s|$ we get by induction that $\mathtt{mce} = \gamma_{\max(\delta st)}$ at the end of the call $\mathtt{DFS\_MIN}(t,\_)$. The claim is proved.

Now, we show by induction on i that before line 4 when considering $t_i \in E(s)$ we have $\mathtt{mce} = \gamma_{\min(\delta st_i)-1}$.

Note that $k = \min(\delta s) = \min(\delta st_1)$. By definition of γ_k, no successor t of s with $\lambda(s,t) < \lambda(s,t_1)$ may be such that δst is on a simple accepting path of length less than $|\gamma_{k-1}|$ (with the convention $|\gamma_{-1}| = \infty$). Hence, the value of $\mathtt{mce}$ remains γ_{k-1} until $t_1 \in E(s)$ is considered. The property holds for $i = 1$.

Assume now that the property holds for some $i < n$. From the claim, we get $\mathtt{mce} = \max(\delta st_i)$ after the iteration for $t_i \in E(s)$. Let $q = \max(\delta st_i)$. Note that $\min(\delta st_{i+1}) = \max(\delta st_i) + 1 = q + 1$. By definition of γ_{q+1} and of the set T, no successor v of s with $\lambda(s,t_i) < \lambda(s,v) < \lambda(s,t_{i+1})$ may be such that δsv is on a simple accepting path of length less than $|\gamma_q|$. Hence, the value of $\mathtt{mce}$ remains γ_q until $t_{i+1} \in E(s)$ is considered and the property still holds for $i + 1$.

Finally, before line 4 when considering $t_n \in E(s)$ we have $\mathtt{mce} = \gamma_{\min(\delta st_n)-1}$. Using the claim, we get $\mathtt{mce} = \max(\delta st_n)$ after the iteration for $t_n \in E(s)$. Note that $\max(\delta st_n) = \max(\delta s)$. By definition of the set T, no successor v of s with $\lambda(s,t_n) < \lambda(s,v)$ may be such that δsv is on a simple accepting path of length less than $|\gamma_{\max(\delta s)}|$. Hence, the value of $\mathtt{mce}$ remains $\gamma_{\max(\delta s)}$ until the end of $\mathtt{DFS\_MIN}(s,\mathtt{mode})$ and the proposition is proved. $\square$

The proof of the next lemma uses auxiliary results (Lemmas 5 and 6 below) on paths that are totally independent of the algorithm.

Lemma 3. *Let δst be a simple path with $\ell = \min(\delta st) < \infty$. Assume that, while considering $t \in E(s)$ in $\mathtt{DFS\_MIN}(s,\_)$, we have $\mathtt{cp} = \delta s$ and $\mathtt{mce} = \gamma_{\ell-1}$ and that for all prefixes $\delta_1 r$ of δs we had $\mathtt{mce} = \gamma_{\min(\delta_1 r)-1}$ at the beginning of the call $\mathtt{DFS\_MIN}(r,\_)$. Then, $\mathtt{DFS\_MIN}(t,\_)$ is called.*

Proof. We let $\alpha' = \delta s$. Assume first that $\ell = 0$, so that $\alpha't$ is a prefix of γ_0. Since $\mathtt{mce} = \gamma_{-1} = \varepsilon$, the test line 4 succeeds. Since $\alpha't$ is simple and $\mathtt{cp} = \alpha'$, the test line 5 fails. Assume that the test line 7 fails. Then, the mode of the algorithm is necessarily **normal**, and in particular there is no accepting state on $\mathtt{cp} = \alpha'$. Moreover, t is not accepting: $\alpha't \cap F = \emptyset$. If the test line 9 also fails, then t has already been visited along a simple path that we denote $\beta't$. By Lemma 2, we have $\beta't \prec_{\mathrm{lex}} \alpha't$. This situation is impossible by Lemma 6. Hence the test line 9 must succeed and $\mathtt{DFS\_MIN}(t,\_)$ is called in this case.

Assume now that $\ell \neq 0$. We have $|\mathtt{cp}| + 1 = |\alpha't| \le |\gamma_\ell|$ since $\alpha't$ is a prefix of γ_ℓ. Further, $|\gamma_\ell| < |\gamma_{\ell-1}|$ by definition of the sequence $(|\gamma_i|)_i$. Since $\mathtt{mce} = \gamma_{\ell-1}$, we deduce that the test line 4 succeeds. Since $\alpha't$ is simple and $\mathtt{cp} = \alpha'$, the test line 5 fails. Assume that the test line 7 fails. We show as before that $\alpha't \cap F = \emptyset$. Assume that the test line 9 also fails. Then, there exists a simple path $\beta't$ such that $\beta't \prec_{\mathrm{lex}} \alpha't$ and $|\beta't| = t{\to}\mathtt{depth}$. If $|\beta't| > |\gamma_\ell|$, then $t{\to}\mathtt{depth} = |\beta't| > |\alpha't| = |\mathtt{cp}| + 1$ and $\mathtt{DFS\_MIN}(t,\_)$ is called on line 11.

Assume now that $|\beta't| \le |\gamma_\ell|$. We want to apply Lemma 5 with $\alpha = \gamma_\ell$. Recall that γ_ℓ is a simple accepting path which is $\sqsubseteq$-minimal in $\mathcal{S}$. Note that $\alpha't$ is a prefix of α which satisfies property (1) of Lemma 5 and it remains to show that $\alpha' t$ is minimal with this property. Since the algorithm is still in mode **normal** (the test line 7 failed), for all prefixes $\delta_1 r$ of α', we had $r{\rightarrow}\mathtt{depth} = \infty$ when the call to DFS_MIN$(r, \mathtt{normal})$ was made. By hypothesis, at the beginning of this call, we had $\mathtt{mce} = \gamma_{\ell_1 - 1}$ where $\ell_1 = \min(\delta_1 r)$. Assume that there is a simple path $\beta_1' r \prec_{\mathrm{lex}} \delta_1 r$. Let $\beta_1'' \sqsubseteq \beta_1'$ be $\sqsubseteq$-minimal with this property. Since $\beta_1'' r$ was not visited before $\delta_1 r$, and since β_1'' is $\sqsubseteq$-minimal, we have $|\beta_1' r| \geq |\beta_1'' r| \geq |\gamma_{\ell_1 - 1}| > |\gamma_\ell| = |\alpha|$ and property (1) of Lemma 5 does not hold for $\delta_1 r$. Therefore, $\alpha' t$ is the shortest prefix of $\alpha = \gamma_\ell$ satisfying (1) and Lemma 5 implies that $|\beta'| > |\alpha'|$. We conclude as above that DFS_MIN$(t, \_)$ is called on line 11. □

Lemma 4. *Let $\delta = \alpha s \beta s$ be a path with $s\beta \cap F \neq \emptyset$, αs simple and $\alpha s \cap \beta = \emptyset$. We can construct a simple accepting path $\delta' = \alpha' s' \beta' s'$ such that $|\delta'| \leq |\delta|$ and αs is a prefix of $\alpha' s'$.*

Proof. Assume that δ is not a simple accepting path. Let t be the first state occuring twice in β. Then, we write $\beta = \beta_1 t \beta_2 t \beta_3$ with $t \notin \beta_1 \beta_2$. If $s\beta_1 t \beta_3 \cap F \neq \emptyset$ then we let $\delta' = \alpha s \beta_1 t \beta_3 s$. The path δ' still satisfies the hypotheses of the lemma (with the same α and s) and we have $|\delta'| < |\delta|$. Hence we can conclude by induction. Otherwise, we let $\delta' = \alpha s \beta_1 t \beta_2 t$. Again, δ' still satisfies the hypotheses of the lemma and $|\delta'| < |\delta|$. Since αs is a prefix of $\alpha s \beta_1 t$, we can again conclude by induction. □

Lemma 5. *Let $\alpha \in \mathcal{S}$ be a simple accepting path which is $\sqsubseteq$-minimal in $\mathcal{S}$. Assume that there exists a prefix $\alpha' t$ of α satisfying*

$$\alpha' t \cap F = \emptyset, \quad \beta' t \prec_{lex} \alpha' t \text{ and } |\beta' t| \leq |\alpha| \text{ for some simple path } \beta' t. \qquad (1)$$

For the shortest prefix $\alpha' t$ of α satsisfying (1) we have $|\beta'| > |\alpha'|$.

Proof. Let α_1 be the greatest common prefix of α' and β'. We write $\alpha' = \alpha_1 \alpha_2$ and $\beta' = \alpha_1 \beta_2$. Note that the transition between the last state of α_1 and the first state of $\beta_2 t$ is strictly smaller than the transition between the last state of α_1 and the first state of $\alpha_2 t$. Hence, for all nonempty prefixes β_2' of $\beta_2 t$ and α_2' of $\alpha_2 t$, we have $\alpha_1 \beta_2' \prec_{\mathrm{lex}} \alpha_1 \alpha_2'$.

Assuming by contradiction that $|\beta_2| \leq |\alpha_2|$ we will build a simple accepting path β with $\beta \prec_{\mathrm{lex}} \alpha$ and $|\beta| \leq |\alpha|$, a contradiction with the $\sqsubseteq$-minimality of α.

Write $\alpha = \alpha' t \alpha''$ and let s be the first state on $\beta_2 t$ which occurs also on $t\alpha''$. We write $\beta_2 t = \beta_2' s \beta_2''$ and $\alpha'' = \alpha_3 s \alpha_4$ with $s \notin \alpha_3$. Below, whenever we state that a path is simple, this follows from the definition of s and α_3 and from the fact that α and $\beta' t$ are simple.

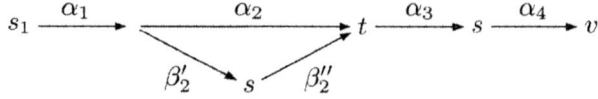

1. Assume that $\alpha_3 s$ contains a final state. Then, $\delta = \alpha_1 \beta_2' s \beta_2'' \alpha_3 s$ is an accepting path which is not necessarily simple. Yet, $\beta' t = \alpha_1 \beta_2' s \beta_2''$ is simple. Hence $\alpha_1 \beta_2' s$ is simple. Moreover, $\alpha_1 \beta_2' s \cap \beta_2'' \alpha_3 = \emptyset$ since α and $\beta_2 t$ are simple and by definition

of s and α_3. Applying Lemma 4, we obtain a simple accepting path β with $|\beta| \leq |\delta| \leq |\alpha|$ and $\alpha_1 \beta_2' s$ is a prefix of β. We deduce that $\beta \prec_{\text{lex}} \alpha$ as announced.

Assume now that $\alpha_3 s \cap F = \emptyset$, so that $\alpha_4 \cap F \neq \emptyset$, and let v be the last state of α. By definition of an accepting path, v is also the seed of the accepting loop.

2. We first show that v does not occur in α_2. Assume by contradiction that $\alpha_2 = \alpha_2' v \alpha_2''$ and consider the simple path $\delta = \alpha_1 \beta_2' s \alpha_4 = \delta' v$. We have $\delta' v \prec_{\text{lex}} \alpha_1 \alpha_2' v$ and $|\delta' v| \leq |\alpha|$, a contradiction with the fact that t is the first such state.

3. If v does not occur in $t\alpha_3$ then we let $\beta = \alpha_1 \beta_2' s \alpha_4$.

4. If v occurs in $t\alpha_3$ then we write $t\alpha_3 = \alpha_3' v \alpha_3''$ and we let $\beta = \alpha_1 \beta_2' s \alpha_4 \alpha_3'' s$.

In both cases, we can check that β is a simple accepting path and that $\beta \prec_{\text{lex}} \alpha$ and $|\beta| \leq |\alpha|$ as desired. $\square$

Lemma 6. *If $\alpha' t$ is a prefix of γ_0 with $\alpha' t \cap F = \emptyset$ then there is no simple path $\beta' t$ with $\beta' t \prec_{lex} \alpha' t$.*

Proof. Assume by contradiction that there exists a prefix $\alpha' t$ of γ_0 such that $\alpha' t \cap F = \emptyset$ and $\beta' t \prec_{\text{lex}} \alpha' t$ for some simple path $\beta' t$. In the following, we assume that $\alpha' t$ is the shortest such prefix of γ_0. We will build a simple accepting path β with $\beta \prec_{\text{lex}} \gamma_0$, a contradiction with the definition of γ_0.

We proceed exactly as in the proof of Lemma 5. The only difference is in case (2) when v occurs in α_2. Here we let $\beta = \alpha_1 \beta_2' s \alpha_4 \alpha_2'' t \alpha_3 s$. Note that we may have $|\beta| > |\gamma_0|$ but we can show that β is a simple accepting path with $\beta \prec_{\text{lex}} \gamma_0$, a contradiction with the $\preceq_{\text{lex}}$-minimality of γ_0. $\square$

3.4   Remarks on the Algorithm

To keep the presentation simple, we have described the algorithm starting from a fresh input. However, one can also start from an automaton already tagged by Algorithm 1. Since no counterexample can go through a black state, this allows us to backtrack in the depth-first search as soon as a black state is seen. This shortens obviously the search by cutting useless parts of the automaton.

Moreover, one can also bound the search by the size of the counterexample produced by Algorithm 1. More precisely, Algorithm 2 is well suited for bounded model-checking. One can give it a bound B for the depth of the research, and it would find successively the counterexamples $\gamma_\ell, \gamma_{\ell+1}, \ldots, \gamma_p$ where ℓ is the first index such that $|\gamma_\ell| < B$. This amounts only to changing the test of line 4 by

$$\left(\texttt{mce} = \varepsilon \textbf{ and } \left(\texttt{length(cp)} + 1 < B\right)\right) \textbf{ or } \left(\texttt{length(cp)} + 1 < \texttt{length(mce)}\right)$$

4   Implementation and Experimental Results

The algorithm presented in Section 2 is quite efficient and visits each state at most twice (in view of Remark 1) in order to find a first counterexample. The second algorithm on the other hand finds the shortest counterexample at the expense of revisiting states much more often. In the worst case, its time complexity is exponential. In order to get the best of the two, we could start with the first algorithm until a first counterexample is found (if any) and then switch to the second algorithm to find the shortest counterexample.

In the prototype used to obtain the experimental results presented below, we actually used SPIN's algorithm for finding the first counterexample instead of our algorithm presented in Section 2. Then we switch to our minimization algorithm of Section 3. The reason is that more in-depth changes have to be carried out on SPIN's code to implement our algorithm of Section 2 and our primary goal was just to minimize the size of the counterexample. We are currently implementing the algorithm of Section 2 and since it is always more efficient than SPIN's one, more improvements can be expected.

In the synchronized product between the model and the LTL automaton built by SPIN, there is a strict alternation between transitions of the model and transitions of the LTL automaton (see [9]). Therefore all accepting paths are of odd length and when minimizing the size of a counterexample we can replace line 4 of Algorithm 2 by `length(cp)+2 < length(mce)`. The test line 4 works in fact for an arbitrary Büchi automaton. This trivial optimization is important for our algorithm since it may revisit states quite often.

We have conducted experiments for various algorithms and specifications. Experiments for which the model does not satisfy the specification and counterexamples exist are gathered in Table 1. We compare our algorithm with `SPIN -i`

Table 1. Experiments for various algorithms when a counterexample does exist

		SPIN -i	Contrex
	counterexample length	55	19
Peterson	states stored	80	85
	states matched	1968	9469
	computation time	0.030s	0.070s
	counterexample length	173	23
Dekker	states stored	539	543
	states matched	48593	$2.5 * 10^6$
	computation time	0.240s	11.420s
	counterexample length	5	5
Dijkstra	states stored	211258	209687
(3 users)	states matched	1.96928e+09	654246
	computation time	71m27.700s	1.780s
	counterexample length	97	17
Hyman	states stored	123	157
	states matched	7389	40913
	computation time	0.080s	0.210s

which tries to reduce the size of the counterexample. Clearly `SPIN -i` does not find the shortest counterexample while we have proved in Section 3 that our algorithm does. The automata of the specifications (never-claims) have been generated by the tool `LTL2BA` [6] both for the verification with `SPIN -i` and with our algorithm. For each experiment, we show, in addition to the size of the minimal counterexample found, the number of *different* states visited by the algorithms (states stored). The last information (states matched) is the number of states (re)visited during the algorithm. Here, each time a state is (re)visited this counter is incremented. The execution time which is indicated is the user time (the system time is negligible in all cases) obtained on a Pentium III 700Mhz with 1Gb of RAM and 1Gb of cache.

As expected, our algorithm needs in general to revisit more states that SPIN's in order to really find the minimal counterexample. Yet, there are cases where SPIN's algorithm is less efficient than ours. The reason is that `SPIN -i` does not test whether a counterexample already exists (test $mce \neq \varepsilon$, line 11 of Algorithm 2). For Dijkstra's algorithm, there is no counterexample in the left part of the graph. Therefore, until the first counterexample has been found, our algorithm does not switch to careful mode, even if a state's depth gets lowered.

5   Conclusion and Open Problems

The main contribution of this paper is the algorithm presented in Section 3 which finds a shortest accepting path in a Büchi automaton. It actually finds a sequence of counterexamples of decreasing length which it can output. It has been implemented and the comparison with SPIN's algorithm clearly demonstrates its superiority in counterexample length. We also proposed an algorithm to find a counterexample, without trying to minimize its length, which is more efficient than SPIN's. It avoids unnecessary revisits of states and hence finds a counterexample more quickly. We plan to implement this algorithm and to compare it experimentally with SPIN. Further, this algorithm detects states that cannot be part of an accepting path (black states). Hence, using it instead of SPIN's before searching for a minimal counterexample should improve the performance of our second algorithm.

Finding a shortest counterexample with a depth-first search algorithm is time consuming because we need to revisit states many times. A general goal for improving the efficiency is to detect more states that need not be revisited.

Another important issue is to be able to deal with partial order reductions. While the first nested-DFS algorithm [5] failed in the presence of partial order reductions, the version of [10] is able to cope with some reductions. We need to investigate whether our algorithms can handle partial order reductions with reasonable memory requirements.

Finally, it would be interesting to find ways to minimize the length of the counterexample with respect to the model and the LTL specification. Instead, existing algorithms search for counterexamples for the model and *a specific automaton* associated with the LTL specification. It is often the case that this specific automaton is not optimal for finding a short counterexample for the LTL formula.

Acknowledgment. The authors wish to thank the anonymous referees for their careful reading of the submitted version of the paper and for their comments.

References

1. E. M. Clarke, O. Grumberg, S. Jha, Y. Lu, and H. Veith. Counterexample-guided abstraction refinement. In *Proceedings of the 12th Conference on Computer Aided Verification (CAV'01)*, volume 1855 of *LNCS*, pages 154–169. Springer, 2001.
2. E. M. Clarke, O. Grumberg, and D. A. Peled. *Model checking*. MIT Press, 1999.
3. E.M. Clarke, O. Grumberg, S. Jha, Y. Lu, and H. Veith. Counterexample-guided abstraction refinement for symbolic model checking. *J. ACM*, 50(5):752–794, 2003.
4. Th. H. Cormen, C. Stein, R. L. Rivest, and Ch. E. Leiserson. *Introduction to Algorithms*. McGraw-Hill Higher Education, 2001.
5. C. Courcoubetis, M. Vardi, P. Wolper, and M. Yannakakis. Memory efficient algorithms for the verification of temporal properties. In *Computer-aided verification '90 (New Brunswick, NJ, 1990)*, volume 3 of *DIMACS Ser. Discrete Math. Theoret. Comput. Sci.*, pages 207–218. Amer. Math. Soc., Providence, RI, 1991.
6. P. Gastin and D. Oddoux. Fast LTL to Büchi automata translation. In G. Berry, H. Comon, and A. Finkel, editors, *Proceedings of the 13th Conference on Computer Aided Verification (CAV'01)*, number 2102 in Lect. Notes Comp. Sci., pages 53–65. Springer, 2001.
7. T.A. Henzinger, R. Jhala, R. Majumdar, and G. Sutre. Lazy abstraction. In *Proc. of POPL'02*, pages 58–70. ACM Press, 2002.
8. G. Holzmann. The model checker spin. *IEEE Trans. on Software Engineering*, 23(5):279–295, May 1997. Special issue on Formal Methods in Software Practice.
9. G. Holzmann. *The SPIN model-checker*. Addison-Wesley, 2003.
10. G. Holzmann, D. Peled, and M. Yannakakis. On nested depth first search. In *Proc. Second SPIN Workshop*, pages 23–32, Rutgers, Piscataway, NJ, 1996. American Mathematical Society.
11. M. Y. Vardi and P. Wolper. An automata-theoretic approach to automatic program verification. In *Proc. 1st Symp. on Logic in Computer Science*, pages 332–344, Cambridge, June 1986.

Black-Box Conformance Testing for Real-Time Systems*

Moez Krichen and Stavros Tripakis

VERIMAG
Centre Equation, 2, avenue de Vignate, 38610 Gières, France. www-verimag.imag.fr.

Abstract. We propose a new framework for black-box conformance testing of real-time systems, where specifications are modeled as non-deterministic and partially-observable timed automata. We argue that such a model is essential for ease of modeling and expressiveness of specifications. The conformance relation is a timed extension of the input-output conformance relation of [29]. We argue that it is better suited for testing than previously considered relations such as bisimulation, must/may preorder or trace inclusion. We propose algorithms to generate two types of tests for this setting: analog-clock tests which measure dense time precisely and digital-clock tests which measure time with a periodic clock. The latter are essential for implementability, since only finite-precision clocks are available in practice. We report on a prototype tool and a small case study.

1 Introduction

Testing is a fundamental step in any development process. It consists in applying a set of experiments to a prototype system, with multiple aims, from checking correct functionality to measuring performance. In this paper, we are interested in so-called *black-box conformance testing*, where the aim is to check conformance of a system to a given specification. The system under test is "black-box" in the sense that we do not have a model of it, thus, can only rely on its observable input/output behavior.

Formal testing frameworks have been proposed (e.g., see [10]), where specifications are described in models with precise semantics and mathematical relations between such models define conformance. Then, under the assumption that the system under test (or *implementation*) can be modeled in the given framework, a set of tests can be automatically derived from the specification to test conformance of the (unknown) model. A number of issues arise, regarding the appropriateness of the models and conformance relation, the correctness of the testing process, its adequacy, its efficiency, and so on. Tools for test generation have been developed for various languages and models, both untimed (e.g., see [17,3,13]) and timed (e.g., see [8,15,12,20,25,26,19]).

---

* Work partially supported by European IST projects "Next TTA" under project No IST-2001-32111 and "RISE" under project No IST-2001-38117, and by CNRS STIC project "CORTOS".

S. Graf and L. Mounier (Eds.): SPIN 2004, LNCS 2989, pp. 109–126, 2004.

In this paper, we propose a new testing framework for real-time systems, based on *timed automata* [1]. Existing works based on similar models (e.g., [14, 16,25,28,11,23,19]) present two major limitations.

First, only restricted subclasses of timed automata are considered. This is problematic, since it limits the class of specifications that can be expressed. For example, [28,19] consider timed automata where outputs are *isolated* and *urgent*. The first condition states that, at any given state, the automaton can only output a single action. Therefore, a specification such as *"when input a is received, output either b or c"* cannot be expressed in this model. Worse, the second condition states that, at any given state, if an output is possible, then time cannot elapse. This essentially means that outputs must be emitted at precise points in time. Therefore, a specification such as *"when input a is received, output b must be emitted within at most 10 time units"* cannot be expressed. Most other works consider deterministic or determinizable subclasses of timed automata. For instance, [25] use *event-recording automata* [2] and [23] use a determinizable timed automata model with restricted clock resets. It is also typically assumed that specifications are *fully-observable*, meaning that all events can be observed by the tester.

The second limitation concerns implementability of tests. Only *analog-clock* tests are considered in the works above. These are tests which can observe the time of inputs precisely and can also react by emitting outputs in precise points in time. For example, a test like *"emit output a at time 1; if at time 5 input b is received, announce PASS and stop, otherwise, announce FAIL"* is an analog-clock test. Analog-clock tests are problematic, since they are difficult, if not impossible, to implement with finite-precision clocks. The tester which implements the test of the example above must be able to emit *a precisely* at time 1 and check whether *b* occurred *precisely* at time 5. However, the tester will typically sample its inputs periodically, say, every 0.1 time units, thus, it cannot distinguish between *b* arriving anywhere in the interval $(4.9, 5.1)$.

In this paper, we lift the above limitations. Our main contributions are the following.

First, we develop a framework which can fully handle *non-deterministic* and *partially observable* specifications. Such specifications arise often in practice: when the model is built compositionally, component interactions are typically non-observable to the external world; abstraction from low-level details often results in non-determinism. In general, timed-automata cannot be determinized [1] and non-observable actions cannot be removed [5]. It can be argued that in practice many models will be determinizable. However, checking this (and performing the determinization) is undecidable [32]. Thus, it is important to offer a modeling framework which is general enough to relief the user from the burden of performing determinization "manually".

Second, we propose a conformance relation, called *timed input-output conformance* or tioco, inspired from the "untimed" conformance relation ioco of [29]. According to ioco, *A* conforms to *B* if for each observable behavior specified in *B*, the possible outputs of *A* after this behavior is a subset of the possible outputs of B. tioco is simply defined by including time delays in the set of observable outputs. This permits to capture the fact that an implementation producing an output too early or too late (or never, whereas it should) is non-conforming. A number of different conformance relations have been considered in previous works. [28] use bisimulation (which in that case reduces to trace equivalence, because of determinism). Bisimulation is also used in [12]. [25] use a must/may preorder. A must/may testing criterion is also considered in [20]. [19] use trace inclusion. [23] use an adaptation of ioco which, under the hypotheses of the model, is shown to be equivalent to trace inclusion. We argue that tioco is more appropriate for conformance testing than the above conformance relations, because it leaves more design freedom to potential implementations (see Section 3).

Finally, we consider both analog-clock and *digital-clock* (or *periodic-sampling*) tests. Analog-clock tests can measure precisely the delay between two events, whereas digital-clock tests can only count how many "ticks" of a periodic clock have occurred between the two events. Digital-clock tests are clearly more realistic to implement. Analog-clock tests can still be useful, however. For instance, when the implementation is discrete-time but its time step is not known a-priori.

The issue of determinization arises during test generation, since most algorithms rely on an implicit determinization of the specification. This presents problems for analog-clock test generation, due to the fact that timed automata are not determinizable in general, as mentioned above. To deal with the problem, we follow the idea of [31]: the automaton is "determinized" *on-the-fly*, during test generation and execution. The algorithm uses standard symbolic reachability techniques for timed automata. With a simple modification of the specification model, similar techniques can be used to generate digital-clock tests. The latter can be generated either on-the-fly or off-line, in which case they are represented as finite trees. We discuss a simple heuristic to reduce the size of these trees by eliminating chains of ticks. We also briefly discuss coverage, proposing a heuristic to generate a test suite which covers the edges of the specification automaton.

We have implemented our test-generation algorithms in a prototype tool, called TTG. The tool is built on top of the IF environment [7] and uses the modeling language of the latter. This language allows to specify systems of many processes communicating through message passing or shared variables and also includes features such as hierarchy, priorities, dynamic creation and complex data types. We have applied TTG to a small case study, presented in Section 6. We have also applied TTG to test behaviors of the K9 Martian Rover executive of NASA [9]. The results of TTG on this case study are reported in [4].

The rest of this paper is organized as follows. Section 2 reviews timed automata and timed automata with inputs and outputs. Section 3 introduces the testing framework. Section 4 defines analog and digital-clock tests. Section 5 presents the test generation methods for the two types of tests. Section 6 discusses a prototype implementation and illustrates the method on a small case study. Section 7 presents the conclusions and future work plans.

2   Timed Automata

Let R be the set of non-negative reals. Given a finite set of *actions* Act, the set $(\mathsf{Act} \cup \mathsf{R})^*$ of all finite-length *real-time sequences* over Act will be denoted $\mathsf{RT}(\mathsf{Act})$. $\epsilon \in \mathsf{RT}(\mathsf{Act})$ is the empty sequence. Given $\mathsf{Act}' \subseteq \mathsf{Act}$ and $\rho \in \mathsf{RT}(\mathsf{Act})$, $P_{\mathsf{Act}'}(\rho)$ denotes the *projection* of ρ to Act', obtained by "erasing" from ρ all actions not in Act'. For example, if $\mathsf{Act} = \{a, b\}$, $\mathsf{Act}' = \{a\}$ and $\rho = a\,1\,b\,2\,a\,3$, then $P_{\mathsf{Act}'}(\rho) = a\,3\,a\,3$. The time spent in a sequence ρ, denoted $\mathsf{time}(\rho)$ is the sum of all delays in ρ, for example, $\mathsf{time}(\epsilon) = 0$ and $\mathsf{time}(a\,1\,b\,0.5) = 1.5$.

We use timed automata [1] with *deadlines* to model urgency [27,6]. A *timed automaton over* Act is a tuple $A = (Q, q_0, X, \mathsf{Act}, \mathsf{E})$ where: Q is a finite set of *locations*; $q_0 \in Q$ is the initial location; X is a finite set of *clocks*; E is a finite set of *edges*. Each edge is a tuple (q, q', ψ, r, d, a), where $q, q' \in Q$ are the source and destination locations; ψ is the *guard*, a conjunction of constraints of the form $x \# c$, where $x \in X$, c is an integer constant and $\# \in \{<, \leq, =, \geq, >\}$; $r \subseteq X$ is a set of clocks to *reset* to zero; $d \in \{\mathsf{lazy}, \mathsf{delayable}, \mathsf{eager}\}$ is the *deadline*; and $a \in \mathsf{Act}$ is the action. We will not allow eager edges with guards of the form $x > c$.

A timed automaton A defines an infinite labeled transition system (LTS). Its states are pairs $s = (q, v)$, where $q \in Q$ and $v : X \to \mathsf{R}$ is a clock *valuation*. $\mathbf{0}$ is the valuation assigning 0 to every clock of A. S_A is the set of all states and $s_0^A = (q_0, \mathbf{0})$ is the initial state. There are two types of transitions. Discrete transitions of the form $(q, v) \xrightarrow{a} (q', v')$, where $a \in \mathsf{Act}$ and there is an edge (q, q', ψ, r, d, a), such that v satisfies ψ and v' is obtained by resetting to zero all clocks in r and leaving the others unchanged. Timed transitions of the form $(q, v) \xrightarrow{t} (q, v + t)$, where $t \in \mathsf{R}, t > 0$ and there is no edge (q, q'', ψ, r, d, a), such that: either $d = \mathsf{delayable}$ and there exist $0 \leq t_1 < t_2 \leq t$ such that $v + t_1 \models \psi$ and $v + t_2 \not\models \psi$; or $d = \mathsf{eager}$ and $v \models \psi$. We use notation such as $s \xrightarrow{a}$, $s \not\xrightarrow{a}$, ..., to denote that there exists s' such that $s \xrightarrow{a} s'$, there is no such s', and so on. This notation extends to timed sequences, in the usual way. A state $s \in S_A$ is *reachable* if there exists $\rho \in \mathsf{RT}(\mathsf{Act})$ such that $s_0^A \xrightarrow{\rho} s$. The set of reachable states of A is denoted $\mathsf{Reach}(A)$.

Timed Automata with Inputs and Outputs: In the rest of the paper, we assume given a set of actions Act, partitioned in two disjoint sets: a set of *input actions* $\mathsf{Act}_{\mathsf{in}}$ and a set of *output actions* $\mathsf{Act}_{\mathsf{out}}$. We also assume there is an *unobservable action* $\tau \notin \mathsf{Act}$. Let $\mathsf{Act}_\tau = \mathsf{Act} \cup \{\tau\}$.

A *timed automaton with inputs and outputs* (TAIO) is a timed automaton over Act_τ. A TAIO is called *observable* if none of its edges is labeled by τ. A TAIO A is called *input-complete* if it can accept any input at any state: $\forall s \in \mathsf{Reach}(A) \,.\, \forall a \in \mathsf{Act}_{\mathsf{in}} \,.\, s \xrightarrow{a}$. It is called *deterministic* if $\forall s, s', s'' \in \mathsf{Reach}(A) \,.\, \forall a \in \mathsf{Act}_\tau \,.\, s \xrightarrow{a} s' \wedge s \xrightarrow{a} s'' \Rightarrow s' = s''$. It is called *non-blocking* if

$$\forall s \in \mathsf{Reach}(A) \,.\, \forall t \in \mathsf{R} \,.\, \exists \rho \in \mathsf{RT}(\mathsf{Act}_{\mathsf{out}} \cup \{\tau\}) \,.\, \mathsf{time}(\rho) = t \wedge s \xrightarrow{\rho} \,. \qquad (1)$$

This condition guarantees that A will not block time in any environment.

The set of *observable timed traces* of a TAIO A is defined to be

$$\mathsf{Traces}(A) = \{P_{\mathsf{Act}}(\rho) \mid \rho \in \mathsf{RT}(\mathsf{Act}_\tau) \wedge s_0^A \xrightarrow{\rho}\}. \tag{2}$$

3 Specifications, Implementations, and Conformance

We now describe our testing framework. We assume that the specification of the system to be tested is given as a non-blocking TAIO A_S. We assume that the implementation (i.e., the system to be tested) can be modeled as a non-blocking, input-complete TAIO A_I. Notice that we do not assume that A_I is known, simply that it exists. Input-completeness is required so that the implementation can accept inputs from the tester at any state (possibly ignoring them or moving to an error state, in case of illegal inputs).

In order to define the conformance relation, we define a number of operators. Given a TAIO A and $\sigma \in \mathsf{RT}(\mathsf{Act})$, A after σ is the set of all states of A that can be reached by some timed sequence ρ whose projection to observable actions is σ. Formally:

$$A \text{ after } \sigma = \{s \in S_A \mid \exists \rho \in \mathsf{RT}(\mathsf{Act}_\tau) \,.\, s_0^A \xrightarrow{\rho} s \wedge P_{\mathsf{Act}}(\rho) = \sigma\}. \tag{3}$$

Given state $s \in S_A$, $\mathsf{elapse}(s)$ is the set of all delays which can elapse from s without A making any observable action. Formally:

$$\mathsf{elapse}(s) = \{t > 0 \mid \exists \rho \in \mathsf{RT}(\{\tau\}) \,.\, \mathsf{time}(\rho) = t \wedge s \xrightarrow{\rho}\}. \tag{4}$$

Given state $s \in S_A$, $\mathsf{out}(s)$ is the set of all observable "events" (outputs or the passage of time) that can occur when the system is at state s. The definition naturally extends to a set of states S. Formally:

$$\mathsf{out}(s) = \{a \in \mathsf{Act}_{\mathsf{out}} \mid s \xrightarrow{a}\} \cup \mathsf{elapse}(s), \qquad \mathsf{out}(S) = \bigcup_{s \in S} \mathsf{out}(s). \tag{5}$$

The *timed input-output conformance relation*, denoted tioco, is defined as

$$A_I \text{ tioco } A_S \equiv \forall \sigma \in \mathsf{Traces}(A_S) \,.\, \mathsf{out}(A_I \text{ after } \sigma) \subseteq \mathsf{out}(A_S \text{ after } \sigma). \tag{6}$$

Due to the fact that implementations are assumed to be input-complete, it can be easily shown that tioco is a transitive relation, that is, if A tioco B and B tioco C then A tioco C. It can be also shown that checking tioco is undecidable. This is not a problem for black-box testing: since A_I is unknown, we cannot check conformance directly, anyway.

Examples: Before we proceed to define tests, we give some examples that illustrate the meaning of our testing framework. In the examples, input actions are denoted $a?$, $b?$, etc, and output actions are denoted $a!$, $b!$, etc. Unless otherwise mentioned, deadlines of output edges are delayable and deadlines of input edges

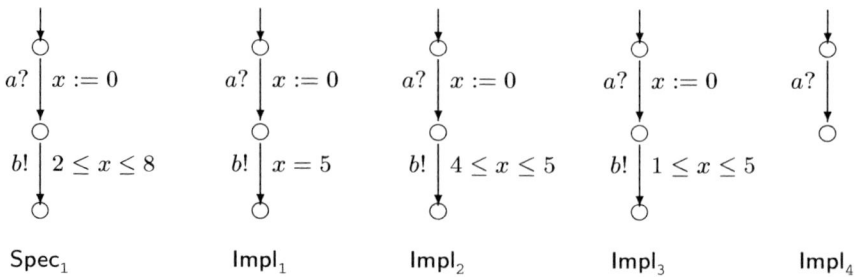

Fig. 1. Examples of specifications and implementations.

are lazy. In order not to overload the figures, we do not always draw input-complete automata. We assume that implementations ignore the missing inputs (this can be modeled by adding self-loop edges covering these inputs).

Consider the specification $\mathsf{Spec_1}$ shown in Figure 1. $\mathsf{Spec_1}$ could be expressed in English as follows: "after the first a received, the system must output b no earlier than 2 and no later than 8 time units". Implementations $\mathsf{Impl_1}$ and $\mathsf{Impl_2}$ conform to $\mathsf{Spec_1}$. $\mathsf{Impl_1}$ produces b exactly 5 time units after reception of a. $\mathsf{Impl_2}$ produces b within 4 to 5 time units. $\mathsf{Impl_3}$ and $\mathsf{Impl_4}$ do not conform to $\mathsf{Spec_1}$. $\mathsf{Impl_3}$ may produce a b after 1 time unit, which is too early. $\mathsf{Impl_4}$ fails to produce a b at all. Formally, $\mathsf{out}(\mathsf{Impl_3}$ after $a\,1) = (0, 4] \cup \{b\}$ and $\mathsf{out}(\mathsf{Impl_4}$ after $a\,1) = (0, \infty)$, whereas $\mathsf{out}(\mathsf{Spec_1}$ after $a\,1) = (0, 7]$.

Now consider specification $\mathsf{Spec_2}$ shown in Figure 2. This specification could be written down as: "if the first input is a then the system should output b within 10 time units; if the first input is c then the system should either output d within 5 time units or, failing to do that, output e within 7 time units". The second branch of $\mathsf{Spec_2}$ is a typical specification of a timeout. If the "normal" result d does not appear for some time, the system itself should recognize the error and output an error message not much later. None of the four implementations of Figure 1 conform to $\mathsf{Spec_2}$, as they do not react to input c (they ignore it). On the other hand, $\mathsf{Impl_5}$ and $\mathsf{Impl_6}$ of Figure 2 are conforming. It is worth noticing that $\mathsf{Impl_6}$ may output a b some time after receiving input f. The fact that input f does not appear in $\mathsf{Spec_2}$ does not affect the conformance of $\mathsf{Impl_6}$. (In fact, $\mathsf{Impl_5}$ and $\mathsf{Impl_6}$ conform not only to $\mathsf{Spec_2}$ but also to $\mathsf{Spec_1}$.) This example illustrates another property of tioco, namely, that an implementation is free to accept inputs not mentioned in the specification and behave as it wishes afterwards. This property is essential for capturing assumptions on the inputs (i.e., on the environment) in the specification. This is why we do not require specifications to be input-complete.

Comparison: [28] define conformance as timed bisimulation (TB), which in their case reduces to timed trace equivalence (TTE), since determinism is assumed. [25] define conformance using a must/may preorder (MMP). None of $\mathsf{Impl_1}$, $\mathsf{Impl_2}$

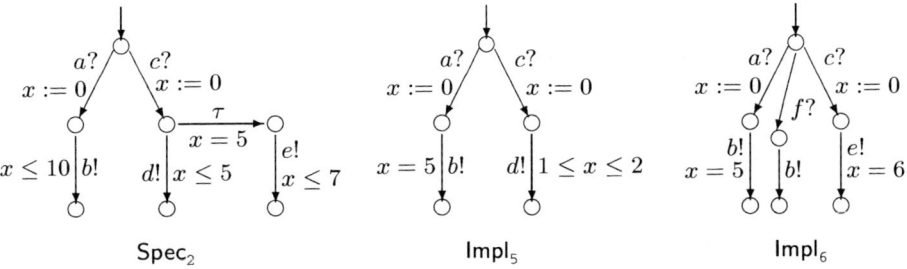

Fig. 2. More examples of specifications and implementations.

conform to Spec_1 w.r.t. TB, TTE or MMP. We believe that this is too strict.[1] [23,19] define conformance as timed trace inclusion (TTI). TTI is generally stricter than tioco: tioco allows an implementation to accept inputs not accepted by the specification, whereas TTI does not. When the specification is input-complete, tioco and TTI are equivalent. A deterministic (and fully observable) specification can be made input-complete without changing its conformance semantics by adding edges covering the missing inputs and leading to a "don't care" location where all inputs and outputs are accepted. This transformation is not always possible for non-deterministic specifications. Moreover, if the transformation is performed, care must be taken to instruct the test generation algorithm not to explore the "don't care" location, so that it does not generate useless tests. We opt for tioco, which avoids these complications in a simple way. For an extensive discussion of various untimed conformance relations, see [30].

4   Tests

A test (or *test case*) is an experiment performed on the implementation by an agent (the *tester*). There are different types of tests, depending on the capabilities of the tester to observe and react to events. Here, we consider two types of tests (the terminology is borrowed from [18]). *Analog-clock* tests can measure precisely the delay between two observed actions and can emit an input[2] at any point in time. *Digital-clock* (or *periodic-sampling*) tests can only count how many "ticks" of a periodic clock have occurred between two actions and emit an input immediately after observing an action or tick. For simplicity, we assume that the tester and the implementation are started precisely at the same time.

---

[1] It should be noted, however, that the issue does not arise in [28] because outputs are assumed to be urgent, thus, Spec_1 cannot be expressed.

[2] We always use terms "input" and "output" to mean input/output of the implementation. Thus, we write "the test emits an input" rather than "emits an output". We follow the same convention when drawing test automata. For example, the edge labeled $a?$ in the TAIO of Figure 3 corresponds to the tester emitting a, upon execution of the test.

In practice, this can be achieved by having the tester issuing the start command to the implementation.

It should be noted that we consider *adaptive* tests (following the terminology of [24]), where the action the tester takes depends on the observation history. Adaptive tests can be seen as *trees* representing the strategy of the tester in a game against the implementation. Due to restrictions in the specification model, which essentially remove non-determinism from the implementation strategy, some existing methods [28,19] generate non-adaptive test *sequences*.

4.1   Analog-Clock Tests

An analog-clock test for a specification A_S over Act_τ is a total function

$$T : \mathsf{RT}(\mathsf{Act}) \rightarrow \mathsf{Act}_{\mathsf{in}} \cup \{\perp, \mathsf{pass}, \mathsf{fail}\}. \tag{7}$$

$T(\rho)$ specifies the action the tester must take once it observes ρ. If $T(\rho) = a \in \mathsf{Act}_{\mathsf{in}}$ then the tester emits input a. If $T(\rho) = \perp$ then the tester waits (lets time elapse). If $T(\rho) \in \{\mathsf{pass}, \mathsf{fail}\}$ then the tester produces a verdict (and stops). To represent a valid test, T must satisfy a number of conditions:

$$\exists t \in \mathsf{R} . \forall \rho \in \mathsf{RT}(\mathsf{Act}) . \mathsf{time}(\rho) > t \Rightarrow T(\rho) \in \{\mathsf{pass}, \mathsf{fail}\} \tag{8}$$

$$\forall \rho \in \mathsf{RT}(\mathsf{Act}) . T(\rho) \in \{\mathsf{pass}, \mathsf{fail}\} \Rightarrow \forall \rho' \in \mathsf{RT}(\mathsf{Act}) . T(\rho \cdot \rho') = T(\rho) \tag{9}$$

Condition (8) states that the test reaches a verdict in bounded time t (called the *completion time* of the test). Condition (9) is a "suffix-closure" property ensuring that the test does not recall a verdict. We also need to ensure that the test does not block time, for instance, by emitting an infinite number of inputs in a bounded amount of time. This can be done by specifying certain conditions on the LTS defined by T. The states of this LTS are sequences $\rho \in \mathsf{RT}(\mathsf{Act})$. The initial state is ϵ. For every $a \in \mathsf{Act}_{\mathsf{out}}$ there is a transition $\rho \xrightarrow{a} \rho \cdot a$. There is also a transition $\rho \xrightarrow{t} \rho \cdot t$ for every $t \in \mathsf{R}$, provided $\forall t' \leq t.T(\rho) = \perp$. If $T(\rho) = b \in \mathsf{Act}_{\mathsf{in}}$ then there is a transition $\rho \xrightarrow{b} \rho \cdot b$. As a convention, all states ρ such that $T(\rho) = \mathsf{pass}$ are "collapsed" into a single sink state pass, and similarly with fail. We require that states of this LTS are non-blocking as in Condition (1), unless pass or fail is reached.

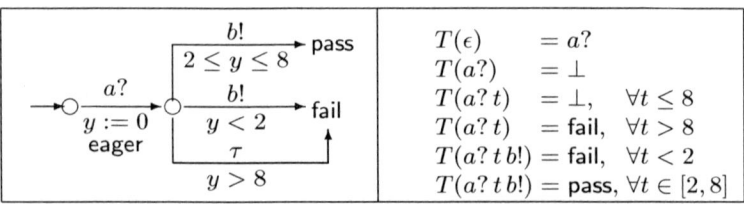

Fig. 3. Analog-clock test represented as a TAIO or a function.

Analog-clock tests can sometimes be represented as TAIO.[3] For example, the test defined in the right part of Figure 3 can be equivalently represented by the TAIO shown in the left part. Function T is partially defined in the figure. The remaining cases are covered by the suffix-closure property of pass/fail — Condition (9). For instance, $T(a?\,9\,b!) = \mathsf{fail}$, because $T(a?\,9) = \mathsf{fail}$.

Execution of the test T on the implementation A_I can be defined as the *parallel composition* of the LTSs defined by T and A_I, with the usual *synchronization* rules for transitions carrying the same label. We will denote the product LTS by $A_I\|T$. The execution of the test reaches a pass/fail verdict after bounded time. However, since the implementation can be non-deterministic or non-observable, the verdict need not be the same in all experiments (i.e., runs of the product). To declare that the implementation passes the test, we require that *all* possible experiments lead to a pass verdict. This implies that in order to gain confidence in pass verdicts, the same test must be executed multiple times, unless the implementation is known to be deterministic.

Formally, we say that A_I *passes* the test, denoted A_I passes T, if state fail is not reachable in the product $A_I\|T$. We say that an implementation passes (resp. fails) a set of tests (or *test suite*) $\mathcal{T}$ if it passes all tests (resp. fails at least one test) in $\mathcal{T}$. We say that $\mathcal{T}$ is *sound with respect to* A_S if $\forall A_I$. A_I tioco $A_S \Rightarrow A_I$ passes $\mathcal{T}$. We say that $\mathcal{T}$ is *complete with respect to* A_S if $\forall A_I$. A_I passes $\mathcal{T} \Rightarrow A_I$ tioco A_S.

Soundness is a minimal correctness requirement. Is is rather weak, since many tests can be sound and useless (by always announcing pass). Completeness, on the other hand, is usually impossible to achieve with a finite test suite (see Section 5.3). We are thus motivated to define another notion. We say that a test T is *strict with respect to* A_S if $\forall A_I$. A_I passes $T \Rightarrow A_I\|T$ tioco A_S. What the above definition says is that a strict test must not announce pass when the implementation has behaved in a non-conforming manner *during the execution of the test*. In the untimed setting, a similar notion of *lax* tests is proposed in [22]. The test shown in Figure 3 is sound and strict w.r.t. Spec_1 of Figure 1. Changing the fail state of the test into pass would yield a test which is still sound, but no longer strict.

4.2   Digital-Clock Tests

Consider a specification A_S over Act_τ and let tick be a new output action, not in Act_τ. A digital-clock test (or *periodic sampling* test) for A_S is a total function

$$D : (\mathsf{Act} \cup \{\mathsf{tick}\})^* \to \mathsf{Act}_{\mathsf{in}} \cup \{\bot, \mathsf{pass}, \mathsf{fail}\}. \tag{10}$$

The digital-clock test can observe all input and output actions, plus the action tick which is assumed to be the output of the tester's digital clock. We assume

---

[3] But not always: the test which moves to pass once it observes a sequence of a's such that the time distance between two a's is 1 cannot be captured by a timed automaton with a bounded number of clocks. This is related to the fact that timed automata are not determinizable whereas a test is by definition deterministic.

that the initial phase of the clock is 0 and its period is 1. We further assume that the clock is never reset, and that ticks have priority over other observable actions (i.e., if tick and a occur at the same time, tick will be always observed before a). With these assumptions, if action a is observed after the i-th and before the $(i+1)$-st tick, then the tester knows that a occurred at some time in the interval $[n, n+1)$.

Validity conditions similar to those for analog-clock apply to digital-clock tests as well. Due to lack of space, we omit the formal definitions. A digital-clock test D defines a LTS with states in $(\mathsf{Act} \cup \{\mathsf{tick}\})^*$ and labels in $\mathsf{Act} \cup \{\mathsf{tick}\} \cup \mathsf{R}$. Given state π, if $D(\pi) \not\subseteq \mathsf{Act_{in}}$ then π has a self-loop transition labeled with t, for all $t \in \mathsf{R}$. The reason such transitions are missing from states such that $D(\pi) = a \in \mathsf{Act_{in}}$ is that we assume that the digital-clock test emits a immediately after the last event in π is observed.

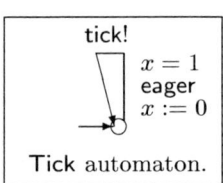

tick!

$x = 1$
eager
$x := 0$

Tick automaton.

Execution of a digital-clock test is defined by forming the parallel product of three LTSs, namely, the ones of the test D, the implementation A_I, and the Tick automaton shown to the left. Tick implicitly synchronizes with A_I through time. Tick explicitly synchronizes with D on transitions labeled tick. The parallel product is built so that tick transitions have priority over other observable transitions. Thus, if s is a state of the product and $s \xrightarrow{\mathsf{tick}}$, then s has no other outgoing transition. The definition of **passes** for digital-clock tests is similar to the one for analog-clock tests, with $A_I \| T$ being replaced by $A_I \| \mathsf{Tick} \| D$. The definitions of soundness, completeness and strictness also carry over in the natural way.

5   Test Generation

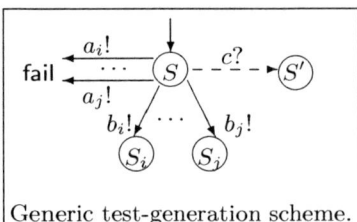

$a_i!$
fail
$a_j!$
S
$c?$
S'
$b_i!$ $\cdots$ $b_j!$
S_i S_j

Generic test-generation scheme.

We adapt the untimed test generation algorithm of [29]. Roughly speaking, the algorithm builds a test in the form of a tree. A node in the tree is a set of states S of the specification and represents the "knowledge" of the tester at the current test state. The algorithm extends the test by adding successors to a leaf node, as illustrated in the figure to the left. For all *illegal* outputs a_i (outputs which cannot occur from any state in S) the test leads to fail. For each legal output b_i, the test proceeds to node S_i, which is the set of states the specification can be in after emitting b_i (and possibly performing unobservable actions). If there exists an input c which can be accepted by the specification at some state in S, then the test may decide to emit this input (dashed arrow from S to S'). At any node, the algorithm may decide to stop the test and label this node as **pass**.

Two features of the above algorithm are worth noting. First, the algorithm is only partially specified. Indeed, a number of decisions need to be made at each node: (1) whether to stop the test or continue, (2) whether to wait or emit an input if possible, (3) which input, in case there are many possible inputs. Some of these choices can be made according to user-defined parameters, such as the desired depth of the test. They can also be made randomly or systematically using some book-keeping, in order to generate a test suite, rather than a single test. We discuss this option in more detail in Section 5.3.

The second feature of the algorithm is that it implicitly *determinizes* the specification automaton. Indeed, building S_i, S_j and so on corresponds to a classical *subset construction*. The latter can be performed either off-line, that is, before the test generation, or on-line, that is, during the test generation or even during the test execution. Test generation during test execution has been termed *on-the-fly* and is supported by the tool Torx [3].

5.1 Generating Analog-Clock Tests

Analog-clock tests cannot be represented as a finite tree, because there is an a-priori infinite set of possible observable delays at a given node. To remedy this, we use the idea of [31]. We represent an analog-clock test as an *algorithm*. The latter essentially performs subset construction on the specification automaton, during the execution of the test. Thus, our analog-clock testing method can be classified as on-the-fly.

More precisely, the test will maintain a set of states S of the specification TAIO, A_S. S will be updated every time an action is observed or some time delay elapses. Since the time delay is not known a-priori, it must be an input to the update function. We define the following operators:

$$\mathsf{dsucc}(S, a) = \{s' \mid \exists s \in S \;.\; s \xrightarrow{a} s'\} \tag{11}$$

$$\mathsf{tsucc}(S, t) = \{s' \mid \exists s \in S \;.\; \exists \rho \in \mathsf{RT}(\{\tau\}) \;.\; \mathsf{time}(\rho) = t \land s \xrightarrow{\rho} s'\} \tag{12}$$

where $a \in \mathsf{Act}$ and $t \in \mathsf{R}$. $\mathsf{dsucc}(S, a)$ contains all states which can be reached by some state in S performing action a. $\mathsf{tsucc}(S, t)$ contains all states which can be reached by some state in S via a sequence ρ which contains no observable actions and takes exactly t time units. The two operators can be implemented using standard data structures for symbolic representation of the state space and simple modifications of reachability algorithms for timed automata [31].

The test operates as follows. It starts at state $S_0 = \mathsf{tsucc}(\{s_0^{A_S}\}, 0)$. Given current state S, if output a is received t time units after entering S, then S is updated to $\mathsf{dsucc}(\mathsf{tsucc}(S, t), a)$. If no event is received until, say, 10 time units later, then the test can update its state to $\mathsf{tsucc}(S, 10)$. If ever the set S becomes empty, the test announces fail. At any point, for an input b, if $\mathsf{dsucc}(S, b) \neq \emptyset$, the test may decide to emit b and update its state accordingly. At any point, the test may decide to stop, announcing pass.

It can be shown that the test defined above is both sound and strict.

5.2   Generating Digital-Clock (Periodic-Sampling) Tests

Since its set of observable events is finite ($\mathsf{Act} \cup \{\mathsf{tick}\}$), a digital-clock test can be represented as a finite tree. In this case, we can decide whether to generate tests on-the-fly or off-line. This is a matter of a space/time trade-off. The on-the-fly method does not require space to store the generated tests. On the other hand, a test computed on-the-fly has a longer reaction time than a test which has been computed off-line.

Independently of which option we choose, we proceed as follows. We first form the product $A'_S = A_S \| \mathsf{Tick}$. We then define the following operator on A'_S:

$$\mathsf{usucc}(S) = \{s' \mid \exists s \in S . \exists \rho \in \mathsf{RT}(\{\tau\}) . s \xrightarrow{\rho} s'\}. \tag{13}$$

$\mathsf{usucc}(S)$ contains all states which can be reached by some state in S via a sequence ρ which contains no observable actions. Notice that, by construction of A'_S, the duration of ρ is bounded: since tick is observable and has to occur after at most 1 time unit, $\mathsf{time}(\rho) \leq 1$.

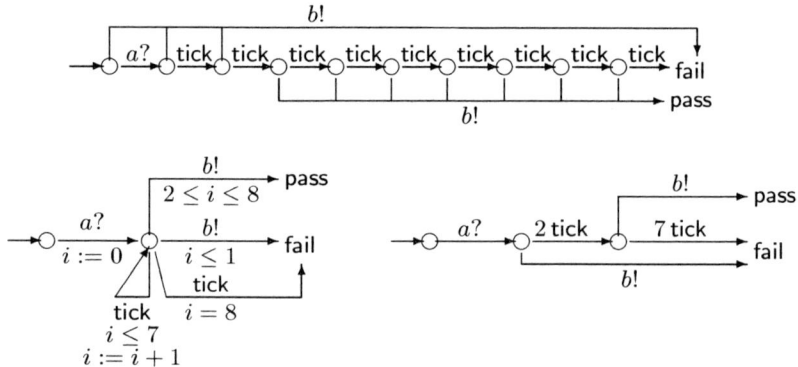

Fig. 4. A digital-clock test (top) and two alternative representations (bottom).

Finally, we apply the generic test-generation scheme presented above. The root of the test tree is defined to be $S_0 = \{s_0^{A_S}\}$. Successors of a node S are computed as follows. For each $a \in \mathsf{Act_{out}} \cup \{\mathsf{tick}\}$, there is an edge $S \xrightarrow{a} S'$ with $S' = \mathsf{dsucc}(\mathsf{usucc}(S), a)$, provided $S' \neq \emptyset$, otherwise there is an edge $S \xrightarrow{a} \mathsf{fail}$. If there exists $b \in \mathsf{Act_{in}}$ such that $S'' = \mathsf{dsucc}(\mathsf{tsucc}(S,0), b) \neq \emptyset$, then the test generation algorithm may decide to emit b at S, adding an edge $S \xrightarrow{b} S''$. Notice the asymmetry in the ways S' and S'' are computed. The reason is that the tester is assumed to emit an input b immediately upon entering S. Thus, S'' should only contain the immediate successors of S by b.

The tests generated in this way are guaranteed to be sound. However, they are not strict in general. This is expected, since the tester cannot distinguish between outputs being produced *exactly* at time 1 or, say, at time 1.5. A sound (but not strict) digital-clock test for Spec_1 of Figure 1 is shown in the top of Figure 4.

Reducing the size of digital-clock tests: Digital-clock tests can sometimes grow large because they contain a number of "chains" of ticks. On the other hand, standard test description languages such as TTCN [21] permit the use of variables and richer data structures. We would like to use such features to make the representation of digital-clock tests more "compact". For example, the test shown in the top of Figure 4 can be equivalently represented as the automaton with counter i, shown in the bottom-left of the figure.

Reducing the size of test representations is a non-trivial problem in general, related to compression and algorithmic complexity theory. In our context, we only use a heuristic which attempts to eliminate tick chains as much as possible. To this purpose, we generalize the labels of the digital-clock test to labels of the form k tick, where k is a positive integer constant. A transition labeled with k tick is taken when the k-th tick is received, counting from the time the source node is entered. Naturally, tick is equivalent to $1\,tick$. Now, consider two nodes S and S' such that: (1) $S \xrightarrow{\text{tick}} S'$, (2) for all $a \in \mathsf{Act}$, the successors of S and S' are identical, (3) $S' \xrightarrow{k\,\text{tick}} S''$. In this case, we remove node S' (and corresponding edges) and add the edge $S \xrightarrow{(k+1)\,\text{tick}} S''$. We repeat the process until no more nodes can be removed. The result of applying this heuristic to the test in the top of Figure 4 is shown in the bottom-right of the figure.

5.3   Coverage

It is generally impossible to generate a finite test suite which is complete, in particular when the specification has loops, which define an infinite set of possible behaviors. This is because implementations can have an arbitrary number of states, while a finite test suite can only explore a bounded number of states. But an implementation could be conforming up to a certain point and not conforming afterwards.

To remedy this fact, test generation methods usually make a compromise: instead of generating a complete test suite, generate a test suite which *covers* the specification.[4] Different coverage criteria have been proposed for untimed systems, such as state coverage (every state of the specification must be "explored" by at least one test), transition coverage (every transition must be explored), and so on. A survey of coverage criteria and their relationships, in the context of software testing, can be found in [33]. In the case of timed automata the state space is infinite, thus, existing methods attempt to cover: either finite abstractions of the state space, e.g., the region graph in [28,16], a time-abstracting partition graph in [25]; or the structural elements of the specification, e.g., [19] propose

---

[4] Some methods [28,12] generate a suite which is complete w.r.t. a given upper bound on the number of states of the implementation.

techniques for edge, location, or definition-use pair coverage and [8] consider various criteria in the context of timed Petri nets.

In the spirit of [19], we propose a heuristic for generating a digital-clock test suite covering the edges of the specification automaton. Notice that we cannot use the technique of [19], which is based on formulating coverage as a reachability problem. Indeed, this technique relies on the assumption that outputs in the specification are urgent and isolated, which results in tests being *sequences*, rather than trees.

Our method aims at covering edges labeled with an input action. Then, edges labeled with outputs will also be covered, since a test must be able to accept any output at any state. Let $\mathcal{T}$ be a test suite and $S \xrightarrow{a} S'$ be an edge in some test of $\mathcal{T}$, with $a \in \mathsf{Act_{in}}$. If e is an edge of A_S labeled with a and enabled at some state in S, then we say that e is *covered* by $\mathcal{T}$. We say that $\mathcal{T}$ covers A_S if all input edges of A_S are covered by $\mathcal{T}$. Then, the test generation algorithm can stop once it has generated a test suite covering A_S.

6   Tool and Case Study

We have built a prototype test-generation tool, called TTG, on top of the IF environment [7]. The IF modeling language allows to specify systems consisting of many processes communicating through message passing or shared variables and includes features such as hierarchy, priorities, dynamic creation and complex data types. The IF tool-suite includes a simulator, a model checker and a connection to the untimed test generator TGV [17]. TTG is implemented independently from TGV. It is written in C++ and uses the basic libraries of IF for parsing and symbolic reachability of timed automata with deadlines.

TTG takes as main input the specification automaton, written in IF language, and can generate two types of tests: (1) analog-clock tests under the assumption that the implementation is discrete-time and has a time step of 1; (2) digital-clock tests with respect to a given Tick automaton. By modifying the Tick automaton, the user can implement different sampling rates, model jitter in the sampling period, and so on. TTG can be executed in an interactive mode, where the user guides the test generation by resolving decision points. TTG can also be asked to generate a single test randomly or the exhaustive test suite, up to a user-defined depth. The depth of a test is the longest path from the initial state to a pass or fail state. The tests are output in IF language.

We have applied TTG to a small case study, which is a modification of the light switch example presented in [19]. The (modified) specification is shown in Figure 5. It models a lighting device, consisting of two modules: the "Button" module which handles the user interface through a touch-sensitive pad and the "Lamp" module which lights the lamp to intensity levels "dim" or "bright", or turns the light off. The user interface logic is as follows: a "single" touch means "one level higher", whereas a "double" touch (two quick consecutive touches) means "one level lower". It is assumed that higher and lower is modulo three, thus, a single touch while the light is bright turns it off.

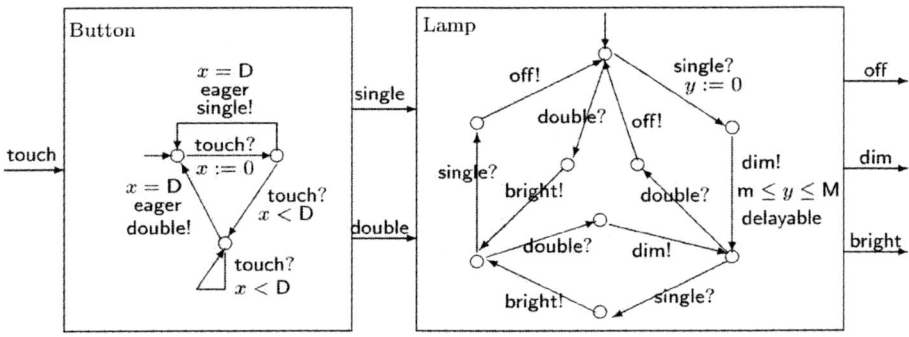

Fig. 5. A lighting device.

The device communicates with the external world through input touch and outputs off, dim, bright. Events single and double are used for internal communication between the two modules through *synchronous rendez-vous* and are non-observable to the external user. The Button module uses the timing parameter D which specifies the maximum delay between two consecutive touches if they are to be considered as a double touch. The Lamp module uses the timing parameters m and M which specify the minimum and maximum delay for the lamp to change intensity (e.g., to warm-up a halogen bulb). In order not to overload the figure, we omit most guards, resets and deadlines in the Lamp module. They are placed similarly to the ones shown in the figure (i.e., resets in inputs, guards and deadlines in outputs).

We have used TTG to generate the exhaustive digital-clock test suite for the above specification, with parameter set $D = 1, m = 1, M = 2$, for various depth levels. We have obtained 68, 180, 591 and 2243 tests, for depth levels 5, 6, 7 and 8, respectively. Notice that these are the sets of all possible tests up to the specified depth: no test selection is performed. Moreover, the current implementation is sub-optimal because it generates tests announcing pass before the maximum depth is reached. Implementation of test selection criteria is underway. One of the tests generated by TTG is shown in Figure 6. The drawing has been produced automatically using the if2eps tool by Marius Bozga.

7 Summary and Future Work

We have proposed a testing framework for real-time systems based on non-deterministic and partially-observable timed-automata specifications. To our knowledge, this is the first framework that can fully handle such specifications. We introduced a timed version of the input-output conformance relation of [29] and proposed techniques to generate analog-clock and digital-clock tests for this relation. We reported on a prototype tool and a simple case-study.

Regarding future work, our priority is to study test selection methods, in order to reduce the number of generated tests. To this aim, we are currently

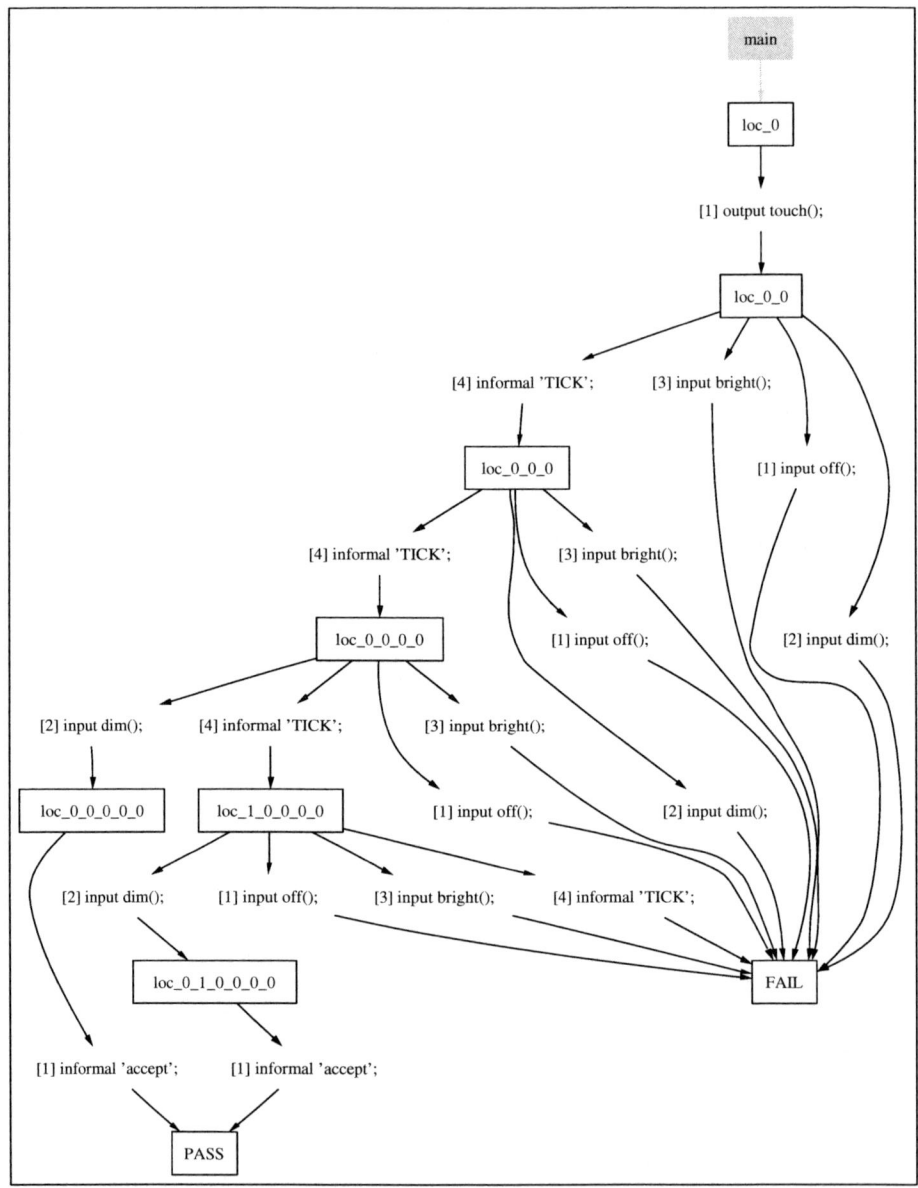

Fig. 6. A test generated automatically by TTG.

implementing the edge-coverage heuristic discussed in Section 5.3. We are also working on reducing the size of generated tests, implementing the reduction heuristic for digital-clock tests discussed in Section 5.2. Another direction that we pursue is to identify classes of specifications for which analog-clock tests can be represented as timed automata. One such class is deterministic and observable specifications. The advantage of a timed automata representation is that it avoids on-the-fly reachability computation, thus reducing the reaction time of the test.

Acknowledgment. We would like to thank Marius Bozga for his help with IF.

References

1. R. Alur and D. Dill. A theory of timed automata. *Theoretical Computer Science*, 126:183–235, 1994.
2. R. Alur, L. Fix, and T. Henzinger. A determinizable class of timed automata. In *CAV'94*, volume 818 of *LNCS*. Springer, 1994.
3. A. Belinfante, J. Feenstra, R.G. de Vries, J. Tretmans, N. Goga, L. Feijs, S. Mauw, and L. Heerink. Formal test automation: A simple experiment. In 12th *Int. Workshop on Testing of Communicating Systems*. Kluwer, 1999.
4. S. Bensalem, M. Bozga, M. Krichen, and S. Tripakis. Testing conformance of real-time applications by automatic generation of observers. In *Runtime Verification (RV'04)*. To appear in ENTCS.
5. B. Berard, A. Petit, V. Diekert, and P. Gastin. Characterization of the expressive power of silent transitions in timed automata. *Fundamenta Informaticae*, 36(2-3):145–182, 1998.
6. S. Bornot, J. Sifakis, and S. Tripakis. Modeling urgency in timed systems. In *Compositionality*, volume 1536 of *LNCS*. Springer, 1998.
7. M. Bozga, J.C. Fernandez, L. Ghirvu, S. Graf, J.P. Krimm, and L. Mounier. IF: a validation environment for timed asynchronous systems. In E.A. Emerson and A.P. Sistla, editors, *Proc. CAV'00*, volume 1855 of *LNCS*, pages 543–547. Springer Verlag, 2000.
8. V. Braberman, M. Felder, and M. Marre. Testing timing behavior of real-time software. In *International Software Quality Week*, 1997.
9. G. Brat, D. Giannakopoulou, A. Goldberg, K. Havelund, M. Lowry, C. Pasareanu, A. Venet, and W. Visser. Experimental evaluation of V&V tools on martian rover software. In *SEI Software Model Checking Workshop*, 2003.
10. E. Brinksma and J. Tretmans. Testing transition systems: An annotated bibliography. In *MOVEP 2000*, volume 2067 of *LNCS*. Springer, 2001.
11. R. Cardell-Oliver. Conformance test experiments for distributed real-time systems. In *ISSTA'02*. ACM Press, 2002.
12. R. Cardell-Oliver and T. Glover. A practical and complete algorithm for testing real-time systems. In *FTRTFT'98*, volume 1486 of *LNCS*, 1998.
13. D. Clarke, T. Jéron, V. Rusu, and E. Zinovieva. STG: A symbolic test generation tool. In *TACAS'02*, volume 2280 of *LNCS*. Springer, 2002.
14. D. Clarke and I. Lee. Automatic generation of tests for timing constraints from requirements. In *3rd Workshop on Object-Oriented Real-Time Dependable Systems (WORDS'97)*, 1997.
15. D. Clarke and I. Lee. Automatic test generation for the analysis of a real-time system: Case study. In *RTAS'97*, 1997.
16. A. En-Nouaary, R. Dssouli, F. Khendek, and A. Elqortobi. Timed test cases generation based on state characterization technique. In *RTSS'98*. IEEE, 1998.

17. J.C. Fernandez, C. Jard, T. Jéron, and G. Viho. Using on-the-fly verification techniques for the generation of test suites. In *CAV'96*, LNCS 1102, 1996.
18. T. Henzinger, Z. Manna, and A. Pnueli. What good are digital clocks? In *ICALP'92*, LNCS 623, 1992.
19. A. Hessel, K. Larsen, B. Nielsen, P. Pettersson, and A. Skou. Time-optimal real-time test case generation using UPPAAL. In *FATES'03*, Montreal, October 2003.
20. T. Higashino, A. Nakata, K. Taniguchi, and A. Cavalli. Generating test cases for a timed I/O automaton model. In *IFIP Int'l Work. Test. Communicat. Syst.* Kluwer, 1999.
21. ISO/IEC. Open Systems Interconnection Conformance Testing Methodology and Framework – Part 1: General Concept – Part 2 : Abstract Test Suite Specification – Part 3: The Tree and Tabular Combined Notation (TTCN). Technical Report 9646, International Organization for Standardization — Information Processing Systems — Open Systems Interconnection, Genève, 1992.
22. C. Jard, T. Jéron, and P. Morel. Verification of test suites. In *TESTCOM 2000*, 2000.
23. A. Khoumsi, T. Jéron, and H. Marchand. Test cases generation for nondeterministic real-time systems. In *FATES'03*, Montreal, October 2003.
24. D. Lee and M. Yannakakis. Principles and methods of testing finite state machines - A survey. *Proceedings of the IEEE*, 84:1090–1126, 1996.
25. B. Nielsen and A. Skou. Automated test generation from timed automata. In *TACAS'01*. LNCS 2031, Springer, 2001.
26. J. Peleska. Formal methods for test automation - hard real-time testing of controllers for the airbus aircraft family. In *IDPT'02*, 2002.
27. J. Sifakis and S. Yovine. Compositional specification of timed systems. In *13th Annual Symposium on Theoretical Aspects of Computer Science, STACS'96*, pages 347–359, Grenoble, France, February 1996. Lecture Notes in Computer Science 1046, Spinger-Verlag.
28. J. Springintveld, F. Vaandrager, and P. D'Argenio. Testing timed automata. *Theoretical Computer Science*, 254, 2001.
29. J. Tretmans. Testing concurrent systems: A formal approach. In J.C.M Baeten and S. Mauw, editors, *CONCUR'99 – 10th Int. Conference on Concurrency Theory*, volume 1664 of *Lecture Notes in Computer Science*, pages 46–65. Springer-Verlag, 1999.
30. J. Tretmans. Testing techniques. Lecture notes, University of Twente, The Netherlands, 2002.
31. S. Tripakis. Fault diagnosis for timed automata. In *Formal Techniques in Real Time and Fault Tolerant Systems (FTRTFT'02)*, volume 2469 of *LNCS*. Springer, 2002.
32. S. Tripakis. Folk theorems on the determinization and minimization of timed automata. In *Formal Modeling and Analysis of Timed Systems (FORMATS'03)*, LNCS. Springer, 2003.
33. H. Zhu, P. Hall, and J. May. Software unit test coverage and adequacy. *ACM Computing Surveys*, 29(4), 1997.

Validation of UML Models via a Mapping to Communicating Extended Timed Automata*

Iulian Ober, Susanne Graf, and Ileana Ober

VERIMAG
2, av. de Vignate
38610 Gières, France
{ober,graf,iober}@imag.fr

Abstract. We present a technique and a tool for model-checking operational UML models based on a mapping of object oriented UML models into a framework of communicating extended timed automata - in the IF format - and the use of the existing model-checking and simulation tools for this format.

We take into account most of the structural and behavioral characteristics of classes and their interplay and tackle issues like the combination of operations, state machines, inheritance and polymorphism, with a particular semantic profile for communication and concurrency. The UML dialect considered here, also includes a set of extensions for expressing timing.

Our approach is implemented by a tool importing UML models via an XMI repository, and thus supporting several commercial and non-commercial UML editors. For user friendly interactive simulation, an interface has been built, presenting feedback to the user in terms of the original UML model. Model-checking and model exploration can be done by reusing the existing IF state-of-the-art validation environment.

1 Introduction

We present in this paper a technique and a tool for validating UML models by simulation and property verification. The reason why we focus on UML is that we feel some of the techniques which emerged in the field of formal validation are both essential to the reliable development of real-time and safety critical systems, and sufficiently mature to be integrated in a real-life development process.

Our past experiences (e.g. with the SDL language [8]) show that this integration can only work if validation takes into account widely used modeling languages. Currently, UML based model driven development encounters a big success with the industrial world, and is supported by several CASE tools furnishing editing, methodological help, code generation and other functions, but very little support for validation.

---

* This work is supported by the OMEGA European Project (IST-33522). See also
http://www-omega.imag.fr

S. Graf and L. Mounier (Eds.): SPIN 2004, LNCS 2989, pp. 127–145, 2004.
© Springer-Verlag Berlin Heidelberg 2004

This work is part of the OMEGA IST project, whose aim is building a basis for a UML based development environment for real-time and embedded systems, including a set of notations for different aspects with common semantic foundations, tool supported verification methods for large systems, including real-time related aspects [11].

1.1 Basic Assumptions

Before going into more detail, in this work we made the following *fundamental assumptions*:

UML is broader than what we need or can handle in automatic validation. In UML 1.4 [33] there are 9 types of diagrams and about 150 language concepts (metaclasses). Some of them are too informal to be useful in validation (e.g. use cases) while for others the coherence and relationships with the rest of the UML model are not clearly (or uniquely) defined (e.g. collaborations, activity diagrams, deployment).

In consequence, in this work we focused on a subset of UML concepts that define an operational view of the modeled system: objects, their structure and their behavior. The choices, which are not fully explained in this paper, are not made ad-hoc. This work is part of a broader project (IST-OMEGA [1]) which aims to define a consistent subset of UML (*kernel language*) to be used in safety critical, real-time applications. See also [12,11].

UML has neither a standard nor a broadly accepted dynamic semantics. As a consequence, one facet of the OMEGA project is a quest for a suitable semantics for UML to be used in complex, safety critical, real-time, possibly distributed applications. Effort is put into: *finding* the right concepts (e.g. communication mechanisms between objects, concurrency model, timing specification features, see [12]), *defining* them formally (a formalization in PVS is available [23]) and *implementing and testing* these concepts in tools.

In this paper *we discuss only the problems of implementing and testing the semantics*, while the definition and formalization are tackled in [12] and [23]. We describe a translation to an automata-based formalism implemented in the IF tool [6,9]. This results in a flexible implementation of the semantics, in which we can easily test the choices of the OMEGA formal semantics and propose changes.

To produce powerful tools we have to build upon the existing. This motivates our choice to do a translation to the IF language [6,9], for which a rich set of tools (for static analysis, model checking with various reduction techniques, model construction and manipulation, test generation, etc.) already exist.

Our claim is that most of this tools work on UML-generated models with only minor updates[1]

Moreover, in order to be usable a validation tool has to accept UML models edited with widely used CASE tools. Our choice to work on the standard XML representation for UML (XMI) is a step into this direction.

---

[1] At least model checking, model construction and manipulation were already tested.

1.2   Our Approach in More Detail

In terms of **language coverage**, in our semantics and in our tool we focus on the operational part of UML: classes with structural and behavioral features, relationships (associations, inheritance), behavior descriptions through state machines and actions. The issues we tackle, like the combination of *operations* and *state machines, inheritance* and *polymorphism, run-to-completion* and *concurrency*, go beyond the previous work done in this area (see section 1.3), which has mainly focused on verification of statecharts. Our choices are outlined in section 2.

Our implementation of the operational semantics of UML models is based on a mapping from UML into an intermediate formal representation IF[5] based on *communicating extended timed automata* (CETA). This choice is motivated by the existence a verification toolset based on this semantic model [6,9] which has been productively used in a number of research projects and case studies, e.g. in [7,17]. The main features of the IF language are presented in section 1.4, and in section 3 we discuss a mapping from UML into this model which respects the semantics given in [12,23].

An important issue in designing real-time systems is the ability to capture quantitative timing requirements and assumptions, as well as time dependent behavior. We rely on the **timing extensions** defined in the context of the Omega project [18,16]. We summarize these extensions and their mapping into IF in section 4.

Another important issue is the formalism in which **properties** of models are expressed. In section 5 we introduce a simple property description language (*observer objects*) that reuses some concepts from UML (like objects, state machines) while remaining sufficiently expressive for a large class of linear properties. The use of concepts that are familiar to most UML users has the potential to alleviate the cultural shock of introducing formal dynamic verification to UML models.

Finally, section 6 presents the *UML validation toolset*. By using the IF tools as underlying simulation and verification engine, the UML tools presented here benefit from a large spectrum of model reduction and analysis techniques already implemented therein, such as *static analysis* and optimizations for state-space reduction, *partial order* reductions, some forms of *symbolic* exploration, model minimization and comparison, etc [6,9].

The techniques and the tool presented in this paper are subject to experimental validation on several larger case studies within the OMEGA project [1].

1.3   Related Work

The application of formal analysis techniques (and particularly model checking) to UML has been a very active field of study in recent years, as witnessed by the number of papers on this subject ([29,30,28,27,26,35,14,15,37,3] are most oftenly cited).

Like ourselves, most of these authors base their work on an existing model checker (SPIN[22] in the case of [29,30,28,35], COSPAN[21] in the case of [37], Kronos[38] for [3] and UPPAAL[25] for [26]), and on the mapping of UML to the input language of the respective tool.

For specifying properties, some authors opt for the property language of the model checker itself (e.g. [28,29,30]). Others use UML collaboration diagrams (e.g. [26,35]) which are too weak to express all relevant properties. We propose to use a variant of UML state machines to express properties in terms of observers.

Concerning language coverage, all previous approaches are restricted to *flat class structures* (no inheritance) and to behaviors, specified *exclusively by statecharts*. In this respect, many important features which make UML an object-oriented formalism (inheritance, polymorphism and dynamic binding of operations) are not dealt with. Our approach is, to our knowledge, the first to try to fill this gap.

Our starting point for handling of UML state machines (not described in detail in this paper) was the material cited above together with previous work on Statecharts ([20,13,31] to mention only a few). In the definition of our concurrency model we have taken inspiration from our previous assessment of the UML concurrency model [32], and from other positions on this topic (see for example [36]) and we respected the operational semantics defined in the OMEGA project [12].

1.4   The Back-End Model and Tools

The validation approach proposed in this work is based on the formal model of communicating extended timed automata and on the IF environment built around this model [6,9,10]. We summarize the elements of this model in the following.

Modeling with communicating extended automata.

IF was developed at VERIMAG in order to provide an instrument for modeling and validating *distributed systems* that can manipulate *complex data*, may involve *dynamic aspects* and *real time constraints*. Additionally, the model allows to describe the semantics of higher level formalisms (e.g. UML or SDL) and has been used as a format for inter-connecting validation tools.

In this model, a system is composed of a set of communicating *processes* that run in parallel (see figure 1). Processes are instances of *process types*. They have their own identity (PID), they may own complex data variables (defined through ADA-like data type definitions), and their behavior is defined by a *state machine*. The state machine of a process type may use composite states and the effect of transitions is described using common (structured) imperative statements.

Processes may inter-communicate via *asynchronous signals*, via *shared variables* or via *rendez-vous*. Parallel processes are composed asynchronously (i.e. by interleaving). The model also allows *dynamic creation* of processes, which is an essential feature for modeling object systems that are by definition dynamic.

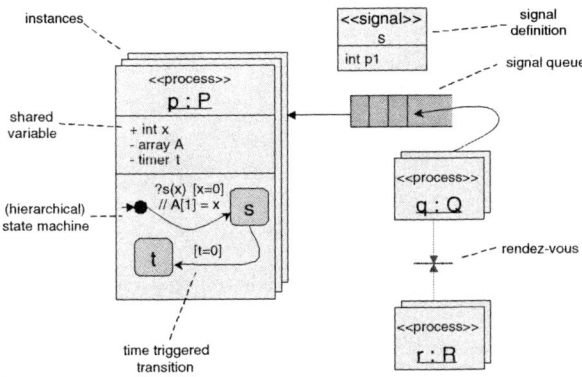

Fig. 1. Constituents of a communicating extended automata model in IF.

The link between system execution and time progress may be described in a precise manner, and thus offers support for modeling real time constraints. We use the concepts from *timed automata with urgency* [4]: there are special variables called *clocks* which measure time progress and which can be used in transition guards. A special attribute of each transition, called *urgency*, specifies if time may progress when the transition is enabled, and by how much (up to infinity or only as long as the time-guard of the transition remains true).

A framework for modeling priority.

On top of the above model, we use a framework for specifying dynamic priorities via partial orders between processes. The framework was formalized in [2]. Basically, a system description is associated with a set of priority directives of the form: $(state\ condition) \Rightarrow p_1 \prec p_2$. They are interpreted as follows: given a system state and a directive, if the condition of the directive holds in that state, then process with ID p_1 has priority over p_2 for the next move (meaning that if p_1 has an enabled transition, then p_2 is not allowed to move).

Property specification with observers.

Dynamic properties of IF models may be expressed using *observer automata*. These are special processes that may monitor[2] the changes in the *state* of a model (variable values, contents of queues, etc.) and the *events* occurring in it (inputs, outputs, creation and destruction of processes, etc.).

For expressing properties, the states of an observer may be classified (syntactically) as *ordinary* or *error*. Observers may be used to express *safety properties*. A re-interpretation of success states as accepting states of a Büchi automaton could also allow observers to express liveness properties.

---

[2] The semantics is that observer transitions synchronize with the transitions of the system.

IF observers are rooted in the observer concept introduced by Jard, Groz and Monin in the VEDA tool [24]. This intuitive and powerful property specification formalism has been adapted over the past 15 years to other languages (LOTOS, SDL) and implemented by industrial case tools like Telelogic's ObjectGEODE.

Analysis techniques and the IF-2 toolbox.

The IF-2 toolbox [6,9] is the validation environment built around the formalism presented before. It is composed of three categories of tools:

1. **Behavioral tools** for simulation, verification of properties, automatic test generation, model manipulation (minimization, comparison). The tools implement techniques such as *partial order reductions* and *symbolic* simulation of time, and thus present a good level of scalability.
2. **Static analysis tools** which provide source-level optimizations that help reducing furthermore the state space of the models, and thus improve the chance of obtaining results from the behavioral tools. Among the state of the art techniques that are implemented we mention *data flow analysis* (e.g. dead variable reduction), *slicing* and simple forms of *abstraction*.
3. **Front-ends and exporting tools** which provide source-level coupling to higher level languages (UML, SDL) and to other verification tools (Spin, Agatha, etc.).

The toolbox has already been used in a series of industrial-size case studies [6,9].

2   Ingredients of UML Models

This section outlines the semantic– and design–related choices with respect to *the UML concepts covered* and *the computation* and to the *execution model* adopted.

2.1   UML Concepts Covered

In this work we consider an operational subset of UML, which includes the following UML concepts: active and passive *classes* - with their *operations* and *attributes*, *associations*, *generalizations* - including polymorphism and dynamic binding of operations, *basic data types*, *signals*, and *state machines*. State machines are not discussed in this paper as they are already tackled in many previous works like [29,30,28,27,26,35,15,37,3].

Additionally to the elements mentioned above, a number of UML extensions for describing timing constraints and assumptions are supported. They were introduced in [16,18] and are discussed in section 4.

2.2   The Execution Model

We describe in this section some of the semantic choices made with respect to the computation and the concurrency model implemented by our method and tools. The purpose is to illustrate some of the particularities of the model and not to give a complete/formal semantics for UML, which may be found in [12, 23].

The execution model chosen in OMEGA and presented here is an extension of the execution model of the Rhapsody UML tool (see [19] for an overview), which is already used in a large number of UML applications. Other execution models can be accommodated to our framework by adapting the mapping to IF accordingly.

Activity groups and concurrency.

There are two kinds of classes: *active* and *passive*, both being described by attributes, relationships, operations and state machines.

At execution, each instance of an active class defines a concurrency unit called *activity group*. Each instance of a passive class belongs to exactly one activity group.

Different activity groups execute concurrently, and objects inside the same an activity group execute sequentially. Groups are sequential on purpose, in order to have some default protection against concurrent access to shared data (passive objects) in the group. The consequence is that requests (asynchronous signals or operation calls) coming from other groups (or even from the same in case asynchronous signals) are placed in a queue belonging to the activity group. They are handled one by one when the whole group is *stable*.

An *activity group* is stable when all its objects are stable. An *object* is stable if it has nothing to execute spontaneously and no pending operation call from inside its group. Note that an object is not necessarily stable when it reaches a stable state in the state machine, as there may be transitions that can be taken simply upon satisfaction of a Boolean condition.

The above notion of stability defines a notion of *run-to-completion* step for activity groups: a step is the sequence of actions executed by the objects of the group from the moment an external request is taken from the activity group's queue by one of the objects, and until the whole group becomes stable. During a step, other requests coming from outside the activity group are not handled and are queued.

Operations, signals and state machines.

In the UML model we distinguish syntactically between two kinds of operations: *triggered* operations and *primitive* operations. Reaction to *triggered operation calls* is described directly in the state machine of a class: the operation call is seen as a special kind of transition trigger, besides asynchronous signals. Triggered operations differ from *asynchronous signals* in that they may have a return value.

Primitive operations have the body described by a method, with an associated action. Their handling is more delicate since they are dynamically bound like in all object-oriented models. This means that, when such an operation call is sent to an object, the most appropriate operation implementation with respect to the actual type of the called object and to the inheritance hierarchy has to be executed.

With respect to call initiation, an object having the control may call a primitive operation on an object from the same activity group at any time, and the call is stacked and handled immediately. However, in case of triggered operation calls, the dynamic call graph between objects should be acyclic, since an object that has already called a triggered operation is necessarily in an unstable state and may not handle any more calls. This type of condition may be verified using the IF mapping.

Signals sent inside an activity group are always put in the group queue for handling in a later run-to-completion step. This choice is made so that there is no intra-group concurrency created by sending signals.

We note that the model described here corresponds to that of concurrent, internally-sequential *components* (activity groups), which make visible to the outside world only the stable states in-between two run-to-completion steps. Such a model has been already successfully used by several synchronous languages.

3 Mapping UML Models to IF

In this section we give the main lines of the mapping of a UML model to an IF system. The idea is to obtain a system that has the same operational semantics as the initial UML model (i.e. the same labeled transition system up to bisimulation). The intermediate layer of IF helps us tackle with the complexity of UML, and provides a semantic basis for re-using our existing model checking tools (see section 6).

The mapping is done in a way that all runtime UML entities (objects, call stacks, pending messages, etc.) are identifiable as a part of the IF model's state. In simulation and verification, this allows tracing back to the UML specification.

3.1 Mapping the Object Domain to IF

Mapping of attributes and associations. Every class X is mapped to a process type P_X that will have a local variable of corresponding type for each attribute or association of X. As inheritance is flattened, all inherited attributes and associations are replicated in the processes corresponding to each heir class.
Activity group management. Each *activity group* is managed at runtime by a special process of a type called GM. This process sequentializes the calls coming from outside the activity group, and helps to ensure the run-to-completion policy. In each P_X there is a local variable *leader*, which points to the GM process managing its activity group.
Mapping of operations and call polymorphism. For each operation $m(p_1 : t_1, p_2 : t_2, ...)$ in class X, the following components are defined in IF:

- a signal $call_{X::m}(waiting : pid, caller : pid, callee : pid, p_1 : t_1, p_2 : t_2, ...)$ used to indicate an operation call. If the call is made in the same activity group, *waiting* indicates the process that waits for the completion of the call in order to continue execution. *caller* designates the process that is waiting for a return value, while callee designates the process corresponding to the object receiving the call (a P_X instance).

- a signal $return_{X::m}(r_1 : tr_1, r_2 : tr_2, ...)$ used to indicate the return of an operation call (sent to the *caller*). Several return values may be sent with it.
- a signal $complete_{X::m}()$ used to indicate completion of computation in the operation (may differ from return, as an operation is allowed to return a result and continue computation). This signal is sent to the *waiting* process (see $call_{X::m}$).
- if the operation is *primitive* (see 2.2), a process type
  $P_{X::m}(waiting : pid, caller : pid, callee : pid, p_1 : t_1, p_2 : t_2, ...)$
  which will describe the behavior of the operation using an automaton. The parameters have the same meaning as in the $call_{X::m}$ signal. The *callee* PID is used to access local attributes of the called object, via the shared variable mechanism of IF.
- if the operation is *triggered* (see 2.2), its implementation will be modeled in the state machine of P_X (see the respective section below). Transitions triggered by a $X :: m$ call event in the UML state machine will be triggered by $call_{X::m}$ in the IF automaton.

The action of invoking an operation $X :: m$ is mapped to the sending of a signal $call_{X::m}$. The signal is sent either directly to the concerned object (if the caller is in the same group) or to the object's *active group manager* (if the caller is in a different group). The group manager will queue the call and will forward it to the destination when the group becomes stable.

The handling of incoming calls is simply modeled by transition loops (in every state[3] of the process P_X) which, upon reception of a $call_{X::m}$ will create a new instance of the automaton $P_{X::m}$ and wait for it to finish execution (see sequence diagram in figure 2).

In general, the mapping of primitive operation (activations) into separate automata created by the called object has several advantages:

- it allows for extensions to various types of calls other than the ones currently supported in the OMEGA semantics (e.g. non-blocking calls). It also preserves modularity and readability of the generated model.
- it provides a simple solution for handling *polymorphic* calls in an inheritance hierarchy: if A and B are a class and its heir, both implementing the method m, then P_A will respond to $call_{A::m}$ by creating a handler process $P_{A::m}$, while P_B will respond to both $call_{A::m}$ and $call_{B::m}$, in each case creating a handler process $P_{B::m}$ (figure 3).
  This solution is similar to the one used in most object oriented programming language compilers, where a "method lookup table" is used for dynamic binding of calls to operations; here, the object's state machine plays the role of the lookup table.

Mapping of constructors. Constructors (take $X :: m$ in the following) differ from primitive operations in one respect: their binding is static. As such, they

---

[3] This is eased by the fact that IF supports hierarchical automata.

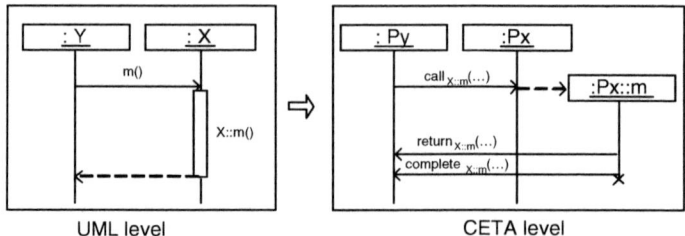

Fig. 2. Handling primitive operation calls using dynamic creation.

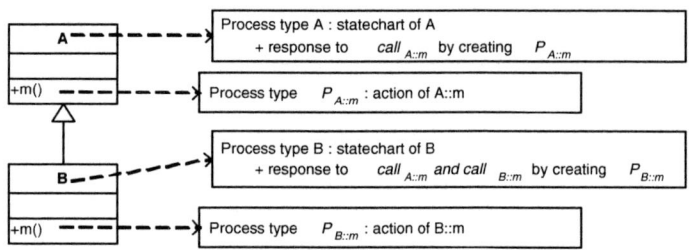

Fig. 3. Mapping of primitive operations and inheritance.

do not need the definition of the $call_{X::m}$ signal and the call (creation) action is directly the creation of the handler process $P_{X::m}$. The handler process begins by creating a P_X object and its strong aggregates, after which it continues execution like a normal operation.

Mapping of state machines. UML state machines are mapped almost syntactically in IF. Certain transformations, not detailed here, are necessary in order to support features that are not directly in IF: entry/exit actions, fork/join nodes, history, etc. Several prior research papers tackle the problem of mapping statecharts to (hierarchical) automata (e.g. [31]). The method we apply is similar to such approaches.

Actions. The action types supported in the original UML model are *assignments, signal output, control structure actions, object creation, method call* and *return.* Some are directly mapped to their IF counterparts, while the others are mapped as mentioned above to special signal emissions (*call, return*) or process creations.

3.2   Modeling Run-to-Completion Using Dynamic Priorities

We discuss here how the concurrency model introduced in section 2.2 is realized using the dynamic partial priority order mechanism presented in 1.4.

As mentioned, the calls or signals coming from outside an activity group are placed in the group's queue and are handled one by one in run-to-completion steps. In IF, the group management objects (GM) handle this simple queuing and forwarding behavior.

In order to obtain the desired run-to-completion (RTC), the following priority protocol is applied (the rules concern processes representing instances of UML classes, and not the processes representing operation handlers, etc.):

- All objects of a group have higher priorities than their group manager:
  $\forall x, y. \, (x.leader = y) \Rightarrow x \prec y$
  This enforces the following property:
  As long as an object inside the group may move, the group manager will not initiate a new RTC step.
- Each GM object has an attribute *running* which points to the presently or most recently running object in the group. This attribute behaves like a token that is taken or released by the objects having something to execute. The priority rule:
  $\forall x, y. \, (x = y.leader.running) \wedge (x \neq y) \Rightarrow x \prec y$
  ensures that
  as long as an object that is already executing has something more to execute (the continuation of an action, or the initiation of a new spontaneous transition), no other object in the same group may start a transition.
- Every object x with the behavior described by a statechart in UML will execute $x.leader.running := x$ at the beginning of each transition. In regard of the previous rule, such a transition is executed only when the previously running object of the group has reached a stable state, which means that the current object may take the *running* token safely.
  The non-deterministic choice of the next object to execute in a group (stated in the semantics) is ensured by the interleaving semantics of IF.

4   UML Extensions for Capturing Timing

In order to build a faithful model of a *real-time* system in UML, one needs to represent two types of timing information:

Time-triggered behavior (*prescriptive modeling*): this corresponds, for example, to the common practice in real-time programming environments to link the execution of an action to the expiration of a delay (represented sometimes by a *timer* object).

Knowledge about the timing of events (*descriptive modeling*): information taken as a *assumption* (hypothesis) under which the system works. Examples are the worst case execution times of system actions, scheduler latency, etc.

In addition to that, a high-level UML model may also contain timing requirements (*assertions*) to be imposed upon the system.

Different UML tools targeting real-time systems adopt different UML extensions for expressing such timing information. A standard UML Real-Time Profile, defined by the OMG [34], provides a common set of concepts for modeling timing, but their definition remains mostly syntactic.

We base our work on the framework defined in [18] for modeling timed systems. The framework reuses some of the concepts of the standard real-time profile [34] (e.g. timers, certain data types), and additionally allows expressing *duration constraints* between various events occurring in the system.

4.1   Validation of Timed Specifications

In this section we present the main concepts taken from [18], that we use in our framework, and we give the principles of their mapping to IF.

For modeling *time-triggered behavior*, we are using *timer* and *clock* objects compatible with those of [34], which are mapped in a straightforward manner to IF.

The modeling of the *descriptive timing information* makes intensive use of the **events** occurring in a UML system execution. An event has an occurrence time, a type and a set of related information depending on its type. The event types that can be identified are listed in section 5.2, as they also constitute an essential part of our property specification language (presented in section 5). All these UML *events* have a corresponding event in IF. For example: the UML event of invoking an operation $X :: m$ corresponds to the event of sending the $call_{X::m}$ signal, etc.

If several events of the same type and with the same parameters may occur during a run, there are mechanisms for identifying the particular event occurrence that is relevant in a certain context.

Between the events identified as above, we may define **duration constraints**. The constraints may be either *assumptions* (hypotheses to be enforced upon the system runs) or *assertions* (properties to be tested on system runs).

The class diagram example in figure 4 shows how these events and duration constraints may be used in a UML model. This model describes a typical client-server architecture in which worker objects on the server are supposed to expire after a fixed delay of 10 seconds. A timing assumption attached to the client says that: *"whenever a client connects to the server, it will make a request before its worker object expires, that is before 10 seconds"*.

For testing or enforcing a timing constraint from the UML model, we are presented with two alternatives:

- if the constraint is *local* to an object, i.e. all involved events are directly observed by the object, the constraint may be tested or enforced by the IF process implementing the object[4]. It will use an additional clock for measuring the duration concerned by the constraint, and a transition to an error state (in case of an assertion) or to an invalid state (in case of an assumption) with an appropriate guard on that clock.
- if the constraint is *not local* to an object (we call it *global*), the constraint will be tested or enforced by an observer running in parallel with the system.

---

[4] This is the case in figure 4. In general, outputs and inputs of a process are directly observed by itself, but they are not visible to other processes.

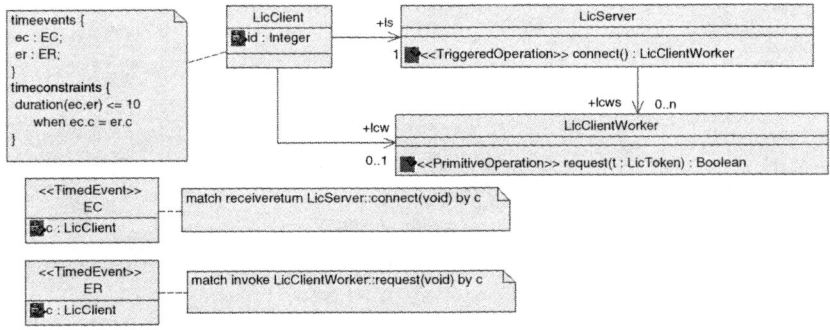

Fig. 4. Using events to describe timing constraints.

The tools will ensure that runs not satisfying a constraint are either ignored – if it is an assumption, or diagnosed as error – if it is an assertion.

5   Dynamic Properties Written as UML Observers

We discuss in this section a technique for specifying and verifying dynamic properties of UML models, that we call *UML observers*. Similarly to IF observer automata (section 1.4), UML observers are special objects which run in parallel with a UML system and monitor its *state* and the *events* that occur.

Syntactically, observers are described by special UML classes stereotyped with ≪*observer*≫. They may own attributes and methods, and may be created dynamically. An important part of the observer is its *state machine*, which is triggered by events occurring in the UML model, as we will see in the following. The main issue in defining UML observers is the choice of visible event types (which include specific UML event types like operation invocation, etc.).

For UML users, the advantage of UML observers compared to other property specification languages is that they use concepts that are known to UML designers (event driven state machines) while remaining sufficiently formal and expressive.

5.1   An Example of Property

Let us take a simple example: assume that we have a point-to-point communication protocol described in UML. Two interfaces TX and RX encapsulate the transmission and reception operations, and, to simplify, at runtime there exists exactly one object implementing each interface. The interface TX has one blocking operation $put(p : Data)$ (where $Data$ is the packet type) and the interface RX has one blocking operation $get()$ that returns a $Data$.

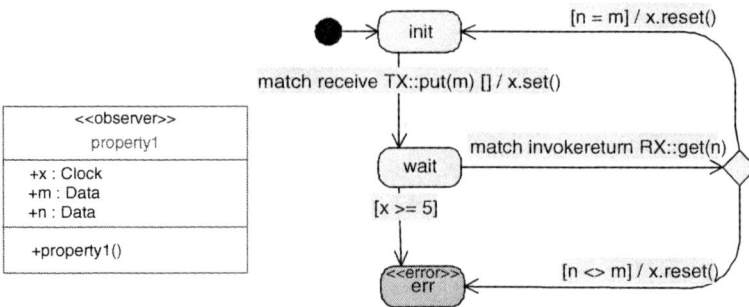

Fig. 5. Example of observer for a safety property.

Assume that we want to express the following reliability property: *whenever put is called with some Data, within at most 5 time units the same Data is received at the other end.* This also supposes that the user at the other end has called *get* within this time frame, reception being signified by the return from *get.* This property is specified in the observer in figure 5.

5.2   Basic Observer Ingredients

An important ingredient of the observer in figure 5 are the event specifications on some transitions. Here, the notion of event and the event types are the ones introduced in [18]:

- Events related to *operation calls:* **invoke, receive** (reception of call), **accept** (start of actual processing of call – may be different from **receive**), **invokereturn** (sending of a return value), **receivereturn** (reception of the return value), **acceptreturn** (actual consumption of the return value).
- Events related to *signal exchange:* **send, receive, consume.**
- Events related to *actions or transitions:* **start, end** (of execution).
- Events related to *states:* **entry, exit.**
- Events related to *timers* (this notion is specific to the model considered in [16,18] and in this work): **set, reset, occur, consume.**

The trigger of an observer transition may be a **match** clause, in which case the transition will be triggered by certain types of events occurring in the UML model. The clause specifies the type of event (e.g. **receive** in figure 5), some related information (e.g. the operation name $TX :: put$) and observer variables that may receive related information (e.g. m which receives the value of the *Data* parameter of *put* in the concerned call).

Besides events, an observer may access any part of the state of the UML model: object attributes and state, signal queues.

As in IF observers, properties are expressed by classifying observer states as *error* or *ordinary*. Note that an observer may be used also to formalize a

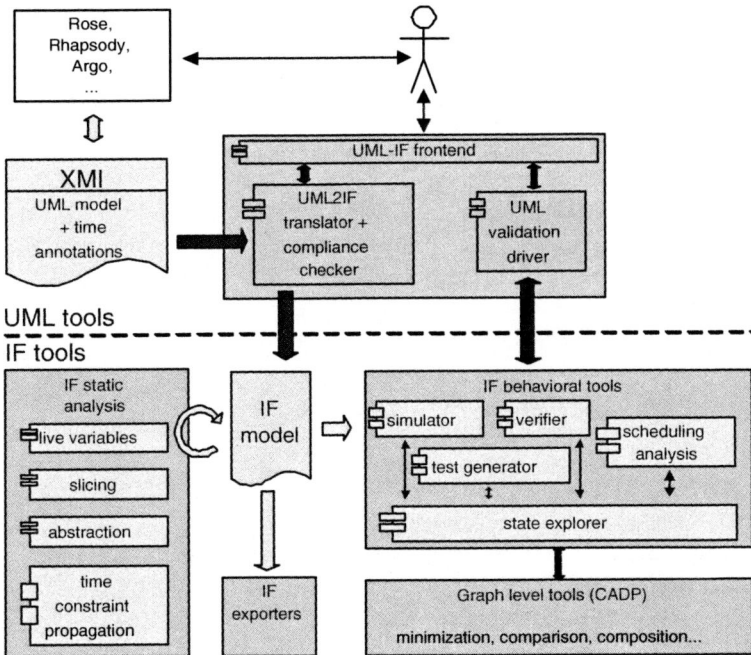

Fig. 6. Architecture of the UML-IF validation toolbox.

hypothesis on system executions, in which case the observer *error* states mark the system states that should be considered *invalid* with respect to the assumptions.
Expressing timing properties.
Certain timing properties may be expressed directly in a UML model using the extensions presented in section 4. However, more complicated properties which involve several events and more arbitrary ordering between them may be written using observers. In order to express quantitative timing properties, observers may use the concepts available in our extension of UML, such as *clocks*.

6   The Simulation and Verification Toolset

The principles presented in the previous sections are being implemented in the UML-IF validation toolbox[5], the architecture of which is shown in figure 6. With this tool, a designer may simulate and verify UML models and observers developed in third-party editors[6] and stored in XMI[7] format. The functionality offered by the tool, is that of an advanced debugger (with step-back, scenario generation, etc.) doubled by a model checker for properties expressed as observers.

---

[5] See http://www-verimag.imag.fr/PEOPLE/ober/IFx.
[6] Rational Rose, I-Logix Rhapsody and Argo UML have been tested for the moment.
[7] XMI 1.0 or 1.1 for UML 1.4

In a first phase, the tool generates an IF specification and a set of IF observers corresponding to the model. In a second phase, it drives the IF simulation and verification tools so that the validation results fed back to the user may be marshaled back to level of the original model. Ultimately, the IF back-end tools will be invisible to the UML designer.

As mentioned in the introduction, by using the IF tools as underlying engine, the UML tools have access to several model reduction and analysis techniques already implemented. Such techniques aim at improving the scalability of the tools, essential in a UML context. Among them, it is worth mentioning *static analysis* and optimizations for state-space reduction, *partial order* reductions, some forms of *symbolic* exploration, model minimization and comparison [6,9].

A first version of this toolset exists and is currently being used on several case studies in the context of the OMEGA project.

7   Conclusions and Plans for Future Work

We have presented a method and a tool for validating UML models by simulation and model checking, based on a mapping to an automata-based model (communicating extended timed automata).

Although this problem has been previously studied [14,29,28,27,26,35], our approach introduces a new dimension by considering the important object-oriented features present in UML: inheritance, polymorphism and dynamic binding of operations, and their interplay with statecharts. We give a solution for modeling these concepts with automata: operations are modeled by dynamically created automata, and thus call stacks are implicitly represented by chains of communicating automata. Dynamic binding is achieved through the use of signals for operation invocation. We also give a solution for modeling run-to-completion and a chosen concurrency semantics using dynamic priorities.

Our experiments on small case studies show that the simulation and model checking overhead introduced by modeling these object-oriented aspects remains low, thus not hampering the scalability of the approach.

For writing and verifying dynamic properties, we propose a formalism that remains within the framework of UML: observer objects. We believe this is an important issue for the adoption of formal techniques by the UML community. Observers are a natural way of writing a large class of properties (linear properties with quantitative time).

In the future we plan to:

- Assess the applicability of our technique to larger models. The tool is already being applied to a set of case studies provided by industrial partners in the OMEGA project.
- Extend the language scope covered by the tool. We plan to integrate the component and architecture specification framework defined in OMEGA.
- Improve the ergonomics and integration of the toolset (e.g. the presentation of validation results in terms of the UML model).

– Study the possibility of using the additional structure available in the object-oriented UML models for improving verification, static analysis, etc.

Acknowledgemens. The authors wish to thank Marius Bozga and Yassine Lakhnech who contributed with ideas and help throughout this work.

References

[1] http://www-omega.imag.fr - website of the IST OMEGA project.

[2] K. Altisen, G. Gössler, and J. Sifakis. A methodology for the construction of scheduled systems. In M. Joseph, editor, *proc. FTRTFT 2000*, volume 1926 of *LNCS*, pages 106–120. Springer-Verlag, 2000.

[3] Vieri Del Bianco, Luigi Lavazza, and Marco Mauri. Model checking UML specifications of real time software. In *Proceedings of 8th International Conference on Engineering of Complex Computer Systems*. IEEE, 2002.

[4] S. Bornot and J. Sifakis. An algebraic framework for urgency. *Information and Computation*, 163, 2000.

[5] M. Bozga, J.Cl. Fernandez, L. Ghirvu, S. Graf, J.P. Krimm, and L. Mounier. IF: An intermediate representation and validation environment for timed asynchronous systems. In *Proceedings of Symposium on Formal Methods 99, Toulouse*, number 1708 in LNCS. Springer Verlag, September 1999.

[6] M. Bozga, S. Graf, and L. Mounier. IF-2.0: A validation environment for component-based real-time systems. In *Proceedings of Conference on Computer Aided Verification, CAV'02, Copenhagen*, LNCS. Springer Verlag, June 2002.

[7] M. Bozga, D. Lesens, and L. Mounier. Model-Checking Ariane-5 Flight Program. In *Proceedings of FMICS'01 (Paris, France)*, pages 211–227. INRIA, 2001.

[8] Marius Bozga, Jean-Claude Fernandez, Lucian Ghirvu, Susanne Graf, Jean-Pierre Krimm, Laurent Mounier, and Joseph Sifakis. IF: An Intermediate Representation for SDL and its Applications. In R. Dssouli, G. Bochmann, and Y. Lahav, editors, *Proceedings of SDL FORUM'99 (Montreal, Canada)*, pages 423–440. Elsevier, June 1999.

[9] Marius Bozga, Susanne Graf, and Laurent Mounier. Automated validation of distributed software using the IF environment. In *2001 IEEE International Symposium on Network Computing and Applications (NCA 2001)*. IEEE, October 2001.

[10] Marius Bozga and Yassine Lakhnech. IF-2.0 common language operational semantics. Technical report, 2002. Deliverable of the IST Advance project, available from the authors.

[11] The Omega consortium (writers: Susanne Graf and Jozef Hooman). The Omega vision and workplan. Technical report, Omega Project deliverable, 2003.

[12] W. Damm, B. Josko, A. Pnueli, and A. Votintseva. Understanding UML: A formal semantics of concurrency and communication in real-time UML. In *Proceedings of FMCO'02*, LNCS. Springer Verlag, November 2002.

[13] Werner Damm, Bernhard Josko, Hardi Hungar, and Amir Pnueli. A compositional real-time semantics of STATEMATE designs. *Lecture Notes in Computer Science*, 1536:186–238, 1998.

[14] Alexandre David, M. Oliver Möller, and Wang Yi. Formal Verification of UML Statecharts with Real-Time Extensions. In R.-D. Kutsche and H. Weber, editors, *Fundamental Approaches to Software Engineering (FASE'2002)*, volume 2306 of *LNCS*, pages 218–232. Springer-Verlag, April 2002.

[15] Maria del Mar Gallardo, Pedro Merino, and Ernesto Pimentel. Debugging UML designs with model checking. *Journal of Object Technology*, 1(2):101–117, August 2002. (http://www.jot.fm/issues/issue 2002 07/article1).

[16] S. Graf and I. Ober. A real-time profile for UML and how to adapt it to SDL. In *Proceedings of SDL Forum 2003 (to appear)*, LNCS, 2003.

[17] Susanne Graf and Guoping Jia. Verification experiments on the MASCARA protocol. In *Proceedings of SPIN Workshop '01 (Toronto, Canada)*, January 2001.

[18] Susanne Graf, Ileana Ober, and Iulian Ober. Timed annotations with UML. In *Proceedings of SVERTS'2003 (Satellite workshop of UML'2003). Available at http://www-verimag.imag.fr/EVENTS/2003/SVERTS*, San-Francisco, 2003.

[19] David Harel and Eran Gery. Executable object modeling with statecharts. *Computer*, 30(7):31–42, 1997.

[20] David Harel and Amnon Naamad. The STATEMATE semantics of statecharts. *ACM Transactions on Software Engineering and Methodology*, 5(4):293–333, 1996.

[21] Z. Har'El and R. P. Kurshan. Software for Analysis of Coordination. In *Conference on System Science Engineering*. Pergamon Press, 1988.

[22] G. J. Holzmann. The model-checker SPIN. *IEEE Trans. on Software Engineering*, 23(5), 1999.

[23] J. Hooman and M.B. van der Zwaag. A semantics of communicating reactive objects with timing. In *Proceedings of SVERTS'03 (Specification and Validation of UML models for Real Time and Embedded Systems)*, San Francisco, October 2003.

[24] C. Jard, R. Groz, and J.F. Monin. Development of VEDA, a prototyping tool for distributed algorithms. *IEEE Transactions on Software Engineering*, 14(3):339–352, March 1988.

[25] H. Jensen, K.G. Larsen, and A. Skou. Scaling up UPPAAL: Automatic verification of real-time systems using compositionality and abstraction. In *FTRTFT 2000*, 2000.

[26] Alexander Knapp, Stephan Merz, and Christopher Rauh. Model checking timed UML state machines and collaborations. In W. Damm and E.-R. Olderog, editors, *7th Intl. Symp. Formal Techniques in Real-Time and Fault Tolerant Systems (FTRTFT 2002)*, volume 2469 of *Lecture Notes in Computer Science*, pages 395–414, Oldenburg, Germany, September 2002. Springer-Verlag.

[27] Gihwon Kwon. Rewrite rules and operational semantics for model checking UML statecharts. In Bran Selic Andy Evans, Stuart Kent, editor, *Proceedings of UML'2000*, volume 1939 of *Lecture Notes in Computer Science*. Springer-Verlag, 2000.

[28] D. Latella, I. Majzik, and M. Massink. Automatic verification of a behavioral subset of UML statechart diagrams using the SPiN model-checker. *Formal Aspects of Computing*, (11), 1999.

[29] J. Lilius and I.P. Paltor. Formalizing UML state machines for model checking. In Rumpe France, editor, *Proceedings of UML'1999*, volume 1723 of *Lecture Notes in Computer Science*. Springer-Verlag, 1999.

[30] Johan Lilius and Ivan Porres Paltor. vUML: A tool for verifying UML models. In *Proceedings of 14th IEEE International Conference on Automated Software Engineering*. IEEE, 1999.

[31] Erich Mikk, Yassine Lakhnech, and Michael Siegel. Hierarchical automata as a model for statecharts. In *Proceedings of Asian Computer Science Conference*, volume 1345 of *LNCS*. Springer Verlag, 1997.

[32] Iulian Ober and Ileana Stan. On the concurrent object model of UML. In *Proceedings of EUROPAR'99*, LNCS. Springer Verlag, 1999.

[33] OMG. Unified Modeling Language Specification (Action Semantics). OMG Adopted Specification, December 2001.

[34] OMG. Response to the OMG RFP for Schedulability, Performance and Time, v. 2.0. OMG ducument ad/2002-03-04, March 2002.

[35] Timm Schäfer, Alexander Knapp, and Stephan Merz. Model checking UML state machines and collaborations. *Electronic Notes in Theoretical Computer Science*, 55(3):13 pages, 2001.

[36] WOODDES. Workshop on concurrency issues in UML. Satelite workshop of UML'2001. See http://wooddes.intranet.gr/uml2001/Home.htm.

[37] Fei Xie, Vladimir Levin, and James C. Browne. Model checking for an executable subset of UML. In *Proceedings of 16th IEEE International Conference on Automated Software Engineering (ASE'01)*. IEEE, 2001.

[38] S. Yovine. KRONOS: A verification tool for real-time systems. *Springer International Journal of Software Tools for Technology Transfer*, 1(1-2), December 1997.

Explicit State Model Checking with Hopper

Michael Jones and Eric Mercer

Brigham Young University
Computer Science, Provo, UT
{jones,egm}@cs.byu.edu

Abstract. The Murφ-based Hopper tool is a general purpose explicit model checker. Hopper leverages Murφ's class structure to implement new algorithms. Hopper differs from Murφ in that it includes in its distribution published parallel and disk based algorithms, as well as several new algorithms. For example, Hopper includes parallel dynamic partitioning, cooperative parallel search for LTL violations and property-based guided search (parallel or sequential). We discuss Hopper in general and present a recently implemented randomized guided search algorithm. In multiple parallel guided searches, randomization increases the expected average time to find an error but decreases the expected minimum time to find an error.

The Hopper[1] tool leverages the Murφ architecture to implement parallel, disk-based and heuristic model checking algorithms. The common theme in the algorithms implemented in Hopper is that they do not use abstraction. Instead, Hopper explores fundamental algorithms for reducing time and space capacity limitations in state generation and storage. Our intention is that algorithms implemented in Hopper can be combined with well-known abstraction techniques. The algorithms studied in Hopper are generic enough to be implemented in any state enumeration context–including software model checking. The current release of Hopper contains parallel and disk based algorithms published by Dill and Stern [1,2] and heuristic search using the heuristic proposed by Edelkamp [3]. Hopper also includes parallel and guided search algorithms developed by the BYU model checking research group [4,5,6]. Hopper is a testbed for ideas that will be incorporated in our forthcoming C/C++ model checker built as an extension of the GNU debugger (GDB). The Hopper distribution includes a suite of 177 benchmark verification problems for Murφ.

This paper describes the architecture and algorithms implemented in Hopper along with a new randomized guided algorithm we have recently implemented. Randomization increases the variance (and the mean) of the search effort required to find a property violation. Search effort is measured by the number of transitions taken. In some problems, increasing the variance (even at the expense of increasing the mean) decreases the expected minimum number of transitions taken in error discovery using in parallel searches.

---

[1] Named after Edward Hopper (1882-1967), an early realist painter. Neither Hopper the artist nor Hopper the tool rely on abstraction.

S. Graf and L. Mounier (Eds.): SPIN 2004, LNCS 2989, pp. 146–150, 2004.

1 Hopper

Hopper is a general purpose explicit state model checker built on the Murφ code base. Hopper, like Murφ, uses a *rule-based* input language for model descriptions. Although it is not process based, like `Promela` or CSP, it is sufficient to describe large complex transition systems [7]. Hopper adds polymorphism to Murφ's code base to implement new algorithms. The design philosophy of Hopper is to minimally alter code in the basic Murφ distribution when adding new functionality through polymorphism. The behavior of key classes is redefined in a separate code base. This design philosophy treats Murφ as an application programmer interface (API) to prototype new algorithms for empirical analysis. Hopper does not support Murφ symmetry reductions in parallel, randomized or disk based algorithms.

Hopper includes an implementation of the Stern and Dill parallel model checking algorithm [1] and the disk based algorithm from [2]. The parallel algorithm in Hopper is implemented with MPICH 1.2.5 for the communication layer and a modified Dijkstra's token-based termination detection algorithm. MPICH is a free MPI implementation that is portable across several different communication fabrics. The modification to Dijkstra's token termination algorithm is required because communication in the parallel algorithm is not limited to a ring topology, as required by Dikjstra's algorithm. The modification adds message count information to the token. Termination is detected when the token travels around the logical ring and both retains the correct color and indicates that the number of messages sent is equal to the number of messages received. After detection, termination is completed by passing a poison pill through the ring. The modified Dijkstra's token termination algorithm is more reliable than the algorithm based on idle time used in [1]. The Hopper implementation has been successfully tested and analyzed on two platforms with 256 processors and different communication fabrics [5].

Hopper also includes a parallel algorithm that uses dynamic partitioning to aggregate memory on multiple computation nodes. The Stern and Dill algorithm uses a static hash function to distribute known reachable states in the model across computation nodes. An imbalanced distribution, however, may not efficiently utilize the aggregated memory since it may prematurely drive a node to its maximum capacity before all reachable state have been enumerated. The dynamic partition algorithm in Hopper constructs the partition function on-the-fly. The Murφ architecture simplifies the use of either the static or dynamic partitioned hash table when running any given search algorithm.

Hopper includes a visualization toolkit for postmortem analysis of parallel model checking algorithm behavior through time. This Java based toolkit reads time stamped entries from Hopper log files. The time series data is then reconstructed and animated. The default configuration shows, for each computation node, the size of its state queue, the total number of states in its hash table, the number of states sent, and the number of states received as dynamic bar charts.

Hopper implements a cooperative parallel search algorithm for finding LTL violations. The bee-based error exploration (BEE) algorithm is designed to operate in a non-dedicated parallel computing environment. It does this by employing a decentralized forager allocation scheme exhibited as a social behavior by honeybee colonies. Forager allocation involves identifying flower patches and allocating foragers to forage for resources at the patches. In LTL search, flower patches map to accept states and foraging maps to finding cycles that contain accept states. The resulting algorithm searches for accept states, then allocates workstations to forage for cycles beginning at accept states. A complete presentation and analysis of the BEE algorithm is given in [4]

Hopper implements property-based guided search in either parallel or sequential modes. The Hopper distribution uses admissible and inadmissible versions of property-based heuristics given by Edelkamp et. al. in [3]. Hopper also implements a Bayes heuristic search (BHS) to improve the expected accuracy of estimates treated as random variables (i.e., functions that assign a real valued probability between 0 and 1 to each possible outcome of an event). A probability density function characterizes the distribution of confidence in the heuristic. If the heuristic is accurate, then most of the probability is close to the actual distance to the target. The BHS algorithm minimizes mean squared error in heuristic estimates using an empirical Bayes [8] meta-heuristic. This is done using sets of sibling states to derive the confidence that should be attributed to each individual estimate. The confidence level is then used to proportionally revise the original estimate toward the mean of the sibling estimates. The theoretical and empirical validation of the approach using a Bayesian model is given in [6]. The analysis shows that the resulting improved heuristic values have smaller total expected mean squared error.

A model database for empirical testing is a final piece of Hopper. The primary obstacle to designing and comparing state enumeration algorithms is a lack of performance data on standardized benchmarks. This lack of data obscures the merits of new approaches to state enumeration. Hopper includes a set of 177 benchmark models with an web portal to add new models and report new benchmark results. The web portal for the database is located at http://vv.cs.byu.edu.

2   Randomized Guided Search

Randomizing the guided search algorithm intends to improve the decentralized parallel search for LTL violations. The decentralized parallel searches will cover more of the search space if they do not all share the same deterministic behavior. Random walk is a trivial, but surprisingly effective, way to distribute the searches. In terms on the expected number of states explored before finding an error, randomized guided search aims to achieve a variance near that of random walk with a mean near that of guided search.

The guided search is randomized by selecting the next state to expand randomly from the first n states in the priority queue. Randomizing next state selection increases the variance of the expected number of states expanded before finding an error. Suppose X is a random variable that represents the *number of states expanded before reaching an error* in a given model for some amount of randomization n. In our experiments, X follows a normal distribution with a mean μ and a variance σ^2. Increasing randomization increases both σ^2 and μ. Randomization can improve search performance because the probability of observing a small value of X increases logarithmically in σ^2–if μ remains unchanged.

Unfortunately, randomization of guided search can increase μ. In other cases, randomization *decreases* μ. In general, increasing randomization in guided best-first search

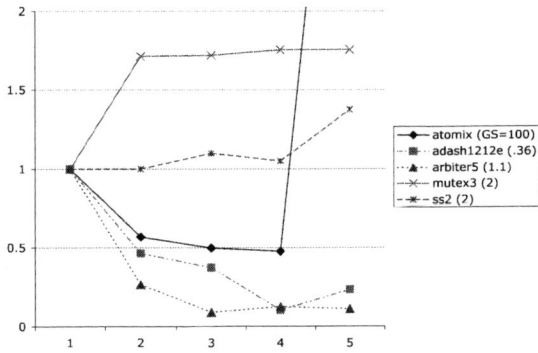

Fig. 1. Ratio of minimum value in 100 samples of randomized guided search and best deterministic search. A ratio less then one indicates that parallel randomization improved search performance.

drives μ toward the number of states expanded by breadth-first search. If breadth-first search expands fewer states than non-randomized guided search, then randomization decreases μ. Otherwise, randomization increases μ.

Taking multiple samples of X logarithmically increases the probability that any one sample will be less than a given threshold. This produces a logarithmic speedup when performing independent randomized guided searches in parallel. This is similar to the amplification of stochastic advantage in a one-sided probabilistic algorithm.

We have implemented the randomized guided search algorithm in Hopper, and we have conducted a series of experiments to asses the impact of randomization on guided search using the BHS algorithm. The amount of randomization was controlled by varying n, the *pickset* which is the number of states in the prefix of the priority queue from which the next state to expand was chosen. Each search result is computed by observing the outcomes of 100 trials and taking the outcome with the smallest number of states expanded. This is done for each model/pickset combination.

We chose five models for which guided search had a wide range of effects. The effect of heuristic guidance on a search problem can be measured using the *guided-speedup* (GS) which is the BFS transition count divided by the guided search transition count. The models used in the experiments have GS ratios ranging from 100 (meaning guided search was 100 times faster) to 0.36 (meaning guided search was almost 3 times slower). The GS ratios for each model are included later in the legend for Figure 1. Each model contains at least one violation of its invariant.

Two sets of experiments were conducted: one to determine the effects of randomization on the adash1212e model (for which guided search was particularly ineffective) and one to determine the effects of randomization on the five models. The adash1212e model was tested with picksets ranging from 2 to 2000 states. As the pickset size increased, the mean number of states expanded decreased. For every pickset size, the minimum number of states explored by any one node was less than both the deterministic BFS and parallel pure random walks.

Each of the 5 models were tested with pickset sizes of 2, 3, 4 and 5. The effect of randomization on the minimum sample drawn from 100 experiments is shown in Figure 1. Figure 1 plots the ratio of the number of transitions taken in the minimum of the 100 samples and the smaller of either the BFS or deterministic guided search. A ratio less than 1 indicates that randomization lead to faster error discovery.

The series of experiments with adash1212e demonstrate that for models in which the heuristic performs extremely poorly increasing randomization results in steadily decreasing search times. For all 5 models, choosing randomly from the first 2 to 4 states in the priority queue gives almost all of the reduction in transition count while avoiding state explosion. These results taken together suggest that choosing from the first four states in the priority queue balances randomization and guidance.

3   Conclusion

Hopper is general purpose model checker built on top of the Murφ code base. It uses Murφ as an API that provides low-level building blocks for new algorithms. Hopper includes several published and unpublished algorithms, as well as a visualization tool and a model database. Recent algorithms in Hopper are a BHS and a parallel randomized guided search. Future work for Hopper includes the implementation of novel disk-based, shared memory and multi-agent search algorithms. Hopper is a testbed for algorithms for increases capacity that can be incorporated into any state enumeration tool, including SPIN.

References

1. Stern, U., Dill, D.L.: Parallelizing the Murϕ verifier. In Grumburg, O., ed.: Computer-Aided Verification, CAV '97. Volume 1254 of Lecture Notes in Computer Science., Haifa, Israel, Springer-Verlag (1997) 256–267
2. Stern, U., Dill, D.L.: Using magnetic disk instead of main memory in the Murϕ verifier. In Hu, A.J., Vardi, M.Y., eds.: Computer-Aided Verification, CAV '98. Volume 1427 of Lecture Notes in Computer Science., Vancouver, BC, Canada, Springer-Verlag (1998) 172–183
3. Edelkamp, S., Lluch-Lafuente, A., Leue, S.: Directed explicit model checking with HSF-SPIN. In: 8th International SPIN Workshop on Model Checking Software. Number 2057 in Lecture Notes in Computer Science, Springer-Verlag (2001)
4. Jones, M.D., Sorber, J.: Parallel search for LTL violations. Software tools for technology transfer (2004) To appear.
5. Jones, M., Mercer, E.G., Bao, T., Kumar, R., Lamborn, P.: Benchmarking explicit state parallel model checkers. In: Workshop on Parrallel and Distributed Model Checking. (2003)
6. Seppi, K., Jones, M., Lamborn, P.: Guided model checking with a Bayesian meta-heuristic. Technical Report VV-0401, Dept. of Computer Science, Brigham Young U. (2004)
7. German, S.M.: Formal design of cache memory protocols in IBM. Formal Methods in System Design **22** (2003) 133–141
8. Bradley P. Carlin, T.A.L.: Bayes and Empirical Bayes Methods for Data Analysis. Chapman & Hall (1996)

SEQ.OPEN: A Tool for Efficient Trace-Based Verification*

Hubert Garavel and Radu Mateescu

INRIA Rhône-Alpes / VASY
655, avenue de l'Europe, F-38330 Montbonnot Saint Martin, France
{Hubert.Garavel,Radu.Mateescu}@inria.fr

Abstract. We report about recent enhancements of the CADP verification tool set that allow to check the correctness of event traces obtained by simulating or executing complex, industrial-size systems. Correctness properties are expressed using either regular expressions or modal μ-calculus formulas, and verified efficiently on very large traces.

1 Introduction

Trace-based verification [3,10,15,16] consists in assessing the correctness of a (software, hardware, telecommunication...) system by checking a set of event traces, i.e., chronological lists of inputs/outputs events sent/received by this system. Although trace-based verification is more limited than general verification on state graphs or Labelled Transition Systems (LTss), it might be the only option for "real" systems that run as "black boxes", disclose none or little information about their internal state, and provide no means for an external observer to control or simply know about their branching structure (i.e., the list of possible transitions permitted in a given state). This is particularly true when the source code of these systems is not available, or cannot be instrumented easily.

The importance of trace-based verification is widely recognized in the hardware community, where traces might be the only information available during the execution of a circuit or the simulation of an HDL model. In particular, there are recent efforts to standardize the use of temporal logics (e.g., SUGAR [4] and FORSPEC [2]) for trace-based verification.

Trace-based verification can be either *on-line* (i.e., verification is done at the same time the trace is generated) or *off-line* (i.e., the trace is generated first, stored in a file and verified afterwards). On-line verification avoids to store the trace in a file, but gets potentially slower if several correctness properties must be checked on the same trace, in which case it might be faster to generate the trace only once and perform all verifications off-line.

In this paper, we present a general solution for off-line trace-based verification, which is easily applicable to the traces generated by virtually any system.

---

* This research was partially funded by Bull S.A. and the European 1st -2001-32360 project "ArchWare".

S. Graf and L. Mounier (Eds.): SPIN 2004, LNCS 2989, pp. 151–157, 2004.

Traces are encoded on a very simple, line-based format. Correctness properties are specified using either regular expressions or μ-calculus formulas, and model checked using dedicated tools of the widespread CADP verification tool set [9]. Notice that on-line trace-based verification could also be addressed by the CADP tools supporting on the fly verification, although this is beyond the scope of this paper.

2   Assumptions on Trace Structure and Representation

Following the "black box" testing paradigm, we assume that the internal state of the system is not available for inspection. Thus, a *trace* is defined as a (de-generated) LTS (S, A, T, s_0) consisting of a set S of *states*, a set A of *actions* (transition labels corresponding to the input/output communications of the system), a *transition relation* $T \subseteq S \times A \times S$, and an *initial state* $s_0 \in S$. Should (a part of) the internal state be observable, then this information could be encoded in the actions without loss of generality [14].

We then assume that the *length*, i.e., the number of states (and transitions) in a trace can be large (e.g., several millions), since traces can be produced by hour- or day-long simulation/execution of the system. In fact, the number of states can be as large as for classical explicit-state verification (with the difference that traces are particular LTSs with a tiny breadth and a huge depth).

We make no special assumption regarding actions. Their contents are unrestricted and may include any sequence of data, including variable-length values such as lists, sets, etc. We therefore represent actions as arbitrary-length character strings. As a consequence, the set A of all possible actions may be very large (or even unbounded), so that it might be prohibitive (or even infeasible) to enumerate its elements. Finally, we make no assumption of regularity or locality in the occurrence of actions. In the worst-case, a trace might contain as many different actions as it contains transitions.

In general, traces might be too large to fit into main memory entirely and must be stored in computer files instead. The CADP tool set provides a textual file format (the SEQ format) for representing traces. So far, this format was mostly used to display the counter-examples generated by CADP model-checkers, but, since this format satisfies the above assumptions, we decided to adopt it for trace-based verification as well. In practice, it is often convenient to store in the same file several traces issued from the same initial state. For this reason, a SEQ file consists of a set of finite traces, separated by the choice symbol "[]", which indicates the existence of several branches starting at the initial state. Each trace consists of a list of character strings (one string per line) enclosed between double quotes, each representing one action in the trace. The SEQ format also admits comments (enclosed between the special characters "\001" and "\002").

3   Principles of the Seq.Open Tool

All the CADP tools that operate on the fly (i.e., execution, simulation, test generation, and verification tools) rely upon the OPEN/CÆSAR [8] software framework. Due to the modularity and reusability brought by OPEN/CÆSAR, it was not needed to develop yet another model checker dedicated to traces encoded in the SEQ format. The proper approach was to design a new tool (named SEQ.OPEN) that connects the SEQ format to OPEN/CÆSAR, thus allowing all the OPEN/CÆSAR tools (including model checkers) to be applied to traces without any modification.

A central feature of OPEN/CÆSAR is its generic API (*Application Programming Interface*) providing an abstract representation for on the fly LTSs. This API clearly separates language-dependent aspects (translation of source languages into LTS models, which is done by OPEN/CÆSAR-*compliant compilers* implementing the API) from the language-independent aspects (on the fly LTS exploration algorithms built on top of the API). In a nutshell, the API consists of two types "LTS state" and "LTS label", equipped with comparison, hash, and print functions, and two operations computing the initial state of the LTS and the transitions going out of a given state.

SEQ.OPEN is an OPEN/CÆSAR-compliant compiler that maps a SEQ file onto the aforementioned API (see Figure 1). A set of n traces contained in a SEQ file can be viewed as an LTS with three types of states: *deadlock states* (terminating states, with 0 successors[1]); *normal states* (intermediate states, with 1 successor); and the *initial state* (common to all traces, with n successors). The user of SEQ.OPEN may decide to explore all the n traces, or only the i-th one ($1 \leq i \leq n$).

An LTS label is implemented by SEQ.OPEN as an offset in the SEQ file (the offset returned by the POSIX function `ftell()` for the double quote opening the label character string). This representation is not canonical: The same label occurring at different places in the file is represented by different offsets.

States also are implemented as offsets. Each deadlock state is represented by the special offset -1. Each normal state s is represented by the offset of the label of the transition going out of s. The initial state is represented by the offset of the first label of the first trace to be considered. Contrary to labels, the state representation is canonical (up to graph isomorphism).

A transition (s_1, a, s_2) of the LTS is encoded by a couple (o_1, o_2), where o_1 is the offset of state s_1 (equal to the offset of label a) and o_2 is the offset of state s_2. The transition relation is implemented as follows. Deadlock states have no successors. For a normal state s with offset o_1, the offset o_2 of its successor is computed by positioning the file cursor at o_1 using the `fseek()` function, reading the character string of the transition label going out of s (possibly skipping comments), then taking for o_2 the offset returned by the `ftell()` function. For

---

[1] All traces end in a deadlock state. If necessary, a distinction can be made between *successful* and *abnormal* termination by considering the action of the last transition preceding the deadlock state.

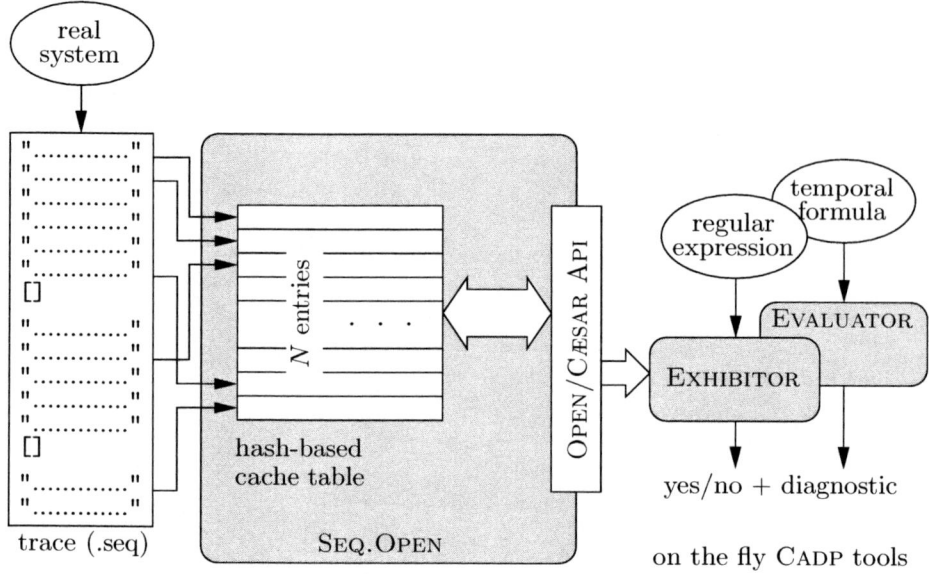

Fig. 1. The Seq.Open Tool

the initial state, the successors are computed only once at initialization. This is done using a preliminary scan of the Seq file, unless the user wants to consider the first trace only (a frequent situation for which no preliminary scan is needed).

To reduce the time overhead induced by calls to `fseek()`, i.e., back and forth skips inside the Seq file, we introduced a hash-based cache table similar to those used in Bdd implementations. This table has a prime number N of entries, which is chosen by the user and remains constant regardless of the number of visited states/transitions. The table speeds up both (1) for a label a known by its offset, the computation of the character string of a, and (2) for a normal state s_1 known by its offset, the computation of the outgoing transition (s_1, a, s_2). Precisely, for a label (resp. normal state) with offset o_1, the table entry of index $o_1 \bmod N$ may contain the character string of label o_1 (resp. the character string of the transition label going out of state o_1, and the successor state offset o_2); if this entry is already occupied by another label (resp. state), its contents will be erased and replaced with information corresponding to the label (resp. state) with offset o_1 (this information will be computed using `fseek()` and `ftell()` as explained above).

The other operations of the Open/Cæsar Api are performed as follows. Comparison of states is simply an equality test of their offsets (since state offsets are canonical). Comparison of labels is done by comparing their character strings (since label offsets are not canonical), a comparison that is sped up when labels are already present in the cache.

4   Verification of Trace Properties

CADP provides two different tools for checking general properties over traces on the fly[2].

EXHIBITOR allows to check linear-time properties expressed as regular expressions over traces. Individual actions in a trace are characterized by boolean formulas consisting of action predicates (plain character strings or UNIX-like regular expressions matching several character strings) combined using boolean connectors such as negation ("~"), disjunction ("|"), and conjunction ("&"). Regular expressions over traces consist of these boolean formulas combined using regular operators such as concatenation (newline character "\n"), choice ("[]"), and iteration ("*" and "+"). A special "<deadlock>" operator characterizes deadlock states. Additional operators inspired from linear temporal logic are provided as shorthand notations: "<until> P" is equivalent to "(~P)*" and "<while> P <until> Q" is equivalent to "(P & ~Q)* \n Q".

EVALUATOR [13] allows to check branching-time properties expressed in alternation-free μ-calculus [7], a specification formalism for which efficient model checking algorithms exist [5] with a linear (time and space) complexity $O(|\varphi| \cdot (|S| + |T|))$, where $|\varphi|$ is the number of operators in the formula φ to be checked, and where $|S|$ and $|T|$ are the respective numbers of states and transitions in the LTS under verification. It was shown recently that on acyclic LTSs (which contain traces as a particular case), the alternation-free μ-calculus has the same expressive power as the full μ-calculus [11]. This result allows, in the case of acyclic LTSs, to benefit from the expressiveness of the full μ-calculus (which subsumes most temporal logics, including CTL and PDL [7], as well as LTL and CTL* [6]) still keeping model checking algorithms with a linear (rather than exponential) complexity. Furthermore, space complexity can be reduced down to $O(|\varphi| \cdot |S|)$ (still maintaining a linear complexity in time) by using specialized algorithms for checking alternation-free μ-calculus formulas on acyclic LTSs [11,12].

Both EXHIBITOR and EVALUATOR provide diagnostic generation features, allowing to exhibit the prefix of the trace illustrating the truth value of a property.

5   Conclusion

We presented a working solution for model checking large event traces. Based upon the generic OPEN/CÆSAR [8] framework, this solution relies on a new software tool, SEQ.OPEN, which enables fast, cache-based handling of large traces stored in computer files. Combined with already existing components of the CADP tool set (such as EXHIBITOR and EVALUATOR), SEQ.OPEN allows to verify trace properties efficiently.

---

[2] For very specific, application-dependent properties, additional tools could be developed using the OPEN/CÆSAR environment.

Due to the extreme simplicity of SEQ.OPEN's line-based trace format, our solution is not "intrusive", in the sense that it is easily applicable to most existing systems without heavy reengineering.

In the setting of hardware systems, our solution was chosen by BULL for validating the traces produced by the VERILOG simulation of the cache coherency protocol used in BULL's NOVASCALE multiprocessor servers. This validation task, previously done by human reviewers, is now fully automated with good performances (7.4 million model checking jobs in 23 hours using a standard 700 MHz Pentium PC).

In the setting of software systems, our solution is used to analyze the traces produced by a multi-threaded virtual machine, which provides the runtime environment for executing the ARCHWARE description language for mobile software architectures.

As for future work, we plan to study trace-based verification algorithms that improve "locality", i.e., produce less faults in the SEQ.OPEN cache table.

Acknowledgements. The authors are grateful to Bruno Ondet (INRIA/VASY) for his contribution to the implementation of SEQ.OPEN, and to Nicolas Zuanon and Solofo Ramangalahy (BULL) for their industrial feedback.

References

1. H. R. Andersen. Model checking and boolean graphs. *TCS*, 126(1):3–30, 1994.
2. R. Armoni, L. Fix, A. Flaisher, R. Gerth, B. Ginsburg, T. Kanza, A. Landver, S. Mador-Haim, E. Singerman, A. Tiemeyer, M. Y. Vardi, and Y. Zbar. The ForSpec Temporal Logic: A New Temporal Property-Specification Language. In *TACAS'2002*, LNCS vol. 2280, pp. 296–311.
3. T. Arts and L-A. Fredlund. Trace Analysis of Erlang Programs. In *ACM SIGPLAN Erlang Workshop (Pittsburgh, PA, USA)*, 2002.
4. I. Beer, S. Ben-David, C. Eisner, D. Fisman, A. Gringauze, and Y. Rodeh. The Temporal Logic Sugar. In *CAV'2001*, LNCS vol. 2102, pp. 363–367.
5. R. Cleaveland and B. Steffen. A Linear-Time Model-Checking Algorithm for the Alternation-Free Modal Mu-Calculus. *FMSD*, 2:121–147, 1993.
6. M. Dam. CTL* and ECTL* as fragments of the modal μ-calculus. *TCS*, 126(1):77–96, 1994.
7. E. A. Emerson and C-L. Lei. Efficient Model Checking in Fragments of the Propositional Mu-Calculus. In *LICS'86*, pp. 267–278.
8. H. Garavel. OPEN/CÆSAR: An Open Software Architecture for Verification, Simulation, and Testing. In *TACAS'98*, LNCS vol. 1384, pp. 68–84. Full version available as INRIA Research Report RR-3352.
9. H. Garavel, F. Lang, and R. Mateescu. An Overview of CADP 2001. *EASST Newsletter*, 4:13–24, 2002. Also available as INRIA Technical Report RT-0254.
10. K. Havelund, A. Goldberg, R. Filman, and G. Rosu. Program Instrumentation and Trace Analysis. In *Monterey Workshop (Venice, Italy)*, 2002.
11. R. Mateescu. Local Model-Checking of Modal Mu-Calculus on Acyclic Labeled Transition Systems. In *TACAS'2002*, LNCS vol. 2280, pp. 281–295. Full version available as INRIA Research Report RR-4430.

12. R. Mateescu. A Generic On-the-Fly Solver for Alternation-Free Boolean Equation Systems. In *TACAS'2003*, LNCS vol. 2619, pp. 81–96.
13. R. Mateescu and M. Sighireanu. Efficient On-the-Fly Model-Checking for Regular Alternation-Free Mu-Calculus. *SCP*, 46(3):255–281, 2003.
14. R. De Nicola and F. W. Vaandrager. *Action versus State based Logics for Transition Systems*. In *Semantics of Concurrency*, LNCS vol. 469, pp. 407–419, 1990.
15. S. Vloavic and E. Davidson. TAXI: Trace Analysis for X86 Implementation. In *ICCD'2002 (Freiburg, Germany)*.
16. A. Ziv. Using Temporal Checkers for Functional Coverage. In *MTV'2002 (Austin, Texas, USA)*.

Model Checking Genetic Regulatory Networks Using GNA and CADP

Grégory Batt, Damien Bergamini, Hidde de Jong,
Hubert Garavel, and Radu Mateescu

INRIA Rhône-Alpes, 655, avenue de l'Europe, Montbonnot,
F-38334 Saint Ismier Cedex, France
{Gregory.Batt,Damien.Bergamini,Hidde.de-Jong,Hubert.Garavel,
Radu.Mateescu}@inria.fr

1 Introduction

The study of genetic regulatory networks, which underlie the functioning of living organisms, has received a major impetus from the recent development of high-throughput genomic techniques. This experimental progress calls for the development of appropriate computer tools supporting the analysis of genetic regulatory processes. We have developed a modeling and simulation method [5, 7], based on piecewise-linear differential equations, that is well-adapted to the qualitative nature of most available biological data. The method has been implemented in the tool Genetic Network Analyzer (GNA) [6], which produces a graph of qualitative states and transitions between qualitative states. The graph provides a discrete abstraction of the dynamics of the system.

A bottleneck in the application of the qualitative simulation method is the analysis of the state transition graph, which is usually too large for visual inspection. In this paper, we propose a model-checking approach to perform this task in a systematic and efficient way. Given that certain properties of biological interest are of a branching nature (see, *e.g.*, the *bistability* property in Section 3), a branching-time temporal logic is necessary. Also, abstractions of state transition graphs can be performed more conveniently by using standard equivalence relations defined on Labeled Transition Systems (LTSs) rather than by implementing *ad hoc* reductions. Therefore, we developed a connection between the qualitative simulator GNA and the widely-used CADP verification toolbox [8], which provides the required analysis functionalities on LTSs.

The connection is established as follows. Firstly, a dedicated translator converts the state transition graph resulting from qualitative simulation into an LTS suitable for automated verification. Then, after instantaneous states have been abstracted away by means of branching bisimulation, various properties characterizing the evolution of protein concentrations are checked by encoding them in regular alternation-free μ-calculus. The diagnostics produced by the CADP model checker make it possible to establish a correspondence between verification results and biological data, for instance by characterizing evolutions leading to equilibrium states. We illustrate the combined use of qualitative simulation and model checking by means of a simple, biologically-inspired example.

S. Graf and L. Mounier (Eds.): SPIN 2004, LNCS 2989, pp. 158–163, 2004.
© Springer-Verlag Berlin Heidelberg 2004

2   Qualitative Simulation of Genetic Regulatory Networks

We consider qualitative models of genetic regulatory networks, based on a class
of piecewise-linear differential equations originally proposed in mathemetical biology [10]. Given a qualitative model of a genetic regulatory network, the qualitative simulation method produces a graph of qualitative states and transitions
between qualitative states, qualitatively summarizing the dynamics of the system [5,7]. In the sequel, we present the method by means of an example.

Figure 1(a) represents a simple genetic regulatory network consisting of two
genes, a and b, and two proteins, A and B. When a gene is expressed, the corresponding protein is synthesized, which, in turn, can regulate the expression of
its own and the other gene. For example, when gene a is expressed, protein A
is synthesized and, depending on whether its concentration is above or below a
threshold, it may inhibit the expression of gene a and/or b. This network can be
described by means of the differential equations (1)-(2), where x_a and x_b denote
the concentration of proteins A and B, θ_a^1, θ_a^2, θ_b^1, and θ_b^2, threshold concentrations and s^-, the decreasing step function. For example, equation (1) states
that protein A is produced (at a rate κ_a), if and only if $s^-(x_a, \theta_a^2)\, s^-(x_b, \theta_b^1) = 1$,
that is, if and only if x_a and x_b are below thresholds θ_a^2 and θ_b^1 respectively. In
addition, protein A is degraded at a rate proportional to its own concentration
($\gamma_a > 0$). The parameter inequalities (3)-(4) constrain the parameter values.

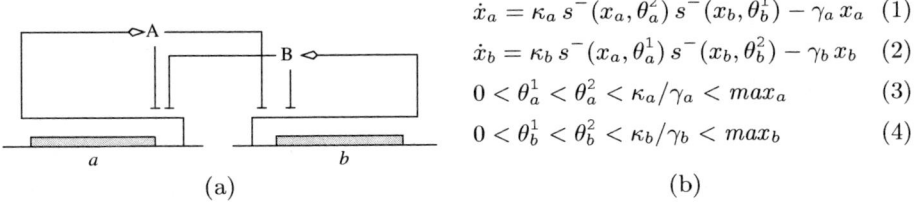

$$\dot{x}_a = \kappa_a\, s^-(x_a, \theta_a^2)\, s^-(x_b, \theta_b^1) - \gamma_a\, x_a \quad (1)$$

$$\dot{x}_b = \kappa_b\, s^-(x_a, \theta_a^1)\, s^-(x_b, \theta_b^2) - \gamma_b\, x_b \quad (2)$$

$$0 < \theta_a^1 < \theta_a^2 < \kappa_a/\gamma_a < max_a \quad (3)$$

$$0 < \theta_b^1 < \theta_b^2 < \kappa_b/\gamma_b < max_b \quad (4)$$

(a)   (b)

Fig. 1.   (a) Example of a genetic regulatory network of two genes, a and b. The notation follows, in a somewhat simplified form, the graphical conventions proposed by
Kohn [11]. (b) Qualitative model, corresponding to the two-gene example, composed
of piecewise-linear differential equations (1)-(2) and parameter inequalities (3)-(4).

The phase space can be partitioned into (hyper)rectangular regions, called
flow domains, where the flow is qualitatively identical, that is, where the sign
of the derivatives is identical for all solutions (see Figure 2(a)). For example, in
flow domain $D^1 = [0, \theta_a^1[\times [0, \theta_b^1[$, the expression $s^-(x_a, \theta_a^2)\, s^-(x_b, \theta_b^1)$ evaluates
to 1 and equation (1) becomes $\dot{x}_a = \kappa_a - \gamma_a x_a$. From the inequalities (3), it
follows that $x_a < \theta_a^1 < \kappa_a/\gamma_a$, so $\dot{x}_a > 0$. To each flow domain D corresponds a
qualitative state QS defined as the tuple $\langle D, S \rangle$, where the vector S represents
the derivative sign of solutions in D. A qualitative state $QS = \langle D, S \rangle$ is called
instantaneous, if all solutions traverse D instantaneously and *persistent* other-
wise. There is a *transition* from $QS^1 = \langle D^1, S^1 \rangle$ to $QS^2 = \langle D^2, S^2 \rangle$, if there

exists a solution reaching D^2 from D^1. The set of qualitative states and transitions between qualitative states together form the *state transition graph*. The state transition graph corresponding to our two-gene example, represented in figure 2(b), contains 18 persistent qualitative states, including two stable (QS^6, QS^{22}) and one unstable (QS^{12}) qualitative equilibrium states.

So, using the simulation method sketched above, the qualitative behavior emerging from genetic regulatory interactions can be predicted. These results are obtained using a version of the GNA tool still under development [6]. The publicly-available version of GNA (GNA 5.0) gives similar results, but uses a slightly coarser partition of the phase space into domains, which makes the interpretation of the properties associated to qualitative states less straightforward.

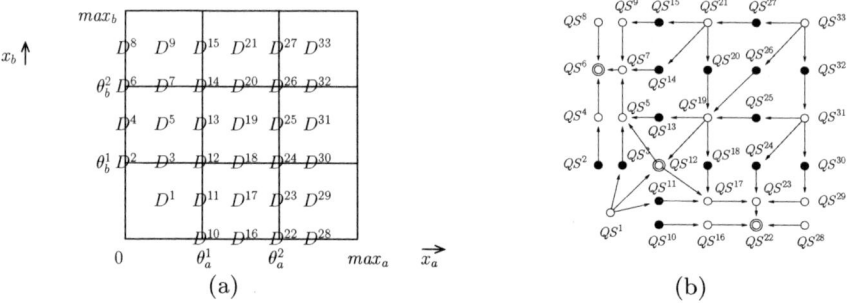

(a)   (b)

Fig. 2. (a) Partition of the phase space into 33 flow domains. Flow domains may be of dimension 2 (*e.g.*, D^1), 1 (*e.g.*, D^{11}) or 0 (*e.g.*, D^{12}). (b) State transition graph, corresponding to the two-gene example in figure 1(a). Filled and unfilled dots correspond to instantaneous and persistent qualitative states, respectively. Qualitative equilibrium states are circled in addition.

3   Transformation of Simulation Results into LTSs

First of all, it is necessary to translate the simulation result into a format suitable for verification. For this purpose, we developed a translator which takes as input a state transition graph produced by qualitative simulation and produces a corresponding LTS encoded in the BCG (*Binary Coded Graph*) format used by CADP [8].

To each qualitative state corresponds a state with a self-transition (loop) in the LTS. The label of this loop encodes all the properties of the corresponding qualitative state: its name, the range and derivative sign of protein concentrations, and additional properties specifying whether the state is instantaneous, persistent, or a stable or unstable equilibrium. Each transition between qualitative states is encoded in the LTS by an invisible transition (labeled by the action "i", noted τ in CCS). Since state transition graphs produced by qualitative simulation of genetic regulatory networks may be disconnected, we create an initial state which is linked to all other states in the LTS via special transitions.

Figure 3(a) shows the translation of the persistent qualitative state QS^1 associated to the flow domain D^1. This qualitative state is encoded in the LTS by a state with a loop labeled "PERS <[0,ta1[x[0,tb1[> A+ B+". Three invisible transitions originate from this state, linking it to the states corresponding to QS^3, QS^{11}, and QS^{12}.

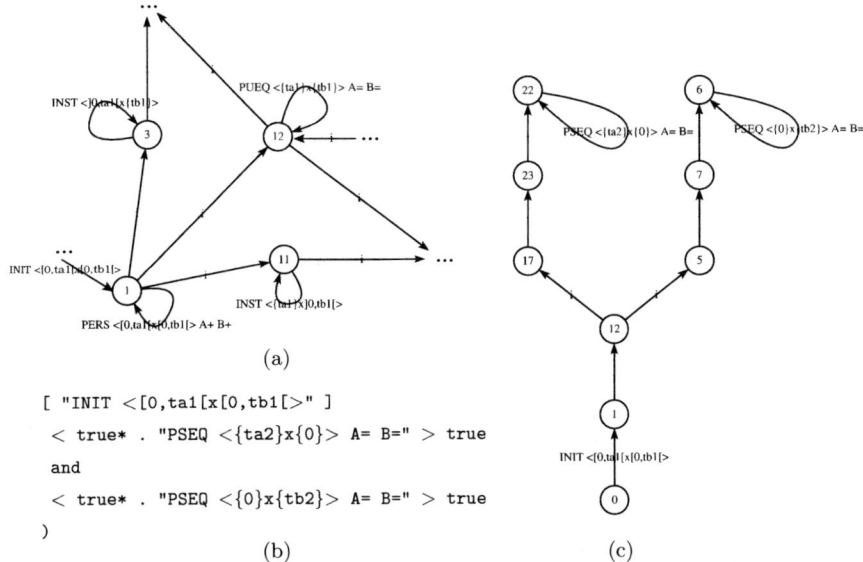

(a)

["INIT <[0,ta1[x[0,tb1[>"]
    < true* . "PSEQ <{ta2}x{0}> A= B=" > true
  and
    < true* . "PSEQ <{0}x{tb2}> A= B=" > true
)

(b)   (c)

Fig. 3. (a) Fragment of the LTS corresponding to the qualitative state QS^1 and its successors. "INST", "PERS", "PSEQ" and "PUEQ" denote qualitative states that are instantaneous, persistent non equilibrium, persistent stable equilibrium, and persistent unstable equilibrium, respectively. The derivative sign of each protein concentration is represented by '=', '-' and '+'. (b) Bistability property formulated in regular alternation-free μ-calculus. (c) Diagnostic produced by model-checking.

A simplified LTS can be obtained from the original LTS by abstracting away the states corresponding to instantaneous qualitative states. By exploiting the fact that in the qualitative model there are never two successive instantaneous states, we can perform this simplification by hiding all labels corresponding to instantaneous qualitative states in the original LTS and minimizing it modulo branching bisimulation using the BCG_MIN tool of CADP. The dynamical properties of interest are preserved in the simplified LTS.

4   Verification Using Temporal Logic

Once the LTS corresponding to the genetic regulatory network has been generated by using GNA together with the translator described in Section 3, we can use the model checking technologies available in CADP to analyze the behaviour of the biological system. The methodology adopted consists of two steps:

- First, each desired property is expressed as a formula in regular alternation-free μ-calculus [12], which is the input language of the EVALUATOR 3.0 model checker of CADP. This temporal logic is a good compromise between expressive power (it subsumes CTL and PDL), user-friendliness (concise formula descriptions due to regular expressions), and model-checking efficiency (algorithms linear w.r.t. formula size and LTS size). Also, generic properties can be encoded as macro definitions and grouped into reusable libraries.
- Second, each property is verified on the LTS using EVALUATOR 3.0, which produces diagnostics (counterexamples and witnesses) illustrating its truth value. The diagnostics obtained, represented as LTSs, can then be inspected visually using the BCG_EDIT graphical LTS editor of CADP. Diagnostics can also be replayed interactively in the LTS by means of the graphical simulator OCIS of CADP.

Figure 3 illustrates the verification of the *bistability property* on the LTS constructed from the genetic regulatory network given in Figure 1. This property states that from an initial state QS^1 in which both proteins A and B have low concentrations (below θ_a^1 and θ_b^1), it is possible to reach two different stable equilibrium states (QS^{22} and QS^6) in which only one protein is present and at a high concentration (at θ_a^2 and at θ_b^2, respectively). The diagnostic (witness) exhibited by EVALUATOR 3.0 is a LTS subgraph containing the paths going from the initial state to the two stable equilibrium states.

Other biologically interesting properties (*e.g.*, reachability of certain equilibrium states, existence of behaviours satisfying certain constraints on protein concentrations) can be verified in a similar way.

5   Conclusion

Our approach for analyzing biological systems consists in connecting GNA, a qualitative simulation tool well-adapted to the available information on genetic regulatory networks, to the widely-used CADP verification toolbox. By translating the state transition graph produced by GNA into a LTS, standard verification technologies become available for analyzing the dynamics of the underlying genetic regulatory network.

Checking properties of qualitative simulation results using temporal logic was originally proposed by Shults and Kuipers [14]. Chabrier and Fages [4] and Peres and Comet [13] have also addressed the formal analysis of genetic regulatory networks using model-checking approaches, but they use rather simple rule-based and Boolean models, respectively. Like us, Alur *et al.* [1], Antoniotti *et al.* [2] and Ghosh *et al.* [9] use hybrid models to analyze biological networks. However, Alur *et al.* and Antoniotti *et al.* use numerical instead of qualitative models. The most closely-related work is the symbolic reachability analysis of Ghosh *et al.*, but the authors ignore the problems related to discontinuities in the right-hand side of the differential equations. Additionally, GNA has been tailored so as to exploit the favorable mathematical properties of the piecewise-linear models, which may make it better capable of analyzing large and complex genetic regulatory networks. In previous work, we used CTL [3], as in [4] and [13], but the use of the more expressive and convenient regular alternation-free μ-calculus, together with the diagnostic generation and interactive simulation facilities offered by CADP, makes it possible to easily express properties, interpret the results of the analysis, and relate them to biological reality.

References

1. R. Alur, C. Belta, F. Ivančíc, V. Kumar, M. Mintz, G.J. Pappas, H. Rubin, and J. Schlug. Hybrid modeling and simulation of biomolecular networks. In M.D. Di Benedetto and A. Sangiovanni-Vincentelli, eds, *Hybrid Systems: Computation and Control (HSCC 2001)*, vol. 2034 of *LNCS*, 19–32. Springer, 2001.
2. M. Antoniotti, B. Mishra, C. Piazza, A. Policriti, and M. Simeoni. Modeling cellular behavior with hybrid automata: bisimulation and collapsing. In C.Priami, ed., *First Int. Work. Comput. Meth. Systems Biol. (CMSB 2003)*, vol. 2602 of *LNCS*, 57–74. Springer, 2003.
3. G. Batt, H. de Jong, J. Geiselmann, and M. Page. Analysis of genetic regulatory networks: A model-checking approach. In P. Salles and B. Bredeweg, eds, *Proc. 17th Int. Work. Qualitative Reasoning (QR-03)*, 31–38, Brasilia, Brazil, 2003.
4. N. Chabrier and F. Fages. Symbolic model checking of biochemical networks. In C.Priami, ed., *First Int. Work. Comput. Meth. Systems Biol. (CMSB 2003)*, vol. 2602 of *LNCS*, 149–162. Springer, 2003.
5. H. de Jong, J. Geiselmann, G. Batt, C. Hernandez, and M. Page. Qualitative simulation of the initiation of sporulation in *B. subtilis*. *Bull. Math. Biol.*, 2004. In press.
6. H. de Jong, J. Geiselmann, C. Hernandez, and M. Page. Genetic Network Analyzer: Qualitative simulation of genetic regulatory networks. *Bioinformatics*, 19(3):336–344, 2003. http://www-helix.inrialpes.fr/gna.
7. H. de Jong, J.-L. Gouzé, C. Hernandez, M. Page, T. Sari, and J. Geiselmann. Qualitative simulation of genetic regulatory networks using piecewise-linear models. *Bull. Math. Biol.*, 2004. In press.
8. H. Garavel, F. Lang, and R. Mateescu. An overview of CADP 2001. *Europ. Assoc. for Soft. Sci. and Tech. (EASST) Newsletter*, 4:13–24, 2002. Also INRIA Technical Report RT-0254 (2001). http://www.inrialpes.fr/vasy/cadp.
9. R. Ghosh, A. Tiwari, and C. Tomlin. Automated symbolic reachability analysis; with application to delta-notch signaling automata. In O. Maler and A. Pnueli, eds, *Hybrid Systems: Computation and Control (HSCC 2003)*, vol. 2623 of *LNCS*, 233–248, Springer, 2003.
10. L. Glass and S.A. Kauffman. The logical analysis of continuous non-linear biochemical control networks. *J. Theor. Biol.*, 39:103–129, 1973.
11. K.W. Kohn. Molecular interaction maps as information organizers and simulation guides. *Chaos*, 11(1):1–14, 2001.
12. R. Mateescu and M. Sighireanu. Efficient on-the-fly model-checking for regular alternation-free mu-calculus. *Sci. Comput. Program.*, 46(3):255–281, 2003.
13. S. Peres and J. P. Comet. Contribution of computational tree logic to biological regulatory networks: Example from *P. aeruginosa*. In C. Priami, ed., *First Int. Work. Comput. Meth. Systems Biol. (CMSB 2003)*, vol. 2602 of *LNCS*, 47–56, Springer, 2003.
14. B. Shults and B. J. Kuipers. Proving properties of continuous systems: Qualitative simulation and temporal logic. *Artif. Intell.*, 92(1-2):91–130, 1997.

Verification of Java Programs Using Symbolic Execution and Invariant Generation

Corina S. Păsăreanu[1] and Willem Visser[2]

[1] Kestrel Technology, NASA Ames Research Center, Moffett Field, CA 94035, USA
pcorina@email.arc.nasa.gov
[2] RIACS/USRA, NASA Ames Research Center, Moffett Field, CA 94035, USA
wvisser@email.arc.nasa.gov

Abstract. Software verification is recognized as an important and difficult problem. We present a novel framework, based on symbolic execution, for the automated verification of software. The framework uses annotations in the form of method specifications and loop invariants. We present a novel iterative technique that uses invariant strengthening and approximation for discovering these loop invariants automatically. The technique handles different types of data (e.g. boolean and numeric constraints, dynamically allocated structures and arrays) and it allows for checking universally quantified formulas. Our framework is built on top of the Java PathFinder model checking toolset and it was used for the verification of several non-trivial Java programs.

1 Introduction

Model checking is becoming a popular technique for the verification of software [1,6,30,21], but it typically can only deal with closed systems and it suffers from the state-explosion problem. In previous work [23] we have developed a verification framework based on *symbolic execution* [24] and model checking that allows the analysis of complex software that take inputs from unbounded domains with complex structure, and helps combat state-space explosion. In that framework, a program is instrumented to add support for manipulating formulas and for systematic treatment of aliasing, so that to enable a standard model checker to perform symbolic execution of the program. The framework is built on top of the Java PathFinder model checker and it was used for test input generation and for error detection in complex Java programs, but it could not be used for proving properties of programs containing loops.

We present here a method that uses the symbolic execution framework presented in [23] for *proving* (light-weight) specifications of Java programs that contain loops. The method requires annotations in the form of method specifications and loop invariants. We present a novel iterative technique that uses invariant strengthening and approximation for discovering these loop invariants automatically. Our technique uniformly handles different types of constraints (e.g. boolean and numeric constraints, constraints on dynamically allocated structures and arrays) and it allows for checking universally quantified formulas. These formulas

S. Graf and L. Mounier (Eds.): SPIN 2004, LNCS 2989, pp. 164–181, 2004.

are necessary for expressing properties of programs that manipulate unbounded data, such as arrays.

Our technique for loop invariant generation works backward from the property to be checked and has three basic ingredients: iterative invariant strengthening, iterative approximation and refinement. Symbolic execution is used to check that the current invariant is inductive: *the base case* checks that the current candidate invariant is true when entering the loop and the *induction step* checks that the current invariant is maintained by the execution of the loop body. Failed proofs of the induction step are used for iterative invariant strengthening, a process that may result in a (possibly infinite) sequence of candidate invariants. At each strengthening step, we further use a novel iterative approximation technique to achieve termination.

For strengthening step k, we use a (finite) set of relevant constraints called the *universe of constraints* U_k. The iterative approximation consists of a sequence of strengthening in which we drop all the constraints that are newly generated (and are not present in U_k). Since U_k is finite, this process is guaranteed to converge to an inductive approximate invariant that is a boolean combination of the constraints in U_k. The intuition here has similarities to *predicate abstraction* techniques [17], that perform iterative computations over a finite set of predicates (i.e. constraints). A failed *base case* proof can either indicate that there is an error in the program or that the approximation that we use at the current step is too strong, in which case we use *refinement*, that consists of enlarging the universe of constraints with new constraints that come from the next candidate invariant (computed at step $k + 1$).

Loop invariant generation has received much attention in the literature, see e.g. [8, 5, 25, 31, 29]. Most of the methods presented in these papers were concerned with the generation of numerical invariants. A recent paper [13] describes a loop invariant generation method for Java programs that uses predicate abstraction. The method handles universally quantified specifications but it relies on user supplied input predicates. We show (in Section 5) how our iterative technique discovers invariants for (some of) the examples from [13] *without* any user supplied predicates.

The main contributions of our work are:

- A verification framework that combines symbolic execution and model checking in a novel way; we extend the basic framework presented in [23] with the ability to handle arrays symbolically and to prove partial-correctness specifications, that may be universally quantified. This results in a flexible and powerful tool that can be used for proving program correctness, in addition to test input generation and model checking.
- A new method for iterative invariant generation. The method handles uniformly different types of constraints (e.g. boolean and numeric constraints, arrays and objects) and it can be used in conjunction with more powerful approximation methods (e.g. widening [9, 7]).
- A series of (small) non-trivial Java examples showing the merits of our method; our method extends to other languages and model checkers.

```
// @ precondition: a != null;
void example(int[] a) {
1:   int i = 0;
2:   while (i < a.length) {
3:     a[i] = 0;
4:     i++;
     }
5:   assert a[0] == 0;
}
```

Fig. 1. Motivating example

Section 2 shows an example analysis in our framework. Section 3 gives background on symbolic execution and it describes our symbolic execution framework for Java programs. Section 4 gives our method for proving properties of Java programs using symbolic execution and invariant generation and Section 5 illustrates its application to the verification of several non-trivial Java programs. We give related work in Section 6 and conclude in Section 7.

2 Example

We illustrate our verification framework using the code shown in Figure 1. This method takes as a parameter an array of integers a and it sets all the elements of a to zero. This method has a **precondition** that its input is not null. The **assert** clause declares a partial correctness property that states that after the execution of the loop, the value of the first element in a is zero.

Using the loop invariant $i \geq 0$, our framework can be used to automatically check that there are no array bounds violations. This is a simple invariant that can be stated without much effort. In order to prove that there are no assertion violations, a more complex loop invariant is needed: $\neg(a[0] \neq 0 \wedge i > 0)$.

Constructing this loop invariant requires ingenuity. Our framework discovers this invariant by iterative approximation. It starts with $I_0 = \neg(a[0] \neq 0 \wedge i \geq a.length)$ which is the weakest possible invariant that is necessary to prove that the assertion is not violated. When checking this invariant to see if it is inductive we find a violation: if the formula $(i+1) \geq a.length \wedge a[0] \neq 0 \wedge 0 < i < a.length$ holds at the beginning of the loop, then I_0 does not hold at the end of the loop. At the next iteration, we strengthen I_0 using $a[0] \neq 0 \wedge 0 < i < a.length$ (i.e. we drop the *new constraint* $(i + 1) \geq a.length$ that is due to the iterative computation in the loop body). This yields the formula: $\neg(a[0] \neq 0 \wedge i \geq a.length) \wedge \neg(a[0] \neq 0 \wedge 0 < i < a.length)$, which simplifies to the desired invariant.

Now suppose we want to verify an additional assertion, which states that, after the execution of the loop, every element in the array a is set to zero: $\forall\ int\ j : a[j] = 0$. This assertion is universally quantified; it refers to the quantified variable j as well to the program variables. We model it by introducing a symbolic constant j, which is a new variable that is not mentioned elsewhere in the program and it is assigned a new, unconstrained symbolic value. Our

```
        int x, y;
1:    if (x > y) {
2:        x = x + y;
3:        y = x - y;
4:        x = x - y;
5:    if (x > y)
6:        assert(false);
      }
```

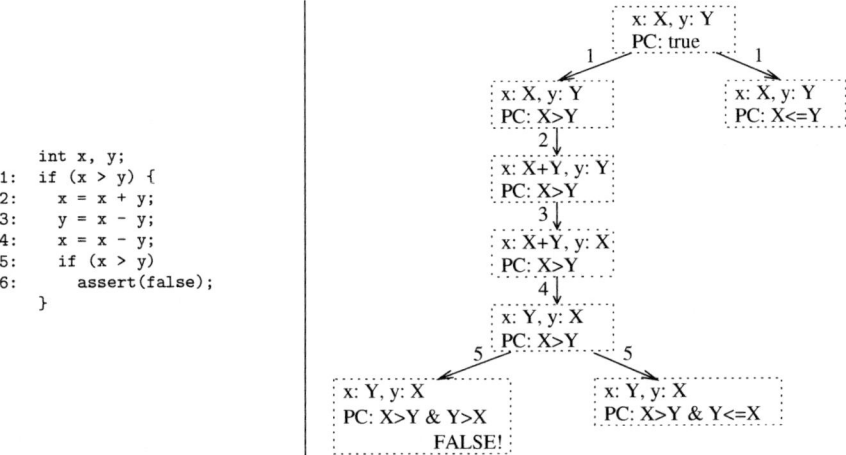

Fig. 2. Code that swaps two integers and the corresponding symbolic execution tree, where transitions are labeled with program control points

symbolic execution framework automatically infers the loop invariant: $\neg(a[j] \neq 0 \wedge i \geq a.length \wedge 0 \leq j < a.length) \wedge \neg(a[j] \neq 0 \wedge j < i \wedge 0 \leq i, j < a.length)$.

Since the symbolic constant j represents some fixed unknown value, this invariant is valid for any value of j. This technique is crucial for checking programs that manipulate unbounded data, such as arrays [13].

3   Symbolic Execution in Java PathFinder

In this section we give some background on symbolic execution and we present the symbolic execution framework used for reasoning about Java programs.

3.1   Background: Symbolic Execution

The main idea behind symbolic execution [24] is to use *symbolic values*, instead of actual data, as input values, and to represent the values of program variables as symbolic expressions. As a result, the output values computed by a program are expressed as a function of the input symbolic values.

The *state* of a symbolically executed program includes the (symbolic) values of program variables, a *path condition* (PC) and a program counter. The path condition is a (quantifier-free) boolean formula over the symbolic inputs; it accumulates constraints which the inputs must satisfy in order for an execution to follow the particular associated path. The program counter defines the next statement to be executed. A *symbolic execution tree* characterizes the execution paths followed during the symbolic execution of a program. The nodes represent program states and the arcs represent transitions between states.

Consider the code fragment in Figure 2, which swaps the values of integer variables x and y, when x is greater than y. Figure 2 also shows the corresponding symbolic execution tree. Initially, PC is *true* and x and y have symbolic values X and Y, respectively. At each branch point, PC is updated with assumptions about the inputs, in order to choose between alternative paths. For example, after the execution of the first statement, both **then** and **else** alternatives of the **if** statement are possible, and PC is updated accordingly. If the path condition becomes *false*, i.e., there is no set of inputs that satisfy it, this means that the symbolic state is not reachable, and symbolic execution does not continue for that path. For example, statement (6) is unreachable.

3.2 Generalized Symbolic Execution

In [23] we describe an algorithm for generalizing traditional symbolic execution to support advanced constructs of modern programming languages, such as Java and C++. The algorithm handles dynamically allocated structures (e.g., lists and trees), method preconditions (e.g., acyclicity of lists), data (e.g., integers and strings) and concurrency. Partial correctness properties are given as assertions in the program and temporal specifications. We have since extended the work in [23] by adding support for symbolic execution of arrays and for checking quantified formulas.

3.3 Symbolic Execution Framework

Our symbolic execution framework automates test case generation and allows model checking concurrent programs that take inputs from unbounded domains with complex structure. To enable a model checker to perform symbolic execution, the original program is instrumented by doing a source to source translation that adds nondeterminism and support for manipulating formulas that represent path conditions. The model checker checks the instrumented program using its usual state space exploration techniques — essentially, the model checker explores the symbolic execution tree of the program. A *state* includes a heap configuration, a path condition on primitive fields, and thread scheduling. Whenever a path condition is updated, it is checked for satisfiability using an appropriate decision procedure, such as the Omega library [27] for linear integer constraints. If the path condition is unsatisfiable, the model checker backtracks.

Note that performing (forward) symbolic execution on programs with loops can explore infinite execution trees. This is why, for systematic state space exploration, the framework presented in [23] uses depth first search with iterative deepening or breadth first search. The framework can be used for test input generation and for finding counterexamples to safety properties. If there is an upper bound on the number of times each loop in the program may be executed, the framework can also be used for proving correctness, since the corresponding symbolic execution tree is finite.

However, for most programs, no fixed bound on the number of times each loop is executed exists and the corresponding execution trees are infinite. In order to prove the correctness of such programs, we have extended our framework with

```
void example() {
  IntArrayStructure a =  new IntArrayStructure();
  Expression i = new IntegerConstant(0);

  while(Expression.pc._update_LT(i,a.length)) {
    a._set(i,new IntegerConstant(0));
    i = i._plus(new IntegerConstant(1));
  }
  assert Expression.pc._update_EQ(a._get(new IntegerConstant(0)),0);
}
```

Fig. 3. Instrumented code

the ability of traversing the symbolic execution tree inductively rather than explicitly, using loop invariants (as presented in the next section).

3.4 Java PathFinder

Our framework uses the Java PathFinder(JPF) [30] model checker to analyze the instrumented programs. As a decision procedure, the framework uses a Java implementation of the Omega library.

JPF is an explicit-state model checker for Java programs that is built on top of a custom-made Java Virtual Machine (JVM). Since it is built on a JVM, it can handle all of the language features of Java, but in addition it also treats nondeterministic choice expressed in annotations of the program being analyzed — annotations are added to the programs through method calls to a special class `Verify`. These features (`Verify.choose_boolean()` and `Verify.choose(n)`) for adding nondeterminism are used to implement the updating of path conditions. JPF also supports a program annotation to forces the search to backtrack (`Verify.ignoreIf(condition)`) when a certain condition evaluates to true— this is used to stop the analysis of infeasible paths (when path conditions are found to be unsatisfiable).

3.5 Instrumentation

The interested reader is referred to [23] for a detailed description of how the code is instrumented for symbolic execution, here we will instead just highlight some key new features.

The main idea is to replace concrete types with corresponding "symbolic types" (i.e. library classes that we provide) and concrete operations with method calls that implement "equivalent" operations on symbolic types. As an illustration of the instrumentation, consider the code from Figure 1. Figure 3 gives part of the resulting code after instrumentation and Figure 4 gives part of the library classes that we provide. Classes `Expression` and `IntArrayStructure` support manipulation of symbolic integers and symbolic integer arrays, respectively. The `static` field `Expression._pc` stores the (numeric) path condition. Method `_update_LT` makes a nondeterministic choice (i.e., a call to `choose_boolean`) to

```
class Expression { ...
 static PathCondition pc;
 Expression _plus(Expression e){
    ...} }

class PathCondition { ...
 Constraints c;
 boolean _update_LT(Expression l,
                    Expression r){
  boolean result;
  result=Verify.choose_boolean();
  if (result)
    c.add_constraint_LT(e1,e2);
  else
    c.add_constraint_GE(e1,e2);
  Verify.ignoreIf(!c.is_sat());
  return result;
 } }
```

```
class IntArrayStructure {
 Vector _v;
 Expression length;
 ...
 ArrayCell _new_ArrayCell(Expression idx) {
  for(int i=0;i<_v.size();i++) {
   ArrayCell cell=(ArrayCell)_v.elementAt(i);
   if(Expression.pc._update_EQ(cell.idx,idx))
    return cell;
  }
  ArrayCell t=new ArrayCell(length,idx,name);
  _v.add(t);
  return t;
 }
 public Expression _get(Expression idx) {
  assert(Expression.pc._update_GE(idx, 0)&&
        Expression.pc._update_LT(idx,length));
  ArrayCell cell = _new_ArrayCell(idx);
  return cell.elem;
 } }
```

Fig. 4. Library classes

add to the path condition the constraint or the negation of the constraint its invocation expresses and returns the corresponding `boolean`. Method is_sat uses the Omega library to check if the path condition is infeasible (in which case, JPF will backtrack). Method _plus constructs a new `Expression` that represents the sum of its input parameters. `IntegerConstant` is a subclass of `Expression` and wraps concrete integer values.

To store the input array elements that are created as a result of a lazy initialization, we use a variable of class `Vector`, for each input array. The _get and _set methods use the elements in this vector to systematically initialize input array elements. When the execution accesses a symbolic array cell, the algorithm nondeterministically initializes it to a new cell or to a cell that was created during a prior cell initialization. The assertion checks in the _get/_set methods establish that there are no array out of bounds errors.

4   Proving Properties of Java Programs

In this section we present a Floyd-Hoare style method [14,20,18] for proving lightweight properties of Java programs. The method requires loop invariants and we present a novel iterative technique for discovering (some of) them automatically.

4.1   Proving Properties Using Symbolic Execution

For simplicity of presentation, we illustrate our methodology on a single-loop program such as the one in Figure 5 (left); multiple loops can be treated similarly, see e.g. [31]. The program consists of some (loop-free) initialization code, a loop with condition C and (loop-free) body and post condition P.

To verify the program, it suffices to find a loop invariant I, i.e. a formula that is true when entering the loop, re-entering the loop during its iteration and

```
init;
while (C) {
  body;
}
assert P;
```

```
1:    init;
2:    assert I; /* base case */
3:    symbolic variables in B;
4:    assume I;
5:    if (C) {
6:        B;
          // oldPC
7:        assert I; /* induction step */
          // PC
      }
8:    else
9:        assert P;
```

Fig. 5. Single loop program (left) and instrumented program for proof (right)

exiting the loop [18]. Moreover, I must be strong enough to produce verifiable results (hence a loop invariant *true* is, in general, not sufficient). In a symbolic execution framework, this amounts to checking the three assertions in the modified program in Figure 5 (right). Here, we replaced the while statement with an if statement; this is equivalent to placing a "cut" in the loop [18]. At this cut point, we consider all the variables that are modified in the loop body initialized to *new* symbolic values, and the path condition initialized to *true*. Note that a symbolic execution from this point on is representative of an arbitrary number of loop unrollings; the "input variables" at the cut point are the variables that are modified by the loop body and their new symbolic values represent all cases. Since the program loop has been cut, this symbolic execution will terminate and have a finite symbolic execution tree.

We check for three assertions :

- the assertion at line (4) is the *base case* of the inductive argument and checks that I holds when entering the loop
- the assertion at line (7) is the *induction step* and checks that, *assuming I* holds at the beginning of the loop, I also holds after the execution of the loop body (i.e. I is inductive)
- the assertion at line (9) checks that I is strong enough for the property to hold (i.e. $I \wedge \neg C \rightarrow P$)

If there are no assertion violations in the loop-free program of Figure 5 (right), then the program of Figure 5 (left) does not violate the property P. With this technique, we can verify properties of complex Java programs using the symbolic execution framework presented in Section 3. However, the technique requires the generation and use of loop invariants.

4.2   Invariant Generation

The generation of loop invariants is an intricate problem that often requires a deep understanding of how these loops work.

We propose a novel technique for generating these loop invariants automatically. The technique works backward, starting from the property to be proved and it has three basic ingredients: iterative invariant strengthening, iterative approximation and refinement.

Iterative Invariant Strengthening. Consider again the example in Figure 5. The check for the actual property (i.e. the assertion at line (9)) is used for defining the initial candidate invariant; the weakest possible choice is $I_0 = \neg(\neg C \wedge \neg P)$. If the base case fails for this candidate invariant, then the program is not verifiable (i.e. it has an assertion violation).

Checking the inductive step generates all the symbolic paths for the loop body. If for some of these paths, the invariant is not inductive, then it must be replaced by a stronger invariant. Assume $PC_1, PC_2, \ldots, PC_n$ are the path conditions for the paths on which the verification of the induction step fails. These path conditions characterize all the "inputs" to the loop body for which the check for the inductive step fails. The invariant is strengthened by replacing it with $I_1 = I_0 \wedge \neg PC_1 \wedge \neg PC_2 \wedge \ldots \wedge \neg PC_n$ and the base case and the inductive step are checked again.

If applied repeatedly, this process can introduce infinitely many new constraints, hence it can lead to an infinite sequence of *exact candidate invariants*[1] $I_1, I_2, \ldots$ We propose to use a simple, but powerful approximation technique to help termination.

Iterative Approximation. At each step $k \geq 0$, we apply our approximation phase for the current candidate invariant I_k. We should first observe that symbolically executing the assumption and the body of the loop once (i.e. executing lines (4) through (6) in the code of Figure 5 (right)) will generate a *finite* number of symbolic execution paths, that contain a finite number of constraints; we call these constraints the *universe of constraints* U_k at step k. U_k contains the constraints from the current invariant together with the constraints generated by symbolically executing the loop body. New constraints (that are not in U_k) may get generated by the symbolic execution of the assertion at line (7).

Let PC be a path condition for some path in the loop body *after* checking and discovering a violation for the assertion at line (7), and let $oldPC$ be the path condition for the same path in the loop body, *before* checking the assertion. As we said, checking for the assertion itself can potentially add new constraints to the path condition (i.e. the set of constraints accumulated in $oldPC$ is a subset of the set of constraints in PC). In the approximation phase, instead of strengthening the invariant using PC, we use $oldPC$, which is *weaker* than PC (i.e. $PC \rightarrow oldPC$); this has the effect of obtaining a stronger invariant. In other words, our approximation consists of a strengthening step in which we drop all the newly generated constraints (e.g. constraints that are present in PC but not in $oldPC$, and hence not in U_k). The approximation phase generates a sequence of *approximate candidate invariants* $I_k^1, I_k^2, \ldots$; since there are only a finite number of constraints in U_k, this process is guaranteed to terminate,

---

[1] We distinguish between *exact* candidate invariants, that are generated during iterative invariant strengthening and *approximate* candidate invariants, that are generated during iterative approximation. If the base case fails for an exact invariant, then the program is not verifiable. But if the base case fails for an approximate invariant, this might indicate that the approximation was too coarse so it needs refinement.

yielding an inductive invariant I_k^l, for some $l > 0$. I_k^l is a boolean combination of the constraints contained in U_k.

Refinement. If the base case fails for an approximate invariant, this may be because the approximation is too strong. This means that the universe of constraints U_k is too coarse for proving the property and it needs to be refined. A simple refinement that we use is to consider U_{k+1} whenever the base case fails for an approximate invariant. This amounts to backtracking to the candidate invariant I_k, computing the next *exact candidate invariant* I_{k+1} and applying the approximation phase at the next iteration. Note that since the set of constraints in I_k is a subset of the set of constraints in I_{k+1}, we have that $U_k \subseteq U_{k+1}$, and hence U_{k+1} will yield finer approximation steps. We should also note that if the program has an error, it will be eventually caught when the proof of the base case will fail for an exact invariant.

Description of General Verification Method. Now that we have seen the basic ingredients, here is how the general method for checking properties works. We use the check for the actual property to come up with the initial candidate invariant I_0. We then check the base case and the inductive step for this invariant.

- if both these checks yield no errors, then we are done, the result is that the property holds for the program and the current invariant is inductive
- if the inductive step fails, we apply *iterative approximation* to get a stronger invariant and we go back to checking the base case and the inductive step
- if the base case fails and the current candidate invariant is *exact*, then we are done, and the result is that the property does not hold for the program; if the base case fails and the current candidate invariant is *approximate*, we apply *refinement* and we check again the base case and the inductive step

If there is an error in the program, our method is guaranteed to terminate, reporting the error. However, if the program is correct with respect to the given property, this iterative method might not terminate (and the refinement might continue indefinitely).

4.3   Illustration

Consider again our motivating example program from Section 2. The program is instrumented to allow symbolic verification and inductive reasoning, as illustrated in Figure 6. Any assertion violation triggers an `AssertionError` exception, which is caught by the program (see lines (3) and (17)-(19) in the instrumented code). Variable `oldPC` stores the value of the path condition before the check of the inductive step; the value of `oldPC` is used in the approximation phase for invariant strengthening. Model checking the program using JPF prints all the path conditions `PC` (together with `oldPC`) for the assertion violations.

We first check the assertion at line (15) - which fails. The initial candidate invariant is then $I_0 = \neg(a[0] \neq 0 \land i \geq a.length)$. We now instrument this

```
void example() {
1:    IntArrayStructure a =  new IntArrayStructure();
2:    Expression i = new IntegerConstant(0);
3:    try {
4:      assert(I); /* base case */
5:      i = new SymbolicInteger();
6:      Expression j = new SymbolicInteger();
7:      Verify.ignoreIf(!I); /* assume I */
8:        if(Expression.pc._update_LT(i,a.length)) {
9:          a._set(i,new IntegerConstant(0));
10:         i = i._plus(new IntegerConstant(1));
11:         ... // oldPC = PC;
12:         assert(I); /* induction step */
13:       }
14:     else
15:         assert Expression.pc._update_EQ(a._get(new IntegerConstant(0)),0);
16:         // assert  Expression.pc._update_EQ(a._get(j),0);
17:   } catch (AssertionError e) {
18:         ... // print oldPC;
19:         ... // print PC;
     } }
```

Fig. 6. Motivating example - verification (excerpts)

formula to enable symbolic execution and add it at lines (4), (7) and (12), then we model check the program and we find a counterexample for the following path condition(s):

$PC = (i+1) \geq a.length \wedge i > 0 \wedge a[0] \neq 0$;
$oldPC = i > 0 \wedge a[0] \neq 0$.

At this point we use iterative approximation, and we use $oldPC$ for strengthening the invariant (i.e. we drop the newly generated constraint $(i+1) \geq a.length$ from PC), yielding the new candidate invariant: $I_0^1 = I_0 \wedge \neg(i > 0 \wedge a[0] \neq 0)$. This invariant suffices to prove the property.

In order to check the additional assertion $\forall j : a[j] = 0$, we declare a new symbolic variable j (at line (6)) and we check for the assertion at line (16), that is instrumented for symbolic execution. The initial candidate invariant is $I_0 = \neg(a[j] \neq 0 \wedge i \geq a.length \wedge 0 \leq j < a.length)$. Model checking the program using this additional invariant gives a counterexample for the following path condition(s):

$PC = (i+1) \geq a.length \wedge a[j] \neq 0 \wedge j < i \wedge 0 \leq i, j < a.length$;
$oldPC = a[j] \neq 0 \wedge j < i \wedge 0 \leq i, j < a.length$.

Using $oldPC$ for strengthening the invariant, we get $I_0^1 = I_0 \wedge \neg(a[j] \neq 0 \wedge j < i \wedge 0 \leq i, j < a.length$ which suffices to prove the property.

4.4   Discussion

We have presented a method that extends the framework presented in [23] with the ability of proving partial-correctness specifications. This yields a flexible framework for checking Java programs. The general methodology for using our framework is to first use it as a model checker, using depth first search with iterative deepening or breadth first search.

If no errors are found up to a certain depth, then there is some confidence that the program is correct (with respect to the given property), and a proof of correctness can be attempted using the method presented in this section. If an error is still present after the model checking phase, it will be found as a base case violation for an exact candidate invariant.

Our approximation consists of dropping newly generated constraints; a potentially more powerful, but more expensive, approximation would be that instead of dropping constraints, to replace them with an appropriate boolean combination of existing constraints from U_k. This has some similarities with the predicate abstraction techniques and we would like to investigate this further. Our technique can also be used in conjunction with other, more powerful methods [9, 8, 7, 32].

Our current system is not fully automated; although we discover all path conditions that lead to an assertion violation automatically, we combine the conditions by hand into a candidate invariant and add it back to the code to check if it is inductive. An implementation of these features is currently underway.

Traditionally, invariant generation has been performed using iterative forward and backward traversal, using different heuristics for terminating the iteration; e.g. convergence can be accelerated by using auxiliary invariants (i.e. already proved invariants or structural invariants obtained by static analysis) [25, 31, 3, 29, 4, 16, 19]. Abstract interpretation introduced the *widening* operator, which was used to compute fixpoints systematically [8, 7, 9]. Alternative methods [5] use constrained based techniques for numeric invariant generation.

Most of these methods use techniques that are *domain specific*. Our method for invariant generation uniformly treats different kinds of constraints. Our method could be viewed as an iterative-deepening search of a sufficient set of constraints that could express an invariant that is strong enough for verifying the property. Each step in this search is guaranteed to terminate, but deepening (refinement) may be non terminating.

5   Experiments

This section shows the application of our framework to the verification of several non-trivial Java programs. We compare our work with the invariant generation method presented in [13]. We also show an example for which our method is not able to infer a loop invariant, in which case it can benefit from more powerful approximation techniques.

Method find. Figure 7 shows an example adapted from [13]. Method find takes as parameters an array of integers a and an array of booleans b. The method returns the index of the first non-zero element of a if one exists and a.length otherwise. The method also sets the i-th element of b to true if the i-th element of a is nonzero, and to false otherwise. The preconditions of the method state that the arrays are not null and of the same length. The assertion states that the index to be returned (spot) is either a.length or b is true at that index.

```
// @ precondition: a != null && b != null && a.length == b.length;
int find(int [] a, boolean [] b) {
1:    int spot = a.length;
2:    for (int i = 0; i < a.length; i++) {
3:       if (spot == a.length && a[i] != 0)
4:          spot = i;
5:       b[i] = (a[i] != 0);
      }
6:    assert (spot == a.length || b[spot]);
7:    return spot;
}
```

Fig. 7. Method `find`

To check that there are no assertion and array bounds violations, our framework infers the following invariant ($k = 0$, two approximation steps):

$\neg(i < 0) \land \neg(i \geq a.length \land 0 \leq spot < a.length \land \neg b[spot]) \land$
$\neg(0 \leq i < a.length \land spot = i \land a[i] = 0) \land$
$\neg(0 \leq i < a.length \land 0 \leq spot < i \land \neg b[spot]) \land$
$\neg(0 \leq i < a.length \land i < spot < a.length).$

This invariant is sufficient to prove the property. As in [13] we checked an additional assertion, which states that, at the end of the method execution, every element of b before spot contains false: $\forall\ int\ j : 0 \leq j < spot \rightarrow \neg b[j]$.

To prove that this assertion holds, our framework generates the following additional invariant:

$\neg(i \geq a.length \land 0 \leq j < spot \land spot \leq a.length \land b[j]) \land$
$\neg(0 \leq i < a.length \land 0 \leq j < i \land spot = a.length \land b[j]) \land$
$\neg(0 \leq i < a.length \land 0 \leq j < spot \land spot = i \land b[j] \land a[i] \neq 0) \land$
$\neg(0 \leq i < a.length \land 0 \leq j < spot \land spot < i \land b[j] \land b[spot]).$

The method presented in [13] starts with a set of "interesting" predicates provided by the user and performs iterative forward *abstract computations* to compute a loop invariant as a combination of these predicates. For proving the first assertion in the example above, the method requires three predicates: $spot = a.length$, $b[spot]$ and $spot < i$, while for proving the second assertion, the method requires four additional predicates: $0 \leq j$, $j < i$, $j < spot$ and $b[j]$.

In contrast, our method does not require any user supplied predicates, although we should note that some of these predicates can be generated by several heuristic methods that are also described in [13]. We should also note that the invariants in [13] are more concise, as they are given in disjunctive normal form. Unlike [13], our method works backward starting from the property to be checked and it naturally discovers the necessary constraints over the program's variables, through symbolic execution and refinement. An interesting future research direction is to use the method presented in [13] in conjunction with ours: at each step k, instead of using approximation we could use the predicate abstraction based method, starting from the set of constraints U_k.

List Partition. Figure 8 (left) shows a list partitioning example adapted again from [13]. Each list element is an instance of the class Node, and contains two

```
Node partition (Node l, int v) {
1:   Node curr = l;                              void m(int n) {
2:   Node prev = null;                           1:   int x = 0;
3:   Node newl = null;                           2:   int y = 0;
4:   Node nextCurr;                              3:   while (x < n) {
5:   while(curr != null) {                       4:     x++;
6:     nextCurr = curr.next;                     5:     y++;
7:     if (curr.elem > v) {                      }
8:        if (prev != null)                      6:   /* hint: x == y; */
9:           prev.next = nextCurr;               7:   while (x != 0) {
10:       if (curr == l)                         8:     x--;
11:          l = nextCurr;                       9:     y--;
12:       curr.next = newl;                      }
13:       assert curr != prev                    10: assert (y == 0);
14:       newl = curr;                           }
     }
15:    else {
16:       prev = curr;
     }
17:    curr = nextCurr;
   }
18: return newl; }
```

Fig. 8. Method `partition` (left) and another example (right)

fields: an integer `elem` and a reference `next` to the following node in the list. The method `partition` takes two arguments, a list `l` and an integer value `v`. It removes every node with value greater than `v` from `l` and returns a list containing all those nodes. The assertion states that `curr` is not aliased with `prev`. Our framework checks that there are no assertion violations and it generates the following sequence of candidate invariants.

$I_0 = \neg(\mathit{curr} = \mathit{prev} \wedge \mathit{curr} \neq \mathit{null} \wedge \mathit{curr}.\mathit{elem} > v).$

$I_0^1 = I_0 \wedge \neg(\mathit{curr} \neq \mathit{prev} \wedge \mathit{curr} \neq \mathit{null} \wedge \mathit{prev} \neq \mathit{null} \wedge \mathit{curr}.\mathit{elem} > v).$

Approximate invariant I_0^1 is too strong (I_0^2 leads to a base case violation). The framework then backtracks and continues with the next exact invariant:

$I_1 = I_0 \wedge \neg(\mathit{curr} \neq \mathit{prev} \wedge \mathit{curr} \neq \mathit{null} \wedge \mathit{prev} \neq \mathit{null} \wedge \mathit{curr}.\mathit{elem} > v \wedge$ $\mathit{prev}.\mathit{elem} > v \wedge \mathit{prev} = \mathit{curr}.\mathit{next}).$

$I_1^1 = I_1 \wedge \neg(\mathit{curr} \neq \mathit{prev} \wedge \mathit{curr} \neq \mathit{null} \wedge \mathit{prev} \neq \mathit{null} \wedge \mathit{curr}.\mathit{elem} > v \wedge$ $\mathit{prev}.\mathit{elem} > v \wedge \mathit{prev} \neq \mathit{curr}.\mathit{next}).$

Approximate invariant I_1^1 is inductive. This example has shown that our framework can handle constraints on structured data. We also successfully applied our framework to the examples presented in [11], where we checked the absence of null pointer dereferences.

Pathological Example. The iterative method for invariant generation presented in Section 4 might not terminate. For example, consider the code in Figure 8 (right)[2].

As our method works backward from the property, we first attempt to compute a loop invariant for the second loop. Our iterative refinement will not

---

[2] Note that several other methods, such as the predicate abstraction with refinement as implemented in the SLAM tool [1] would also not terminate on this example.

terminate for this loop. Considering increasing the number of exact strengthening steps does not help. Intuitively, the method does not converge because the constraint $x = y$ (and its negation) is "important" for achieving termination, but this constraint does not get discovered by repeated symbolic executions of the code in the loop body.

The programmer can provide additional helpful constraints by hand in the form of "hints", to boost the precision of the iterative approximation method. For example, the hint at line (6) in the code of Figure 8 (right) has the effect of nondeterministically adding the constraint (and its negation) to the current path condition, and hence these constraints are also added to the universe of constraints at each strengthening step. With this hint, we get the following loop invariant for the second loop ($k = 0$, two approximation steps):

$$\neg(y \neq 0 \wedge x = 0) \wedge \neg(y \leq 0 \wedge x > 0) \wedge \neg(y > 0 \wedge x \neq y).$$

Using this invariant as the postcondition for the first loop, we then get the following loop invariant for the first loop, which suffices to prove the property:

$$\neg(x \geq n \wedge x \neq y) \wedge \neg(x < 0) \wedge \neg(x \geq 0 \wedge x < n \wedge x \neq y).$$

We should note that more powerful techniques such as linear equalities abstract domain [22] would work for this example. We would like to use our framework in conjunction with more powerful abstraction techniques (such as [22]) or with alternative dynamic methods for discovering loop invariants (e.g. the Daikon tool [12] could be used to provide useful "hints").

6   Related Work

Throughout the paper, we have discussed related work on invariant generation. Here we link our approach to software verification tools. King [24] developed EFFIGY, a system for symbolic execution of programs with a fixed number of integer variables. EFFIGY supported various program analyses (such as assertion based correctness checking) and is one of the earliest systems of its kind.

Several projects aim at developing static analyses for verifying program properties. The Extended Static Checker (ESC) [10] uses a theorem prover to verify partial correctness of classes annotated with JML specifications. ESC has been used to verify absence of such errors as null pointer dereferences, array bounds violations, and division by zero. However, tools like ESC rely heavily on specifications provided by the user and they could benefit from invariant generation techniques such as ours.

The Three-Valued-Logic Analyzer (TVLA) [28] is a static analysis system for verifying rich structural properties, such as preservation of a list structure in programs that perform list reversals via destructive updating of the input list. TVLA performs fixed point computations on shape graphs, which represent heap cells by shape nodes and sets of indistinguishable runtime locations by summary nodes. Our approximation technique has similarities to widening operations used in static analysis. We would like to explore this connection further.

The pointer assertion logic engine (PALE) [26] can verify a large class of data structures that can be represented by a spanning tree backbone, with possibly additional pointers that do not add extra information. These data structures include doubly linked lists, trees with parent pointers, and threaded trees. Shape analyses, such as TVLA and PALE, typically do not verify properties of programs that perform operations on numeric data values.

There has been a lot of recent interest in applying model checking to software. Java PathFinder [30] and VeriSoft [15] operate directly on a Java, respectively C program. Other projects, such as Bandera [6], translate Java programs into the input language of verification tools. Our work would extend such tools with the ability to prove partial-correctness specifications. The Composite Symbolic Library [33] uses symbolic forward fixed point operations to compute the reachable states of a program. It uses widening to help termination but can analyze programs that manipulate lists with only a fixed number of integer fields and it can only deal with closed systems.

The SLAM tool [1] focuses on checking sequential C code with static data, using well-engineered predicate abstraction and abstraction refinement tools. It does not handle dynamically allocated data structures. Symbolic execution is used to map abstract counterexamples on concrete executions and to refine the abstraction, by adding new predicates discovered during symbolic execution. We should note that tools like SLAM perform abstraction on each program statement, whereas our method performs approximation (which can be seen as a form of abstraction) only when necessary, at loop headers. This indicates that our method is potentially cheaper in terms of the number of predicates (i.e. constraints) required. Of course, further experimentation is necessary to support this claim. There are many similarities between predicate abstraction and our iterative approximation method and we would like to compare the two methods in terms of relative completeness (as in [2, 9]).

7   Conclusion

We presented a novel framework based on symbolic execution for the verification of software. The framework uses annotations in the form of method specifications and loop invariants. We presented a novel iterative technique for discovering these loop invariants automatically. The technique works backward from the property to be checked and it systematically applies approximation to achieve termination. The technique handles uniformly both numeric constraints and constraints on structured data and it allows for checking universally quantified formulas. We illustrated the applicability of our framework to the verification of several non-trivial Java programs. Although we made our presentation in the context of Java programs, JPF, and the Omega library, our framework can be instantiated with other languages, model checkers and decision procedures. In the future, we plan to investigate the application of widening and other more powerful abstraction techniques in conjunction with our method for invariant generation. We also plan to extend our framework to handle multithreading and richer properties. We would also like to integrate different (semi) decision procedures and constraint solvers that will allow us to handle floats and non-linear constraints. We believe that our framework presents a promising flexible approach for the analysis of software. How well it scales to real applications remains to be seen.

References

1. T. Ball, R. Majumdar, T. Millstein, and S. Rajamani. Automatic predicate abstraction of C programs. In *Proc. PLDI*, pages 203–213, 2001.
2. T. Ball, A. Podelski, and S. K. Rajamani. Relative completeness of abstraction refinement for software model checking. In *Proc. TACAS*, 2002.
3. S. Bensalem, Y. Lakhnech, and H. Saidi. Powerful techniques for the automatic generation of invariants. In *Proc. CAV*, 1996.
4. N. Bjorner, A. Browne, M. Colon, B. Finkbeiner, Z. Manna, H. Sipma, and T. Uribe. Verifying temporal properties of reactive systems: A STeP tutorial. *FMSD*, 16:227–270, 2000.
5. M. Colon, S. Sankaranarayanan, and H. Sipma. Linear invariant generation using non-linear constraint solving. In *Proc. CAV*, 2003.
6. J. Corbett, M. Dwyer, J. Hatcliff, S. Laubach, C. Păsăreanu, Robby, and H. Zheng. Bandera : Extracting finite-state models from Java source code. In *Proc. ICSE'00*.
7. P. Cousot and R. Cousot. On abstraction in software verification. In *Proc. CAV'02*.
8. P. Cousot and N. Halbwachs. Automatic discovery of linear restraints among variables of a program. In *Proc. 5th POPL*, 1978.
9. G. Delzanno and A. Podelski. Widen, narrow and relax. Technical report.
10. D. L. Detlefs, K. R. M. Leino, G. Nelson, and J. B. Saxe. Extended static checking. Research Report 159, Compaq Systems Research Center, 1998.
11. N. Dor, M. Rodeh, and M. Sagiv. Checking cleanness in linked lists. In *Proc. SAS*, 2000.
12. M. D. Ernst, A. Czeisler, W. G. Griswold, and D. Notkin. Quickly detecting relevant program invariants. In *Proc. ICSE*. ACM, 2000.
13. C. Flanagan and S. Qadeer. Predicate abstraction for software verification. In *Proc. POPL*, 2002.
14. R. W. Floyd. Assigning meanings to programs. In *Proc. Symposia in Applied Mathematics 19*, pages 19–32, 1967.
15. P. Godefroid. Model checking for programming languages using VeriSoft. In *Proc. POPL*, pages 174–186, Paris, France, Jan. 1997.
16. S. Graf and H. Saidi. Verifying invariants using theorem proving. In *Proc. 8th CAV*, pages 196–207, 1996.
17. S. Graf and H. Saidi. Construction of abstract state graphs with PVS. In *Proc. 9th CAV*, pages 72–83, 1997.
18. S. L. Hantler and J. C. King. An introduction to proving the correctness of programs. *ACM Comput. Surv.*, 8(3):331–353, 1976.
19. K. Havelund and N. Shankar. Experiments in theorem proving and model checking for protocol verification. In *Proc. FME*, pages 662–681, 1996.
20. C. A. R. Hoare. An axiomatic basis for computer programming. *Commun. ACM*, 12(10):576–580, 1969.
21. G. Holzmann. *The Spin Model Checker: Primer and Reference Manual.* 2003.
22. M. Karr. Affine relationships among variables of a program. *Acta Informatica*, 6, 1976.
23. S. Khurshid, C. S. Păsăreanu, and W. Visser. Generalized symbolic execution for model checking and testing. In *Proc. TACAS*, 2003.

24. J. C. King. Symbolic execution and program testing. *Commun. ACM*, 19(7):385–394, 1976.
25. Z. Manna and A. Pnueli. *The Temporal Logic of Reactive and Concurrent Systems: Specification*. 1992.
26. A. Moeller and M. I. Schwartzbach. The pointer assertion logic engine. In *Proc. PLDI*, Snowbird, UT, June 2001.
27. W. Pugh. The Omega test: A fast and practical integer programming algorithm for dependence analysis. *Communications of the ACM*, 31(8), Aug. 1992.
28. M. Sagiv, T. Reps, and R. Wilhelm. Solving shape-analysis problems in languages with destructive updating. *ACM Trans. Prog. Lang. Syst.*, January 1998.
29. A. Tiwari, H. Rues, H. Saidi, and N. Shankar. A technique for invariant generation. In *Proc. TACAS*, 2001.
30. W. Visser, K. Havelund, G. Brat, and S. Park. Model checking programs. In *Proc. ASE*, Grenoble, France, 2000.
31. B. Wegbreit. The synthesis of loop predicates. *Communications of the ACM*, 17(2):102–112, 1974.
32. P. Wolper and B. Boigelot. Verifying systems with infinite but regular state spaces. In *Proc. CAV*, pages 88–97, 1998.
33. T. Yavuz-Kahveci and T. Bultan. Automated verification of concurrent linked lists with counters. In *Proc. SAS*, 2002.

Polynomial Time Image Computation with Interval-Definable Counters Systems

Alain Finkel and Jérôme Leroux

Laboratoire Spécification et Vérification,
CNRS UMR 8643 & ENS de Cachan,
61 av. du Président Wilson,
94235 Cachan cedex, France
{finkel,leroux}@lsv.ens-cachan.fr

Abstract. The model checking of counters systems often reduces to the effective computation of the set of predecessors $\mathrm{Pre}^*(X')$ of a Presburger-definable set X'. Because there often exists an integer $k \geq 0$ such that $\mathrm{Pre}^{\leq k}(X') = \mathrm{Pre}^*(X')$ we will first look for an *efficient* algorithm to compute the set $\mathrm{Pre}(X)$ in function of X. In general, such a computation is exponential in the size of X. In [BB03], the computation is proved to be polynomial for a restrictive class of counters systems. In this article we show that for any counters systems, the computation is polynomial. Then we show that the computation of $\mathrm{Pre}^{\leq k}(X')$ is polynomial in k (and exponential in the dimension m) for effective counters systems with interval-definable sets.

1 Introduction

Model checking infinite-state transition systems often reduces to the effective computation of the potentially infinite set of predecessors Pre^*. More precisely, the safety model checking can be expressed as the following problem.

Given as inputs: an infinite-state transition system, a set S_0 of initial states, and a set S_{bad} of non-safe states;
the question is $S_0 \cap \mathrm{Pre}^*(S_{bad}) = \emptyset$?

To succeed in computing the limit $\mathrm{Pre}^*(S_{bad})$ of the infinite non-decreasing sequence $(\mathrm{Pre}^{\leq i}(S_{bad}))_i$, we need three properties:

- The convergence of the sequence $\exists k;\ \mathrm{Pre}^*(S_{bad}) = \mathrm{Pre}^{\leq k}(S_{bad})$, and
- An efficient algorithm for computing $\mathrm{Pre}(X)$ from X,
- An efficient algorithm for computing $(\mathrm{Pre}^{\leq i}(X))$ from X,

The convergence of $(\mathrm{Pre}^{\leq i}(S_{bad}))_i$ with S_{bad} an upward closed is insured for Well Structured Transition Systems (WSTS) [FS01], but even for simple WSTS (for instance, lossy channel systems), the index k such that $\mathrm{Pre}^*(S_{bad}) = \mathrm{Pre}^{\leq k}(S_{bad})$ may be very large [Sch02]. However, even if the convergence is not guaranteed by the theory (for instance when the set of initial states is not upward-closed), in practice we observe that often, the sequence $(\mathrm{Pre}^{\leq i}(S_0))_i$ converge [Del00] [BB03] and it often converges quickly ([Bra] [Bab]). This explains

S. Graf and L. Mounier (Eds.): SPIN 2004, LNCS 2989, pp. 182–197, 2004.

that we will focus our attention on the second problem, to obtain an efficient algorithm for computing $\text{Pre}(X)$ from X and then, on the third problem for efficiently computing $(\text{Pre}^{\leq i}(X))$. We would like to understand what are the conditions insuring an efficient computation of the sequence $(\text{Pre}^{\leq i}(S_{bad}))_i$ and then, may be, to better understand the good performances of some recent tools: BRAIN, BABYLON.

We first have to fix the model of our infinite-state transition systems, the type of infinite sets and the way to represent these sets.

Infinite-state transition systems. We will focus on programs with integer variables and more precisely on counters systems in which a transition is defined by a Presburger function relating the values of the counters before and after the transition is fired. This model is very general (our model restricts neither the number of counters nor the upward closed guards [FMP99]) and powerful ([FL02], [Ler03a]) so the price to pay is the undecidability of reachability properties. Generally, the transition relation will be effectively given by a saturated digit automaton [Ler03a].

Representations of Presburger-definable sets. In order to effectively compute $\text{Pre}(X')$, one generally needs to find a class of infinite sets which has the following properties: (1) closure under union, (2) closure under Pre, (3) membership and inclusion are decidable with a good complexity, and (4) there exists a canonical representation.

Semi-linear basis/periods and Presburger formulas are not canonical representations of Presburger-definable sets (which are also semi-linear sets). Recall that Number Decision Diagrams (NDD) ([Boi98], [WB00], [BC96]), provide a m-digit by m-digit representation of vectors in $\mathbb{N}^m$ whereas Saturated Digit Automata (SDA) use a digit-by-digit representation of vectors in $\mathbb{N}^m$. We prove that NDD and SDA have the same expressiveness but the theory of SDA enjoys an useful characterization of the minimal SDA associated with a set X.

Our computation problems. Now we may precise the input of our two computation problems.

1. The first problem is to compute $\text{Pre}_S(X')$:
   Input: a counters system S and a saturated digit automaton $\mathcal{A}'$ that represents a set $X' \subseteq \mathbb{N}^m$.
   Question: Can we compute in polynomial time in the size of $\mathcal{A}'$, a saturated digit automaton $\mathcal{A}$ representing $X = \text{Pre}_S(X')$?

2. The second problem is to compute the kth element $\text{Pre}_S^{\leq k}(X)$:
   Input: a counters system S, a saturated digit automaton $\mathcal{A}'$ that represents a set $X' \subseteq \mathbb{N}^m$ and an integer k.
   Question: Can we compute in polynomial time in k, a saturated digit automaton $\mathcal{A}$ representing $X = \text{Pre}_S^{\leq k}(X')$?

Related works. We use the approach called the *regular model checking*: for channel systems, Semi-Linear Regular Expressions [FPS00] and Constrained

Queue-content Decision Diagrams [BH99] have been proposed; for lossy channel systems [ABJ98], the tools LCS (in the more general tool TREX [ABS01] [Tre]) uses the downward-closed regular languages and the corresponding subset of Simple Regular Expressions for sets and it represents them by finite automata to compute Post*; for stack automata, regular expressions or finite automata are sufficient to represent Pre* and Post* [BEF⁺00]; for Petri nets and parameterized rings, [FO97] uses regular languages and Presburger arithmetics (and acceleration) for sets. For Transfer and Reset Petri nets [DFS98], the tool BABYLON [Bab] utilizes the upward closed sets and represents them by Covering Sharing Trees [DRV01], a variant of BDD; for counters automata, the tool BRAIN [Bra] uses linear sets and represent them by their linear bases and periods; for extended counters automata, the tools FAST [Fas], [FL02], [BFLP03] and LASH [Las] utilize semi-linear sets and represents them by NDD, moreover, these two tools are able to accelerate loops [Boi] [FL02]; MONA [Mon] [KMS02] and FMONA [BF00] use formula in WS1S to represent sets; the tool CSL-ALV [BGP97] [Alv] uses linear arithmetic constraints for sets and manipulates formula with the OMEGA solver and the automata library of LASH.

In [BB03], the computation of $\mathrm{Pre}_S(X')$ is proved to be polynomial for a complex subclass of counters systems.

Our results.

1. We introduce SDA as a canonical representation of set of vectors of integers. Even if SDA have the same expression power than NDD, there exists an elegant theoretical characterization of the minimal SDA associated with a set X which is useful for computing the size of the minimal SDA.
2. We show that for counters systems S, the set of immediate predecessors $\mathrm{Pre}_S(X')$ is computable in polynomial time in the size of the SDA that represents X'. This result generalizes a recent result of [BB03].
3. We characterize the affine functions whose the inverse image of any interval-definable set remains interval-definable. Then we prove that the asymptotic size of the minimal SDA that represents $\mathrm{Pre}_S^{\leq k}(X')$ is polynomial in k and exponential in m.

Plan of the paper. Saturated Digit Automata are introduced in section 3 and compared with NDD. In the next section 4, we define counters systems and prove that the computation of $\mathrm{Pre}(X')$ is polynomial in X'. In the last section 5, the asymptotic size of the minimal SDA representing $\mathrm{Pre}_S^{\leq k}(X')$ is proved to be polynomial in k.

2   Preliminaries

The cardinal of a finite set X is written $\mathrm{card}(X)$.

The set of rationals, integers and positive integers are respectively written $\mathbb{Q}$, $\mathbb{Z}$ and $\mathbb{N}$. The set of vectors with m components in a set X is written X^m. The i-th component of a vector $x \in X^m$ is written $x_i \in X$; we have $x = (x_1, \ldots, x_m)$. For any vector $v, v' \in \mathbb{Q}^m$ and for any $t \in \mathbb{Q}$, we define $t.v$ and $v + v'$ in $\mathbb{Q}^m$ by $(t.v)_i = t.v_i$ and $(v + v')_i = v_i + v'_i$. The vector $\mathbf{e}_i \in \mathbb{N}^m$ is defined as $(\mathbf{e}_i)_j = 1$ if $j = i$ and $(\mathbf{e}_i)_j = 0$ otherwise.

The set of square matrices of size m in $\mathbb{Q}$ is written $\mathcal{M}_m(\mathbb{Q})$. A function $f : D \to \mathbb{N}^m$ with $D \subseteq \mathbb{N}^m$ is affine if there exists a square matrix $M \in \mathcal{M}_m(\mathbb{Q})$ and a vector $v \in \mathbb{Q}^m$ such that $f(x) = M.x + v$ for every $x \in D$. Remark that rational matrices are needed for representing some affine functions like $f : 2.\mathbb{N} \to \mathbb{N}$ defined by $f(x) = \frac{x}{2}$.

The set of words over a finite alphabet Σ is written Σ^*. The concatenation of two words σ and σ' in Σ^* is written $\sigma\sigma'$. The empty word in Σ^* is written ϵ.

A finite automaton $\mathcal{A}$ is a tuple $\mathcal{A} = (Q, \Sigma, \Delta, Q_0, F)$; Q is the finite set of states, Σ is the finite alphabet, $\Delta \subseteq Q \times \Sigma \times Q$ is the transition relation, $Q_0 \subseteq Q$ is the set of initial states and $F \subseteq Q$ is the set of final states. The size of a finite automaton $\mathcal{A}$ is $|\mathcal{A}| = \mathrm{card}(Q)$. A finite automaton $\mathcal{A}$ is said deterministic if the set Q_0 is reduced to one element $Q_0 = \{q_0\}$ and if there exists a function δ defined over a subset of $Q \times \Sigma$ into Q such that $\Delta = \{(q, \delta(q, a)); \; q \in Q; \; a \in \Sigma\}$. A deterministic automaton is said complete if the function δ is defined over the whole set $Q \times \Sigma$. A path P in a finite automaton $\mathcal{A}$ from a state q to a state q' is a finite sequence $q = q_0, (q_0, a_1, q_1), q_1, \ldots, (q_{n-1}, a_n, q_n), q_n = q'$ with $n \geq 0$ such that (q_{i-1}, a_i, q_i) is a transition in Δ. The label of P is the word $\sigma = a_1 \ldots a_n \in \Sigma^*$. Such a path is also written $q \xrightarrow{\sigma} q'$. The state q' is said reachable from q and q is said co-reachable from q'. The language accepted by a finite automaton $\mathcal{A}$ is $\mathcal{L}(\mathcal{A}) = \{\sigma \in \Sigma^*; \; \exists q_0 \in Q_0; \; \exists q_f \in F; \; q_0 \xrightarrow{\sigma} q_f\}$.

Let us recall the two considered logics:

- The Presburger logic ([Ber77]) is built with the following formulas:

$$\phi := \sum_{i \in I} c_i.v_i = c \,|\, \exists v \; \phi \,|\, \forall v \; \phi \,|\, \phi \vee \phi \,|\, \phi \wedge \phi \,|\, \neg \phi \,|\, true \,|\, false$$

  where $(c_i)_{i \in I}$ is a finite sequence of $\mathbb{N}$, $c \in \mathbb{N}$ and $(v_i)_{i \in I}$, v are in a finite set V of variables.
- The interval logic ([Str98] (a.k.a simple constraint [AAB00]) is defined by the following formulas:

$$\phi := v_i = c \,|\, \phi \vee \phi \,|\, \phi \wedge \phi \,|\, \neg \phi \,|\, true \,|\, false$$

A set $X \subseteq \mathbb{N}^m$ is said Presburger-definable (resp. interval-definable) if it can be defined by a Presburger formula (resp. by a formula in the interval logic).

3   Saturated Digit Automata

Recall that there exist two natural ways in order to associate to a word σ a vector in $\mathbb{N}^m$ following that the first letter of σ is considered as an "high bit" or a "low bit". In this article, we consider the "low bit" representation (even if the other one, just seems to be symmetrical, results proved in the paper cannot be easily extended to the other one).

Let us consider an integer $r \geq 2$ called the *basis of decomposition* and an integer $m \geq 1$ called the *dimension of the represented vectors*. A *digit* b is an element of the finite alphabet $\Sigma_r = \{0, \ldots, r-1\}$. In general ([Boi98] [WB00],

[BC96]), a vector in $\mathbb{N}^m$ is only associated to words of digits whose the length is multiple of m. However, as shown in this article, an extension to any word of any length can be useful.

Like in [Ler03a,Ler03b], function $\gamma_\sigma : \mathbb{N}^m \to \mathbb{N}^m$ is defined by the induction $\gamma_{\sigma.\sigma'} = \gamma_\sigma \circ \gamma'_\sigma$ and $\gamma_b((x_1, \dots, x_m)) = (r.x_m + b, x_1, \dots, x_{m-1})$ for any digit b. Let us remark that if m divides the length of $\sigma = (b_{1,1} \dots b_{1,m}) \dots (b_{n,1} \dots b_{n,m})$, then the following equality holds:

$$\gamma_\sigma((0, \dots, 0)) = \sum_{i=1}^n r^{i-1}(b_{i,1}, \dots, b_{i,m})$$

Naturally, the vector $\rho_m(\sigma) = \gamma_\sigma((0, \dots, 0))$ is called the *vector associated to* σ. Thanks to the function $\rho_m : \Sigma_r^* \to \mathbb{N}^m$, we can now define the Saturated Digit Automata and the Number Decision Diagrams.

Definition 1. *A* Saturated Digit Automaton (SDA) $\mathcal{A}$ *that represents a set* $X \subseteq \mathbb{N}^m$ *is a deterministic and complete automaton over* Σ_r *such that* $\mathcal{L}(\mathcal{A}) = \rho_m^{-1}(X)$. *Such a set* X *is called SDA-definable.*

Definition 2. *A* Number Decision Diagram (NDD) $\mathcal{A}$ *([Boi98] [WB00]) that represents a set* $X \subseteq \mathbb{N}^m$ *is a deterministic and complete automaton over* Σ_r *such that* $\mathcal{L}(\mathcal{A}) = \rho_m^{-1}(X) \cap (\Sigma_r^m)^*$.

Remark 1. NDD also allow to represent vectors in $\mathbb{Z}^m$ with "high" or "low" bit first representation. Whereas the results proved in this article can be extended to $\mathbb{Z}^m$, an extension to "high" bit first representation seems difficult.

The following proposition shows that SDA and NDD represent the same sets of $\mathbb{N}^m$.

Proposition 1.   – *From any NDD* $\mathcal{A}$, *we can effectively compute in time* $O(r.|\mathcal{A}|)$ *a SDA* $\mathcal{A}'$ *that represents the same subset, such that* $|\mathcal{A}'| \leq |\mathcal{A}|$.
  – *From any SDA* $\mathcal{A}$, *we can effectively compute in time* $O(r.m.|\mathcal{A}|)$ *an NDD* $\mathcal{A}'$ *that represents the same subset, such that* $|\mathcal{A}'| \leq m.|\mathcal{A}|$

Proof. (Sketch). Let us consider a NDD $\mathcal{A}$ that represents a set X. By replacing the set of final states F of $\mathcal{A}$ by the set $F' = \{q \in Q; \exists q_f \in F; q \xrightarrow{0^*} q_f\}$, we deduce a SDA $\mathcal{A}'$ that represents X.

Now, let us consider a SDA $\mathcal{A}$ that represents a set X. As $\mathcal{L}(\mathcal{A}) = \rho^{-1}(X)$, the "synchronized product" of $\mathcal{A}$ and the automaton with m states that recognizes the language $(\Sigma_r^m)^*$ provides a NDD $\mathcal{A}'$ that also represents X.

Remark 2. As any Presburger-definable set can be effectively represented by a NDD [WB00], the same result holds for SDA.

We have introduced the class of SDA rather than using the NDD because the minimal SDA that represents a set X is given by the "residues" of X.

Definition 3. *The set* $\sigma^{-1}.X = \gamma_\sigma^{-1}(X)$ *is called the residue of* $X \subseteq \mathbb{N}^m$ *by* $\sigma \in \Sigma_r^*$.

From $\gamma_{\sigma_1.\sigma_2} = \gamma_{\sigma_1} \circ \gamma_{\sigma_2}$, we deduce the equality $\sigma_2^{-1}.\sigma_1^{-1}.X = (\sigma_1.\sigma_2)^{-1}.X$ that enables us to give the following definition.

Definition 4. *Let* $X \subseteq \mathbb{N}^m$ *be such that its set of residues* $Q(X) = \{\sigma^{-1}.X;\ \sigma \in \Sigma_r^*\}$ *is finite. The deterministic and complete automaton* $\mathcal{A}(X)$ *is defined by:*

$$
\begin{cases}
\mathcal{A}(X) = (Q(X), \Sigma_r, \delta, q_0, F) \\
\delta(q, b) = b^{-1}.q \\
q_0 = X \\
F = \{q \in Q(X);\ (0, \dots, 0) \in q\}
\end{cases}
$$

Lemma 1. *For any* $X \subseteq \mathbb{N}^m$ *and* $\sigma \in \Sigma_r^*$, *we have* $\sigma^{-1}.\rho^{-1}(X) = \rho^{-1}(\sigma^{-1}.X)$.

Proof. We have $w \in \sigma^{-1}.\rho^{-1}(X)$ iff $\sigma.w \in \rho^{-1}(X)$ iff $\rho(\sigma.w) \in X$ iff $\gamma_\sigma(\rho(w)) \in X$ iff $\rho(w) \in \sigma^{-1}.x$ iff $w \in \rho^{-1}(\sigma^{-1}.X)$. □

The following theorem is really important because it proves that the structure of the minimal SDA that represents a set X can be obtained just by studying the set of residues of X.

Theorem 1. *A set* $X \subseteq \mathbb{N}^m$ *is SDA-definable if and only if its set of residues is finite. Moreover, in this case,* $\mathcal{A}(X)$ *is the unique minimal SDA that represents* X.

Proof. Assume that $Q(X)$ is a finite set. We are going to show that $\mathcal{A}(X)$ is a SDA that represents X by proving that $\mathcal{L}(\mathcal{A}(X)) = \rho^{-1}(X)$. We have $\sigma \in \mathcal{L}(\mathcal{A}(X))$ iff $(0, \dots, 0) \in \sigma^{-1}.X = \gamma_\sigma^{-1}(X)$. Therefore $\sigma \in \mathcal{L}(\mathcal{A}(X))$ iff $\rho(\sigma) = \gamma_\sigma((0, \dots, 0)) \in X$. Hence, we have proved that $\mathcal{L}(\mathcal{A}(X)) = \rho^{-1}(X)$. In particular $\rho(\mathcal{L}(\mathcal{A}(X))) = X$ and $\rho^{-1}(\rho(\mathcal{L}(\mathcal{A}(X)))) = \mathcal{L}(\mathcal{A}(X))$. We have proved that $\mathcal{A}(X)$ is a SDA that represents X.

Now, assume that X is SDA-definable and let us prove that $Q(X)$ is finite. The language $\mathcal{L} = \rho^{-1}(X)$ is regular. As the minimal deterministic and complete automaton that recognizes $\mathcal{L}$ is unique, there exists a unique minimal SDA that represents X. Recall that the set of states of this minimal automaton is given by $\{\sigma^{-1}.\mathcal{L}\}$. From lemma 1, we deduce that $Q(X) = \{\rho(\sigma^{-1}.\mathcal{L})\}$. Therefore, $Q(X)$ is finite and by uniqueness of the minimal automaton, $\mathcal{A}(X)$ is the unique minimal SDA that represents X. □

Remark 3. Find a theorem equivalent to the previous one for the class of NDD seems difficult.

4   Polynomial Time Computation of $Pre_S(X')$

For counters systems S, the computation of the set of immediate predecessors $Pre_S(X')$ for the SDA representation, is proved to be polynomial in time.

Definition 5. *A saturated digit automaton $\mathcal{A}$ represents a function $f : \mathbb{N}^m \to \mathbb{N}^m$ if it represents the following set of $\mathbb{N}^{2m}$:*

$$\{(x_1, x'_1, \ldots, x_m, x'_m); \ (x'_1, \ldots, x'_m) = f((x_1, \ldots, x_m))\}$$

Naturally, a function f is said *SDA-definable* if there exists a saturated digit automaton that represents f.

Remark 4. The previous definition can be extended to binary relation.

Definition 6. *A counters system S is a tuple $S = (\mathbb{N}^m, \Sigma, (f_a)_{a \in \Sigma})$ where Σ is a finite set of actions and $f_a : \mathbb{N}^m \to \mathbb{N}^m$ is a SDA-definable function.*

Remark 5. In practice, the function f_a is given by Presburger formula. However, remark 2 shows that any Presburger definable set is SDA-definable.

The set of immediate predecessors of $X' \subseteq \mathbb{N}^m$ is naturally defined by $Pre_S(X') = \bigcup_{a \in \Sigma} f_a^{-1}(X')$.

Remark 6. Any counter automaton can be "simulated" by a counter system just by added another counter bounded by the number of control states.

The size $|S|$ of an effective counters system S represented by a sequence of SDA $(\mathcal{A}_a)_{a \in \Sigma}$ is $|S| = \sum_{a \in \Sigma} |\mathcal{A}_a|$.

Theorem 2. *Let $g : \mathbb{N}^m \to \mathbb{N}^m$ and $X' \subseteq \mathbb{N}^m$ be represented respectively by the SDA $\mathcal{A}^f$ and by the SDA $\mathcal{A}'$. The set $g^{-1}(X')$ can be effectively represented by a SDA in time $O(r.(|\mathcal{A}'| + 1)^{|\mathcal{A}^g|})$.*

Proof. Let us denote by $Q_\perp^g$ the set of states $q^g \in Q^g$ such that there does not exist a path from q^g to a final state. Symmetrically, we define $Q'_\perp$. Let $K = (Q_\perp^g \times Q') \cup (Q^g \times Q'_\perp)$. We are going to prove that the following automaton $\mathcal{A} = (Q, \Sigma_r, \delta, \{q_0\}, F)$ is a SDA that represents $g^{-1}(X)$:

$$\begin{cases} Q = \mathcal{P}(Q' \times Q^g) \\ \delta(q, b) = \{(\delta'(q', b'), \delta^g(q^g, bb')); \ (q', q^g) \in q; \ b' \in \Sigma_r\} \backslash K \\ q_0 = \{(q'_0, q_0^g)\} \backslash K \\ F = \{q_f \in Q; \ \exists q \in Q; \ q \cap (F' \times F^g) \neq \emptyset; \ q_f \xrightarrow{0^*} q_f\} \end{cases}$$

Let us prove that the number of reachable states of $\mathcal{A}$ is bounded by $(|Q'|+1)^{|Q^g|}$. Let q be a reachable state of $\mathcal{A}$ and let us prove that for any (q'_1, q^g) and (q'_2, q^g) in q, we have $q'_1 = q'_2$. There exists a sequence $b_1, \ldots, b_n$ in Σ_r such that $q =$

$\delta(q_0, b_1 \ldots b_n)$. By definition of $\mathcal{A}$, there exists two sequences $b'_{1,1}, \ldots b'_{n,1}$ and $b'_{1,2}, \ldots, b'_{n,2}$ in Σ_r such that

$$\begin{cases} q^g = \delta^g(q_0^g, b_1 b'_{1,1} \ldots b_n b'_{n,1}) \\ q^g = \delta^g(q_0^g, b_1 b'_{1,2} \ldots b_n b'_{n,2}) \\ q'_1 = \delta'(q'_0, b'_{1,1} \ldots b'_{n,1}) \\ q'_2 = \delta'(q'_0, b'_{1,2} \ldots b'_{n,2}) \end{cases}$$

As (q^g, q'_1) is not in K, we have $q_g \notin Q_\perp^g$. So, there exists a word $\sigma \in \Sigma_r^*$ and a final state $q_f^g \in F^g$ such that $q^g \xrightarrow{\sigma} q_f^g$ is an accepting path in $\mathcal{A}^g$. As $\mathcal{A}^g$ is a SDA, by replacing σ by $\sigma.0$, we can assume that $|\sigma|$ is even. We have $\sigma = b_{n+1} b'_{n+1} \ldots b_k b'_k$ where $b_i, b'_i \in \Sigma_r$. Let x'_1 x'_2 and x be the vectors in $\mathbb{N}^m$ defined by:

$$\begin{cases} x'_1 = \rho_m(b'_{1,1} \ldots b'_{n,1} b'_{n+1} \ldots b'_k) \\ x'_2 = \rho_m(b'_{1,2} \ldots b'_{n,2} b'_{n+1} \ldots b'_k) \\ x = \rho_m(b_1 \ldots b_k) \end{cases}$$

As $b_1 b'_{1,1} \ldots b_n b'_{n,1} b_{n+1} b'_{n+1} \ldots b_k b'_k$ and $b_1 b'_{1,2} \ldots b_n b'_{n,2} b_{n+1} b'_{n+1} \ldots b_k b'_k$ are two accepted words in $\mathcal{L}(\mathcal{A}^g)$, we have $x'_1 = g(x) = x'_2$. As $b'_{1,1} \ldots b'_{n,1} b'_{n+1} \ldots b'_k$ and $b'_{1,2} \ldots b'_{n,2} b'_{n+1} \ldots b'_k$ are two words with the same length that represent the same vector $x'_1 = x'_2$, we have $b'_{1,1} \ldots b'_{n,1} b'_{n+1} \ldots b'_k = b'_{1,2} \ldots b'_{n,2} b'_{n+1} \ldots b'_k$. In particular, we have proved that $q'_1 = \delta'(q'_0, b'_{1,1} \ldots b'_{n,1}) = \delta'(q'_0, b'_{1,2} \ldots b'_{n,2}) = q'_2$. Therefore, the number of reachable states of $\mathcal{A}$ is bounded by $(|Q'| + 1)^{|Q^g|}$.

Now, let us prove that $\mathcal{L}(\mathcal{A}) \subseteq \rho_m^{-1}(g^{-1}(X))$. Consider an accepting path $q \xrightarrow{w} q_f$ in $\mathcal{A}$. There exists a path $q_f \xrightarrow{0^i} q$ such that $q \cap (F' \times F^g) \neq \emptyset$. Let us decompose the word $w.0^i$ as a sequence of digits $w.0^i = b_1 \ldots . b_n$. There exists a word $b'_1 \ldots b'_n$ such that $b_1 b'_1 \ldots b_n b'_n \in \mathcal{L}(\mathcal{A}^g)$ and such that $b'_1 \ldots b'_n \in \mathcal{L}(\mathcal{A}')$. Let $x = \rho_m(b_1 \ldots b_m)$ and $x' = \rho_m(b'_1 \ldots b'_m)$. Remark that $\rho_{2.m}(b_1 b'_1 \ldots b_n b'_n) = (x_1, x'_1, \ldots, x_m, x'_m)$. Therefore $x' = g(x)$. Moreover, from $b'_1 \ldots b'_n \in \mathcal{L}(\mathcal{A}')$, we deduce $x' \in X'$. So $x \in g^{-1}(X)$. As $\rho_m(w) = \rho_m(w.0^i) = \rho_m(b_1 \ldots b_n)$, we have proved $w \in \rho_m^{-1}(g^{-1}(X))$.

Finally, let us prove that $\rho_m^{-1}(g^{-1}(X)) \subseteq \mathcal{L}(\mathcal{A})$. Consider $w \in \rho^{-1}(g^{-1}(X'))$ and let $x = \rho_m(w)$ and $x' = g(x)$. There exists a word $\sigma \in \mathcal{L}(\mathcal{A}^g)$ such that $\rho_{2.m}(\sigma) = (x_1, x'_1, \ldots, x_m, x'_m)$. As $\mathcal{A}^g$ is a SDA, we can replace σ by $\sigma.0^j$ for any $j \geq 0$. In particular, $|\sigma|$ can be assumed even and greater than $2.|w|$. Let us write $\sigma = b_1 b'_1 \ldots b_n b'_n$ such that $b_i, b'_i \in \Sigma_r$ and remark that $x = \rho_m(b_1 \ldots b_n)$ and $x' = \rho_m(b'_1 \ldots b'_n)$. Hence $q_0 \xrightarrow{b_1 \ldots b_n} q$ is a path in $\mathcal{A}$ such that $q \cap (F' \times F^g) \neq \emptyset$. As $\rho_m(b_1 \ldots b_n) = \rho_m(w)$ and $|w| \leq n$, there exists $i \geq 0$ such that $b_1 \ldots b_n = w.0^i$. By definition of F, we have $w \in \mathcal{L}(\mathcal{A})$. $\square$

Corollary 1. *Let S be a counters system. The minimal SDA $\mathcal{A}(\text{Pres}(X'))$ is computable in polynomial time in function of $\mathcal{A}(X')$.*

Proof. Just remark that $\text{Pres}(X') = \bigcup_{a \in \Sigma} f_a^{-1}(X')$. By using an Hopcroft algorithm [Hop71], we can compute the minimal SDA $\mathcal{A}(\text{Pres}(X'))$ from a SDA $\mathcal{A}$ that represents $\text{Pres}(X')$ in time $O(|\mathcal{A}|.\ln(|\mathcal{A}|))$. $\square$

The previous corollary shows that $\mathcal{A}(\mathrm{Pre}_S(X'))$ can be computed in polynomial time in the size of $\mathcal{A}(X')$ for counters system S. Remark that the complexity is also exponential in $|S|$. However, in the computation of $\mathrm{Pre}_S^{\leq k}(X')$, the size $|S|$ does not depend on k. Moreover, in practice, the size of S is small compared to the size of $\mathcal{A}(X')$.

Remark 7. In the case of the computation of the immediate successors $\mathrm{Post}_S(X) = \bigcup_{a \in \Sigma} f_a(X)$, the number of states of $\mathcal{A}(\mathrm{Post}_S(X))$ can be exponential in the number of states of $\mathcal{A}(X)$. This exponential blow up provides from the fact that $f(X)$ correspond to a "projection" for the function $f : \mathbb{N}^m \to \mathbb{N}^m$ defined by $f(x_1, \dots, x_m) = (0, x_2, \dots, x_m)$ ([Ler03b]).

5   Asymptotic Size of $\mathrm{Pre}_S^{\leq k}(X')$

The polynomial time computation of $\mathrm{Pre}_S(X')$ is a first step to be able to efficiently compute the set of predecessors in k steps. If each step multiplies the size of the SDA by 2, after k steps, the size of the SDA that represents the set of predecessors is greater than 2^k. In this section, we give sufficient conditions such that this exponential blow up cannot appear.

Definition 7. *A counters system S is affine if for any $a \in \Sigma$, there exists an affine function $f_a : D_a \to \mathbb{N}^m$, $D_a \subseteq \mathbb{N}^m$, such that $x\mathcal{R}_a x'$ iff $x' = f_a(x)$.*

Precisely, we show that if D_a and X' are definable in the interval logic (almost all the counters systems studied in practice, satisfy this condition [Str98], [Del00], [BB02], [FS01], [FL02]), the asymptotic size in k of $\mathcal{A}(\mathrm{Pre}_S^{\leq k}(X'))$ is polynomial in k.

The size of $\mathcal{A}(X)$ is first bounded in the *granularity* of the set X defined as bellow.

Definition 8. *The granularity of an interval-definable set X is the least integer $\mathrm{gran}(X) \geq 0$, such that X is the set of vectors accepted by a formula in the interval logic with $c < \mathrm{gran}(X)$:*

$$\phi := v_i = c|\phi \vee \phi|\phi \wedge \phi|\neg\phi|true|false$$

Proposition 2. *For any interval-definable set X, we have:*

$$|\mathcal{A}(X)| \leq (r.\mathrm{gran}(X))^m + 2^{3^m}$$

Proof. Recall that the size of the SDA $\mathcal{A}(X)$ is equal to the number of elements in $\{\gamma_\sigma^{-1}(X); \sigma \in \Sigma_r^*\}$. We first prove that for any word $\sigma \in (\Sigma_r^m)^*$ and for any interval-definable set X such that $r^{|\sigma|/m} \geq \mathrm{gran}(X)$, the granularity of $\gamma_\sigma^{-1}(X)$ is bounded by 1. Next, we show that there exists at most 2^{3^m} interval-definable sets whose the granularity is bounded by 1. Finally, from these two results, we prove the proposition.

So, let us first consider $\sigma \in (\Sigma_r^m)^*$ and an interval-definable set X such that $r^{|\sigma|/m} \geq \mathrm{gran}(X)$ and let us prove that $\mathrm{gran}(\gamma_\sigma^{-1}(X)) \leq 1$. Remark that if $\mathrm{gran}(X) = 0$ then $X = \mathbb{N}^m$ or $X = \emptyset$. As in these two cases, we have $|\mathcal{A}(X)| = 1$, we can assume that $\mathrm{gran}(X) \geq 1$. From $\gamma_\sigma^{-1}(X \cap Y) = \gamma_\sigma^{-1}(X) \cap \gamma_\sigma^{-1}(Y)$, $\gamma_\sigma^{-1}(\mathbb{N}^m \backslash X) = \mathbb{N}^m \backslash \gamma_\sigma^{-1}(X)$, we can assume that there exists $i \in \{1, \ldots, m\}$ such that $X = \{x \in \mathbb{N}^m; \ x_i = \mathrm{gran}(X) - 1\}$. We have $\gamma_\sigma^{-1}(X) = \{x \in \mathbb{N}^m; \ (\gamma_\sigma(x))_i = \mathrm{gran}(X) - 1\} = \{x \in \mathbb{N}^m; \ x_i = c\}$ where $c = \frac{\mathrm{gran}(X) - 1 - \rho_m(\sigma)}{r^{|\sigma|/m}} < 1$. Remark that if $c \notin \mathbb{N}$ then $\gamma_\sigma^{-1}(X) = \emptyset$ and if $c \in \mathbb{N}$ then $c = 0$. In these two cases, we have proved that $\mathrm{gran}(\gamma_\sigma^{-1}(X)) \leq 1$.

Next, let us prove that there exists at most 2^{3^m} interval-definable sets X such that $\mathrm{gran}(X) \leq 1$. Remark that such a set is a finite union of sets defined by a formula of the form $\bigwedge_{i \in I}(x_i = 0) \bigvee_{i' \in I'}(x_{i'} \neq 0)$ where $I, I' \subseteq \{1, \ldots, m\}$ and $I \cap I' = \emptyset$. So, there exists at most 2^{3^m} interval-definable sets whose the granularity is bounded by 1.

Finally, let X be an interval-definable set such that $\mathrm{gran}(X) \geq 1$ and consider $k \geq 0$ such that $r^k \geq \mathrm{gran}(X) \geq r^{k-1}$. The number of states of $\mathcal{A}(X)$ is bounded by $\sum_{i=0}^{m.k-1} r^i + 2^{3^m} \leq (r.\mathrm{gran}(X))^m + 2^{3^m}$. $\qquad\square$

Next, we characterize the affine function f such that the inverse image of an interval-definable set remains interval-definable.

Definition 9. *Let X be a subset of $\mathbb{N}^m$, $n \geq 0$ and $I \subseteq \{1, \ldots, m\}$, the set $X_{I,n}$ is defined by:*

$$X_{I,n} = \{x \in X; \ \forall i \in I, x_i = n; \ \forall i \notin I, x_i < n\}$$

Proposition 3. *For any interval-definable set X and for any $n \geq \mathrm{gran}(X)$, we have:*

$$X = \bigcup_{I \subseteq \{1, \ldots, m\}} X_{I,n} + \sum_{i \in I} \mathbb{N}.\boldsymbol{e}_i$$

Proof. Let us consider a formula ϕ in the logic $\phi := v_i = c|\phi \vee \phi|\phi \wedge \phi|\neg\phi|true|false$ such that $c < \mathrm{gran}(X)$ and such that the set of vectors satisfying ϕ is equal to X. By developing ϕ, we can assume that ϕ is a finite disjunction of formula of the form $\bigwedge_{j \in J_{\neq}}(v_j \neq c_j) \bigwedge_{j \in J_=}(v_j = c_j)$ where $J_{\neq} \cap J_= = \emptyset$ and $c_j < \mathrm{gran}(X)$. Remark that we can assume that $\phi = \bigwedge_{j \in J_{\neq}}(v_j \neq c_j) \bigwedge_{j \in J_=}(v_j = c_j)$ to prove the proposition.

Let $x \in X$ and let us prove that $x \in \bigcup_{I \subseteq \{1, \ldots, m\}} X_{I,n} + \sum_{i \in I} \mathbb{N}.\boldsymbol{e}_i$. Let us consider the set $I = \{i \in \{1, \ldots, m\}; \ x_i \geq n\}$. As for any $j \in J_=$, we have $x_j = c_j < \mathrm{gran}(X)$, we deduce $I \subseteq \{1, \ldots, m\} \backslash J_=$. Let us consider the vector $y \in \mathbb{N}^m$ defined by $y_i = n$ if $i \in I$ and $y_i = x_i$ otherwise. As x satisfies ϕ, the vector y also satisfies ϕ. Therefore $y \in X_{I,n}$. From $x \in y + \sum_{i \in I} \mathbb{N}.\boldsymbol{e}_i$, we deduce the inclusion $X \subseteq \bigcup_{I \subseteq \{1, \ldots, m\}} X_{I,n} + \sum_{i \in I} \mathbb{N}.\boldsymbol{e}_i$. Let us prove the converse inclusion. Let $x \in \bigcup_{I \subseteq \{1, \ldots, m\}} X_{I,n} + \sum_{i \in I} \mathbb{N}.\boldsymbol{e}_i$. There exists $I \subseteq \{1, \ldots, m\}$ such that $x \in X_{I,n} + \sum_{i \in I} \mathbb{N}.\boldsymbol{e}_i$. Let $y \in X_{I,n}$ such that $x \in y + \sum_{i \in I} \mathbb{N}.\boldsymbol{e}_i$. As $y \in X_{I,n} \subseteq X$, y satisfies ϕ. As for any $i \in I$, we have $y_i = n$, we have $I \subseteq \{1, \ldots, m\} \backslash J_=$. From $x \in y + \sum_{i \in I} \mathbb{N}.\boldsymbol{e}_i$, we deduce that x satisfies ϕ. Therefore $x \in X$. $\qquad\square$

Proposition 4. *Let $f : D \to \mathbb{N}^m$ with $D \subseteq \mathbb{N}^m$ be an affine function. The two following assertions are equivalent:*

- *D is interval-definable.*
- *For any interval-definable set X', $f^{-1}(X')$ is interval-definable.*

Moreover, in this case, we have $\operatorname{gran}(f^{-1}(X')) \leq \operatorname{gran}(X') + \operatorname{gran}(D)$.

Proof. Remark that if $f^{-1}(X')$ is interval-definable for any interval-definable set X', then in particular, as $\mathbb{N}^m$ is interval-definable, the definition domain $D = f^{-1}(\mathbb{N}^m)$ is also interval-definable. So let us consider an affine function $f : D \to \mathbb{N}^m$ such that $D \subseteq \mathbb{N}^m$ is interval-definable and let X' be an interval-definable set. We first prove that we can assume that $\operatorname{gran}(X') \geq 1$. In fact, if $\operatorname{gran}(X') = 0$, then $X' = \emptyset$ or $X' = \mathbb{N}^m$. In the first case, we have $f^{-1}(X') = \emptyset$ and the set $f^{-1}(X')$ is an interval-definable set such that $\operatorname{gran}(f^{-1}(X')) = 0 \leq \operatorname{gran}(X') + \operatorname{gran}(D)$ and in the second case, we have $f^{-1}(X') = D$ and the set $f^{-1}(X')$ is interval-definable and verify $\operatorname{gran}(f^{-1}(X')) = \operatorname{gran}(D) \leq \operatorname{gran}(X') + \operatorname{gran}(D)$. So, we can assume that $\operatorname{gran}(X') \geq 1$.

As f is an affine function, there exists a square matrix $M \in \mathcal{M}_m(\mathbb{Q})$ and a vector $v \in \mathbb{Q}^m$ such that $f(x) = M.x + v$ for any $x \in D$. Proposition 3 shows that the sets X' and D can be decomposed as follow where $D_I = D_{I,\operatorname{gran}(D)}$ and $X'_I = X'_{I,\operatorname{gran}(X')}$:

$$D = \bigcup_{J \subseteq \{1,\dots,m\}} D_J + \sum_{j \in J} \mathbb{N}.\mathbf{e}_j$$

$$X' = \bigcup_{I \subseteq \{1,\dots,m\}} X'_I + \sum_{i \in I} \mathbb{N}.\mathbf{e}_i$$

We have:

$$
\begin{aligned}
&f^{-1}(X') \\
&= \bigcup_{J \subseteq \{1,\dots,m\}} \{x \in D_J + \sum_{j \in J} \mathbb{N}.\mathbf{e}_j; \ f(x) \in X'\} \\
&= \bigcup_{J \subseteq \{1,\dots,m\}} \bigcup_{d \in D_J} d + \{x \in \sum_{j \in J} \mathbb{N}.\mathbf{e}_j; \ f(d) + M.x \in X'\} \\
&= \bigcup_{\substack{J \subseteq \{1,\dots,m\} \\ I \subseteq \{1,\dots,m\}}} \bigcup_{\substack{d \in D_J \\ x' \in X'_I}} d + \{x \in \sum_{j \in J} \mathbb{N}.\mathbf{e}_j; \ f(d) + M.x \in x' + \sum_{i \in I} \mathbb{N}.\mathbf{e}_i\}
\end{aligned}
$$

Let us consider a subset J such that D_J is not empty. In this case let us consider $d \in D_J$ and remark that for every $j \in J$, we have $d + \mathbb{N}.\mathbf{e}_j \subseteq D$. Therefore $f(d) + \mathbb{N}.M.\mathbf{e}_j \subseteq \mathbb{N}^m$. So, for every $j \in J$ and for every $i \in \{1,\dots,m\}$ we have $M_{ij} \geq 0$.

Now, let us consider a subset I such that X'_I is not empty and consider $x' \in X'_I$. Remark that we have just to prove that the following set is interval-definable and has a granularity bounded by $\operatorname{gran}(X')$:

$$\{x \in \sum_{j \in J} \mathbb{N}.\mathbf{e}_j;\ f(d) + M.x \in x' + \sum_{i \in I} \mathbb{N}.\mathbf{e}_i\}$$

$$
= \bigcap_{i \notin I} \{x \in \sum_{j \in J} \mathbb{N}.\mathbf{e}_j;\ f(d)_i + \sum_{j \in J} M_{ij}.x_j = x'_i\}
$$
$$
\bigcap_{i \in I}\ \bigcap_{c_i \in \{0, \dots, x'_i - 1\}} \{x \in \sum_{j \in J} \mathbb{N}.\mathbf{e}_j;\ f(d)_i + \sum_{j \in J} M_{ij}.x_j \neq c_i\}
$$

Remark that for every $i \notin I$, we have $x'_i - f(d)_i < \mathrm{gran}(X')$ and for any $i \in I$ and for any $c_i \in \{0, \dots, x'_i - 1\}$, we have $c_i - f(d)_i < x'_i = \mathrm{gran}(X')$. Let us consider the sequence $(\alpha_j)_{j \in \{1, \dots, m\}}$ in $\mathbb{N}$ defined by $\alpha_j = M_{ij}$ if $j \in J$ and $\alpha_j = 0$ otherwise. We have just to prove that for every $k < \mathrm{gran}(X')$ the following set is interval-definable and has a granularity bounded by $\mathrm{gran}(X')$:

$$\{x \in \sum_{j \in J} \mathbb{N}.\mathbf{e}_j;\ \sum_{j \in J} \alpha_j.x_j = k\} = \left(\sum_{j \in J} \mathbb{N}.\mathbf{e}_j\right) \cap \{x \in \mathbb{N}^m;\ \sum_{j=1}^{m} \alpha_j.x_j = k\}$$

The granularity of the set $\sum_{j \in J} \mathbb{N}.\mathbf{e}_j$ is bounded by 1 and as $\mathrm{gran}(X') \geq 1$, we have just to prove that for any sequence $(\alpha_j)_{j \in \{1, \dots, m\}}$ in $\mathbb{N}$ and for any $k < \mathrm{gran}(X')$, the following set has a granularity bounded by $\mathrm{gran}(X')$:

$$\{x \in \mathbb{N}^m;\ \sum_{j=1}^{m} \alpha_j.x_j = k\}$$

Let us consider the set $J' = \{j \in \{1, \dots, m\};\ \alpha_j \geq 1\}$ and let $Y = \{y \in \mathbb{N}^m;\ \forall j \notin J\ y_j = 0;\ \sum_{j=1}^{m} \alpha_j.y_j = k\}$. Remark that for any $y \in Y$ and for any $i \in \{1, \dots, m\}$, we have $y_j \leq k$. Therefore Y is finite. Moreover, from $\{x \in \mathbb{N}^m;\ \sum_{j=1}^{m} \alpha_j.x_j = k\} = Y + \sum_{j \notin J'} \mathbb{N}.\mathbf{e}_j$, we are done.   □

We can now bound the asymptotic size of $\mathcal{A}(\mathrm{Pre}_S^{\leq k}(X'))$ in function of k.

Theorem 3. *Let S be an affine counters system with interval-definable definition domains and let X' be an interval-definable set. The asymptotic size in k of $\mathrm{Pre}_S^{\leq k}(X')$ is in $O(k^m)$.*

Proof. Let $c_S = \max_{a \in \Sigma} \mathrm{gran}(D_a)$. From proposition 4, we deduce that for an interval-definable set X', the set $\mathrm{Pre}_S(X')$ is interval-definable and $\mathrm{gran}(\mathrm{Pre}_S(X')) \leq \mathrm{gran}(X') + c_S$. Therefore $\mathrm{gran}(\mathrm{Pre}_S^{\leq k}(X')) \leq c' + k.c_S$ where $c' = \mathrm{gran}(X')$. From the proposition 2, we deduce $|\mathcal{A}(\mathrm{Pre}_S^{\leq k}(X'))| \leq (r.(c' + c_S.k))^m + 2^{3^m}$.   □

Corollary 2. *Let S be an affine counters system with interval-definable definition domains and X' be an interval-definable set. We can compute in polynomial time in k the minimal SDA $\mathcal{A}(\mathrm{Pre}_S^{\leq k}(X'))$.*

Remark 8. When the sets D_a and X' are *upward closed* (an upward closed set X is a subset of $\mathbb{N}^m$ such that $X + \mathbb{N}^m = X$), the sequence $\mathrm{Pre}_S^{\leq k}(X')$ converges as any increasing sequence of upward closed sets.

Remark 9. The bound $O(k^m)$ follows directly from proposition 2. In the proof of these proposition, we have assumed that no sharing appears in the SDA representing an interval-definable set. However, in practice, SDA are like BDD and the asymptotic size of $\mathcal{A}(\mathrm{Pre}_S^{\leq k}(X'))$ is in $O(m.\ln(k))$ rather than $O(k^m)$.

When the sets D_a and X' are just Presburger-definable, the following proposition 5 shows that the asymptotic size in k of $\mathcal{A}(\mathrm{Pre}_S^{\leq k}(X'))$ may be exponential.

Proposition 5. *Let* $S = (\mathbb{N}^2, \{a\}, (f_a))$ *where* $f_a(x_1, x_2) = (r.x_1, x_2)$ *over* $D_a = \mathbb{N}^2$, *and let* $X' = \{(x'_1, x'_2) \in \mathbb{N}^2; \ x'_1 = x'_2\}$. *For any integer* $k \geq 0$, *we have:*

$$|\mathcal{A}(\mathrm{Pre}_S^{\leq k}(X'))| \geq r^{k-1}$$

Proof. Let X_i be the subset of $\mathbb{N}^m$ defined for any $i \geq 0$ by $X_i = \{(x, r^i.x); \ x \in \mathbb{N}\}$. We have $\mathrm{Pre}_S^{\leq k}(X') = \bigcup_{i=0}^k X_i$. Assume by contradiction that there exists a SDA $\mathcal{A} = (Q, \Sigma_r, \delta, \{q_0\}, F)$ that represents $\mathrm{Pre}_S^{\leq k}(X')$ and such that $\mathrm{card}(Q) < r^{k-1}$. Let us consider the finite language $\mathcal{L} = (00 + \cdots + (r-1)0)^{k-1}10$. For any word $\sigma \in \mathcal{L}$, we have $\delta(q_0, \sigma) \in Q$. As $\mathrm{card}(Q) < r^{k-1} = \mathrm{card}(\mathcal{L})$, there exist two words $\sigma \neq \sigma'$ in $\mathcal{L}$ such that $\delta(q_0, \sigma) = \delta(q_0, \sigma')$. Let $y, y' \in \mathbb{N}$ such that $\rho_2(\sigma) = (y, 0)$ and $\rho_2(\sigma') = (y', 0)$. We have $y, y' \in \{r^{k-1}, \ldots, r^k - 1\}$. Let us consider a word $w \in \Sigma_r^*$ such that $\rho_2(w) = (0, y)$. From $\rho_2(\sigma.w) = \rho_2(\sigma) + r^k.\rho_2(w) = (y, r^k.y)$, we deduce that $\rho_2(\sigma.w) \in X_k$. As $\mathcal{A}$ is a SDA that represents $\bigcup_{i=0}^k X_i$, we have proved that $\sigma.w \in \mathcal{L}(\mathcal{A})$. From $\delta(q_0, \sigma) = \delta(q_0, \sigma')$, we deduce that $\sigma'.w \in \mathcal{L}(\mathcal{A})$. Therefore $(y', r^k.y) = \rho_2(\sigma'.w) \in \bigcup_{i=0}^k X_i$. There exists $i \in \{0, \ldots, k\}$ such that $(y', r^k.y) \in X_i$. We have $r^k.y = r^i.y'$. From $y \geq r^{k-1}$ and $y' < r^k$, we deduce $i > k - 1$. Hence $i = k$ and we have proved that $y = y'$. As σ and σ' have the same length and as $\rho_2(\sigma) = \rho_2(\sigma')$, we have $\sigma = \sigma'$. We have a contradiction. □

References

[AAB00]   Aurore Annichini, Eugene Asarin, and Ahmed Bouajjani. Symbolic techniques for parametric reasoning about counter and clock systems. In *Proc. 12th Int. Conf. Computer Aided Verification (CAV'2000), Chicago, IL, USA, July 2000*, volume 1855 of *Lecture Notes in Computer Science*, pages 419–434. Springer, 2000.

[ABJ98]   Parosh Aziz Abdulla, Ahmed Bouajjani, and Bengt Jonsson. On-the-fly analysis of systems with unbounded, lossy FIFO channels. In *Proc. 10th Int. Conf. Computer Aided Verification (CAV'98), Vancouver, BC, Canada, June-July 1998*, volume 1427 of *Lecture Notes in Computer Science*, pages 305–318. Springer, 1998.

[ABS01]   Aurore Annichini, Ahmed Bouajjani, and Mihaela Sighireanu. TReX: A
           tool for reachability analysis of complex systems. In *Proc. 13th Int. Conf.
           Computer Aided Verification (CAV'2001), Paris, France, July 2001*, vol-
           ume 2102 of *Lecture Notes in Computer Science*, pages 368–372. Springer,
           2001.
[Alv]   ALV homepage. http://www.cs.ucsb.edu/~bultan/composite/.
[Bab]   BABYLON homepage.
           http://www.ulb.ac.be/di/ssd/lvbegin/CST/-index.html.
[BB02]   Constantinos Bartzis and Tevfik Bultan. Efficient symbolic representations
           for arithmetic constraints in verification. Technical Report ucsb cs:TR-
           2002-16, University of California, Santa Barbara, Computer Science, 2002.
[BB03]   Constantinos Bartziz and Tevfik Bultan. Efficient image computation in
           infinite state model checking. In *Proc. 15th Int. Conf. Computer Aided
           Verification (CAV'2003), Boulder, CO, USA, July 2003*, volume 2725 of
           Lecture Notes in Computer Science, pages 249–261. Springer, 2003.
[BC96]   Alexandre Boudet and Hubert Comon. Diophantine equations, Presburger
           arithmetic and finite automata. In *Proc. 21st Int. Coll. on Trees in Algebra
           and Programming (CAAP'96), Linköping, Sweden, Apr. 1996*, volume 1059
           of *Lecture Notes in Computer Science*, pages 30–43. Springer, 1996.
[BEF+ 00] A. Bouajjani, J. Esparza, A. Finkel, O. Maler, P. Rossmanith, B. Willems,
           and P. Wolper. An efficient automata approach to some problems on
           context-free grammars. *Information Processing Letters*, 74(5–6):221–227,
           2000.
[Ber77]   Leonard Berman. Precise bounds for Presburger arithmetic and the reals
           with addition: Preliminary report. In *Proc. 18th IEEE Symp. Foundations
           of Computer Science (FOCS'77), Providence, RI, USA, Oct.-Nov. 1977*,
           pages 95–99, Providence, Rhode Island, 31 October–2 November 1977.
           IEEE.
[BF00]   J.-P. Bodeveix and M. Filali. FMona: a tool for expressing validation tech-
           niques over infinite state systems. In *Proc. 6th Int. Conf. Tools and Al-
           gorithms for the Construction and Analysis of Systems (TACAS'2000),
           Berlin, Germany, Mar.-Apr. 2000*, volume 1785 of *Lecture Notes in Com-
           puter Science*, pages 204–219. Springer, 2000.
[BFLP03]   Sébastien Bardin, Alain Finkel, Jérôme Leroux, and Laure Petrucci. FAST:
           Fast Acceleration of Symbolic Transition systems. In *Proc. 15th Int.
           Conf. Computer Aided Verification (CAV'2003), Boulder, CO, USA, July
           2003*, volume 2725 of *Lecture Notes in Computer Science*, pages 118–121.
           Springer, 2003.
[BGP97]   Tevfik Bultan, Richard Gerber, and William Pugh. Symbolic model-
           checking of infinite state systems using Presburger arithmetic. In *Proc.
           9th Int. Conf. Computer Aided Verification (CAV'97), Haifa, Israel, June
           1997*, volume 1254 of *Lecture Notes in Computer Science*, pages 400–411.
           Springer, 1997.
[BH99]   Ahmed Bouajjani and Peter Habermehl. Symbolic reachability analysis of
           FIFO-channel systems with nonregular sets of configurations. *Theoretical
           Computer Science*, 221(1–2):211–250, 1999.
[Boi]   Bernard Boigelot. On iterating linear transformations over recognizable
           sets of integers. *Theoretical Computer Science*. To appear.
[Boi98]   Bernard Boigelot. *Symbolic Methods for Exploring Infinite State Spaces*.
           PhD thesis, Université de Liège, 1998.

[Bra]   BRAIN homepage.
            http://www.cs.man.ac.uk/~voronkov/BRAIN/index.html.
[Del00]   Gorgio Delzanno. Automatic verification of parameterized cache coherence protocols. In *Proc. 12th Int. Conf. Computer Aided Verification (CAV'2000), Chicago, IL, USA, July 2000*, volume 1855 of *Lecture Notes in Computer Science*, pages 53–68. Springer, 2000.
[DFS98]   Catherine Dufourd, Alain Finkel, and Philippe Schnoebelen. Reset nets between decidability and undecidability. In *Proc. 25th Int. Coll. Automata, Languages, and Programming (ICALP'98), Aalborg, Denmark, July 1998*, volume 1443 of *Lecture Notes in Computer Science*, pages 103–115. Springer, 1998.
[DRV01]   Gorgio Delzanno, Jean-Francois Raskin, and Laurent Van Begin. Attacking symbolic state explosion. In *Proc. 13th Int. Conf. Computer Aided Verification (CAV'2001), Paris, France, July 2001*, volume 2102 of *Lecture Notes in Computer Science*, pages 298–310. Springer, 2001.
[Fas]   FAST homepage. http://www.lsv.ens-cachan.fr/fast/.
[FL02]   Alain Finkel and Jérôme Leroux. How to compose Presburger-accelerations: Applications to broadcast protocols. In *Proc. 22nd Conf. Found. of Software Technology and Theor. Comp. Sci. (FST&TCS'2002), Kanpur, India, Dec. 2002*, volume 2556 of *Lecture Notes in Computer Science*, pages 145–156. Springer, 2002.
[FMP99]   Alain Finkel, Pierre McKenzie, and Claudine Picaronny. A well-structured framework for analysing Petri nets extensions. Research Report LSV-99-2, Lab. Specification and Verification, ENS de Cachan, Cachan, France, February 1999.
[FO97]   Laurent Fribourg and Hans Olsén. Proving safety properties of infinite state systems by compilation into Presburger arithmetic. In *Proc. 8th Int. Conf. Concurrency Theory (CONCUR'97), Warsaw, Poland, Jul. 1997*, volume 1243 of *Lecture Notes in Computer Science*, pages 213–227. Springer, 1997.
[FPS00]   Alain Finkel, S. Purushothaman Iyer, and Grégoire Sutre. Well-abstracted transition systems. In *Proc. 11th Int. Conf. Concurrency Theory (CONCUR'2000), University Park, PA, USA, Aug. 2000*, volume 1877 of *Lecture Notes in Computer Science*, pages 566–580. Springer, 2000.
[FS01]   Alain Finkel and Phillipe Schnoebelen. Well structured transition systems everywhere! *Theoretical Computer Science*, 256(1–2):63–92, 2001.
[Hop71]   John E. Hopcroft. An $n \log n$ algorithm for minimizing the states in a finite-automaton. In Z. Kohavi, editor, *Theory of Machines and Computations*, pages 189–196. Academic Press, 1971.
[KMS02]   Nils Klarlund, A. Møller, and M. I. Schwartzbach. MONA implementation secrets. *Int. J. of Foundations Computer Science*, 13(4):571–586, 2002.
[Las]   LASH homepage.
            http://www.montefiore.ulg.ac.be/~boigelot/research/lash/.
[Ler03a]   Jérôme Leroux. The affine hull of a binary automaton is computable in polynomial time. In *5th Int. Workshop on Verification of Infinite-State Systems*, Electronic Notes in Theor. Comp. Sci., 2003. to appear.
[Ler03b]   Jérôme Leroux. *Algorithmique de la vérification des systèmes à compteurs. Approximation et accélération. Implémentation de l'outil Fast*. PhD thesis, Ecole Normale Supérieure de Cachan, Laboratoire Spécification et Vérification. CNRS UMR 8643, décembre 2003.
[Mon]   MONA homepage. http://www.brics.dk/mona/index.html.

[Sch02]   Philippe Schnoebelen. Verifying lossy channel systems has nonprimitive recursive complexity. *Information Processing Letters*, 83(5):251–261, 2002.

[Str98]   Karsten Strehl. Using interval diagram techniques for the symbolic verification of timed automata. Technical Report 53, Computer Engineering and Networks Lab (TIK), Swiss Federal Institute of Technology (ETH) Zurich, Gloriastrasse 35, CH-8092 Zurich, July 1998.

[Tre]   TREX homepage. `http://www.liafa.jussieu.fr/~sighirea/trex/`.

[WB00]   Pierre Wolper and Bernard Boigelot. On the construction of automata from linear arithmetic constraints. In *Proc. 6th Int. Conf. Tools and Algorithms for the Construction and Analysis of Systems (TACAS'2000), Berlin, Germany, Mar.-Apr. 2000*, volume 1785 of *Lecture Notes in Computer Science*, pages 1–19. Springer, 2000.

Using Fairness to Make Abstractions Work

Dragan Bošnački[1], Natalia Ioustinova[2], and Natalia Sidorova[1]

[1] Eindhoven University of Technology
Den Dolech 2, P.O. Box 513, 5612 MB Eindhoven, The Netherlands
{d.bosnacki,n.sidorova}@tue.nl
[2] Department of Software Engineering, CWI
P.O. Box 94079, 1090 GB Amsterdam, The Netherlands
Natalia.Ioustinova@cwi.nl

Abstract. Abstractions often introduce infinite traces which have no corresponding traces at the concrete level and may lead to failure of the verification. Refinement does not always help to eliminate those traces. In this paper, we consider a timer abstraction that introduces a cyclic behaviour on abstract timers and we show how one can exclude cycles by imposing a strong fairness constraint on the abstract model. By employing the fact that the loop on the abstract timer is a self-loop, we render the strong fairness constraint into a weak fairness constraint and embed it into the verification algorithm. We implemented the algorithm in the DTSPIN model checker and showed its efficiency on case studies. The same approach can be used for other data abstractions that introduce self-loops.

1 Introduction

Abstraction techniques are widely used to make the verification of complex/parameterised/infinite systems feasible. Abstraction, intuitively, means replacing one semantical model by an abstract, in general, simpler one. The abstraction needs to be *safe*, which means that every property checked to be true on the abstract model, holds for the concrete one as well. This allows the transfer of positive verification results from the abstract model to the concrete one.

The concept of safe abstraction is well-developed within the *Abstract Interpretation* framework [8,9,12]. The relation between the concrete model and its safe abstraction is formalized there as a requirement on the relation between the data operations of the concrete system and their abstract counterparts. Every value of the concrete state space is mapped by the *abstraction function* α into an abstract value that "describes" the concrete value. As an example consider the abstraction of integers into their signs in which e.g. -3 is mapped by α into **neg**. For every operation (function) f on the concrete level, an abstraction f^α needs to be defined which "mimics" f. In general, the abstraction can be *nondeterministic*. For example, addition $(+)$ over the integers is abstracted into an operation $(+^\alpha)$ such that **pos** $+^\alpha$ **neg** may yield **pos** or **neg** nondeterministically. This is formally captured by letting f^α be a function into the powerset over the domain of abstract values.

S. Graf and L. Mounier (Eds.): SPIN 2004, LNCS 2989, pp. 198–215, 2004.
© Springer-Verlag Berlin Heidelberg 2004

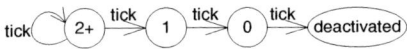

Fig. 1. Abstracted timer

Working within the Abstract Interpretation framework guarantees the preservation (in the direction from the abstract to the concrete model) of the truth of formulas of temporal logics without existential quantification over paths, e.g. $\Box L_\mu^+$ (i.e., all formulas of the μ-calculus without negation and containing only the $\Box$ operator) or next-free LTL [20,11]. Counterexamples can be spurious. In case a counterexample is found, the abstraction should be refined and the refined model is then model-checked. Such a sequence of refinements can happen to be infinite; in this case one needs different techniques to prove or disprove the property.

In this paper we consider a simple abstraction for (discrete) timers similar to the one from [10]. This abstraction is often used to prove that a property holds for all instantiations of settings of a timer that are greater than or equal to some value k. It leaves all values below k unchanged and maps all other values to the abstract value k^+. Being a deterministic operation on the concrete model, the time progress operation *tick* becomes non-deterministic on the abstract one (see Fig. 1). That introduces infinite traces with $k^+ \xrightarrow{tick} k^+$ being chosen whenever *tick* is enabled. As a result, the timer never expires, which, in general, does not correspond to any trace of the concrete model. For instance, properties of the form $\Box(\phi \to \Diamond \psi)$ get disproved on the abstract model whenever they depend on the fact that the timer in question eventually expires after being set. Refining the model by taking a greater value for k, we still keep the loop at k_{new}^+. So, refinement gives no solution to this problem.

The systems we consider are specified as parallel compositions of communicating processes. A process consists of a number of locations, variables and a number of transitions connecting the locations and changing the valuations of variables. Processes can communicate by rendezvous/buffered message passing and through shared memory. There are explicit timing constraints in the specification imposed by timer operations.

We assume that the properties are given in the universal fragment of the μ-calculus, $\Box L_\mu$, consisting of formulas in which the negations are applied only to atomic propositions. The verification methodology we propose works for any formula of the universal fragment without negation $\Box L_\mu^+$ and, under certain conditions that occur relatively often in practice (for instance, if the formula does not refer to abstracted variables (timers)), for the whole $\Box L_\mu$.[1]

---

[1] Since any $\Box L_\mu$ formula can be rewritten into an equivalent $\Box L_\mu^+$ formula, and any formula of the universal unrestricted μ-calculus has an equivalent formula in $\Box L_\mu$ (see e.g. [20]), this is not a significant loss of generality.

To exclude the infinite loop $k^+ \xrightarrow{tick} k^+$ that causes spurious counterexamples, we impose a strong fairness condition Φ^α on the abstract model, which we call *t-fairness*: "For any trace where $k^+ \xrightarrow{tick} (k-1)$ is infinitely often enabled, $k^+ \xrightarrow{tick} (k-1)$ is infinitely often taken or t is infinitely often set to a new value". We show that the concrete property Φ that corresponds to the t-fairness condition Φ^α trivially holds on the concrete model. Therefore, in order to prove a formula ϕ on the concrete system we check the validity of the formula $\Phi^\alpha \rightarrow \phi^\alpha$ on the abstract one, where ϕ^α is the corresponding abstract version of ϕ. If $\Phi^\alpha \rightarrow \phi^\alpha$ holds, we conclude that ϕ holds on the concrete system. It should be emphasized though that we use fairness only to eliminate unwanted traces in the abstract system. We do not lift fairness constraints from the concrete system to the abstract system.

By exploiting some specifics of the class of systems we are working with, we show that the strong fairness criterion can be reformulated into a weak fairness one. When one deals with explicit model checking, this is often a significant advantage because algorithmically, it could be easier to deal with the latter. Moreover, when one stays in the realm of explicit-state model checking, it is much more efficient to build the t-fairness check into the model checking algorithm, instead of expressing it as a formula. In this case, one can check for the validity of ϕ on the abstract model, assuming a built-in t-fairness check. The t-fairness check algorithm we propose here is inspired by Choueka's flag algorithm [5], and it is a version of the algorithm for weak process fairness which is implemented in SPIN.

We implemented our algorithm in DTSPIN [3] (a discrete-time version of the Spin model checker [15]) and tested the prototype implementation on some examples from the literature with encouraging results.

Related work. Counter abstractions similar to the timer abstraction we use are quite standard and they can be traced to [21]. Such abstractions are often applied to abstract (discrete) timers for the verification of *safety* properties (see e.g. [10]). We study here the verification of *liveness* properties, which gives rise to the use of fairness requirements on the abstract model.

There are several papers that deal with the problem of eliminating spurious execution sequences caused by abstraction. The closest to our approach is the theory of linear abstraction from [17] (also described in [18]). The general method of data abstraction presented there can also suffer from the problem of spurious execution sequences. To eliminate those, it is suggested to augment the system under consideration by an auxiliary monitoring module (executed synchronously with the system) and then to abstract the system obtained by such a composition. In one of the examples, [17] features a three-valued counter abstraction ($\{0, 1, 2^+\}$, using our notation). Thus, one could apply the idea of a monitoring process to eliminate extra sequences introduced by self-loops to abstract states. However, this would lead to a solution based on strong fairness on the transition level. The monitor labels the "critical" transitions with -1 or $+1$. The (strong) fairness criterion requires that if a -1 transition is executed infinitely often then also a $+1$ transition is executed infinitely often. This ensures leaving the artificial self-loops in the abstract state space introduced by the abstraction. As it was already emphasized, we show that in the context of timer abstraction, such a straightforward strong fairness can be transformed into a weak one, which is a significant advantage in the context of explicit model checking.

In [22] the authors present a three-valued counter abstraction in the context of the verification of parameterized systems, i.e., networks of N identical concurrent processes, where N is an arbitrary finite number. The counters count the number of processes at a particular control (program) location. The solution to the problem of spurious execution sequences also in this case boils down to strong fairness. To this end two new variables *from* and *to* are introduced. The unwanted self-looping sequences are eliminated by the natural requirement that for each process location l if the processes enter l infinitely many times, then they must also leave it infinitely many times.

The problem of parameterized networks of processes is also treated in [1], with a solution for the spurious sequences which resembles both of the above given approaches. The role of the monitors from [17] is played by "ranking functions", similar to the ones used to ensure the termination of sequential programs. The ranking functions count how many processes have executed a particular transition in the concrete system. By abstracting a ranking function value, similarly to [22], one obtains a separation of the "critical" transitions into "negative" and "positive" ones. The "marking algorithm" which solves the problem of spurious sequences is based on strong fairness. The efficiency remarks in favor of our solution in the context of explicit model checking would also apply to [1] and [22].

α-SPIN [13] is an extension of SPIN with abstraction. The abstraction framework of α-SPIN is based on the Abstract Interpretation theory and in that regard it is similar to our approach. However, to the best of our knowledge, there is no work that deals with spurious executions in the context of α-SPIN. Another approach to use abstractions in combination with SPIN can be found in [15].

The paper is organised as follows: In Section 2 we describe the timer abstraction and introduce the notion of t-fairness. In Section 3 we present the verification algorithm. In Section 4 we describe our implementation of t-fairness in DTSPIN. In Section 5 we discuss some experimental results. Finally in Section 6 we give some conclusions.

2   Timer Abstraction and Fairness

Currently, model checkers provide some facilities to (automatically) reduce a state space, like partial-order reduction techniques. These techniques deal mainly with the control flow of a model. On the contrary, data (values stored and transmitted in a system), whose domain is often infinite or very large, are not handled by them; it is a task of a user to present data in a verification model in a finite form of reasonable size. Depending on the property to be verified, the actual values of data may sometimes be ignored or replaced by some abstract values. In an abstract model, the operations on data are mimicked by new ones on the abstract data. The main requirement for an abstraction is that the abstract system behaviour should correctly reflect the behaviour of the original system with respect to a verification task in the sense that (1) an abstraction should capture all essential points in the system behaviour, i.e., be not "too abstract", and (2) an abstraction should be safe.

Abstraction and Abstract Interpretation Framework. We first give a brief overview of the formal aspects of abstraction (see [1,20] for more detail).

Let the semantics of a concrete system M be given with the corresponding transition system $T = (S, R)$, where S is a set of states and $R \subseteq S \times S$ is a transition relation. Given an abstract state space ${}_\alpha S$ and a total *description* relation $\rho_s \subseteq S \times {}_\alpha S$, we derive the pair of (monotonic) functions α and $\tilde{\gamma}$, where $\alpha : 2^S \to 2^{{}_\alpha S}$ is the point-wise lifting of ρ_s to the sets of states, i.e. $\alpha = post[\rho_s]$, and $\tilde{\gamma} : 2^{{}_\alpha S} \to 2^S$ is the inverse image of ρ_s, i.e. $\tilde{\gamma} = pre[\rho_s]$ (*post* and *pre* are the standard relation post- and preimage.) Intuitively, ρ_s induces a simulation relation between T and ${}_\alpha T$ (c.f. [20]). We say that ${}_\alpha T = ({}_\alpha S, {}_\alpha R)$ is an abstraction of T with regard to α, denoted as $T \sqsubseteq_\alpha {}_\alpha T$ iff $\forall Q \subseteq {}_\alpha S :$ $post[R](\tilde{\gamma}(Q)) \subseteq \tilde{\gamma}(post[{}_\alpha R](Q))$. As a consequence, a given formula ϕ holds on T if it holds on ${}_\alpha T$, under condition that $\tilde{\gamma}(\mathcal{I}^\alpha(\phi)) \subseteq \mathcal{I}(\phi)$ for corresponding interpretations $\mathcal{I}, \mathcal{I}^\alpha$. The preservation result holds for formulas of temporal logics without existential quantification over paths, e.g. $\Box L_\mu^+$ or LTL [20,11].

Given an abstraction function α, let ϕ, ϕ^α be μ-calculus formulas with the corresponding sets of atomic propositions $\mathcal{P}, \mathcal{P}^\alpha$. The semantics of ϕ and ϕ^α is given with the interpretation functions $\mathcal{I} : \mathcal{P} \to 2^S$ and $\mathcal{I}^\alpha : \mathcal{P}^\alpha \to 2^{{}_\alpha S}$, respectively. Let p^α be the proposition that corresponds to the subset $\mathcal{I}^\alpha(p) = \alpha(\mathcal{I}(p)) - \alpha(\overline{\mathcal{I}(p)})$ of the abstract state space ${}_\alpha S$. We say then that p^α is a *contracting* abstraction of p under α [17]. (Note that p^α can be considered as interpretation of p under $\mathcal{I}^\alpha : \mathcal{P} \to 2^{{}_\alpha S}$.) We call ϕ^α a contracting abstraction of formula ϕ if ϕ^α is obtained by replacing each atomic proposition p in ϕ with its contracting abstraction p^α.

Abstraction function α is *consistent*[2] with $\mathcal{I}$ iff for each $p \in \mathcal{P} : \alpha(\mathcal{I}(p)) \cap \alpha(\overline{\mathcal{I}(p)}) = \emptyset$, i.e. the images by α of the interpretations of p and $\neg p$ are not contradictory [20]. (Consistency of $\tilde{\gamma}$ with $\mathcal{I}^\alpha$ is defined analogously.) In this case, we call the contracting abstraction ϕ^α a consistent abstraction of ϕ. Note that for all $s \in S, s^\alpha \in {}_\alpha S$ such that $s^\alpha \in \alpha(\{s\})$, $s \models p$ iff $s^\alpha \models p^\alpha$ precisely when p^α is consistent, and $s \models p$ if $s^\alpha \models p^\alpha$ when p^α is contracting.

Theorem 1. *Let $T = (S, R)$ and ${}_\alpha T = ({}_\alpha S, {}_\alpha R)$ be two transition systems such that $T \sqsubseteq_\alpha {}_\alpha T$, with interpretation functions $\mathcal{I}, \mathcal{I}^\alpha$ defined as above. Given a $\Box L_\mu^+$ (resp. $\Box L_\mu$) formula ϕ, let ϕ^α be a contracting (resp. consistent with $\mathcal{I}$) abstraction of ϕ. Then ${}_\alpha T \models \phi^\alpha$ implies $T \models \phi$.*

Proof. The theorem is a corollary of Theorem 2, item 1 B, from [20]: Observe that $\tilde{\gamma}(\mathcal{I}^\alpha(p)) \subseteq \mathcal{I}(p)$ and that the consistency of α with $\mathcal{I}$ implies the consistency of $\tilde{\gamma}$ with $\mathcal{I}^\alpha$.   □

---

[2] Consistent abstraction corresponds to the notion of precise abstraction from [17].

Often it is more convenient to apply abstractions directly on the model M than on its transition system T. Such an abstraction on the level of M is well-developed within the *Abstract Interpretation* framework [8,9,12]. The requirement that Abstract Interpretation imposes on the relation between the concrete model M and its safe abstraction M^α can be formalized as a requirement on the relation between the data and the operations of the concrete system and their abstract counterparts as follows: Each value of the concrete domain Σ is mapped by a *description function* ρ_d into a value from the abstract domain $_\alpha\Sigma$. The abstract value "describes" the concrete value. We assume an ordering $\preceq$ on the abstract domain $_\alpha\Sigma$ according to the "precision" of abstract values: given a concrete value x and its abstract description $x^\alpha = \rho_d(x)$, we say that any $y^\alpha \in {_\alpha\Sigma}$ such that $x^\alpha \preceq y^\alpha$ is a *less precise* description of x.

For every operation (function) f on the concrete data domain, an abstract function f^α is defined, which "mimics" f. (For simplicity, we assume f to be a unary operation.) In general, the abstraction can be nondeterministic. This is formally captured by letting f^α be a function into the *powerset* over the domain of abstract values. The requirement of mimicking is then formally phrased with the following *safety statement*: $\forall x \in \Sigma \; \exists y \in f^\alpha(\rho_d(x)) : \rho_d(f(x)) \preceq y$.

A state s can be seen as a valuation vector $\langle v_0, v_1, \dots, v_{n-1} \rangle$ and, thus, $S = \Sigma_0 \times \dots \times \Sigma_{n-1}$, with $\Sigma_0, \dots, \Sigma_{n-1}$ being the corresponding data domains. Assuming the same set of variables as in M, the state space of M^α is $_\alpha S = {_\alpha\Sigma_0} \times \dots \times {_\alpha\Sigma_{n-1}}$. We relate S and $_\alpha S$ via the description relation, which in our case is the function $\rho_s : S \to {_\alpha S}$ defined as $\rho_s(s) = \langle \rho_{d0}(v_0), \dots, \rho_{dn-1}(v_{n-1}) \rangle$, where $\rho_{d0}, \dots, \rho_{dn-1}$ are description functions for the corresponding variables. (We assume a trivial (identity) mapping as description function for unabstracted variables.)

Let M^α be obtained by replacing each constant c and function f of M with their abstract versions, $T^\alpha = (S^\alpha, R^\alpha)$ be the transition system that corresponds to M^α, and let the safety statement hold for all functions. Obviously $S^\alpha = {_\alpha\Sigma_0} \times \dots \times {_\alpha\Sigma_{n-1}} = {_\alpha S}$. Moreover, for "usual" modelling languages, like PROMELA, $R^\alpha \supseteq {_\alpha R}$, which can be shown e.g. following 4.4.1 from [9]. This trivially implies $_\alpha T \sqsubseteq_{\alpha'} T^\alpha$, where α' is the identity function. Thus, by Theorem 1 a given formula ϕ^α is preserved from T^α via $_\alpha T$ to T, i.e., from M^α to M.

Timer Abstraction. We employ the concept of timers to specify timing conditions imposed on the system. Each timer is related to a certain process and modelled by a timer variable. We denote the value of a timer t at a state s as $[\![t]\!]_s$. A timer can be activated by setting. Timer variables are mapped to integers; -1 represents a deactivated timer and larger values stand for active timers. A setting step $set(t, e)$ leads to the change of the timer value to the value given by expression e. A predicate $expire(t)$ is *true* iff $[\![t]\!] = 0$. The transitions are assumed to be instantaneous. Time progression is modelled as a special transition called *tick* that decreases values of *all* active timers by 1 and leaves deactivated timers unmodified. Further, we refer to a segment of time separated by time progress steps as a *time slice*. We leave the semantics of time partially open here, since our approach does not depend on it. (We revisit this issue in Section 3.)

To prove that some property holds for all settings of a timer that are greater or equal to some value k, one often uses a timer abstraction similar to the one of [10]. For a timer t, the concrete domain of timer values $\Sigma = \mathbb{N} \cup \{-1\}$ is replaced with the abstract domain $_\alpha\Sigma_t = \{-1, 0, \ldots, k_t - 1, k_t^+\}$, where the value k_t is a positive value defined by the user assuming that the verification property still holds even if we do not distinguish between the values of the timer greater or equal to k_t. We overload the notation by using c $(-1 \leq c < k_t)$ as an abstract value representing the single concrete value i, while c^+ describes the set of concrete values $\{c, c+1, c+2, \ldots\}$.

The description function ρ_{d_t} is defined as $\rho_{d_t}(c) = c$, if $c < k_t$, and $\rho_{d_t}(c) = k_t^+$, otherwise. Abstract operations on timers are defined in an intuitive way: setting a timer to value x becomes setting it to value $\rho_{d_t}(x)$, $expire^\alpha(a)$ is *true* iff $a = 0$, and $tick^\alpha$ is a non-deterministic operation that changes the value of a timer from a to b according to the following rules: (1) if $a = -1$ then $b = -1$, (2) if $0 \leq a < k_t$ then $b = a - 1$ (where "$-$" works on abstract values as on integers), (3) if $a = x^+$ then $b \in \{x^+, x - 1\}$.

Lemma 2. *System M^α built from system M according to the rules given above is a safe abstraction of M.*

Proof. By a simple check that the safety statement is satisfied.   □

From now on we assume that systems under consideration have no deadlocks and infinite zero-time cycles (infinite traces with a finite number of $tick$'s). The absence of zero-time cycles can be checked on the abstract model by verifying the property $\Box\Diamond tick^\alpha$, which is a consistent abstraction of $\Box\Diamond tick$. The absence of deadlocks follows straightforward from the fact that time can progress even when no other action is possible in the system, and thus $tick$ action is still possible.

Fair timer abstraction. An abstracted system contains more behavior than the original one. Therefore, positive verification results can be transferred from the abstract to the concrete system, while counterexamples can be spurious. Abstraction refinement is a common technique used in case spurious counterexamples are found (see e.g. [6]), though just a change of the granularity level does not always help—the sequence of refinements can turn out to be infinite.

Suppose we use the timer abstraction described above to prove that some property holds for all timer settings greater than or equal to some k_t. Due to the non-determinism introduced with the abstract version of $tick$, it becomes possible that the timer once set will never expire. That means that the states that are always reachable in the concrete system are not reached in the abstract system if $k_t^+ \xrightarrow{tick} k_t^+$ step is always chosen. Such a trace gives a spurious counterexample: In the concrete system the timer expires after a finite number of time slices. The only possible refinement is taking the same abstraction with a greater value of k. But the same trace where the timer never expires is still possible, so a counterexample would be produced again. Therefore, we need a different technique to cope with the problem.

Imposing a strong fairness condition that requires that for any trace where transition $k_t^+ \xrightarrow{tick} (k_t - 1)$ is infinitely often enabled it is infinitely often taken, gives incorrect results: One can easily build a (concrete) model where a timer t is infinitely often set to a new value (before it expires), so it can be seen every time as a new variable in the one-assignment setting. This observation leads us to the following definition of t-*fairness*:

Definition 3. *Given an LTS T of a system with a set of abstract timers $TVar^\alpha$, we say that a trace of T is t-fair iff for any $t \in TVar^\alpha$ the following holds: $k_t^+ \xrightarrow{tick} (k_t - 1)$ is infinitely often enabled implies that $k_t^+ \xrightarrow{tick} (k_t - 1)$ is infinitely often executed or $set(t, x)$, $x \in {}_\alpha \Sigma_t$, is infinitely often executed.*

This definition has a *strong fairness* pattern. Interestingly, due to the fact that the loop introduced on a timer with the abstraction is a *self-loop*, this requirement can be reformulated as a condition with a *weak fairness* pattern:

Lemma 4. *A trace ξ of T is t-fair iff for any $t \in TVar^\alpha$ the following holds: if there exists an infinite suffix σ of ξ such that $[\![t]\!]_{s_j} = k_t^+$ for every state of σ, then $set(t, k_t^+)$ is infinitely often executed along the trace.*

Proof. Let p, q, and r denote the propositions (from Def. 3) "$k_t^+ \xrightarrow{tick} (k_t - 1)$ is enabled", "$k_t^+ \xrightarrow{tick} (k_t - 1)$ is executed", and "$set(t, x)$, $x \in {}_\alpha \Sigma_t$, is executed", respectively.

$$\Box \Diamond p \to (\Box \Diamond q \vee \Box \Diamond r). \tag{1}$$

We can split the proposition r into a disjunction of two propositions r_1 and r_2: "$set(t, k_t^+)$ is executed" and "$set(t, x)$, where $x \neq k_t^+$, is executed", respectively. After straightforward transformations, (1) becomes

$$\neg(\Box \Diamond p \wedge \Diamond \Box(\neg q \wedge \neg r_1)) \vee \Box \Diamond r_2. \tag{2}$$

We will show that $\Box \Diamond p \wedge \Diamond \Box(\neg q \wedge \neg r_1)$ (*), is semantically equivalent to $\Diamond \Box p'$, where p' denotes the proposition "the value of t is k_t^+".

The conjunct $\Box \Diamond p$ says that $k_t^+ \xrightarrow{tick} (k_t - 1)$ is infinitely often enabled. Since we assume the absence of zero-time cycles, by the timer abstraction definition, this is equivalent to the proposition "timer t has value k_t^+ infinitely often". The conjunct $\Diamond \Box(\neg q \wedge \neg r_1)$ says that after some point in the execution sequence neither $k_t^+ \xrightarrow{tick} (k_t - 1)$ nor $set(t, x)$, with $x \neq k_t^+$, are executed. As these transitions are the only ones that can change the value of t from k_t^+ to a value different than k_t^+, we can conclude that from some point the value of t will remain k_t^+ forever.

For the other direction, we first observe that if t has value k_t^+ from some point on, then $k_t^+ \xrightarrow{tick} (k_t - 1)$ is enabled infinitely many times. (Again, we use the absence of zero-time cycles, i.e., a *tick* transition is executed infinitely often along any execution sequence.) Also, the other conjunct of (*) follows immediately: As $k_t^+ \xrightarrow{tick} (k_t - 1)$ and $set(t, x)$, where $x \neq k_t^+$, are the only statements which can change the value of the abstract timer t, they also cannot be executed after some point on.

Thus, we can replace (*) with the equivalent proposition $\Diamond\Box p'$ and rewrite (2) as $\Diamond\Box p' \to \Box\Diamond r_2$, which is the (weak t-fairness) condition of Lemma 4. $\Box$

Thus we can express the t-fairness criterion by the LTL formula $\Phi^\alpha = \bigwedge_{t \in TVar^\alpha}(\Diamond\Box p \to \Box\Diamond q)$, where p and q are propositions corresponding to the terms "$[\![t]\!]_{s_j} = k_t^+$" and "$set(t, k_t^+)$" from Lemma 4, respectively. Though Φ^α is formulated on states *and transitions*, it can be easily encoded as a property defined on the states of the system. (To express the fact that some transition q is infinitely often taken, one can e.g. extend the model with introducing a boolean variable b_q that is negated every time the transition is taken and replace $\Box\Diamond q$ with $\Box\Diamond b_q \wedge \Box\Diamond\neg b_q$.)

One can see the analogy between Φ^α and the definition of *weak fairness for processes*, where a timer set to k_t^+ corresponds to an enabled process and an execution of the *set* operation corresponds to an execution of an action by the process. Further, one can show that the t-fairness criterion Φ^α is a consistent abstraction of the LTL formula $\Phi = \bigwedge_{t \in TVar}(\Diamond\Box p' \to \Box\Diamond q')$, where p', q' are defined as "$[\![t]\!]_{s_j} \geq k_t$" and "$set(t, x)$, where $x \geq k_t$", respectively. This can be done by a simple check that p and q are consistent abstractions of p' and q', respectively. Indeed, let $s^\alpha \in \alpha(\{s\})$. Timer t has the value k_t^+ in the abstract state s^α iff t has a value greater than or equal to k_t in s. Similarly, t is set to some x which is greater than or equal to k_t by a transition which has s as the target state iff it is set by a transition in the abstract state which ends up in the state s^α with $[\![t]\!]_{s^\alpha} = k_t^+$.

Suppose we want to verify that $T \models \phi$ for some $\Box L_\mu^+$ (resp. $\Box L_\mu$) formula ϕ and a concrete system T without infinite zero-time traces. The "concrete" version of the abstract t-fairness condition, Φ, holds on any trace of T: If from some point on the value of timer t remains greater than or equal to k_t, then the timer must be infinitely often set to some value greater than k_t. Otherwise, since *tick* happens infinitely often, the value of t will eventually become less than k_t. Thus, $T \models \phi$ iff $T \models (\Phi \to \phi)$.

By Theorem 1 we know that instead of verifying $T \models (\Phi \to \phi)$ on the concrete system, we can verify its contracting (resp. consistent) abstraction $(\Phi \to \phi)^\alpha$ on the abstract system. By the definition of contracting (consistent) abstraction, the last formula is equivalent to $\Phi^\alpha \to \phi^\alpha$. In case ϕ does not refer to variables (timers) that are abstracted, the abstraction α is trivially a consistent abstraction for all atomic propositions in ϕ and we have $\phi^\alpha = \phi$. If ϕ does mention abstracted timers, one has to derive the contracting abstraction ϕ^α of ϕ. Finally, by Theorem 1, $T^\alpha \models (\Phi^\alpha \to \phi^\alpha)$ implies $T \models (\Phi \to \phi)$ and thus also $T \models \phi$.

Thus, by imposing t-fairness condition on the abstract model, we eliminate spurious counterexamples caused by unfair non-deterministic choices made by abstract functions.

3   Incorporating t-Fairness into the Verification Algorithm

To express the formula Φ^α as an LTL formula defined on the states of the system, one needs to introduce additional variables (see Section 2). Therefore it is computationally expensive to verify the formula $\Phi^\alpha \to \phi^\alpha$ and it is more convenient to incorporate the t-fairness requirement into the verification algorithm that verifies ϕ^α by considering t-fair traces only. In this section we describe how to embed the t-fairness check into a model-checking algorithm for LTL.

Since there is a strong analogy between t-*fairness* and *weak process fairness*, one can easily adapt any algorithm for model checking under weak process fairness. The algorithm we propose here is inspired by the weak process fairness algorithm used in SPIN [15,2], which is a combination of the Nested Depth First Search (NDFS) algorithm [7] and Choueka's flag algorithm [5]. In the automata-theoretic approach, to verify a property expressed by an LTL formula, the negation of the formula is translated into a Büchi automaton, which is combined with the transition system representing the state space of the system. If the language accepted by the resulting automaton is empty, the property is satisfied. As a result, the model checking problem is reduced to a graph theoretic problem of finding *acceptance cycles*, i.e., cycles that contain states from a special designated set of accepting states. The absence of acceptance cycles means that the property holds for the system. Further on we assume that we work directly with the labelled transition system (LTS), which is the product of the Büchi automaton and the LTS of the system.

Given an LTS $T = (S, Act, \longrightarrow_T, s_{init}, F)$ of a composition of the transition system of a given abstract system with the Büchi automaton that represents the negation of a property to be verified, where S is a finite state space, Act is a set of actions, $\longrightarrow_T \subseteq S \times Act \times S$ is a transition relation, $s_{init} \in S$ is an initial state and $F \subseteq S$ is a set of accepting states. Our goal is to construct an extension of T that contains an acceptance cycle iff there exists a t-fair acceptance cycle in T. (We say that a cycle $s_0 \xrightarrow{a_0} ... s_n \xrightarrow{a_n} s_0$ is t-fair iff $\forall t \in TVar^\alpha$ there exists i, $(0 \le i \le n)$, such that $[\![t]\!]_{s_i} \ne k_t^+$ or $a_i = set(t, k_t^+)$.) Therefore, we will define this extension in such a way that any acceptance cycle would be t-fair by construction.

Let the abstract system have N abstract timers. Then we construct the extended LTS $T' = (S', Act', \longrightarrow_{T'}, s'_{init}, F')$ in the following way: The set of states of the extended system is a set of pairs (s, c), where $s \in S$ and $0 \le c \le N$. We call (s, c) a c-*replica* of s. (Note that not every replica (s, c) of a reachable state s of T will be reachable in T'). 0-replicas are the basic replicas of the states, while replicas $1, \ldots, N$ allow to track the behaviour of abstract timers $t_1, \ldots, t_N$, respectively. All the accepting states and the initial state of T' are 0-replicas of the accepting states and the initial state of T, respectively. All transitions from accepting states lead to 1-replicas only. Transitions from a c-replica (s, c), related to timer t_c, lead either to the c-replicas, or, when they guarantee t-fair behaviour w.r.t. timer t_c, to the next $((c+1) \bmod (N+1))$ replica. Since all the acceptance states are 0-*replicas*, any acceptance cycle contains for every abstract timer at least one transition that guarantees t-fairness.

The verification algorithm starts the construction of T' from the initial state $(s_{init}, 0)$ and proceeds by adding the 0-replicas in accordance with the transition function $\longrightarrow_T$ until an accepting state is met. If an accepting state s is encountered, the algorithm adds a dummy τ-step that connects the 0-replica of s with the 1-replica of the same state. A move from a c-replica with $1 \leq c \leq N$ to the $((c+1) \mod (N+1))$-replica happens when a state is encountered in which t_c has a value different from k_t^+ or a step setting timer t_c is taken, i.e. *when the t-fairness condition for t_c is fulfilled.* (A move from a 0-replica to a 1-replica is possible only by τ-steps connecting the replicas of the same accepting state.) For the rest, the algorithm adds states following the transition function $\longrightarrow_T$.

Theorem 5. *Given an LTS $T = (S, Act, \longrightarrow_T, s_{init}, F)$ with abstract timers $t_1, \ldots, t_N$ and its smallest extension $T' = (S', Act', \longrightarrow_{T'}, s'_{init}, F')$ that satisfies the following conditions:*

1. $Act' = Act \cup \{\tau\}$;
2. $s'_{init} = (s_{init}, 0)$;
3. $(s, 0) \xrightarrow{a}_{T'} (s_1, 0)$ *if* $(s, 0) \in S'$ *and* $s \xrightarrow{a}_T s_1$ *and* $s \notin F$;
4. $(s, 0) \xrightarrow{\tau}_{T'} (s, 1)$ *if* $(s, 0) \in S'$ *and* $s \in F$;
5. $(s, c) \xrightarrow{a}_{T'} (s_1, c_1)$ *if* $(s, c) \in S'$ *and* $c > 0$ *and* $s \xrightarrow{a}_T s_1$ *with* $c_1 = ((c+1) \mod (N+1))$ *if* $(\llbracket t_c \rrbracket_s \neq k_{t_c}^+$ *or* $a = set(t_c, k_{t_c}^+))$, *and* $c_1 = c$ *otherwise*;
6. $F' = S' \cap \{(s, 0) \mid s \in F\}$.

Then the following statements hold:

1. $(S, Act, \longrightarrow_T, s_{init})$ *and* $(S', Act', \longrightarrow_{T'}, s'_{init})$ *are branching bisimilar.*
2. *T contains a reachable t-fair acceptance cycle iff T' contains a reachable acceptance cycle.*

Proof. 1. Consider $Q \subseteq S \times S'$ where $(s, s') \in Q$ iff $s' = (s, c)$ where $0 \leq c \leq N$. It is straightforward to check by case analysis that Q is a weak bisimulation. Since system T is τ-free, T and T' are branching bisimilar [24].

2. Notice that all acceptance cycles of the extended state space are t-fair by construction: An acceptance cycle contains at least one accepting state; this state is a 0-replica and has outgoing transitions to 1-replicas only. As transitions from a c-replica lead either to c-replicas, or to "neighbour" $((c+1) \mod (N+1))$-replicas $(0 \leq c \leq N)$, for any c, the cycle includes a c-replica $(s, c), s \in S$. Every move from a c-replica to its neighbour satisfies the t-fairness condition for timer t_c, so for every abstract timer there is a transition in the cycle satisfying the t-fairness condition and thus the cycle is t-fair.

Due to the bisimulation result, any acceptance cycle of T' (which is always t-fair) has a corresponding t-fair acceptance cycle in T.

In the opposite direction: Assume that there is a trace $s_{init} \xrightarrow{a_0} s_1 \xrightarrow{a_1} \ldots$ in T that contains a fair acceptance cycle. Then there are s_i, s_j such that $s_i = s_j$ with $j > i$. The path π from s_i to s_j contains at most $m = (j - i)$ distinct states. Trace $\sigma = s_{init} \xrightarrow{a} \ldots s_i \ldots s_i \ldots s_i$ going through the cycle $N + 1$ times is also the valid trace of T. Due to the bisimulation result, there is a trace σ' in T' that

Procedure 6 (**dfs**(s, c)).

add (s, c) to S'	add a pair to the state space
if $c = 0$ and $s \in F$	0-replica and state s is accepting
then if $(s, 1) \notin S'$ then $dfs(s, 1)$;	τ-step from 0-replica to 1-replica
else	
for all $s \xrightarrow{a}_T s_1$ do	for all transitions enabled in s
if $c > 0$ and $(a = set(t_c, k_{t_c}^+)$ or $[\![t_c]\!]_s \neq k_{t_c}^+)$	t-fairness condition
then $c_1 = (c + 1)$ mod N	the next replica number
else $c_1 = c$;	the same replica number
if $(s_1, c_1) \notin S'$ then $dfs(s_1, c_1)$;	recursive call
od;	

Fig. 2. Generating t-fair extension of S

mimics σ. The suffix ξ' of σ' that mimics passing through the cycle $N + 1$ times contains at least $m(N + 1) + 1$ states. The states of ξ' are replicas of the states of π, therefore at most $m(N + 1)$ of them are distinct. Thus, there is at least one state that is present in ξ' twice, and ξ' is a cycle.

Now we shall show that ξ' is an *acceptance* cycle. We denote the suffix of σ corresponding to ξ' as ξ and pick up an arbitrary state s of ξ. Then ξ' contains some state (s, c), $0 \leq c \leq N$. Assume that $c > 0$. Since ξ is a t-fair cycle, there are some states q_1, q_2 reachable from s such that $q_1 \xrightarrow{a}_T q_2$ and $([\![t_c]\!]_{q_1} \neq k_t^+$ or $a = set(t_c, k_t^+))$. Hence there exists a transition from the c-replica q_1 to the $((c + 1)$ mod $N)$-replica q_2 in ξ'. Proceeding in the same way, we will obtain transitions leading to some $((c + 2)$ mod $N)$-replica, etc., and eventually we arrive at a 0-replica. Thus, we conclude that ξ' contains at least one 0-replica of some state. In T', transitions from 0-replicas of non-accepting states lead to 0-replicas, and transitions from 0-replicas of accepting states lead to 1-replicas. Since ξ contains an accepting state, due to the bisimulation result, ξ' contains an accepting state as well and thus it is an accepting cycle of T'.   □

We call the extension T' a *t-fair extension* of T. An algorithm that generates the extended state space in a depth first search (DFS) manner is given in Fig. 2. It is straightforward to prove the following claim:

Lemma 7. *Given an LTS T, let T' be a system produced from system T by applying Procedure 6. Then T' is a t-fair extension of T.*

To detect acceptance cycles, DFS is extended with a cycle-check procedure (Fig. 3). Whenever Procedure 8 detects an accepting state, it starts Procedure 9, which is again a DFS, that reports an accepting state if the seed state is matched within the cycle-check. Here we omit a detailed description of the NDFS algorithm and refer the interested reader to [7].

Procedure 8 (ndfs$_1$(s, c)).

add $(s, c, 0)$ to S'	add a pair to the state space
if $c = 0$ and $s \in F$	0-replica, and state s is accepting
then if $(s, 1, 0) \notin S'$ then $ndfs_1(s, 1)$;	τ-step from 0-replica to 1-replica
else	
for all $s \xrightarrow{a}_T s_1$ do	for all transitions enabled in s
if $c > 0$ and $(a = set(t_c, k_{t_c}^+)$ or $[\![t_c]\!]_s \neq k_{t_c}^+)$	t-fairness condition
then $c_1 = (c + 1) \bmod N$	the next replica number
else $c_1 = c$;	the same replica number
if $(s_1, c_1, 0) \notin S'$ then $ndfs_1(s_1, c_1)$;	recursive call
od;	
if $c = 0$ and $s \in F$ then $seed := (s, 0, 1)$; $ndfs_2(s, 0)$;	set the seed and start ndfs$_2$

Procedure 9 (ndfs$_2$(s, c)).

add $(s, c, 1)$ to S'	add a pair to the state space
if $c = 0$ and $s \in F$	0-replica, and state s is accepting
then if $(s, 1, 1) \notin S'$ then $ndfs_2(s, 1)$;	τ-step from 0-replica to 1-replica
else	
for all $s \xrightarrow{a}_T s_1$ do	for all transitions enabled in s
if $c > 0$ and $(a = set(t_c, k_{t_c}^+)$ or $[\![t_c]\!]_s \neq k_{t_c}^+)$	t-fairness condition
then $c_1 = (c + 1) \bmod N$	the next replica number
else $c_1 = c$;	the same replica number
if $seed = (s, c_1, 1)$ then REPORT CYCLE!	seed is matched, report the cycle
else if $(s_1, c_1, 1) \notin S'$ then $ndfs_2(s_1, c_1)$;	recursive call
od;	

Fig. 3. NDFS version of Procedure 6

The correctness of the algorithm is given by the following claim:

Theorem 10. *Given an LTS T , Procedure 8 called with $(s_{init}, 0)$ reports an acceptance cycle iff there exists a reachable t-fair acceptance cycle in T .*

Proof. Follows from the correctness of the NDFS algorithm from [7] by observing that the algorithm is actually NDFS from [7] applied on the extended state space T'.   □

The last result completes the series of claims that guarantee the soundness of the verification approach proposed in this paper. If no acceptance cycle is detected then the verified property holds for t-fair traces of the abstract system and therefore also for the concrete system.

Time complexity of the NDFS Algorithm in Fig. 3 is $O(N \cdot |T|)$, where N is the number of timers, while $|T|$ is the size (states and transitions) of the abstract system state space. Memory space needed to save T' is virtually the same as the one for T. Instead of keeping each of the N replicas (s, i), $(1 \leq i \leq N)$ one can save only the "useful" part s plus additional $2(N + 1)$ bits, like it is done for process fairness in SPIN. The first $N + 1$ bits correspond to the replicas in the main depth first search of the NDFS algorithm, while the second group of $(N + 1)$ bits corresponds to the nested DFS. If bit i of the first group is set then this means that the state (s, i) has been visited by the algorithm. Similarly for the second group. As the description of s is usually much greater than $2(N + 1)$ bits, the bookkeeping overhead is negligible.

4 T-Fairness in DTSpin

DTSPIN [3] is a discrete-time extension of SPIN [15] that has all verification features of SPIN. It was successfully applied for debugging and verification of timed models of industrial size protocols (see e.g. [4,16]). DTSPIN is designed for the verification of systems where delays are significantly larger than the duration of the events within the system. Therefore, system transitions are assumed to be instantaneous. DTSPIN employs the concept of timers to express time aspects of a system. In DTPROMELA, the input language of DTSPIN, timers are modelled by variables of a predefined type *timer*. The data domain and the operations on timers are defined as in Section 2.

Since the system transitions are assumed to be instantaneous, time progress has the least priority in the system and may take place only when the system is *blocked*. A special process *Timer* ticks all the active timers down in case the system is blocked. DTSPIN employs PROMELA's statement *timeout* to check whether the system is blocked. To ensure that time progression has the least priority, the usage of *timeout* is reserved for the implementation of time progression and forbidden in DTPROMELA specifications. Note that by the definition of *tick*, all DTPROMELA models are *deadlock-free*.

To implement the timer abstraction defined in Section 2, we extend DT-PROMELA with a new data type $timer^\alpha$ for abstract timers and define the operations on them as macros. The abstract version of *tick*, $tick^\alpha$, decreases values of active abstract timers if they are different from k_t^+. If a timer has the k_t^+ value, the non-deterministic choice is made between decreasing the value of the timer to $(k_t - 1)$ and leaving it unmodified. Our fairness algorithm from Section 3 is implemented by means of a PAN2TFPAN Java program that transforms the *pan* verifier generated by SPIN for the verification of the property without t-fairness into a new one that checks the property under t-fairness. The transformation is automatic and does not require any interaction with the user.

The user applies thus the following scheme for the verification: (1) Choose timers of a concrete model that should be abstracted and define a k_t value for each of those timers; (2) Redefine the type of the chosen times to $timer^\alpha$ and redefine the *set* operations according to the k_t values; (3) Check whether the abstract system is free from zero-time cycles, i.e. check whether *tick* happens infinitely often. This is done by checking LTL formula: $\Box\Diamond timeout$. (In DT-SPIN, time progresses if the statement *timeout* of PROMELA is *true*. Since this statement is forbidden to use in DTPROMELA specifications, $\Box\Diamond timeout$ expresses the absence of zero-time cycles.) (4) Formulate the abstract version of the property to check and generate the *pan* verifier for this property; (5) Transform the *pan* verifier with PAN2TFPAN to the new *pan* verifier, which will check the property under the *t*-fairness condition. Positive verification results imply that the property holds for the concrete system as well. If the property gets violated on the abstract system, the counterexample is generated, and the user checks whether the counterexample is spurious or not.

5   Experimental Results

In this section we describe some experimental results that show the efficiency of our approach. Our test cases are the positive acknowledgment retransmission protocol (PAR) [23] and Fischer's mutual exclusion protocol [19]. We compare the results obtained when we specify *t*-fairness as LTL formulas according to strong fairness and weak fairness patterns (we will refer to it as verifying with strong/weak fairness respectively) with the results obtained with our prototype implementation of the algorithm from Section 3 in DTSPIN, which we refer to as built-in *t*-fairness. Our prime goal here is to compare the performance of the three methods rather than to verify the protocols.

Experiments with the Positive Acknowledgment Retransmission Protocol (PAR). PAR [23] is a classical example of a communication protocol where time issues are essential for the correct functionality of the protocol. PAR involves a sender, a receiver, a message channel and an acknowledgment channel. The sender receives a frame from the upper layer, sends it to the receiver via the message channel and waits for a positive acknowledgment from the receiver via acknowledgment channel. When the receiver delivered the message to the upper layer, it sends the acknowledgment to the sender. After the positive acknowledgment is received, the sender becomes ready to send the next message. The channels delay the delivery of messages. Moreover, they can lose or corrupt messages. Therefore, the sender handles lost frames by timing out. If the sender times out, it re-sends the message. As known, the protocol functions correctly only under the following condition: the timeout of sender should be greater than the sum of delays on channels.

We specified PAR in DTPROMELA using concrete timers to represent delays on the channels and the sender timeout. Our goal was to check that if the channels do not lose messages continuously, no message reordering occurs and no message gets lost, under condition that the timeout of the sender is greater than the sum of the (given) delays on the channels. To prove the property for an arbitrary message sequence we used a well-known canonical abstraction [14, 25] and defined two abstract environment processes: one representing an upper layer for the sender and another one for the upper layer of the receiver. Then we abstracted the sender's timer to check the property for *all* values greater than the sum of the channels' delays.

Table 1. PAR

pattern	states	transitions	memory(Mb)	time
strong fairness	825761	5.10962e+06	52.286	0:21.00
weak fairness	227569	1.49527e+06	15.320	0:05.98
built-in t-fairness	100275	390012	6.693	0:01.56

Without t-fairness, the property gets violated, since there exists a trace where the abstract timer of the sender never expires, staying in the loop $k_t^+ \xrightarrow{tick} k_t^+$ (we obtained a t-unfair trace as counterexample). Under the t-fairness condition, we proved that the property holds. Table 1 contains information on the time and memory consumption for the verification with DTSPIN of the property formulated with the strong and weak fairness patterns and for the verifier with built-in t-fairness.

Fischer's mutual exclusion protocol. Our second test example is Fischer's mutual exclusion protocol. The protocol uses time constraints and a shared variable to ensure mutual exclusion in a system that consists of N processes running in parallel and competing for a critical section. We assume that each process has a unique id from 1 to N. The initial value of the shared variable x is 0. When a process observes that x is 0, it waits for *at most* δ_1 time units and then writes its id to x. After that, it waits for *at least* δ_2 time units, and if x still equals the process id, the process enters the critical section. The process stays in the critical section for some time and then leaves it.

We have specified Fischer's mutual exclusion protocol in DTPROMELA using concrete timers to represent delays not larger than δ_1 and abstract timers to represent delays which are at least δ_2. As known, mutual exclusion is ensured provided that $\delta_1 < \delta_2$. We have checked the property that if there comes a request of access to the critical section, one of the processes will get it. Table 2 contains results for strong, weak and built-in t-fairness for the case of two, three

Table 2. Fischer's mutual exclusion

pattern	num. of proc.	states	transitions	memory(Mb)	time
strong fairness	2	41384	171586	4.363	0:00.46
weak fairness	2	4705	13053	2.724	0:00.08
built-in t-fairness	2	1236	4181	1.573	0:00.01
strong fairness	3	3.28599e+06	2.01406e+07	190.539	1:01.79
weak fairness	3	115874	362068	8.561	0:01.22
built-in t-fairness	3	21592	110332	2.700	0:00.26
strong fairness	4	out of memory			
weak fairness	4	2.60665e+06	9.2549e+06	151.729	0:38.34
built-in t-fairness	4	346903	2.45733e+06	20.927	0:05.69

and four processes. Note that the number of abstracted timers in this example is equal to the number of processes.

The experiments were done on AMD Athlon(TM) XP 2400+ with 1Gb of memory. In all experiments, the verification with built-in t-fairness took significantly less time and memory than the verification with strong and weak fairness patterns expressed as LTL formulas. The prototype implementation PAN2TFPAN and the models can be found at www.cwi.nl/~ustin/tfair.html.

6   Conclusion

In this paper we considered a timer abstraction that introduces a cyclic behavior on abstract timers that is not present at the concrete level. This could lead to spurious counterexamples for liveness properties. We showed how one can eliminate those by imposing a strong fairness constraint on the traces of the abstract model. Using the fact that the loop on the abstract timer is a self-loop for this abstract timer (though there is possibly no self-loop on the corresponding LTS), we transformed the strong fairness constraint into a constraint which has a weak fairness pattern, and embedded it into the verification algorithm. Our experiments with the prototype implementation of the algorithm were encouraging. We conjecture that the ideas in this paper can also be used for other data abstractions that introduce self-loops on the abstracted data.

References

1. K. Baukus, Y. Lakhnech, and K. Stahl. Verification of parameterized protocols. *Journal of Universal Computer Science*, 7(2):141–158, 2001.
2. D. Bošnački. Partial-order reduction in presence of rendez-vous communication with unless constructs and weak fairness. In *Theoretical and Practical Aspects of SPIN Model Checking, 5th and 6th Int. SPIN Workshops*, volume 1680 of *Lecture Notes in Computer Science*. Spriner-Verlag, 1999.
3. D. Bošnački and D. Dams. Integrating real time into Spin: A prototype implementation. In *Proc. of Formal Description Techniques and Protocol Specification, Testing, and Verification*. Kluwer Academic Publishers, 1998.
4. D. Bošnački, D. Dams, L. Holenderski, and N. Sidorova. Verifying SDL in Spin. In *TACAS 2000*, volume 1785 of *Lecture Notes in Computer Science*. Springer-Verlag, 2000.
5. Y. Choueka. Theories of automata on ω-tapes: a simplified approach. *Journal of Computer and System Science*, 8:117–141, 1974.
6. E. Clarke, O. Grumberg, S. Jha, Y. Lu, and H. Veith. Counterexample-guided abstraction refinement. In *Int. Conference on Computer Aided Verification (CAV'00)*, volume 1855 of *Lecture Notes in Computer Science*. Springer, 2000.
7. C. Courcoubetis, M. Vardi, P. Wolper, and M. Yannakakis. Memory efficient algorithms for the verification of temporal properties. *Formal Methods in System Design*, 1:275–288, 1992.
8. P. Cousot and R. Cousot. Abstract interpretaion: A unified lattice model for static analysis of programs by construction or approximation of fixpoints. In *Proc. of POPL '73*. ACM, January 1973.

9. D. Dams. *Abstract Interpretation and Partition Refinement for Model Checking.* PhD dissertation, Eindhoven University of Thechnology, July 1996.
10. D. Dams and R. Gerth. The bounded retransmission protocol revisited. *Electronic Notes in Theoretical Computer Science*, 9, 1999.
11. D. Dams, R. Gerth, and O. Grumberg. Abstract interpretation of reactive systems: Abstraction preserving ∀CTL*, ∃CTL*, and CTL*. In *Proc. of PROCOMET '94*. IFIP, North-Holland, June 1994.
12. D. Dams, R. Gerth, and O. Grumberg. Abstract interpretation of reactive systems. *ACM Transactions on Programming Languages and Systems (TOPLAS)*, 19(2), 1997.
13. M. M. Gallardo, J. Martine, P. Merino, and E. Pimentel. αSpin: Extending Spin with abstraction. In *9th Int. SPIN Workshop, Grenoble, France 2002*, volume 2318 of *Lecture Notes in Computer Science*, pages 254–258, 2002.
14. S. Graf. Verification of a distributed cache memory by using abstractions. In *Workshop on Computer-Aided Verification, CAV'94, Stanford.* LNCS 818, Springer Verlag, 1994.
15. G. J. Holzmann. *The SPIN Model Checker: Primer and Reference Manual.* Addison Wesley, 2003.
16. N. Ioustinova, N. Sidorova, and M. Steffen. Closing open SDL-systems for model checking with DT Spin. In *Proc. of Formal Methods Europe (FME'02)*, volume 2391 of *Lecture Notes in Computer Science*. Springer-Verlag, 2002.
17. Y. Kesten and A. Pnueli. Control and data abstraction: The cornerstones of practical formal verification. *Int. Journal on Software Tools for Technology Transfer*, 2(4):328–342, 2000.
18. Y. Kesten and A. Pnueli. Verification by augmented finitary abstraction. *Information and Computation*, 163(1):203–243, 2000.
19. L. Lamport. A fast mutual exclusion algorithm. *ACM Transactions in Computer Systems*, 5(1):1–11, 1987.
20. C. Loiseaux, S. Graf, J. Sifakis, A. Bouajjani, and S. Bensalem. Property preserving abstractions for the verification of concurrent systems. *Formal Methods in System Design*, 6(1):11–44, 1995.
21. B. D. Lubachevsky. An approach to automating the verification of compact parallel coordination programs I. *Acta Informatica*, 21:125–169, 1984.
22. A. Pnueli, J. Xu, and L. Zuck. Liveness with $(0, 1, \infty)$-counter abstraction. In *Computer Aided Verification : 14th Int. Conference, CAV 2002, Copenhagen, Denmark, July 27-31, 2002. Proc.*, volume 2404 of *Lecture Notes in Computer Science*, pages 107 – 122. Springer, 2002.
23. A. S. Tanenbaum. *Computer Networks.* Prentice Hall Int. Inc., 1981.
24. R. J. van Glabbeek and R. P. Weijland. Branching time and abstraction in bisimulation semantics. In *Proc. IFIP'89*, pages 613–618. North-Holland, 1989.
25. P. Wolper. Expressing interesting properties of programs in propositional temporal logic. In *Proc. 13th ACM Symp. on Principles of Programming Languages*, pages 184–192, St. Petersburgh, January 1986.

A Scalable Incomplete Test for Message Buffer Overflow in Promela Models

Stefan Leue, Richard Mayr, and Wei Wei

Department of Computer Science
Albert-Ludwigs-University Freiburg
Georges-Koehler-Allee 51, D-79110 Freiburg, Germany
{leue,mayrri,wwei}@informatik.uni-freiburg.de

Abstract. In Promela, communication buffers are defined with a fixed length, and buffer overflows can be handled in two different ways: block the send statement or lose the message. Both solutions change the semantics of the system, compared to one with unbounded channels. The question arises, if such buffer overflows can ever occur in a given system and what buffer lengths are sufficient to avoid them. We describe a scalable incomplete boundedness test for the communication buffers in Promela models, which is based on overapproximation and static analysis. We first reduce Promela models to systems of communicating finite state machines (CFSMs) and then apply further abstractions that leave us with a system of linear inequalities. Those represent the message sending and receiving effect that the control flow cycles of every process have on any message buffer. The test tries to establish the existence of a linear combination of the effect vectors so that at least one message can occur an unbounded number of times. If no such linear combination exists then the system is bounded. We discuss the complexity of this test and present experimental results using our implementation in the IBOC system. Scalability of the test is in part due to the fact that it is polynomial for the type of sparse control flow graphs derived from Promela models. Also, the analysis is local, i.e., it avoids the combinatorial state space explosion due to concurrency of the models. We also present a method to derive upper bound estimates for the maximal occupancy of each individual message buffer. Previously, we have applied this approach to UML RT models, while in this paper we focus on the additional problems specific to Promela code: determining the potential message types of any channel, tracking potential contents of variables, channels passed as arguments to processes, channel assignments, channel arrays and parallel process creation.

1 Introduction

In Promela, the input language of the SPIN model checker [7], inter-process communication can be done via shared global variables or by message passing via communication channels that operate as first-in first-out (FIFO) buffers. These buffers are defined with a fixed length, and buffer overflows (i.e., an attempt to send a message to a full buffer) can be handled by SPIN in two different ways: block the send statement or lose the message. Both solutions change the semantics of the system, compared to one with unbounded channels. The question arises whether such buffer overflows can ever occur in

S. Graf and L. Mounier (Eds.): SPIN 2004, LNCS 2989, pp. 216–233, 2004.
© Springer-Verlag Berlin Heidelberg 2004

a given system and what buffer lengths are sufficient to avoid them. Our paper presents an automated test for the occurrence of these buffer overflows in Promela.

Of course, possible buffer overflows can be detected by simulation, or by encoding this question into an LTL model checking problem. However, this normally involves fully exploring the state space. Here we propose a type of boundedness analysis that avoids exhaustively checking all the computations of the model. We describe a scalable incomplete boundedness test for the communication buffers in Promela models, which is based on overapproximation and static analysis. For the test, we first interpret all communication buffers in the model as having unbounded length (instead of the fixed length in their definition) and then try to prove their boundedness, i.e., to establish upper bounds on the maximal reachable occupancy of every buffer. To do this, we first reduce Promela models to systems of communicating finite state machines (CFSMs) and then apply further abstractions that leave us with a system of linear inequalities. Those represent the summary message sending and receiving effect that the control flow cycles of every process have on any message buffer. The test tries to establish the existence of a linear combination of the resulting effect vectors so that at least one message can occur an unbounded number of times. If no such linear combination exists then the system is bounded. By similar techniques it is also possible to derive upper bound estimates for the maximal occupancy of each individual message buffer.

Our test is: (i) Incomplete: Since boundedness for systems of CFSMs is undecidable [4] we work with an overapproximation of the Promela model. Hence, not every instance of a bounded system can be detected. (ii) Safe: If our test returns the result 'bounded' for the overapproximation then the original Promela model is also bounded. The computed upper bounds for maximal occupancy of each individual message buffer also carry over to the original Promela model. (iii) Scalable: Scalability of the test is in part due to the fact that it is polynomial for the type of sparse control flow graphs derived from Promela models. Also, the analysis is local, i.e., it avoids the combinatorial state space explosion due to concurrency of the models.

In precursory work [10] we have successfully applied this approach to boundedness checking of communication channels in UML RT [14,15] models, using our implementation in the IBOC (*IMCOS Boundedness Checker*) tool that we are currently developing. Promela differs from UML RT in a number of important aspects. In UML RT the different parallel processes in the system are represented by so-called *capsules* which communicate with each other only by message passing. These message passing channels are a priori assumed to be unbounded and the topology of the communication structure is defined statically at compile time. The capsule behaviors are defined through hierarchical state machines whose transitions are triggered solely by message-receive events. These transition can also be labeled with arbitrary programming language code (which we abstract from in our UML RT analysis). Promela, on the other hand, is a concurrent programming language with concurrent processes, referred to as *proctypes*. It's control structure is much more flexible and versatile than that of UML RT, although state machines can easily be modeled in Promela. As opposed to UML RT, in Promela communication between proctypes can be via message passing or shared variables, and the communication topology can be dynamically changed.

However, once the static code analysis is completed and the message passing effect vectors have been determined, the boundedness analysis for the Promela case is identical to the analysis in the UML RT case. The focus of this paper is therefore on the specific problems that have to be addressed when analyzing Promela code in order to determine the message passing effect vectors. Issues that we will consider include

- the identification of message types, since in receive statements these can be referred to by variables whose values are not statically known;
- the passing of channel names as formal parameters during proctype instantiation;
- the replication of identical proctype instances;
- the assignment of channel variables;
- the use of channel array data structures where the arrays are indexed by variables not known statically;
- and the impact of unbounded proctype creation.

Paper Outline. For the sake of self-containedness of this paper we review the principle of our boundedness test in Section 2. In Section 3 we describe the solutions to the specific issues in the application of the analysis to Promela. Experimental results are discussed in Section 4. We discuss related work in Section 5 and conclude in Section 6.

2   Boundedness Analysis

For the sake of self-containedness of this paper we now summarize the general principle of our boundedness analysis. A more detailed description can be found in [10].

First, we consider a sequence of conceptual abstractions for Promela models. In every step we obtain a coarser overapproximation of the previous model, for which the boundedness problem is easier to solve. All behavior of the original system is also possible in the overapproximations, i.e., they are monotonous w.r.t. simulation preorder. Furthermore, the abstractions preserve the (upper bounds on the) number of messages in every communication channel (buffer) of the Promela model. In practice, in the IBOC tools, all these abstractions are done in a single step.

Level 0: Promela code. We start with the original system model described in Promela, except that we a priori assume that buffers have arbitrary length. For this model (Promela with arbitrary length buffers) boundedness is, of course, undecidable, since the buffers could be used to simulate a Turing-machine tape.

Level 1: CFSMs. First, we abstract from the general program code in the model, i.e., variables, arithmetic, etc. We retain only the finite control structure of the program and the message passing behavior via unbounded buffers representing the communication channels. We obtain a system of communicating finite-state machines (CFSMs), sometimes also called FIFO-channel systems [1]. For the CFSM model boundedness is also undecidable [4].

Level 2: Parallel-Composition-VASS. In the next step we abstract from the order of the messages in the buffers and consider only the number of messages of any given type. For example, the buffer with contents abbacb would be represented by the integer vector $(2, 3, 1)$, representing 2 messages of type a, 3 messages of type b and 1 message of type c. Also we abstract from the ability to test explicitly whether a given buffer is empty. We so obtain a vector addition system with states (VASS) [3]. More exactly, we obtain a *parallel-composition-VASS*. This is a VASS whose finite-control is the parallel composition of several finite automata. Each part of this parallel composition corresponds to the finite control of some part of CFSM of level 1, and to the finite control of a process in the original Promela model. (Parallel-composition-VASS are as expressive, but more succinct than normal VASS.) The boundedness problem for parallel-composition-VASS is polynomially equivalent to the boundedness problem for Petri nets, which is *EXPSPACE*-complete [17].

Level 3: Parallel-Composition-VASS with Arbitrary Input. We now abstract from activation conditions of cycles in the control-graph of the VASS and assume instead that there are always enough messages, represented by tokens, present to start the cycle. As far as boundedness is concerned, we replace the problem 'Is the system bounded if starting at the given initial configuration?' by the problem 'Is the system bounded for any finite initial configuration?', also referred to as the *structural boundedness problem*. It has been shown in [10] that this structural boundedness problem for parallel-composition-VASS is co-$\mathcal{NP}$-complete, unlike for standard Petri nets where it is polynomial [12,6].

Level 4: Independent Cycle System. Finally, we abstract from the fact that certain cycles in the control graph depend on each other. Instead we assume that all cycles are independent and any combination of them is executable infinitely often, provided that the combined effect of this combination on all places is non-negative. The *un*boundedness problem for this abstracted model then becomes the following question: Is there any linear combination (with non-negative integer coefficients) of the effects of simple cycles in the control graph, such that the combined effect is non-negative on all places and strictly positive on at least one place? Since we consider an overapproximation, the original Promela model is surely bounded if the answer to this question is 'no'. Since these effects of simple cycles can be represented by integer vectors, we get the following problem. Given a set of integer vectors, does there exist a linear combination (with non-negative integer coefficients) of them, such that the result is non-negative in every component and strictly positive in at least one. This problem can be solved in time polynomial in the number of vectors by using linear programming techniques.

However, the important aspect is that the time required is only polynomial in the number of simple cycles, unlike at level 3, where the problem is co-$\mathcal{NP}$-hard even for a linear number of simple cycles. This is very significant, since for instances derived from typical Promela models, the number of simple cycles is usually small. This is because the typical control-flow graphs of Promela code are (like in programming languages) sparse and often very local. (This is also the general reason why caching works.) Thus the number of different simple cycles derived from this code is typically polynomial rather than (in the worst case) exponential.

Overall Boundedness Test. From every simple cycle found in the control structure, a vector can be derived which describes its effect on the unbounded system part. Here, for the Promela model, the vector describes how many messages were altogether added to the buffer. For every buffer and every message type there is one component in each of the effect vectors. The component can be negative if in the cycle more messages of this type were removed from a buffer than added to it. The resulting semilinear system is unbounded if and only if there exists a linear combination with non-negative coefficients of the effect-vectors that is non-negative in every component and strictly positive in at least one component. Formally, this can be described as follows: Let $v_1, \ldots, v_n \in \mathbb{Z}^k$ be the effect-vectors of all simple cycles and let v^j be the j-th component of the vector v. The question then is

$$\exists x_1, \ldots, x_n \in \mathbb{N}_0. \sum_{i=1}^{n} x_i v_i \geq \mathbf{0} \wedge \exists j. \left(\sum_{i=1}^{n} x_i v_i \right)^j > 0.$$

This can easily be transformed into a system of linear inequations and solved by standard linear programming tools. If this condition is true then our overapproximation is unbounded, but not necessarily also the Promela model. The unboundedness could simply be due to the coarseness of the overapproximation. On the other hand, if the condition above is false, then our overapproximation is bounded, and thus our original Promela model is also bounded. Thus, this test yields an answer of the form "BOUNDED" in case no linear combination of the effect vectors satisfying the above constraint can be found, and "UNKNOWN" when such a linear combination exists.

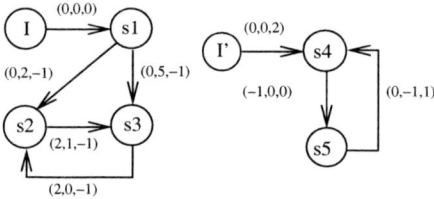

Fig. 1. Effect Graphs of a 2-Process Model

Example. Figure 1 describes effect graphs obtained from two communicating processes. The left process sends messages 'a' or 'b' to the right one, and the right process sends messages 'c' to the left one. The three components of the vector describe how many messages 'a', 'b' or 'c' are written (positive values) or read (negative values) in a step. For example, in the step from s_2 to s_3 two messages 'a' and one message 'b' are written and one message 'c' is read. From this graph we obtain the effect vectors $v_1 = (4, 1, -2)$ and $v_2 = (-1, -1, 1)$ for the simple cycles. To represent the > 0 condition in the linear inequation system we add a constraint $3x_1 - x_2 \geq 1$. The linear inequation solver returns infeasibility of this system of inequations, and we thus conclude a result of "BOUNDED".

Computing Bounds for Individual Buffers. A more refined problem is to compute upper bounds on the reachable lengths of individual buffers in the system. In particular, some buffers might be bounded even if the whole system is unbounded. Since normally not all buffers can reach maximal length simultaneously, the analysis is done individually for each buffer B. This can be done by solving a linear programming problem that maximizes a linear target function f_B (length of B) on an abstraction level 4 system description. The basic idea is the following. Let p be a path from the initial configuration to a configuration where B has maximal length. Then p can be decomposed into a cyclic part p_c and an acyclic part p_a. Since at abstraction level 4 we assume total independence of simple cycles, the effect of p_c can be described by a linear combination of the vectors describing the effects of simple cycles. It thus suffices to maximize f_B on this linear combination. Determining the maximal contribution of the acyclic part p_a is harder since one has to consider all possible combinations of acyclic paths in all parallel processes. (This is generally exponential in the number of parallel processes.) Therefore we only compute an upper bound on the effect of p_a as follows: Let n be the number of parallel processes and p_a^i the part of p_a in the i-th process. Let $E(x)$ be the effect vector of path x. Then $E(p_a) := \sum_{i=1}^{n} E(p_a^i)$. Now we compute vectors r_i which are upper bounds on $E(p_a^i)$, i.e., $\forall p_a^i . r_i \geq E(p_a^i)$. The r_i are computed (in polynomial time) by maximizing individually every component of the possible effect of paths p_a^i. (For example, if in process i there are two acyclic paths with effects $(3, 1)$ and $(1, 2)$ then $r_i = (3, 2)$.) It follows that $E(p_a) = \sum_{i=1}^{n} E(p_a^i) \leq \sum_{i=1}^{n} r_i$ and thus $E(p) = E(p_c) + E(p_a) \leq E(p_c) + \sum_{i=1}^{n} r_i$. It only the remains to solve the linear optimization problem of f_B on $E(p)$ over $E(p_c)$ as explained above.

Example. Having established boundedness of the example of Figure 1, we now compute the estimated upper bound for each buffer. First we compute the effect vectors for all non-cyclic paths. They are listed in Table 1 where $init$ and $init'$ are the initial states of the state machines. Then we take the maxima of the individual components from those effect vectors and construct the overapproximated maximal effect vectors for process Left as $r_1 = (2, 5, 0)$ and for Right as $r_2 = (0, 0, 2)$. Thus the sum is $\sum_{i=1}^{n} r_i = (2, 5, 2)$. We obtain the following two optimization problems (1-4 and 5-8) for the two buffers left-to-right and right-to-left:

$$max : 2 - 2x_1 + x_2 \quad (1)$$
$$2 + 4x_1 - x_2 \geq 0 \quad (2)$$
$$5 + x_1 - x_2 \geq 0 \quad (3)$$
$$2 - 2x_1 + x_2 \geq 0. \quad (4)$$

$$max : 7 + 5x_1 - 2x_2 \quad (5)$$
$$2 + 4x_1 - x_2 \geq 0 \quad (6)$$
$$5 + x_1 - x_2 \geq 0 \quad (7)$$
$$2 - 2x_1 + x_2 \geq 0. \quad (8)$$

Linear Programming returns a value of 6 for the objective function (1) and a value of 18 for the objective function (5). These values represent the estimated bounds for the communication buffers 1 and 2, respectively.

Table 1. The Effect Vectors for all Non-Cyclic Paths in Figure 1

The non-cyclic path	The effect vectors	The non-cyclic path	The effect vectors
$< init, s1 >$	(0,0,0)	$< init, s1, s2 >$	(0,2,-1)
$< init, s1, s2, s3 >$	(2,3,-2)	$< init, s1, s3 >$	(0,5,-1)
$< init, s1, s3, s2 >$	(2,5,-2)	$< init', s4 >$	(0,0,2)
		$< init', s4, s5 >$	(-1,0,2)

3   Promela-Specific Issues

Given a Promela model the first step in the model analysis is to extract from it a system of CFSMs that consists of all state machines of all potentially executing processes. SPIN can automatically generate a state machine representation for every proctype definition in the model [1]. The state machine of each actually instantiated process is then obtained from the state machine of its process type by replacing all formal arguments by the corresponding actual arguments. Figure 2 shows a simple Promela model and the corresponding system of CFSMs. There are two process instances at run time, one of process type P and the other of process type Q. Each transition in the state machine representation corresponds to a basic statement in the Promela code [2] of its process type. The source state of the transition denotes the entry point of the corresponding statement and the target state denotes the exit point of the statement. Every transition has a guard which is determined by the implicit executability condition of the corresponding statement. The executability of a statement describes under which condition the statement is executable. For instance, the transition from the state 4 to the state 3 is labeled by its corresponding statement $C?msg1$. The statement is executable if and only if there is a message $msg1$ available in the channel C.

```
mtype = { msg0, msg1 };
chan C = [2] of { mtype };
active proctype P(){
        C!msg0;
        do
        :: C?msg1 -> C!msg0
        od}
active proctype Q(){
        C!msg1;
        do
        :: C?msg0 -> C!msg1
        od}
```

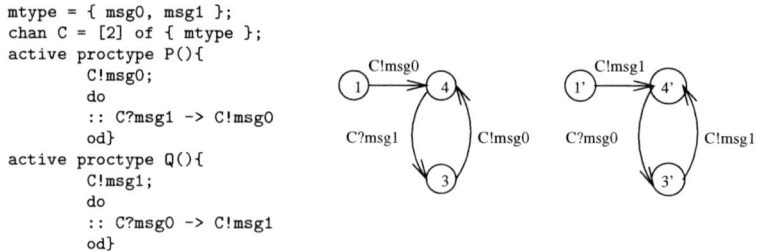

Fig. 2. A simple Promela model and the corresponding state machines.

We apply code abstraction to the resulting system of CFSMs. We replace all the statements in the state machines by their message passing effects. The resulting system is called the system of effect graphs. The remaining steps of the analysis, including cycle detection and translating the summary effects of all the cycles into a linear programming problem, are not different from the corresponding steps for UML RT models as described in [10]. In the remainder of this section we discuss several issues that have to be addressed during the Promela code abstraction in order to extract effect vectors from the Promela code that ensure an overapproximation of the system. The resolution of these issues greatly influences the resulting systems of effect graphs, in particular how coarse the overapproximation is.

---

[1] This is accomplished by invoking the spin -d option.

[2] A basic statement is defined in the Promela language as an indivisible statement such as an assignment statement or a receive statement.

3.1   Identifying Message Types

Each component of an effect vector corresponds to a distinct message type. To construct effect vectors we must determine all distinct message types occurring in the model. Before we discuss this problem, we first review the syntactic structure of messages and the message passing semantics in Promela. The structures of the messages are defined in the declarations of the channels that store them. Consider the following channel declarations:

```
chan C1 = [2] of { mtype, int, bool }; chan C2 = [2] of { int, bool };
```

Messages can contain any finite number of fields. Each field can be of any well-formed type except arrays. In particular, the channel type $chan$ is allowed. There is a special type called $mtype$ that contains user-defined symbolic constants. In the Promela model in figure 2 $mtype$ is declared as containing two constants: $msg0$ and $msg1$. In any model, there can be at most one $mtype$ declaration. A $mtype$ field is not necessarily contained in every message. For instance, the messages in the channel $C2$ only contain an integer field and a boolean field.

Consider a send statement of the form $Ch!e_1, e_2, ..., e_n$ where each e_i ($1 \leq i \leq n$) can be an arbitrary Promela expression. The statement is executable if the channel Ch is not full. Nevertheless, under our a priori assumption of unboundedness of channels, the send statement is never blocked. The send statement sends the message $(val(e_1), val(e_2), ..., val(e_n))$ to the channel, where $val(e_i)$ is the run-time value of e_i.

For a receive statement $Ch?e_1, e_2, ..., e_n$[3], each e_i ($1 \leq i \leq n$) can be a variable, the evaluation $eval(v)$ of some variable v, or a constant. $eval(v)$ can be regarded as a constant. But its value is unknown statically. The statement is executable if all the constant expressions match the relative fields in the available message. Otherwise, it is blocked. If e_i is some variable v then, if the statement is executable, the corresponding field of the received message is stored into v.

The constants in a receive statement distinguish among messages containing different values of the relative fields. This allows users to associate with each message a proper piece of code for manipulation. We observe that these constants are often of type $mtype$. The variables in a receive statement can never block the execution. They are used to retrieve the relative fields from the received message. Consider the Promela model in Figure 3. The two receive statements in the model use constants of type $mtype$ to discriminate between the messages of type *exact* and *inexact*. The variable x stores the data upon receiving, no matter whether the received message type is *exact* or *inexact*, and no matter which integer is transmitted with the message.

For the purpose of our analysis one can regard two messages which have the same structure but disagree on at least one field as being of different types. However, the number of the message types recognized in this way can be very large. It is also not necessary based on the following observation. In the previous example, the messages

---

[3] Promela knows additional forms of the send and receive primitives, denoted by *!!* and *??*, respectively. They are variants of the basic send and receive statement and only differ in the order in which they add and remove messages from the communication channels. Since our analysis abstracts from the order of messages in the buffer anyway, we do not distinguish these primitives here and map them to their respective base form.

```
mtype = {exact, inexact}
chan C = [2] of {mtype, int}
active proctype P(){
    int x;
    do
    :: C?exact, x -> keep(x)
    :: C?inexact, x -> dump(x)
    od
}
```

(1,0)   (0,1)

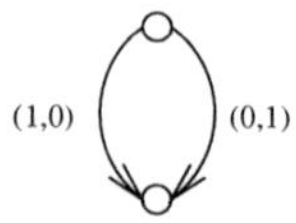

Fig. 4. Nondeterministic effect graph

Fig. 3. Receive statements

```
mtype = {msg0, msg1};
chan C = [2] of {mtype};
chan D = [2] of {mtype};
proctype P(chan X; chan Y){
    do
    :: X?msg0; Y!msg0; Y!msg0
    od}
init{   run P(C, D);
        run P(D, D)}
```

Fig. 5. Channel parameters.

$(exact, 5)$ and $(inexact, 5)$ must be of different types because the model discriminates between them. On the contrary, the messages $(exact, 5)$ and $(exact, 7)$ need not to be of different types since the model treats them in exactly the same way. Only the first field of the messages is used to indicate the message types.

Based on the discussion so far, we propose the following solution to identify message types. For any channel Ch that stores messages with $mtype$ fields, we identify the types of the messages in Ch as pairs $(Ch, mconst)$ where $mconst$ is an $mtype$ constant. We include the channel name into message types because more than one channel can store messages with the same structure, and messages exchanged in different channels must be distinguished. For any channel Ch that stores messages without $mtype$ field, there is only one type, denoted as (Ch), for all the messages in Ch. In this way there are two message types identified for the model in Figure 3: $(C, exact)$ and $(C, inexact)$. This solution simply abstracts away all the non-$mtype$ fields of messages.

This abstraction approach becomes coarse if, in any model, some constants in some receive statements are of other types than $mtype$. For instance, if we have a receive statement $C?(exact, 5)$ in the model in Figure 3, the model discriminates between the messages containing the integer 5 and the messages containing other integers. Then the previously identified types are not sufficient to distinguish messages such as $(exact, 5)$ and $(exact, 7)$. Thus, for any channel Ch and receive statement $Ch?e_1, e_2, ..., e_i, ..., e_n$, where e_i is a constant c_i, those messages containing c_i in their i-th fields and those messages containing other constants in their i-th fields must be of different message types.

We propose a finer abstraction as follows. For any channel Ch that is declared as $chan\, Ch = [k]$ of $\{type_1, type_2, ..., type_n\}$, the message types are those $(Ch, < d_1, d_2, ..., d_n >)$ such that

- D_i is the domain of the type $type_i$.
- $P(D_i)$ is a partition over D_i and $P(D_i) = \{\{const_1\}, \{const_2\}, ..., \{const_m\}, D_i - \bigcup_{j=1}^{j=m}\{const_j\}\}$ such that each constant $const_j \in D_i$ $(1 \leq i \leq m)$ is the i-th expression in some receive statement $Ch?e_1, e_2, ..., const_j, ..., e_n$.
- $d_i \in P(D_i)$.

For the example in Figure 3 augmented with the receive statement $C?exact, 5$, assuming I as the integer domain, we then have four message types as follows: $(C, < exact, \{5\} >)$, $(C, < exact, I - \{5\} >)$, $(C, < inexact, \{5\} >)$ and $(C, < inexact, I - \{5\} >)$.

3.2 Tracking *mtype* Variables

If an expression in a send or receive statement is a variable or the evaluation of a variable, its run-time value is not known statically. This affects our abstraction when the relative field of messages is used to identify the message types. For instance, assume that we have a send statement $C!x, y$ in the model in Figure 2 where x is a *mtype* variable and y is an integer variable. We identify all the message types as $(C, exact)$ and $(C, inexact)$. In other words, the integer field of messages is abstracted away. Which type the sent message has depends only on the variable x. Since we can not generally determine the run-time values for x, we model the statement as sending nondeterministically any message whose *mtype* field is either *exact* or *inexact*. Therefore, in the resulting effect graph, there are two transitions. Both are leaving from the state corresponding to the entry point of the statement and lead to the state corresponding to the exit point, as shown in Figure 4. The left transition is labeled by the effect $(1, 0)$ denoting that a message of the type $(C, exact)$ is sent. The right transition is labeled by the effect $(0, 1)$, denoting that a message of the type $(C, inexact)$ is sent. Thus one obtains a nondeterministic choice between two transitions, as shown in Figure 4.

As mentioned before, there is at most one *mtype* declaration in a model. All constants of type *mtype* can be used by any send or receive operation on any channel. However, most channels usually use only a small portion of all *mtype* constants. If we can determine for each channel the range of the *mtype* constants it uses, we only need to consider those constants in the range for the nondeterministic modeling of message passing. So we could obtain a finer overapproximation. Our approach works by statically tracking possible values of *mtype* variables. *mtype* constants are numerical symbols. The Promela language allows for arithmetic operations on *mtype* constants or variables. If $mtype = \{msg0, msg1\}$, $msg0$ and $msg1$ are internally represented by the compiler as integers 2 and 1, respectively. The statement $v = msg0 + msg1$ is syntactically valid and the *mtype* variable v is assigned the value 3. Note that this value is outside the range of the integers for representing a *mtype* constant in this example. However, Spin does not report such a range error. Arithmetic operations over the *mtype* domain make it extremely hard to track *mtype* variables. Due to these reasons, we exclude the usage of arithmetic operations over *mtype* from our analysis. Hence there are only three ways to change the value of a *mtype* variable: through an assignment, through a receive statement, or through argument passing.

We propose a solution to determine the ranges for the channels for the coarser approach of identifying message types. That means all non-*mtype* fields of messages are abstracted away. The rules for updating the ranges for *mtype* variables and channels are given as follows, where v_1 and v_2 are *mtype* variables, *mconst* is a *mtype* constant, and Ch is a channel:

- Initially all the *mtype* variables and channels have the empty set as the ranges for them.
- For the assignment $v_1 = mconst$, add *mconst* to the range of v_1.
- For the assignment $v_1 = v_2$, add all the constants in the range of v_2 to the range of v_1.
- For the send statement $Ch!e_1, ..., v_1, ..., e_n$, add all the constants in the range of v_1 to the range of Ch.
- For the send statement $Ch!e_1, ..., mconst..., e_n$, add *mconst* to the range of Ch.

- For the receive statement $Ch?e_1, ..., v_1, ..., e_n$, add all the constants in the range of Ch to the range of v_1.
- Assume a process type defined as *proctype* $P(...; mtype \ v_1; ...)$. For *run* $P(..., v_2, ...)$, add all the constants in the range of v_2 to the range of v_1.
- Assume a process type defined as *proctype* $P(...; mtype \ v_1, ...)$. For *run* $P(..., mconst, ...)$, add *mconst* to the range of v_1.

After determining the range of a channel Ch, we may reduce the number of distinct message types. For instance, if the domain of the *mtype* constants is D and the range of Ch is $D_{ch} \subset D$, then any message type $(Ch, mconst)$ can be discarded if $mconst \in D - D_{ch}$.

3.3   Channel Arguments

In Promela models, process types can be parameterized. For any process type that has formal arguments as channels, its instances with different instantiations of the channel arguments have different message passing behaviors. Consider the Promela model in Figure 5, where two running instances of process P are created. We refer to them as p_1 and p_2. The process p_1, instantiated as $P(C, D)$, accepts two different channels as the actual arguments. The process p_2 instantiated as $P(D, D)$ accepts the same channel D for both the formal arguments X and Y. We can easily observe that p_1 alone does not cause any unboundedness, while p_2 floods the channel D by messages $msg0$.

3.4   Replication of Proctypes

As shown above, different instances of some procedure with different channel arguments differ w.r.t. the boundedness of the channels. However, several parallel instances of some proctype with the same channel arguments do not contribute more to a potential unboundedness than just one, as far as our analysis is concerned. This is because in our abstraction level 4 (see Section 2) we assume all control-flow cycles to be independent. Thus two parallel copies of a procedure do not contribute more different control-flow cycles than just one.

3.5   Channel Assignments

The channel names specified in a Promela model are actually variables of the type $chan$. At run time, Spin maintains a set of actual channels called queues, and each channel variable keeps a pointer to a specific queue. The queue pointed to by a channel variable can be changed through channel assignments. Consider the Promela model in Figure 6. The channel C and D initially point to two separate queues. After the assignment $C = D$, C points to the same queue as pointed by D. It's easy to see that this queue is flooded by messages $msg0$.

A simple abstraction works as follows. Wherever we find a channel assignment $Ch_1 = Ch_2$ in the model, we merge the channels Ch_1 and Ch_2 into a single channel. That means one does not discriminate between the messages in Ch_1 and the messages in Ch_2. This is an overapproximation since we abstract from message orders. This solution is relatively coarse because a channel assignment does not necessarily affect all parts of

```
mtype = { msg0, msg1 };
chan C = [2] of { mtype };
chan D = [2] of { mtype };
active proctype P(){
    C = D;
    do
    :: C?msg0; D!msg0; D!msg0
    od}
```

```
mtype = { msg0, msg1 };
chan C = [2] of { mtype };
chan D = [2] of { mtype };
active proctype P(){
    do
    :: C?msg0; D!msg0; D!msg0
    od;
    C = D;}
```

Fig. 6. A Promela model   **Fig. 7.** A Promela model

the model. Consider the Promela model in Figure 7. Apparently the channel assignment $C = D$ does not affect the loop in the process type P where C and D still point to separate queues.

We propose a finer overapproximation based on the notion of strongly connected components (SCCs). A SCC in a directed graph is a subgraph in which any vertex is reachable from any other vertex. If we collapse all the vertices in the same SCC into a single vertex, we obtain a directed acyclic graph (DAG). In the DAG each vertex denotes a SCC in the original graph. Each transition from the state SCC_1 to the state SCC_2 corresponds to a transition in the original graph from one of the states in SCC_1 to one of the states in SCC_2. We derive the DAGs from the state machines of the running processes that contain channel assignments. It's obvious that a channel assignment in some SCC can only affect those SCCs reachable from it in the DAG of SCCs. For parallel processes, a channel assignment in one process can affect every part of every other process running in parallel. In this setting the effect vectors are constructed with separate components for different channels. However, at program locations where two channels are possibly identical, messages are nondeterministically sent to either channel. This encoding has the same effect as the unification of channels described above.

3.6 Channel Arrays

A set of channels can be declared as an array, e.g., *chan C[3] = [5] of { mtype}*. The channel array C consists of three channels indexed by integers between 0 and 2. For instance, the statement $C[1]!msg$ sends a message to the channel indexed at 1. When an index is a variable, its value is generally not known statically. For instance, the statement $C[i]!msg$ uses an integer variable i to index the array element. A simple solution is to model the statement as nondeterministically sending the message to any element of C, assuming that the run-time values of i always fall inside the range of the channel array indices. A finer approach is to statically track the index variable i to determine its range in a similar way as tracking $mtype$ variables. However we cannot exclude arithmetic operations over integers. Whenever an arithmetic expression is met in an assignment, or in a receive statement, or in an argument passing, we have to set the range of the affected variable to the range of the channel array indices.

3.7 Unbounded Process Creations

The SPIN model checker limits the number of parallel processes to an implementation dependent constant which is in most installations 255. If one takes such a limit for granted then process creation alone could not lead to channel unboundedness. However, the Promela language could just as well be interpreted without this limitation. Here we show how unbounded parallel process creation could lead to channel-unboundedness (even in the absence of cycles in the control-flow graphs), and how our method could handle this problem.

Unbounded process creations can result in unbounded channels. There are two kinds of unbounded process creations. One kind is through local loops as demonstrated by the Promela model in Figure 8. The instance p of the process type P repeatedly creates instances of the process type Q. There is an execution where every new instance of Q immediately sends a message $msg0$ to the channel C after p creates it, and then stops there for p to create another new instance of Q. This floods C with messages $msg0$.

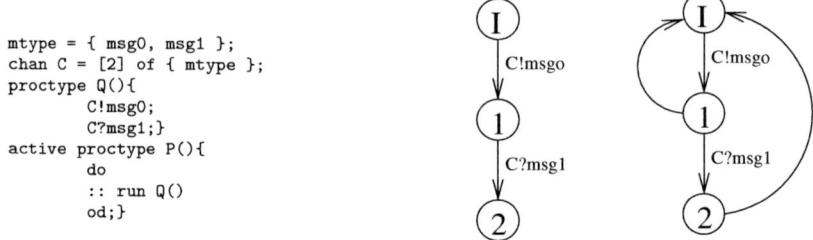

Fig. 8. A Promela model (left), the state machine of a running process of Q (middle), and the modified state machine with replication transitions (right).

The unboundedness of C can not be detected from the state machine of any instance of Q as shown in the middle of the figure. A straightforward solution is to add an extra backward transition from each state in the state machine to the initial state. These transitions are called replication transitions. The modified state machine is on the right in the figure. Now we can determine the loop $(I, 1, I)$ as the cause of the flooding of channel C.

The other kind of unbounded process creations is through self-creations or mutual creations. An example for self-creation is the Promela model in Figure 9. The channel C is unbounded because any new instance of P is self-created and every instance sends a message to the channel. The unboundedness is not detected from the state machine of any running process of P as shown in the middle of the figure. Similarly we use replication transitions to detect self-creations. But we only need to add a replication transition for those states corresponding to the entry points of self-creations. So in the modified state machine on the right of the figure, there is no backward transition from state 2. The execution of any instance of P can never reach there before it creates a new instance.

Now consider the situation that the unbounded process creations are through *mutual* invocation, as demonstrated by the Promela model in Figure 10. An instance of P creates an instance of Q that creates an instance of R. This instance of R creates in turn another new instance of P. The channel C is flooded with messages $msg0$ at run time.

```
mtype = { msg0, msg1 };
chan C = [2] of { mtype };
active proctype P(){
        C!msg0;
        run P()}
```

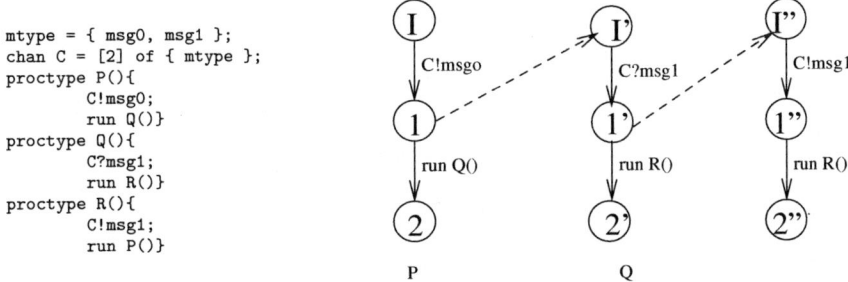

Fig. 9. A Promela model (left), the state machine of a running process of P (middle), and the modified state machine with replication transitions (right).

One way of dealing with this is to use replication transitions again to detect the unboundedness caused by mutual creations. But for any process, the replication transition would not target its own initial state since it is not self-created. Instead, for instance, the replication transition from the state 1 of the state machine of a P instance transfers the control to the initial state of the state machine of a Q instance. In this way, several previously independent state machines are united to one much larger state machine. Thereby our boundedness analysis would no longer be local to individual processes, but had to consider the complete system, which would significantly increase its complexity. In fact, unlike before, the time required would then be exponential in the number of parallel components, even if each individual component contains only a polynomial number of simple cycles.

```
mtype = { msg0, msg1 };
chan C = [2] of { mtype };
proctype P(){
        C!msg0;
        run Q()}
proctype Q(){
        C?msg1;
        run R()}
proctype R(){
        C!msg1;
        run P()}
```

Fig. 10. A Promela model (left), the united state machines with replication transitions (right).

A second solution would be to add local replication transitions, just like in Figure 9, in every process which can, directly or indirectly, call itself. This is a safe, but coarser, overapproximation of the solution in Figure 10. The advantage is that one avoids inter-process transitions and thus keeps the boundedness analysis local and efficient.

4   Experimental Results

In this section we present experimental results using a prototype implementation of our analysis algorithms in the IBOC tool. As case studies we use the *2-Proctype* model that is given in Figure 11, a Promela model of the *Alternating Bit Protocol*, and a Promela model of the CORBA *General Inter-ORB Protocol* (GIOP) [9][4]. IBOC uses to LPSOLVE tool for the linear programming tasks. All experiments were performed on a two processor 1GHz Pentium III PC with 2 GB of memory. Table 2 gives some statistics regarding the complexity of these models as well as the computational effort for the analysis with IBOC.

```
mtype = { c, b, a };
chan AB = [25] of { mtype };
chan BA = [25] of { mtype };                              active proctype B(){
active proctype A(){                                         BA!c;
  s1:  if                                                    BA!c;
       :: BA?c -> AB!b; AB!b; goto s2                        goto s4;
       :: BA?c -> AB!b; AB!b; AB!b; AB!b; AB!b; goto s3   s4: if
       fi;                                                   :: AB?a -> goto s5
  s2:  if                                                    fi;
       :: BA?c -> AB!a; AB!a; AB!b; goto s3               s5: if
       fi;                                                   :: AB?b -> BA!c; goto s4
  s3:  if                                                    fi;}
       :: BA?c -> AB!a; AB!a; goto s2
       fi}
```

Fig. 11. The 2-Proctype Promela Model.

Table 2. Model Complexity Statistics and Computational Effort for Analysis

	2-Proctype	Alternating Bit	CORBA GIOP
Processes	2	3	5
States	20	12	135
Transitions	21	22	163
Message types	3	8	108
Channels	2	4	11
Reported cycles	3	13	2638
Generated vectors	2	13	752
Runtime for cycle detection [sec.]	0.062	0.218	7.187
Runtime for boundedness check [sec.]	0.000	0.031	0.098
Runtime for computing bounds [sec.]	0.032	-	1.265

In IBOC, the full range of abstractions as discussed in Section 3 is not yet implemented. We use the finer abstraction proposed in Section 3.1 to identify message types. We are tracking *mtype* variables as discussed in Section 3.2. Since we can not exclude arithmetic operations over the integer domain, whenever we encounter an arithmetic expression in an assignment to a variable, we set the integer domain as the range of the variable. We collect all process creation statements to record channel argument passing for each running process. We adopt the coarser of the abstractions proposed in Section 3.5 to deal with channel assignments. We use some tracking of integer variables to narrow down channel array index values. We don't consider the unbounded process creation problem at all since SPIN allows no more than 255 concurrent proctype instances.

---

[4] The Promela sources for the IBOC model that we use are freely available from URL http://tele.informatik.uni-freiburg.de/leue/sources/giop/giop-sttt.tar.

IBOC returned a result of "BOUNDED" for the 2-Proctypes model. The estimated bounds were 20 for the channel AB and 6 for the channel BA which allows us to reduce the channel size compared to the values in the original model. This entails a significant state space reduction. Note that neither the boundedness result nor the estimated bounds could easily be derived from the model by manual inspection.

"UNKNOWN" was returned for the model of the Alternating Bit Protocol. When such a verdict is returned, IBOC indicates control flow cycles that possibly contribute to the unbounded growth of a channel. For this model IBOC identified the cycle in which the sender sends messages to the system as a potential source of unboundedness. This is quite plausible since in the sender can flood the Alternating Bit protocol in an unconstrained fashion. In the sequel we will refer to the potentially unbounded cycles that IBOC identifies as *counterexamples*.

The GIOP model is a real-life communication protocol with significant complexity. It amongst other features it supports server object migration between different Object Request Brokers (ORBs). IBOC returned an "UNKNOWN" result for the GIOP model and provided two counterexamples within a very reasonable runtime. One counterexample is the cycle where a GIOP client ORB forwards a user request message to the GIOP agent ORB. The execution of this cycle can cause unboundedness if there are an unbounded number of user requests. The other counterexample is the cycle where server objects register their migration from one ORB to another. If we allow migrations to happen at any time, the system is flooded by an unbounded number of register messages. We eliminated these two sources of unboundedness from the GIOP system and applied IBOC again to the modified model. We obtained a result "BOUNDED" which indicates that the two counterexamples were indeed the only sources of unboundedness in the system. While some of the buffer bound estimates were larger than the ones assumed in [9], there were also some channels with smaller estimates. For instance, the size of the channel *toServer* in [9] is 3 while its estimate is 1.

5 Related Work

There is a long history of work on the handling of infinite communication buffers in automated system analysis. An overapproximation using the assumption that buffers may loose messages is proposed in [1]. Sufficient syntactic conditions for the *un*boundedness of communication channels in CFSM systems are proposed in [8]. There is a history of checking properties of Petri-Nets using linear programming techniques (c.f. [11,5]) but these approaches do not encompass boundedness tests. We are not aware of any work prior to ours that addresses buffer capacity estimation for CFSM-type models. Various attempts have been made to define formal operational semantics for Promela [13,2,16]. Note that our analysis largely relies on the recognition of statically analyzable features of Promela models, such as the control flow cycles, and many of the semantic subtleties of Promela were abstracted away. As a consequence our work does not depend on the availability of a completely specified and unanimously agreed semantics definition for Promela.

6   Conclusion

We presented an incomplete test for buffer overflows in Promela models as well as a conservative estimate for the maximal occupancy of Promela message channels. The experimental results we presented indicate that the analysis method scales well to problems of realistic size. We also illustrated that the analysis produces useful results, in particular the maximal occupancy estimates help in finding smaller models.

In comparison to the UML RT analysis presented in [10] the analysis of Promela code imposes more challenges on the employed code abstraction techniques. Due to its syntactically more constrained nature, the determination of message types and the identification of communication channels is not an issue.

Current research focuses on the improvement of counterexample handling and the identification of sources of unboundedness. As we discussed above, IBOC attempts to point the user to potential sources of unboundedness. Determining the non-spuriousness of a counterexample and the ensuing abstraction refinement are currently entirely handcraft, and we are currently working towards more automated support at this end.

Acknowledgements. The third author was supported through the DFG funded project IMCOS (grant number LE 1342/1). We thank all involved students, in particular Quang Minh Bui, for their effort in developing IBOC.

References

1. P. Abdulla and B. Jonsson. Verifying Programs with Unreliable Channels. In *LICS'93*. IEEE, 1993.
2. William R. Bevier. Towards an operational semantics of promela in acl2. In *Proceedings of the Third SPIN Workshop, SPIN97*, 1997.
3. A. Bouajjani and R. Mayr. Model checking lossy vector addition systems. In *Proc. of STACS'99*, volume 1563 of *LNCS*. Springer Verlag, 1999.
4. D. Brand and P. Zafiropulo. On communicating finite-state machines. *Journal of the ACM*, 2(5):323–342, April 1983.
5. J. Esparza and S. Melzer. Verification of safety properties using integer programming: Beyond the state equation. *Formal Methods in System Design*, 16:159–189, 2000.
6. J. Esparza and M. Nielsen. Decidability issues for Petri nets - a survey. *Journal of Informatics, Processing and Cybernetics*, 30(3):143–160, 1994.
7. Gerard J. Holzmann. *The Spin Model Checker - Primer and Reference Manual*. Addison-Wesley, 2004.
8. T. Jeron and C. Jard. Testing for unboundedness of fifo channels. *Theoretical Computer Science*, (113):93–117, 1993.
9. M. Kamel and S. Leue. Formalization and validation of the general inter-orb protocol (GIOP) using Promela and SPIN. In *Software Tools for Technology Transfer (STTT)*, volume 2, pages 394–409, 2000.
10. S. Leue, R. Mayr, and W. Wei. A scalable incomplete test for the boundedness of UML RT models. In *Proceedings of TACAS 2004*, LNCS. Springer Verlag, 2004.
11. S. Melzer and J. Esparza. Checking system properties via integer programming. In H.R. Nielson, editor, *Proc. of ESOP'96*, volume 1058 of *Lecture Notes in Computer Science*, pages 250–264. Springer Verlag, 1996.

12. G. Memmi and G. Roucairol. Linear algebra in net theory. In *Net Theory and Applications*, volume 84 of *LNCS*, pages 213–223, 1980.
13. V. Natarajan and G.J. Holzmann. Outline for an operational semantics of promela. In Jean-Charles Grégoire, Gerard J. Holzmann, and Doron A. Peled, editors, *The SPIN Verification System. Proceedings of the Second SPIN Workshop 1996.*, volume 32 of *DIMACS*. AMS, 1997.
14. B. Selic, G. Gullekson, and P.T. Ward. *Real-Time Object-Oriented Modelling*. John Wiley & Sons, Inc., 1994.
15. B. Selic and J. Rumbaugh. Using UML for modeling complex real-time systems. http://www.rational.com/media/whitepapers/umlrt.pdf, March 1998.
16. Carsten Weise. An incremental formal semantics for promela. In *Proceedings of the Third SPIN Workshop, SPIN97*, 1997.
17. H. Yen. A unified approach for deciding the existence of certain Petri net paths. *Information and Computation*, 96(1):119–137, 1992.

Translation from Adapted UML to Promela for CORBA-Based Applications

J. Chen and H. Cui

School of Computer Science, University of Windsor
Windsor, Ont. Canada N9B 3P4
{xjchen,cui}@uwindsor.ca

Abstract. Nowadays, many distributed applications take advantage of the transparent distributed object systems provided by CORBA middlewares. While greatly reduce the design and coding effort, the distributed object systems may also introduce subtle faults into the applications, which on the other hand, complicate the validation of the applications. In this paper, we present our work on applying SPIN to check the correctness of the designs of CORBA-based applications, taking into account those characteristics of CORBA that are essential to the correctness of the applications. In doing so, we provide adaptations to UML, so that the CORBA-based applications can be modeled with succinct yet sufficient details of the underlying middlewares. An automated translation tool is developed to generate Promela models from such UML design models. The translation tool embeds the behavioral details of the middleware automatically. In this way, the software developers can stay in their comfort zone while design faults, including those caused by the underlying distributed object systems can be pinpointed through the verification or the simulation with SPIN.

Keywords: Distributed Object Systems, Middleware, Formal Specification and Verification, Model Checking, UML, SPIN, CORBA.

1 Introduction

Nowadays, many distributed applications take advantage of middlewares. A middleware encapsulates the heterogeneity of the distributed computing environment and provides a consistent logic communication media for distributed applications. This greatly reduces the design and coding effort. Many general object-oriented distributed applications choose distributed object system (DOS) middlewares, where objects are made available by the middleware beyond process boundaries. To promote the interoperability of DOS middlewares, a widely accepted standard, CORBA, is established by OMG. Today, most DOS middlewares are either CORBA-compatible or similar to CORBA on architecture level.

However, distributed object systems may also introduce subtle faults into the applications. This is because application designers usually tend to overlook

S. Graf and L. Mounier (Eds.): SPIN 2004, LNCS 2989, pp. 234–251, 2004.

the differences between a local object and a remote object made transparently available. For example, phenomena like the serialization or blocking of remote object invocations may occur due to various reasons such as the resource configuration of the remote objects or the synchronization mode of the invocation itself. Overlooking such phenomena may under certain circumstances affect the business logic of the applications.

In this paper, we present our work on applying SPIN [6,7] to check the correctness of the designs of CORBA-based applications, taking into account those characteristics of CORBA that are essential to the correctness of the applications.

Formal verification techniques, such as SPIN model checker, rely on formal specifications of the design documents. However, it is hard for ordinary software developers to grasp formal specification languages. One of the possible solutions is to define an automated translation from graphical, easy-to-use design models into the formal specification languages. For object-oriented applications, UML has been recognized as an industrial standard and is commonly used for software design. Here we assume that the design specifications of CORBA-base distributed applications are given in UML notations. As the UML notations stretch over almost all aspects of software artifacts, translating the entire domain of UML notations is not feasible. We choose to adapt and translate an essential subset of UML class diagram, statechart diagram and deployment diagram, which provide sufficient information about the dynamic behavior of the applications.

When building a verification model for a CORBA-based application, the behavior of a remote object should not be over-simplified as that of a local object. On the other hand, as the verification process is always resource intensive, the verification model must be succinct and should not accommodate a *complete* middleware model. In this paper, we construct an abstracted CORBA middleware model in Promela, considering those and only those characteristics of CORBA that are essential to the correctness of the applications, namely: (i) *binding*: the connection of a client to a remote object; (ii) *thread policy*: the POA (Portable Object Adaptor) policy which governs the service of remote objects; (iii) *synchronization mode*: the mode for client-side remote method invocations.

Accordingly, we made a few adaptations to UML notations, including (i) stereotypes for classes, methods and interfaces; (ii) pre-defined classes for client binding, remote method invocations and thread policies; and (iii) pre-defined component types for describing CORBA facilities (POAs and ORBs). These adaptations serve as the interface of the abstract CORBA middleware model. In this way, we preserve the clarity of the design models: The CORBA middleware remains a black-box in the design models. While generating the corresponding Promela model from such design models, our CORBA-middleware model is integrated automatically.

We have developed a translation tool called CUP, which generates the corresponding Promela source code from adapted UML diagrams. A concrete system is created from a UML deployment diagram using the elements defined in

UML class diagrams. The behavior of the elements is defined in UML statechart diagrams. The statechart diagrams in our design model are built upon parameterized method calls, change events, guard conditions and value assignment actions. Currently, CUP takes as its input only specially formatted XML file that represents the UML diagrams. The files are actually simplified standard XMI representation of the UML diagrams. We plan to use the XMI representations as the input of CUP in the future.

To reduce verification complexity, we translate most of the methods into Promela *inlines*, which is the most efficient way to simulate method calls in Promela [6]. For this purpose, we require that the behavior of a class is defined on per-method basis. Consequently, we eliminate all concurrency elements in a statechart diagram (sync, fork, join, concurrent regions in composite states). Instead, the concurrency is achieved through some specially stereotyped methods, which are specified as *running on its own execution thread*.

To further reduce the complexity, we define specially named composite states in statechart diagrams to identify atomically executed blocks. Thus, transitions dealing with only local variables can be organized into atomic execution blocks which eliminates some interleavings that do not affect the truthfulness of the correctness properties.

We assume that readers have basic knowledge of Promela/SPIN and UML. In Section 2, we give a brief introduction to parts of CORBA relevant to our work. A motivating example is described in Section 3. This example is used through out the paper to demonstrate the UML adaptation, translation and the verification results. Our adapted UML design model for CORBA-based applications is introduced in Section 4. In Section 5, we explain the generation of Promela code from the design model, especially the realization of the distributed object systems. Conclusion, related work and some final remarks are given at the end.

2   A Brief Introduction to CORBA

CORBA is a widely accepted standard for DOS middlewares established by OMG. A CORBA middleware makes objects in a distributed application accessible beyond process boundaries. The core component of the middleware is the object request brokers (ORB), which is responsible for finding a proper remote object to service a client (binding), communicating the method invocation requests to the remote objects and transferring the result back to the clients when it becomes available. An ORB may be *single-threaded* or *multi-threaded*. To be remotely accessible, a remote object must be managed by a POA object and registered to the naming space. The POA is the interface between the objects and the ORB. A POA manages remote objects, interprets the invocation requests made to the objects and activates proper servant threads to service the requests. How a POA performs is determined by its *policies*. The policy we are interested in is the *thread policy*, which specifies the thread model used for the servant threads:

- *main-thread.* All POAs in an ORB with this thread policy will share a servant thread provided by the ORB for all method invocations.
- *thread-per-POA.* The POA will create one servant thread to handle all method invocations.
- *thread-pool(n).* The POA will create a set of n servant threads to handle method invocations.
- *thread-per-object.* The POA will create a servant thread for each remote object it manages.
- *thread-per-client.* The POA will create a servant thread for method invocations from each client of an object it manages.
- *thread-per-request.* The POA will create a servant thread for each method invocation request.

POA thread models can be used in either *single-threaded* or *multi-threaded* ORB. However, in a *single-threaded* ORB, the performance of any POA will be the same as that of a *main-thread* one.

Since method invocations may share a thread in ORB or POA according to the thread policies, internal blocking is introduced to the application, which may cause deadlocks or request re-ordering.

To find a remote object for service, a client must identify to the ORB, the remote object(s) it wishes to connect to and the ORB will locate the proper remote object for it accordingly. This process is called *binding*. Common binding options are:

- Request to bind to a specific remote object. The object is identified by its unique identifier.
- Request to bind to a remote object of a certain type. The type is identified by the remote interface of the object.
- Request to bind to a remote object of a certain type in a certain POA. The POA is identified by its unique identifier.

A remote method may be invoked in different synchronization modes. Typically, the invocation is *synchronous*: the client blocks until the remote method call returns. When a method requires no return values, the invocation can be made *asynchronously*: the client will continue its execution as soon as the request is received on the other end, without waiting for its completion. If the method invocation involves lengthy computation, *deferred synchronous* call is useful. In this invocation mode, the client continues execution after issuing the request, and *pulls* the result of the remote method call sometime later.

In the next section, we give a motivating example to show the design of distributed applications with CORBA middleware and the possible faults that may be introduced.

3   A Motivating Example

In an *auction* system, multiple clients (bidders) can compete for items. A bidder can withdraw from bidding at any time, and the bidding of an item terminates when all bidders have withdrawn from the competition for that item, or when the pre-set price limit for that item is reached. When the bidding of an item terminates, whoever offered the highest bid first will succeed in the bidding. Suppose for fault-tolerance purpose, there are two servers running concurrently to service the bidders. Each of them maintains a local copy of the bidding status. A bidder is allowed to connect to any one of the servers, yet for fairness reason, only one connection is allowed for each bidder. The auction server will refuse a connection if another connection from the same bidder (determined by its identifier) already exists.

Let us assume that such a system is designed using CORBA middleware in the following way: Two remote objects are used as auction servers. The bidding status is represented as replicated local data of these objects. The two auction servers synchronize with each other through remote method invocations to keep the bidding status consistent. When two servers try to update the bidding status simultaneously, a token is used to determine which server should update first. An active object is used to represent a bidder. Each bidder object connects to an auction server through a client that is bound randomly to an auction server. To make a bidding request, the client invokes a remote method on the auction server it is connected to.

Below are some of the properties of the applications we are interested in and that can be verified with model checking tools:

- The design should be deadlock-free.
- The bidding process should eventually complete.
- One and only one of the bidders will eventually succeed in bidding an item.
- The successful bidder must hold a bid higher than or equal to the other bidders.
- The successful bid should be no higher than the pre-set price limit.

The correctness of such properties may vary depending on whether we model the middleware behavior or simply treat the remote object invocations similar as local calls. For example, an application according to the above design runs well under *multi-threaded* ORBs and *thread-per-client* POAs but it may run into deadlock if we use *thread-per-object* POAs. In the latter case, suppose bidder b_1 made a bidding request to auction server s_1 and bidder b_2 made a bidding request to auction server s_2 simultaneously. Server s_1 tries to synchronize with server s_2 on behalf of b_1: it makes a remote method invocation on auction server s_2 for the update of the bidding status, while vice versa, server s_2 tries to synchronize with server s_1. However, both these method invocations are blocked because the only servant threads on server object s_1 and s_2 are already occupied by bidders b_1 and b_2 respectively when they made the method invocations on their respect server object. As b_1 and b_2 will not release the servant threads of s_1 and s_2 respectively while they wait for the results of their bidding requests, the execution runs into a deadlock state. Such a deadlock situation cannot be identified if we model remote method invocations in the same way as local ones.

4   Adapted UML Diagrams

In this section, we introduce our UML design model for CORBA-based applications as the input of the CUP tool.

The design model consists of a set of self-executable active objects, ORB and POA components and remote object components deployed into the POA components. Each object and component is assigned a unique and publicly known integer ID. We assume all objects and components are persistent. We do not consider the creation, de-activation and destruction of any active objects, remote object components, POA or ORB components.

Correspondingly, the input model of the CUP tool consists of a UML deployment diagram, which creates and deploys all object instances in the application, UML class diagrams and the UML state chart diagrams, which are for the specification of the objects. Each method defined in the class diagram is associated with a statechart diagram to specify its behavior. The behavior of a class is specified by the collection of its method statechart diagrams.

In the following, we introduce the syntax and the semantics of the adapted deployment diagrams, class diagrams and statechart diagrams.

4.1   The Deployment Diagram

The deployment diagram specifies the following aspects of the application:

- The object and component instances and their unique identifiers;
- The *deployment relationship* between remote objects and POAs, between POAs and ORBs, is used to specify the management relationship among them.
- The thread policies for POAs and ORBs are specified by deploying a *Policy* object to a POA or an ORB.

The deployment diagram contains two nodes: a CORBA node and a *Clients* node.

The CORBA node forms the server-side of the application. It contains one or more ORB components. An ORB component contains a root POA component and possibly a *Policy* object. The latter defines the thread policy of the ORB. If omitted, the default thread policy is *single-threaded*. The root POA component contains zero or more remote object components and zero or more POA components. Each POA component also contains zero or more remote object components and zero or more POA components. A remote object is expressed as a component which implements a remote object interface. A POA component may contain a *Policy* object, which defines the thread policy of the POA. The thread policy of root POA is always *main-thread*. A POA without a *Policy* object inherits the thread policy of its parent POA.

The *Clients* node contains a set of *Process* components. They form the client-side of the application. Each *Process* component contains an active object, which is self-executable and serves as the starting point of the execution.

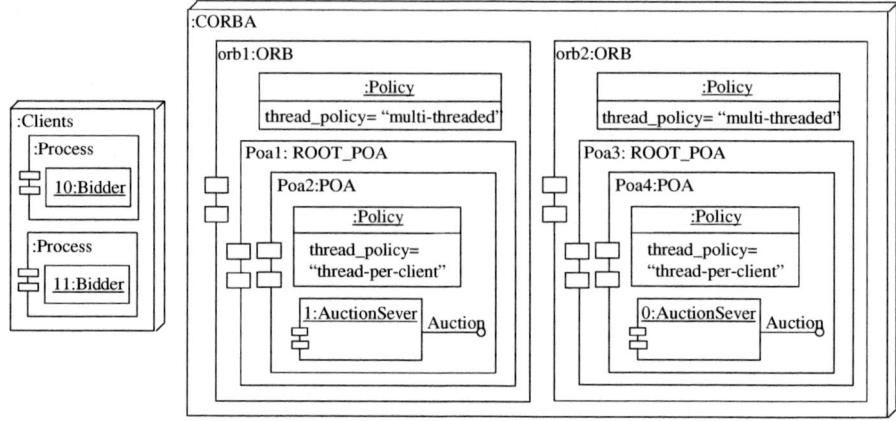

Fig. 1. Deployment diagram of the online auction example

Figure 1 shows the deployment diagram of the auction example, in which two bidders participate in the auction of an item. Here, the CORBA node contains two ORB components *orb1* and *orb2*, both specified as *multi-threaded*. In the root POA of *orb1*, we have POA component *Poa2* whose thread policy is *thread-per-client*. With this policy, it manages a remote object of class *AuctionServer* with identifier 1. The *Clients* node contains two *Process* components with active objects 10 and 11 respectively of class *Bidder*.

4.2   The Class Diagrams

The class diagrams in our model contains active object classes, remote object interfaces and classes that implement remote object interfaces. To distinguish the specific roles of the classes in the applications, we define class stereotype *Active* for active object classes and interface stereotype *IDL* for remote interfaces. An active object is self-executable. To specify the starting point of the execution, we define method stereotype *Main*. An *Active* class must contain one and only one *Main*-stereotyped method, which starts the execution. We also define a similar method stereotype called *Thread*. A *Thread*-stereotyped method is not self-executable. However, when it is called, it will execute on its own execution thread, running concurrently with its caller. A *Thread*-stereotyped method must have neither output nor return parameters.

Figure 2 shows the class diagram for the auction example. Here, an instance of class *Bidder* is an *active* object, and its attribute *serverC* is a *Stub*. In the statechart diagrams, it will be bound to an *Auction* remote object and thus become a client of the object. Similarly, the attribute *interServer* in an *Auction-Server* object will become a client of the other *Auction* remote object for server synchronization.

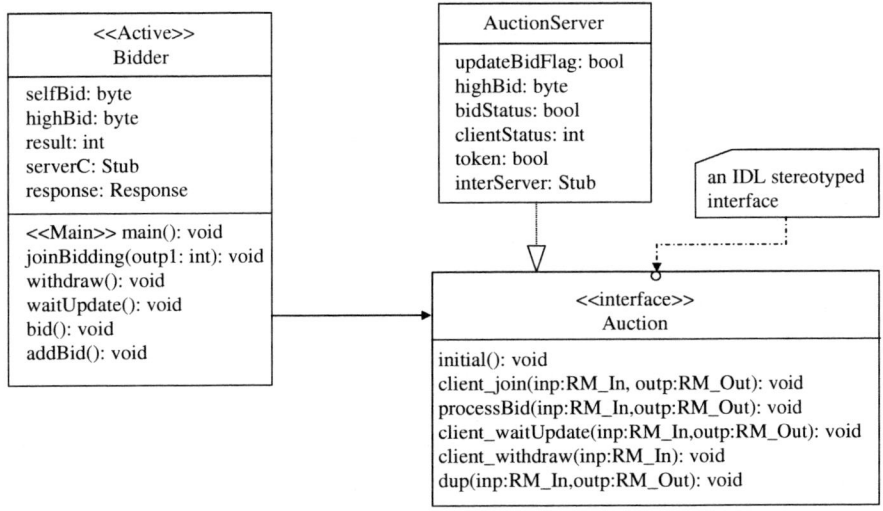

Fig. 2. Class diagram in online auction example

Note that these diagrams are for illustration only. Our CUP tool currently works only on text-based, specially formatted input.

As shown in this figure, to keep the verification model manageable, we uniform the parameters of the remote methods such that: (i) The method must have no return value; (ii) The method must take an *RM_In* object as its input parameter and possibly an *RM_Out* object as its output parameter. As default, the data classes *RM_In* and *RM_Out* contain two integer parameters each. Designers can override these classes if needed, but the parameters must be of type integer or its subtype.

With the restriction, the interface to any remote method is statically determined. That, combined with the statically created remote objects, greatly simplifies the realization of the binding and the remote method invocation process.

As shown in the figure above, two pre-defined CORBA-related classes, namely *Stub* and *Response*, are used to facilitate remote method invocations. A *Stub* object represents a client to a remote object. The *Request* object in CORBA, which is used for dynamic method invocation, is omitted in our model since the restrictions we put on the model reduced much of the dynamic method invocation tasks. For simplicity, the core of the dynamic method invocation, namely the deferred remote method calls, is packed into the *Stub* object. The *Response* class is for getting the result of deferred remote method calls.

Figure 3 shows the details of the class definitions of the *Stub* and *Response*.

The *Stub* class contains six methods: two binding methods, three remote call methods and an *unbind* method.

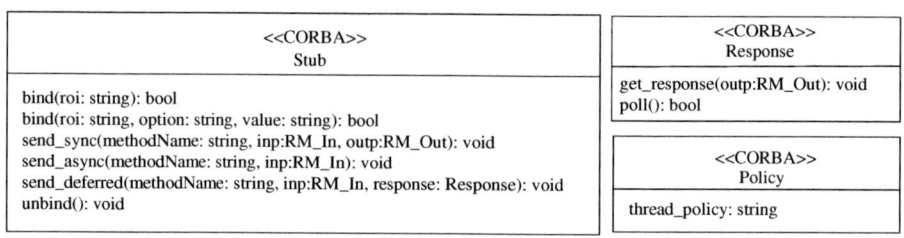

Fig. 3. The Stub and Response classes

A *Stub* object becomes a client to a remote object through its binding methods. The first parameter in both methods defines the type of the remote object to which the *Stub* object will be bound. Its value must be set as one of the *IDL*-stereotyped interface name.

- The binding method with no binding option will randomly bind the *Stub* object to a remote object which implements that interface.
- If the *option* parameter is given value *POA*, the method will bind the *Stub* object to a remote object component implementing the given interface in the specific POA component. The parameter *value* indicates the id of that POA.
- If the *option* parameter is given value *OBJ*, the method will bind the *Stub* object to a specific remote object. The parameter *value* indicates the id of that object. The object must implement the given interface.

After binding, the remote method calls to that object can be made through the *Stub* object. The remote methods can be called synchronously through the *send_sync* method, asynchronously through the *send_async* method or deferred synchronously through the *send_deferred* method. The parameter *methodName* in these methods specifies the remote method that should be called. The parameters *inp* and *outp* contain input and output parameters respectively. The *Response* object is for getting result of deferred method calls. The result of the method invocation can be pulled at any time by calling the *get_response* method of the *Response* object.

A *Stub* object can also be disconnected from the remote object by calling the *unbind* method. After disconnection, the bind methods can be called again to bind the object to a remote object.

Another class shown on Figure 3 is the *Policy* class. Instances of this class define the thread policy for ORB or POA components. (See Figure 1).

A *Policy* object contains a string attribute *thread_policy*, which defines the thread policy of a POA or ORB component. The legal values of *thread_policy* for POA are *thread-per-client*, *thread-per-obj*, *thread-per-POA*, *thread-per-ORB*, *thread-pool(n)* and *thread-per-request*. The legal values for ORB are *single-threaded* and *multi-threaded*. We assume a multi-threaded ORB has unlimited

method clientJoin in AuctionServer

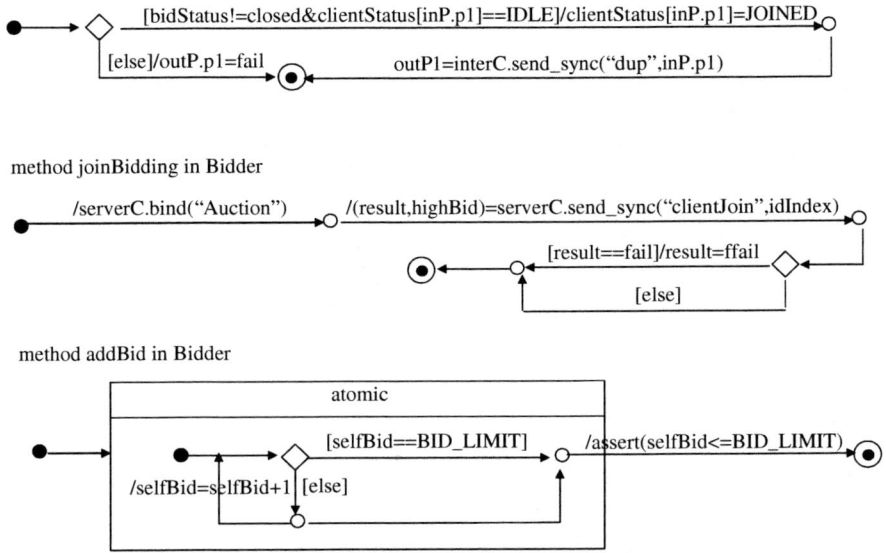

method joinBidding in Bidder

method addBid in Bidder

Fig. 4. Partial statechart diagram in online auction example

thread resource and will never block. We also do not consider the inter-ORB communication at this stage.

4.3   The Statechart Diagrams

As we mentioned in the Introduction, in the design model, a statechart diagram defines the behavior of a method. It is built upon parameterized method calls, change events, guard conditions and value assignment actions. Unlike in traditional state diagrams, in UML statechart diagrams, a transition with a guard condition is executable only if the condition is true at the time the system leaves the starting state of the transition. Correspondingly, change event is defined in UML statechart diagrams: A transition with a change event is executable whenever the boolean condition used in the event becomes true. Both cases are reflected in CUP.

In the statechart diagram of method *joinBidding* (the second statechart diagram) in Figure 4, a *serverC* stub is bound to an arbitrary remote object of *AuctionServer*. With this binding, remote method *clientJoin* (see the first statechart diagram) is called in synchronous mode.

We eliminate all concurrency elements in a statechart diagram (sync, fork, join, concurrent regions in composite states). Instead, the concurrency is achieved through calls to *Thread*-stereotyped methods when necessary.

To reduce the verification complexity of the model, we add special semantics for composite states named *atomic*: they identify atomically executed blocks. For example, in the statechart diagram of method *addBid* in Figure 4, since generating a new bid is a sequence of local actions which do not involve any shared data, they are specified as an *atomic* composite state for an atomic sequence of actions. It reduces the verification complexity without any side-effect.

For verification purpose, we add special semantics for states whose name starting with *end, progress* or *accept*. They will be translated into their corresponding Promela labels [6], which play important roles during the verification. We also allow users to insert Promela assertion statements in the transition actions as correctness properties. For example, in the statechart diagram *addBid* in Figure 4, the assertion statement verifies if the new bid generated will be no greater than the pre-set price limit.

Due to space limit, we will not discuss statechart diagrams in more details here (cf. [1]).

5   Promela Model for CORBA Distribute Object Systems

In the previous section, we have introduced our adaptation of UML for CORBA-based applications. In this section, we explain the corresponding Promela model. Basically, the Promela model is generated according to the following rules:

- Each POA component is translated into a global channel which holds remote method call requests and a set of *servant thread processes* according to its thread policy. The servant threads repeatedly remove the request it should process from the POA channel, invoke proper method inline to service the call and send results (if any) through the return channel provided in the request back to the caller.
- An ORB component with *single-threaded* policy is translated into a global channel which holds remote method call requests and a *dispatcher process* which repeatedly removes element from the channel and dispatches it to proper POA channel.
- An ORB component with *multi-threaded* policy is omitted in the Promela model: The remote method call requests are sent directly to the POA channels.
- An active object is translated into a data attribute, a set of method inlines (each corresponding to a method) and a set of Promela process prototype (each corresponding to a *Main* or *Thread*-stereotyped method). A process of a *Main*-stereotyped method prototype will be activated by the *init* process of Promela.
- A remote object component is translated into an attribute of a customized data type and a set of method inlines. One or more servant thread processes of its POA will be assigned to service remote method invocations to this object, using the data attributes and the method inlines.
- The binding is extracted from ORBs and is realized by a sole Promela process called *cup_bind*.

- The data class *RM_In* and *RM_Out* are translated into two customized Promela datatypes *CUP_RM_In* and *CUP_RM_Out*.
- A *Response* object is translated into an attribute of data type *CUP_Response*, which contains a channel for retrieving the result of a remote method call.
- A *Stub* object is translated into an attribute of data type *CUP_Stub*, which contains two channels and two integers: Channel *invocation* is for sending remote method calls and channel *response* is for getting the result of a synchronized remote method call; Integer *objID* and *stubID* are for the binding purpose.

Table 5 shows the definitions of *CUP_Response* and *CUP_Stub*.

Table 1. CUP data types for the Stub and the Response classses

```
typedef CUP_Stub
{
    int stubID, objID;
    chan invocation;      / * for sending remote method calls * /
    / * return channel : outputParameters * /
    chan response = [0] of {CUP_RM_Out};
}
typedef CUP_Response      / * for deferred method calls * /
{
    chan responseChan = [1] of {CUP_RM_Out};     / * outputParameters * /
}
```

The binding of a *Stub* object is translated into the proper initialization of the invocation channel and the *objID* attribute. We chose to use a sole Promela process instead of one for each ORB to handle all binding requests and each binding request is serviced by an atomic block. This puts less strain on the state space. Since the variables modified by the binding process is local to the stub or to the generated servant thread, such implementation is free from side-effect.

All binding requests are sent through a global channel *cup_bind_request*. The request contains three *mtype* integers representing the unique id of the *Stub* object, the type of the remote object and the binding option (CUP_RANDOM, CUP_POA or CUP_OBJ). It also contains an integer for POA or remote object id.

The binding process interprets the requests, finds a proper remote object according to the binding options and returns the proper invocation channel together with the remote object id to another global channel *cup_bind_result* to be picked up by the requester. If the remote object is managed by a POA which belongs to a *single-threaded* ORB, the request channel of that ORB will be sent back. Otherwise, the request channel of the POA will be sent back. If the chosen object is managed by a *thread-per-client* policy POA, the binding process also starts a servant process to service that stub.

The following shows the definition of the binding channels and the translation of the binding for a *Stub* object *stub*:

$chan\ cup\_bind\_request = [0]\ of\ \{mtype, mtype, mtype, int\};$
$chan\ cup\_bind\_result = [0]\ of\ \{chan,\ int\};$

stub.bind("Auction") is translated into

$cup\_bind\_request!stub\_T.stubID, CUP\_IDL\_Auction, CUP\_RANDOM, scratch;$
$cup\_bind\_request?stub\_T.invocation, stub\_T.objID;$

Note that each variable name may be assigned with some suffixes during the translation. As such details are omitted here (cf. [1]), we use T to represent such possible suffix here for readability.

A remote method call is translated into sending of a remote method call element to the invocation channel. For example, suppose an invocation request for method m with input parameter ip is made through a *Stub* object named s. If the method has an output parameter op, then UML synchronous remote method call

$s.send\_sync("m", ip, op)$

will be translated by CUP into

$s\_T.invocation!s\_T.stubID, CUP\_SYNC, s\_T.response, s\_T.objID,$
$\qquad CUP\_METHOD\_m, ip\_T);$
$stub\_T.response?op\_T;$

The element contains the id for the stub object, the synchronization flag, the response channel, the remote object id, the remote method id and the input parameter. Here, CUP_METHOD_m is the generated unique identifier for method m.

Each remote method call element is extracted from the invocation channel by a servant process, interpreted and serviced. The functionality and the quantity of the servant threads are determined by the thread policy of POAs:

- A servant process is created for each ORB which has at least one *thread-per-ORB* policy POA to service all calls made to the request channel of the ORB (to invoke a remote method managed by one of the POAs).
- A set of servant processes is created for each POA that does not have a *thread-per-ORB* policy. They service specific calls made to the request channel of the POA:
    - *thread-per-client*: A servant process is created for each stub object which is a client of a remote object managed by the POA to service the calls from the stub object.
    - *thread-per-obj*: A servant process is created for each remote object managed by the POA to service the calls to the object.
    - *thread-per-POA*: A servant process is created to service all the calls to the POA.
    - *thread-pool(n)*: A set of n servant processes is created to service all the calls to the POA.

- *thread-per-request*: A servant process is created for each invocation request. The process terminates after the call is completed.

To service a call, a servant thread will first determine a proper inline to invoke, according to the method identifier and the remote object identifier sent as part of the request. Then the inline will be invoked with the input parameter from the request, and the output parameter, if any, will be updated in the inline and finally be sent back to the return channel provided in the request.

Due to the limit of space, we will not discuss the generation of the inlines here.

6 Related Work

To boost the acceptance of formal verification techniques, various researchers have been exploiting ways to loosen the restriction that a system must be described formally for verification purpose. An alternative is to derive formal descriptions automatically from existing software artifacts, so that the software developers can get relief from learning a formal specification language and further writing correct specifications in it. Since UML is well accepted by the software industries as graphical design notations, people have been studying the formalization of UML descriptions. In particular, people have discussed various issues regarding the translation from formalized UML statechart diagrams into PROMELA [10,11,14,13].

Our work also involves such a translation. Its details, which is out of the scope of the present paper, is reported in [1]. The most prominent feature in our translation of UML statechart diagrams (as well as class diagrams and deployment diagrams) is that our focus is application-oriented. While other UML → Promela translation tools are available, ours specifically deals with the parameterized remote and local method calls and exempt signal events. We allow rich transition syntax while put much restrictions on states, especially those related to the concurrency control. The result is an efficient translation that translates each statechart into a Promela process or a Promela inline. In this regard, our translation shares some commonality with the Java Pathfinder [5]. Our treatment greatly reduced the number of processes in the translated code. We also distinguish between change events and guard conditions, which is not addressed in other translators. Our focus has been put on introducing the realization of the CORBA distributed object system in Promela, which simplifies the verification task for distributed applications built on CORBA-based middlewares.

The verification of distributed computing environment has also gained much of our attention. Various works have been conducted to verify the correctness of communication protocols on different layers. For example, the specifications of CORBA ORB (Object Request Broker) properties are discussed in [2]. The descriptions of CORBA GIOP (General Inter-ORB Protocol) in PROMELA can be found in [8]. The motivation behind these works is to check the correctness of the protocols themselves. Our work, on the other hand, is targeted at the correctness of the design models of the applications built on top of the CORBA middleware. In doing so, we have not only abstracted and formalized the CORBA-middleware but also embedded it automatically into the design notations during the translation of the adapted UML diagrams.

There are two main middleware families: the DOS middlewares, and the message-oriented middleware. While we have reported our work for the former, one can also find related work for the publish-subscribe middleware, one of the major message-oriented middlewares [3]. In the work of [3], the authors used *reusable, parameterized state machine models* to define the behavior of a *generic* publish-subscribe middleware, and developed translation tool to transform it, together with the descriptions of the components of the applications, into a specific verification model for SMV. The middleware interfaces we used here are an object-based, generic form in UML to describe the *reusable, parameterized state machine*.

A similar work that involves both the formalism of CORBA and its integration into the design specifications of the applications can be found in [9]. There, the authors have presented a technique on modeling the behavior of CORBA ORB in Finite State Processes (FSP) [12] so that the related model checking tool Labeled Transition System Analyzer (LTSA) [12] can apply. To incorporate the modeling of the ORB into the specification of the design models in UML, the authors suggested to use the *stereotypes* on class diagrams to define the threading policy (single-threaded class or multithreaded class), and on method invocations in statechart diagrams to define the synchronization modes of the calls. In reality, however, the thread policy is defined on ORBs and POAs, and instances of the same class (of the application) may be managed by different POAs possibly with different thread policy. Here we have explicitly defined dedicated components for POAs and ORBs, each with an attribute to specify the corresponding thread policy.

There are quite some model-checking tools available off-the-shelf. We chose SPIN because it is a popular, mature and powerful tool. It allows us to benefit from a lot of important features it provides, e.g. on-the-fly verification, support for both rendezvous and buffered message passing, efficient partial order reduction. Our focus is on the transparency and the efficiency of the translated model. For efficiency, our model is basically static and methods are implemented as PROMELA inlines to reduce resource consumption. If desired, CUP can be modified without difficulty to utilize the extensions of SPIN such as dSPIN [4], which may provide some additional features.

7   Conclusion and Final Remark

CUP is for those users who have little knowledge of formal verification techniques but desire to use them. Especially, we consider applying model checking tools to CORBA-based applications.

The major issue of the tool is how to model the applications so that the chosen model checking tool can work effectively. Even with the effectiveness of SPIN, we still need to make our best effort to reduce the complexity of the generated Promela model, because the difficulty comes from two dimensions: one is the complexity of the application logic, and another is from the realization of CORBA-based middleware.

On the aspect of the application logic, we translated most statechart diagrams into Promela inlines, for which we have to generate method invocation graph and create different suffix for labels, method names and variable names accordingly. We also added special semantics to composite states to identify atomically executed blocks. On the aspect of middleware modeling, we first simplified naming, binding, etc. The naming is omitted and binding request are serviced by a single process with each binding request modeled as an atomic block. Each servant thread is modeled as a Promela process. By minimizing the processes used for remote method calls, the complexity is reduced and the resulting model can remain manageable.

We verified the Promela source file generated by current version of CUP for the auction application on a Toshiba Satellite notebook computer with Microsoft Windows XP, Pentium(R) 4 with CPU 3.06GHz speed and 512M memory. The verification to check deadlock on the model with two bidders passed in 160 minutes in exhaustive checking, and less than 7 minutes in supertrace checking with over 99% coverage. We also verified some LTL formulas while polishing the auction application. We have identified errors in verifying:

- One and only one of the bidders should finally succeed and the others should finally fail.
  #define ppp ((Bidder[0].result == fsucc)& (Bidder[1].result == ffail))
  #define qqq ((Bidder[1].result == fsucc)& (Bidder[0].result == ffail))
  LTL: <>(ppp—qqq)
  error: Both bidder fails.
  reason: Bidder may not bid at all before withdrawing.
  solution: Let bidder bid at least once before withdrawing.
- The success bidder should hold the highest bid.
  #define rr1 ((Bidder[0].result == fsucc)&(Bidder[0].selfBid== Auction[0].highBid))
  #define rr2 ((Bidder[1].result == fsucc)&(Bidder[1].selfBid== Auction[0].highBid))
  LTL: <>(rr1|rr2)
  error: the final bid is higher than the *highBid* in *Auction Server*.
  reason: error in auction server synchronization.
  solution: change made in the *dup* method.

Compared with the simplified version of our work where middleware is not modeled and the remote objects are treated as access-free local objects, CUP has apparently added some overhead to the execution cost to handle each client thread and each remote method call issued by a client thread. This overhead is determined by many factors. Intuitively, the impact of the overhead on handling the client thread decreases with the increase of the workload of the client thread, and the impact of the overhead on handling the remote method call header increases with the frequency of the remote calls: If the clients makes frequent yet short remote method calls, it will cause a great deal of overhead.

We have run the auction example with two bidders under the thread-per-client mode, and with different pre-set price limits 2, 3, 4, 5, 6. See below:

Price Limit= 6 → Depth= 628 States= 5.5e+007 Transitions = 7.23034e+007
Price Limit = 5 → Depth= 586 States= 3.1e+007 Transitions = 4.0888e+007
Price Limit = 4 → Depth= 570 States= 1.4e+007 Transitions = 1.86401e+007
Price Limit = 3 → Depth= 566 States= 5e+006 Transitions = 6.79471e+006
Price Limit = 2 → Depth= 531 States= 1e+006 Transitions= 1.3985e+006

The workload of the client threads and the number of remote method calls in each client thread increase with the pre-set price limit. From the above data, we can see that the impact of the thread overhead (¡e+006) is negligible when the price limit increases. On the other hand, the overhead on the remote method calls remains constant and cannot be ignored.

The state explosion problem due to the increased complexity of the application itself is unavoidable in CUP: typically, the number of states will increase exponentially with the number of active servant threads. For example, if three bidders instead of two compete for an item with price limit 3, the number of state increases rapidly to 3.5e+008.

Acknowledgements. The author would like to thank the anonymous reviewers for helpful comments on the preliminary version of this paper submitted to SPIN 2004. This work is supported in part by the Natural Sciences and Engineering Research Council of Canada under grant number RGPIN 209774.

References

1. H. Cui. Correctness of distributed systems with middleware. Master's Thesis. School of Computer Science, University of Windsor, April 2003.
2. G. Duval. Specification and verification of an object request broker. In *Proc. of the 20th International Conference on Software Engineering*, pages 43–52, 1998.
3. D. Garlan, S. Khersonsky, and J. Kim. Model checking publish-subscribe systems. In *Proceedings of the 10th International SPIN Workshop on Model Checking Software (SPIN'03), LNCS 2648*, pages 166–180, 2003.
4. J. Hatcliff, X. Deng, M. Dwyer, G. Jung, and V. P. Ranganath. An integrated development, analysis, and verification environment for component-based systems. In *Proc. of the 25th International Conference on Software Engineering*, pages 160–173. IEEE, 2003.
5. K. Havelund and T. Pressburger. Model checking Java programs using Java PathFinder. *International Journal on Software Tools for Technology Transfer*, 2(4):366–381, April 2000.
6. G. Holzmann. *The Design and Validation of Computer Protocols*. Prentice Hall, 1991.
7. G. Holzmann. The model checker SPIN. *IEEE Transactions on Software Engineering*, 23(5), May 1997.

8. M. Kamel and S. Leue. Formalization and validation of the general inter-ORB protocol (GIOP) using Promela and Spin. *Software Tools for Technology Transfer*, 2(4):394–409, 2000.

9. N. Kaveh and W. Emmerich. Deadlock detection in distributed object systems. In *Proc. of the Joint 8th European Software Engineering Conference (ESEC) and 9th ACM SIGSOFT Symposium on the Foundations of Software Engineering (FSE-9)*, pages 44–51. ACM Press, 2001.

10. D. Latella, I. Majzik, and M. Massink. Automatic verification of a behavioural subset of UML statechart diagrams using the SPIN model-checker. *Formal Aspects of Computing*, 11:637–664, 1999.

11. J. Lilius and I. Paltor. Formalizing UML state machines for model checking. In *Proc. of the 2nd International Conference on Unified Modeling Language (UML'99), LNCS 1723*, pages 430–445. Springer-Verlag, 1999.

12. J. Magee and J. Kramer. *Concurrency: Models and Programs – From Finite State Models to Java Programs*. John Wiley, 1999.

13. E. Mikk, Y. Lakhnech, M. Siegel, and G. Holzmann. Implementing statecharts in PROMELA/SPIN. In *Proc. of the 2nd IEEE Workshop on Industrial Strength Formal Specification Techniques*, pages 90–101, 1998.

14. T. Schafer, A. Knapp, and S. Merz. Model checking UML state machines and collaborations. *Electronic Notes in Theoretical Computer Science*, 47:1–13, 2001.

Verifying Commit-Atomicity Using Model-Checking*

Cormac Flanagan

Department of Computer Science
University of California at Santa Cruz
Santa Cruz, CA 95064
cormac@cs.ucsc.edu

Abstract. The notion that certain procedures are *atomic* provides a
valuable partial specification for many multithreaded software systems.
Several existing tools verify atomicity by showing that every interleaved
execution *reduces* to an equivalent serial execution (in which the actions of each atomic procedure are not interleaved with actions of other
threads). However, experiments with these tools have highlighted a number of interesting procedures that, although atomic, are not reducible.

This paper presents a more complete technique for verifying atomicity.
Essentially, this technique explores non-serial and serial executions of the
multithreaded system simultaneously to ensure that every non-serial execution yields the same final state as the corresponding serial execution.
Using the SPIN model checker, we have applied this technique to verify
the atomicity of a number of irreducible procedures that could not be
handled by previous reduction-based tools for checking atomicity.

1   Multithreading and Atomicity

The development and validation of multithreaded software systems is an important yet challenging problem. In particular, standard techniques such as testing
and manual code inspection are often inadequate for multithreaded systems, due
to the large number of possible thread interleavings. Model checking provides
a promising technique for ensuring that a system's implementation satisfies its
specification under all possible thread interleavings.

A prerequisite of model checking is developing an appropriate specification.
For many interesting software systems, writing a sufficiently-complete specification is non-trivial. As an example, consider the filesystem procedure `create`,
which creates a new file. A specification of the exact effect of `create` on the
concrete filesystem state would be quite verbose. Alternatively, we could specify
the behavior of `create` on an abstraction of the filesystem state, but we would
then need an abstraction invariant relating concrete and abstract states, and
such abstraction invariants are also quite complex.

---

* This work was partly supported by the NSF under Grant CCR-03411797 and by
  faculty research funds granted by the University of California at Santa Cruz.

S. Graf and L. Mounier (Eds.): SPIN 2004, LNCS 2989, pp. 252–266, 2004.

For many multithreaded procedures such as **create**, the notion of *atomicity* provides a lightweight yet valuable partial specification. Informally, a procedure is atomic if for every (arbitrarily-interleaved) program execution, there is an equivalent execution with the same overall behavior where the atomic procedure is executed serially, that is, the procedure's execution is not interleaved with actions of other threads. This atomicity guarantee reduces the challenging problem of reasoning about the procedure's behavior in a *multithreaded* context to the simpler problem of reasoning about the procedure's *sequential* behavior. The latter problem is significantly more amenable to standard techniques such as testing and manual code inspection. In addition, many programming errors associated with improper synchronization can be detected as atomicity violations.

We formalize this notion of atomicity by modeling multithreaded program execution as a transition system and using two transition relations. The *standard* transition relation $\rightarrow$ interleaves steps of the various threads in an arbitrary manner. The *serial* transition relation $\mapsto$ also interleaves steps of the various threads, provided no thread is executing an atomic procedure. Once a thread enters an atomic procedure, then the serial transition relation executes that procedure to completion, without interleaved steps of other threads.

Reasoning about program behavior is much easier under the serial semantics ($\mapsto$) than under the standard semantics ($\rightarrow$), since each atomic block can be understood sequentially, without the need to consider all possible interleaved actions of concurrent threads. However, standard language implementations only provide the standard semantics ($\rightarrow$), which admits additional transition sequences and behaviors, and a program that behaves correctly according to the serial semantics may still behave erroneously under the standard semantics. Thus, in addition to being correct with respect to the serial semantics, the program should also use sufficient synchronization to ensure the atomicity of each block of code that is intended to be atomic. That is, for any program execution $\sigma_0 \rightarrow^* \sigma$ from the initial state σ_0 (where, for simplicity, we assume no thread is executing an atomic block in σ), there should exist an equivalent serial execution $\sigma_0 \mapsto^* \sigma$. We call this the *atomicity requirement* on program executions, and correctly synchronized programs should satisfy this requirement.

Over the past year, a number of tools have been developed for verifying this atomicity requirement, using techniques such as theorem proving [11], static typing systems [9,10], dynamic analysis [8,23], and model checking [13]. All these approaches are based on *reduction*, either Lipton's theory of reduction [16] or partial order reduction [21].

Reduction suffices to verify the atomicity of many procedures with straight-forward synchronization, but is often inadequate for procedures that use more subtle synchronization. This paper introduces *commit-atomicity*, which is a more general technique for verifying atomicity. This technique is based on exploring serial and non-serial executions of the program simultaneously, and checking that both executions yield the same final state. Commit-atomicity is capable of verifying the atomicity of many procedures that cannot be handled by existing atomicity-checking tools based on reduction.

The presentation of our results proceeds as follows. The following section reviews reduction and provides an illustration of limitations of that technique. Section 3 introduces a semantics for multithreaded programs that we use as the basis for our formal development. Section 4 describes our technique for verifying commit-atomicity during model checking. Section 5 provides an evaluation of this technique using the SPIN model checker on four benchmark programs. Section 6 discusses related work, and we conclude with Section 7.

2   Reduction

The essential idea behind reduction is to transform an interleaved (non-serial) execution of an atomic procedure into a serial execution of that procedure by commuting adjacent actions of concurrent threads. For example, consider the first execution trace in the diagram below, in which one thread executes a procedure that (1) acquires a lock m, (2) reads a variable x protected by that lock, (3) updates x, and then (4) releases m. The execution of this procedure is interleaved with some actions b_1, b_2, b_3 of a second thread, which do not access x. Hence, the read and write of x by the first thread commute with the operations of the second thread. In addition, the acquire operation right-commutes and the release operation left-commutes with the operations of the second thread, as illustrated by the following diagram. Hence, via reduction, we obtain an equivalent serial execution with the same final state in which the actions of the procedure are not interleaved with operations of other threads. Thus, reduction suffices to prove that the first execution trace is serializable, that is, it has an equivalent serial trace. If every execution trace through the procedure is serializable, we say the procedure is *atomic*.

Reduction example

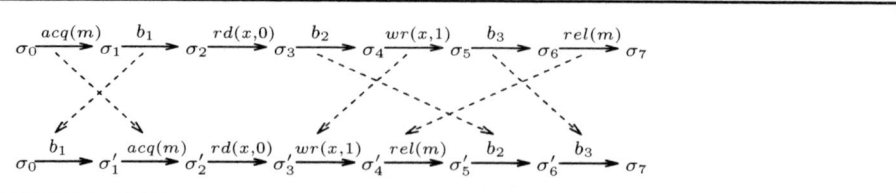

Reduction suffices to verify the atomicity of many procedures that follow straightforward synchronization disciplines. However, during our experiments with atomicity-checking tools based on reduction, we repeatedly encountered procedures that, although atomic, are not reducible. As an example, the procedure `acquire` shown on the next page uses a combination of busy-waiting and a compare-and-swap (CAS) operation to acquire a mutually-exclusive lock m (represented as a boolean). The operation CAS(m,false,r) has no effect and returns false if $m \neq$ false. However, if $m =$ false, then the operation CAS(m,false,r) swaps m and r and returns true.

Procedures acquire and do_transaction

```
void acquire() {                  void do_transaction() {
    boolean r := true;                while (true) {
    while (r==true) {                     acquire(mutex);
        CAS(m,false,r);                   int t := data;
    }                                     release(mutex);
}
                                          // long computation
                                          int fdata := f(t);

                                          acquire(mutex);
                                          if (t==data) {
                                              data := fdata;
                                              release(mutex);
                                              return;
                                          }
                                          release(mutex);
                                      }
                                  }
```

A non-serial execution of `acquire` is shown in column (a) below, in which the acquire operation performed by thread T1 is interleaved with an operation of thread T2 that resets m to `false`. This execution reduces to the serial execution of column (b), since the operation of T2 can commute to the start of the execution sequence, before `acquire` begins.

Executions of acquire

(a) Non-serial execution	(b) Serial execution	(c) Non-serial execution
T1: acquire() begins	T2: m := false	T1: acquire() begins
T1: r := true	T1: acquire() begins	T1: r := true
T1: assume r == true	T1: r := true	T1: assume r == true
T2: m := false	T1: assume r == true	T1: CAS(m,false,r) fails
T1: CAS(m,false,r) ok	T1: CAS(m,false,r) ok	T1: assume r == true
T1: assume r != true	T1: assume r != true	T2: m := false
T1: acquire() ends	T1: acquire() ends	T1: CAS(m,false,r) ok
		T1: assume r != true
		T1: acquire() ends

Column (c) shows an alternative non-serial execution of `acquire` in which the CAS operation initially fails, and the busy-waiting loop iterates until the CAS operation succeeds. Note that since the execution of column (c) contains more instructions in column (b), we clearly cannot commute the execution of column (c) into the serial execution of column (b). Thus, even though the execution of column (c) is equivalent to the serial execution of column (b), in the sense that both executions yield the same final state, reduction is inadequate to verify this equivalence. Thus, the procedure `acquire` is atomic yet not reducible, and current atomicity checking tools based purely on reduction (using either type systems [9,10], dynamic analysis [8,23], or model checking [13]) cannot verify the atomicity of `acquire`. The Calvin-R tool [11] uses a combination of iterated abstraction and reduction to verify such atomicity properties, but requires additional programmer annotations to "guide" the right abstraction. Commit-atomicity is intended to verify such atomicity properties automatically.

Another example of an atomic yet irreducible procedure is the procedure do_transaction shown above. In this example, the global variable data is protected by mutex, and the procedure do_transaction updates data according to data := f(data). However, the calculation of f(data) requires a long computation. To avoid holding mutex while computing f(data), the procedure acquires mutex, reads data, and releases mutex. The procedure then computes f(data), and, if data has not changed, updates data with f(data). If data has changed, then the transaction is retried.

The procedure do_transaction is atomic, in the sense that each execution is equivalent to some serial execution. However, in every serial execution, the procedure returns during the first iteration of the loop, but there are many non-serial executions where the loop iterates many times. Thus, these non-serial executions cannot reduce to the equivalently-behaved serial executions, and so reduction is again inadequate to verify the atomicity of do_transaction. In contrast, commit-atomicity is capable of verifying the atomicity of both of these irreducible procedures.

3 Multithreaded Programs

To provide a formal basis for reasoning about atomicity, we start by formalizing an execution semantics for multithreaded programs. In this semantics, a multithreaded program consists of a number of concurrently executing threads, each of which has an associated thread identifier $i \in Tid$. The threads communicate through a shared store $\sigma \in Store$, and system execution starts in an initial store σ_0. The exact structure of the store is left unspecified as it is orthogonal to our development. The behavior of each thread i is specified by a partial function

$$T_i : Store \rightarrow Store$$

which performs a single step of that thread.

3.1   Standard Semantics

The standard semantics of the entire multithreaded program is defined as a non-deterministic interleaving of steps of the various threads. The transition relation $\sigma \rightarrow \sigma'$ performs a single step of an arbitrarily chosen thread. We use $\rightarrow^*$ to denote the reflexive-transitive closure of $\rightarrow$.

Standard semantics: $\sigma \rightarrow \sigma'$

$$\sigma \rightarrow \sigma' \quad \text{iff} \quad \exists i \in Tid. \ T_i(\sigma, \sigma')$$

3.2   Serial Semantics

We assume that each thread in the multithreaded program contains a number of atomic blocks, and that each atomic block has a particular *commit point* where, from the perspective of other threads, the entire block appears to happen atomically. We assume that for each thread i the function

$$A_i : Store \rightarrow \{Outside, PreCommit, PostCommit\}$$

indicates the *phase* of thread i, that is, whether thread i is

1. outside an atomic block (*Outside*);
2. in the pre-commit phase of atomic block (*PreCommit*);
3. or in the post-commit phase of atomic block (*PostCommit*).

This phase information might be determined by examining the program counter of thread i recorded in the store. We require that no atomic block is active in the initial state; that the phase of one thread is not affected by step of a different thread; and that each thread cannot directly transition from the post-commit phase of one atomic block to the pre-commit phase of a subsequent atomic block (it must have an intermediate state that is outside any atomic block). We formalize these requirements as follows:

- $A_i(\sigma_0) = Outside$ for all $i \in Tid$.
- if $T_i(\sigma, \sigma')$ then $\forall j \neq i.\ A_j(\sigma) = A_j(\sigma')$.
- if $T_i(\sigma, \sigma')$ then $A_i(\sigma) \neq PostCommit$ or $A_i(\sigma') \neq PreCommit$.

The relation $\mathcal{A}(\sigma)$ holds if any thread is inside an atomic block:

$$\mathcal{A}(\sigma) \stackrel{\text{def}}{=} \exists i \in Tid.\ A_i(\sigma) \neq Outside$$

The following *serial* transition relation $\mapsto$ is similar to the standard relation $\rightarrow$, except that a thread cannot perform a step if another thread is inside an atomic block. Thus, the serial relation $\mapsto$ does not interleave the execution of an atomic block with instructions of concurrent threads.

Serial semantics: $\sigma \mapsto \sigma'$

$$\sigma \mapsto \sigma' \quad \text{iff} \quad \exists i \in Tid.\ (T_i(\sigma, \sigma') \wedge \forall j \neq i.\ A_j(\sigma) = Outside)$$

Reasoning about program behavior is much easier under the serial semantics ($\mapsto$) than under the standard semantics ($\rightarrow$) that is provided by standard language implementations. However, a program that behaves correctly according to the serial semantics may still behave erroneously under the standard semantics. Thus, in addition to being correct under the serial semantics, the program should also use sufficient synchronization to ensure the atomicity of each block of code that is intended to be atomic. That is, for any program execution $\sigma_0 \rightarrow^* \sigma$ where $\neg\mathcal{A}(\sigma)$, there should exist an equivalent serial execution $\sigma_0 \mapsto^* \sigma$. We call this the *atomicity requirement* on program executions, and correctly synchronized programs should satisfy this requirement. (The restriction $\neg\mathcal{A}(\sigma)$ avoids consideration of partially-executed atomic blocks.)

4 Model Checking Commit-Atomicity

In this section, we present an instrumented semantics that detects violations of the atomicity requirement described above. The instrumented semantics only admits execution sequences that are serializable, and goes wrong on non-serializable sequences. To determine whether a given execution sequence is serializable, the instrumented semantics extends the state space with a *shadow store* $\rho \in State$. Program operations in the pre-commit or post-commit phase of an atomic block operate as expected on the normal store σ, and do not affect the shadow store ρ. However, when an atomic block commits, the entire atomic block is executed in a serial manner on the shadow store. Thus, the shadow store reflects the serial execution of all commited atomic blocks. The shadow store is used to verify the serializability of the given execution sequence.

The instrumented transition relation $(\sigma, \rho) \Rightarrow (\sigma', \rho')$ is defined below. If no atomic block is executing on the shadow store (that is, $\neg\mathcal{A}(\rho)$), then the instrumented semantics performs a step of an arbitrary thread on the normal store. If this step is in the pre-commit or post-commit phase of an atomic block, then no action is performed on the shadow store, via the rules [PRE-COMMIT] and [POST-COMMIT]. However, if the step is the commit action of an atomic block, then the serial execution of that atomic block on the shadow store is initiated via the rule [COMMIT]. As expected, commit actions include transitions from the *PreCommit* to *PostCommit* phase of an atomic block. However, commit actions also include:

- transitions from *Outside* to *PostCommit*, where an action enters and immediately commits an atomic block;
- transitions from *PreCommit* to *Outside*, where an action commits and immediately exits an atomic block; and
- transitions from *Outside* to *Outside*, where the "atomic block" only contains a single action.

Instrumented semantics: $(\sigma, \rho) \Rightarrow (\sigma', \rho')$ **and** $(\sigma, \rho) \Rightarrow wrong$

[PRE-COMMIT]   [POST-COMMIT]   [COMMIT]

$$\frac{\neg\mathcal{A}(\rho) \quad T_i(\sigma, \sigma') \quad A_i(\sigma') = PreCommit}{(\sigma, \rho) \Rightarrow (\sigma', \rho)}$$

$$\frac{\neg\mathcal{A}(\rho) \quad T_i(\sigma, \sigma') \quad A_i(\sigma) = PostCommit}{(\sigma, \rho) \Rightarrow (\sigma', \rho)}$$

$$\frac{\neg\mathcal{A}(\rho) \quad T_i(\sigma, \sigma') \quad A_i(\sigma) \in \{PreCommit, Outside\} \quad A_i(\sigma') \in \{PostCommit, Outside\} \quad T_i(\rho, \rho')}{(\sigma, \rho) \Rightarrow (\sigma', \rho')}$$

[SHADOW]   [WRONG]

$$\frac{A_i(\rho) \in \{PreCommit, PostCommit\} \quad T_i(\rho, \rho')}{(\sigma, \rho) \Rightarrow (\sigma, \rho')}$$

$$\frac{\neg\mathcal{A}(\sigma) \quad \neg\mathcal{A}(\rho) \quad \sigma \neq \rho}{(\sigma, \rho) \Rightarrow wrong}$$

Once the execution of an atomic block on the shadow store is initiated via [COMMIT], then the execution of that atomic block continues in a serial (non-interleaved) manner via the rule [SHADOW] until it completes. Thus, in any reachable instrumented state (σ, ρ), the shadow store reflects the serial execution of all commited atomic blocks. If no thread is currently inside an atomic block (that is, $\neg\mathcal{A}(\sigma)$), then we expect that the operations on the shadow store are a serialization of the operations on the normal store, and hence that $\sigma = \rho$. If the serial execution on the shadow store and the interleaved execution on the normal store yield different results (that is, $\sigma \neq \rho$), then we cannot verify that the execution sequence is serializable, and the instrumented execution *goes wrong* via the rule [WRONG].

Since atomic blocks are executed in a serial manner on the shadow store, two threads should never be simultaneously executing atomic blocks on the shadow store. Hence, we say the shadow store ρ is *well-formed* if

$$\forall i, j \in Tid.(A_i(\rho) \neq Outside \wedge A_j(\rho) \neq Outside \implies i = j)$$

The following lemma states that the instrumented semantics performs a sequence of interleaved operations on the normal store, and a sequence of serial operations on the shadow store.

Lemma 1. *If $(\sigma, \rho) \Rightarrow^* (\sigma', \rho')$ and ρ is well-formed then $\sigma \rightarrow^* \sigma'$ and $\rho \mapsto^* \rho'$ and ρ' is well-formed.*

Proof   We prove the case where $(\sigma, \rho) \Rightarrow (\sigma', \rho')$ via a single transition by case analysis on the transition rule used. This proof generalises to longer transition sequences by induction.

- [PRE-COMMIT] or [POST-COMMIT]: Since $T_i(\sigma, \sigma')$, we have $\sigma \rightarrow \sigma'$. In addition, since $\rho' = \rho$, we trivially have $\rho \mapsto^* \rho'$ and ρ' is well-formed.
- [COMMIT]: Since $T_i(\sigma, \sigma')$, we have $\sigma \rightarrow \sigma'$. In addition, since $\neg\mathcal{A}(\rho)$, we have $\mathcal{A}_j(\rho) = Outside$ for all $j \in Tid$. Together with $T_i(\rho, \rho')$, we then have $\rho \mapsto \rho'$. Also from $T_i(\rho, \rho')$, we have $\mathcal{A}_j(\rho') = Outside$ for all $j \neq i$, so ρ' is well-formed.
- [SHADOW] Since $\mathcal{A}_i(\rho) \neq Outside$ and ρ is well-formed, we have $\mathcal{A}_j(\rho) = Outside$ for all $j \neq i$. Together with $T_i(\rho, \rho')$, we then have $\rho \mapsto \rho'$ and that ρ is well-formed. Finally, since $\sigma' = \sigma$, we have $\sigma \rightarrow^* \sigma'$. $\square$

In addition, the instrumented semantics includes all evaluation sequences possible under the standard semantics, except that the instrumented semantics records additional information in the shadow store. We assume that all atomic blocks terminate, that is, if $A_i(\rho_1) \neq Outside$ then there exists $\rho_2, \ldots, \rho_n$ such that $A_i(\rho_n) = Outside$ and $T_i(\rho_k, \rho_{k+1})$ for all $0 < k < n$.

Lemma 2. *If $\sigma \rightarrow^* \sigma'$ and atomic blocks terminate then for all well-formed ρ there exists ρ' such that $(\sigma, \rho) \Rightarrow^* (\sigma', \rho')$.*

Proof   We first prove the base case where $\sigma \rightarrow \sigma'$ via a single transition because $T_i(\sigma, \sigma')$. The proof then generalises to longer transition sequences via induction.

- Suppose $\neg\mathcal{A}(\rho)$ and $\mathcal{A}_i(\sigma') = PreCommit$. In this case $(\sigma, \rho) \mapsto (\sigma', \rho)$ via [PRE-COMMIT].

- Similarly, suppose $\neg\mathcal{A}(\rho)$ and $\mathcal{A}_i(\sigma) = PostCommit$. In this case $(\sigma, \rho) \mapsto (\sigma', \rho)$ via [POST-COMMIT].
- Suppose $\neg\mathcal{A}(\rho)$ and neither of the above cases hold. That is, $\mathcal{A}_i(\sigma') \neq PreCommit$ and $\mathcal{A}_i(\sigma) \neq PreCommit$. Then $(\sigma, \rho) \mapsto (\sigma', \rho')$ via [COMMIT], where $T_i(\rho, \rho')$.
- Suppose $\mathcal{A}(\rho)$. Then there exists $i \in Tid$ such that $\mathcal{A}_i(\rho) \neq Outside$. Since atomic blocks terminate, then there exists $\rho_2, \ldots, \rho_n$ such that $\mathcal{A}_i(\rho_n) = Outside$ and $T_i(\sigma, \rho_2)$ and for all $1 < k < n$, we have $\mathcal{A}_i(\rho_k) \neq Outside$ and $T_i(\rho_k, \rho_{k+1})$. Hence, $(\sigma, \rho) \mapsto^* (\sigma, \rho_n)$ via a sequence of [SHADOW] transitions to a state (σ, ρ_n) where $\neg\mathcal{A}(\rho_n)$, and one of the above cases then applies to this state.   □

Finally, any instrumented execution that does not go wrong satisfies the atomicity requirement.

Theorem 1. *If $\sigma \to^* \sigma'$ and $\neg\mathcal{A}(\sigma)$ and $\neg\mathcal{A}(\sigma')$ and atomic blocks terminate, then either*

1. $\sigma \mapsto^* \sigma'$, or
2. $(\sigma, \sigma) \Rightarrow^* wrong$.

Proof   Since $\sigma \to^* \sigma'$, by Lemma 2 there exists ρ' such that $(\sigma, \sigma) \Rightarrow^* (\sigma', \rho')$. Since atomic blocks terminate, there exists ρ'' such that $(\sigma', \rho') \Rightarrow^* (\sigma', \rho'')$ and $\neg\mathcal{A}(\rho'')$. If $\sigma' \neq \rho''$ then $(\sigma', \rho'') \Rightarrow wrong$ via [WRONG], yielding case 2 of this theorem. Otherwise $\sigma' = \rho''$ and $\sigma \mapsto^* \sigma'$ by Lemma 1, yielding case 1 of this theorem.   □

Thus, given any standard execution $\sigma_0 \to^* \sigma'$ (where $\neg\mathcal{A}(\sigma_0)$ and $\neg\mathcal{A}(\sigma')$ and σ_0 is well-formed), we can inspect the corresponding instrumented execution $(\sigma_0, \sigma_0) \Rightarrow (\sigma', \rho')$, which must exist by Lemma 2. If this instrumented execution does not go wrong, then by Theorem 1, we know that the original execution $\sigma_0 \to^* \sigma'$ is equivalent to some serial execution $\sigma_0 \mapsto^* \sigma'$. Thus, by using model checking to ensure that no instrumented execution goes wrong, we can therefore verify that the program satisfies the atomicity requirement.

5   Evaluation

We have applied commit-atomicity to verify several example programs that could not be handled by earlier atomicity-checking tools based on reduction. This section presents the example programs we used and reports on the performance of our verification technique.

5.1   Busy-Waiting Lock Acquire

Our first benchmark uses the busy-waiting lock acquire function described in Section 2. This benchmark contains an integer variable `data` protected by the mutex m. The code for each thread contains a loop that first acquires the mutex, updates data, and then releases the mutex. Our correctness specification is that each iteration of the loop should appear to execute atomically (and hence two threads should never update data at the same time). This correctness of specification is included in the code via the construct *atomic* { ... }. We consider two version of this benchmark in order to calibrate the ability of our technique to handle large procedures. In the first version acquire1, the critical section only contains a single line of code, whereas in the second version acquire2, the critical section contains 100 lines of code that manipulate data.

Busy-waiting lock acquire benchmark

```
Variables:                Code for each thread:

    boolean m;                while (true) {
    int data;                     atomic {
                                      acquire(); // see impl in Section 2
Initially:
                                      // critical section
    m := false;                   // read-modify-write data
    data := 0;
                                      m := false;
                                  }
                              }
```

5.2   Dekker's Mutual Exclusion Algorithm

Our second example is Dekker's algorithm, a classic algorithm for mutual exclusion between two threads that uses subtle synchronization. The critical section of each thread updates a shared variable data. Our correctness specification is that, because the mutual exclusion code is correct, the body of the while loop of each thread should appear to execute atomically. This specification is expressed using the construct *atomic* { ... }.

Dekker's mutual exclusion benchmark

```
Variables:        Thread₁:                      Thread₂:
                      while (true) {                while (true) {
    boolean a₁;         atomic {                      atomic {
    boolean a₂;             a₁ := true;                   a₂ := true;
    int data;              if (¬a₂) {                    if (¬a₁) {
                               // critical section            // critical section
Initially:                     // read, write data           // read and write data
                           }                             }
    a₁ := false;           a₁ := false;                  a₂ := false;
    a₂ := false;         }                             }
    data := 0;        }                             }
```

5.3   Transaction Retry

Our third benchmark re-uses the procedure do_transaction from Section 2, with the requirement that each transaction should be performed atomically.

Transaction benchmark

Variables:	Code for each thread:

`boolean mutex;`
`int data;`
 	
Initially:
 	
`mutex := false;`
`data := 0;`
	`while (true) {`
	    `atomic {`
	        `do_transaction();`
	    `}`
	`}`

5.4   Bluetooth Device Driver

The Bluetooth benchmark is a simplified model of one of the bluetooth device drivers in Windows NT described in [22]. There are two dispatch functions in this simplified device driver: `BCSP_PnpAdd` and `BCSP_PnpStop`. The function `BCSP_PnpAdd` is called by the operating system to perform I/O in the driver. The second dispatch function `BCSP_PnpStop` is called by the operating system to stop the driver. In our benchmark, one thread calls `BCSP_PnpStop`, and all the remaining threads call `BCSP_PnpAdd`.

Our correctness specification is that each dispatch function should execute atomically. In particular, each call to `BCSP_PnpAdd` should either operate normally or return immediately because the device driver is already stopped.

5.5   Experimental Results

We tested each benchmark using various numbers of concurrent threads, as shown in Figure 1. For each of the five benchmarks, we manually generated two Promela programs that capture the semantics of the benchmarks under the standard semantics ($\rightarrow$) and instrumented semantics ($\Rightarrow$), respectively. Figure 1 compares the cost of model checking these benchmarks under these two semantics. For each benchmark/threads/semantics configuration, the figure reports the size of the reachable state space and the memory and time required for model checking. An entry of "-" indicates that the SPIN model checker ran out of memory on that configuration. We performed these experiments under Windows XP on a 1.7GHz Pentium M laptop with 1GB of memory.

For each variable x in the original program, we declared two variables x and s_x in the Promela code for the instrumented semantics, to represent the value of x in the normal store and shadow store, respectively. Thus, the size of each state in the Promela code for the instrumented semantics is twice as large as for the standard semantics. In addition to this increase in the size of each state, the experimental results in Figure 1 indicate that the size of the reachable state space for the instrumented semantics is significantly larger than for the standard semantics. That is, the overhead of atomicity checking contributes to the state explosion problem on these benchmarks. However, commit-atomicity does provide a means of verifying atomicity in these benchmarks, which could not be accomplished with previous reduction-based tools. In addition, our results

Benchmark	Threads	Standard semantics ($\rightarrow$)			Instrumented semantics ($\Rightarrow$)		
		states	space (MB)	time (s)	states	space (MB)	time (s)
dekker	2	3104	1.7	0.02	3601	1.8	0.05
acquire1	2	135	1.6	0.02	278	1.6	0.02
acquire1	3	468	1.6	0.02	1795	1.7	0.03
acquire1	4	4361	1.9	0.05	20935	3.4	0.16
acquire1	5	16369	6.0	0.15	118242	16.9	0.99
acquire1	6	62806	11.5	0.58	658038	113.4	7.21
acquire1	7	299952	70.8	4.42	-	-	-
acquire2	2	3335	1.7	0.03	8278	2.0	0.04
acquire2	3	12864	2.4	0.09	58795	5.4	0.24
acquire2	4	153854	45.6	1.32	714359	96.7	4.91
acquire2	5	541601	85.3	5.97	-	-	-
transaction	2	836	1.6	0.02	4730	1.9	0.05
transaction	3	25557	6.0	0.11	532457	78.1	2.21
transaction	4	826627	99.3	4.68	-	-	-
bluetooth	2	91	1.6	0.02	116	1.6	0.02
bluetooth	3	568	1.6	0.02	1187	1.6	0.03
bluetooth	4	4762	1.9	0.05	16383	3.1	0.09
bluetooth	5	47163	5.2	0.13	271111	33.1	1.46
bluetooth	6	527668	48.6	1.79	-	-	-

Fig. 1. Summary of benchmark programs and model checking performance.

for the acquire2 benchmark indicate that this technique is capable of handling moderately-large procedures (in this case containing 100 lines of code).

During our experiments, the bluetooth benchmark initially went wrong under the instrumented semantics, revealing the same synchronization bug that was discovered in [22] via an assertion violation. After fixing this bug, none of the benchmarks went wrong under the instrumented semantics, indicating that all these programs satisfy their intended atomicity properties.

6   Related Work

Lipton [16] first proposed reduction as a way to reason about concurrent programs without considering all possible interleavings. Although he focused primarily on checking deadlock freedom, reduction has subsequently been extended to support proofs of general safety and liveness properties [6,3,15,4,19].

Reduction has been applied to verify atomicity in a static type system for Java programs [10,9]. This type system for atomicity was inspired by the Calvin-R [11] static checking tool for multithreaded programs, which relates each procedure's specification to its implementation via a combination of simulation and reduction. The Atomizer is a dynamic analysis tool for detecting atomicity violations by running an instrumented version of the program [8]. In recent work, Wang and Stoller [23] also developed several algorithms for checking atomicity dynamically. The use of model checking for verifying atomicity is being explored by Hatcliff *et al* [13], and they present two approaches, based on Lipton's theory of reduction and partial order reductions, respectively. Their experimental results suggest that verifying atomicity via model-checking is feasible for unit-testing. All of these approaches can only verify the atomicity of reducible procedures, and thus are insufficient for the examples considered in this paper.

Atomicity is a semantic correctness condition for multithreaded software. It is related to strict serializability [20], a correctness condition for database transactions, and linearizability [14], a correctness condition for concurrent objects. It is possible that techniques for verifying atomicity can be leveraged to develop lightweight checking tools for related correctness conditions.

Many other researchers have proposed using atomicity as a language primitive, essentially implementing the serial semantics $\mapsto$. Lomet [18] first proposed the use of atomic blocks for synchronization. The Argus [17] and Avalon [7] projects developed language support for implementing atomic objects. Persistent languages [1,2] attempt to augment atomicity with data persistence in order to introduce transactions into programming languages. A more recent approach to supporting atomicity uses lightweight transactions implemented in the run-time system [12]. An alternative is to generate synchronization code automatically from high-level specifications [5].

7   Conclusion

In an effort to avoid errors due to unexpected interactions between concurrent threads, programmers often design procedures that are intended to be atomic. Reduction suffices to verify the atomicity of procedures that use straightforward synchronization, but is often inadequate for more subtle synchronization disciplines.

This paper introduces a novel technique called commit-atomicity for verifying atomicity in multithreaded programs. This technique is based on executing serial and non-serial versions of the programs simultaneously, and checking that both versions yield the same final state. This technique is capable of verifying atomicity of variety of procedures, including procedures that could not be handled using existing atomicity-checking tools based on reduction.

Commit-atomiciy does introduce a significant model checking overhead. An important area for future research is the development of hybrid atomicity-checking tools that use reduction to verify many procedures, but is capable of leveraging commit-atomicity as necessary to verify procedures that use more complicated synchronization disciplines.

References

1. M. P. Atkinson, K. J. Chisholm, and W. P. Cockshott. PS-Algol: an Algol with a persistent heap. *ACM SIGPLAN Notices*, 17(7):24–31, 1981.
2. M. P. Atkinson and D. Morrison. Procedures as persistent data objects. *ACM Transactions on Programming Languages and Systems*, 7(4):539–559, 1985.

3. R.-J. Back. A method for refining atomicity in parallel algorithms. In *PARLE 89: Parallel Architectures and Languages Europe*, volume 366 of *Lecture Notes in Computer Science*, pages 199–216. Springer-Verlag, 1989.

4. E. Cohen and L. Lamport. Reduction in TLA. In *Proceedings of the International Conference on Concurrency Theory*, volume 1466 of *Lecture Notes in Computer Science*, pages 317–331. Springer-Verlag, 1998.

5. X. Deng, M. Dwyer, J. Hatcliff, and M. Mizuno. Invariant-based specification, synthesis, and verification of synchronization in concurrent programs. In *International Conference on Software Engineering*, pages 442–452, 2002.

6. T. W. Doeppner, Jr. Parallel program correctness through refinement. In *Proceedings of the ACM Symposium on the Principles of Programming Languages*, pages 155–169, 1977.

7. J. L. Eppinger, L. B. Mummert, and A. Z. Spector. *Camelot and Avalon: A Distributed Transaction Facility*. Morgan Kaufmann, 1991.

8. C. Flanagan and S. N. Freund. Atomizer: A dynamic atomicity checker for multithreaded programs. In *Proceedings of the ACM Symposium on the Principles of Programming Languages*, 2004.

9. C. Flanagan and S. Qadeer. A type and effect system for atomicity. In *Proceedings of the ACM Conference on Programming Language Design and Implementation*, pages 338–349, 2003.

10. C. Flanagan and S. Qadeer. Types for atomicity. In *Proceedings of the ACM Workshop on Types in Language Design and Implementation*, pages 1–12, 2003.

11. S. N. Freund and S. Qadeer. Checking concise specifications for multithreaded software. In *Workshop on Formal Techniques for Java-like Programs*, 2003.

12. T. L. Harris and K. Fraser. Language support for lightweight transactions. In *Proceedings of the ACM Conference on Object-Oriented Programming, Systems, Languages and Applications*, pages 388–402, 2003.

13. J. Hatcliff, Robby, and M. B. Dwyer. Verifying atomicity specifications for concurrent object-oriented software using model-checking. In *Proceedings of the International Conference on Verification, Model Checking and Abstract Interpretation*, 2004.

14. M. P. Herlihy and J. M. Wing. Linearizability: A correctness condition for concurrent objects. *ACM Transactions on Programming Languages and Systems*, 12(3):463–492, 1990.

15. L. Lamport and F. B. Schneider. Pretending atomicity. Research Report 44, DEC Systems Research Center, 1989.

16. R. J. Lipton. Reduction: A method of proving properties of parallel programs. *Communications of the ACM*, 18(12):717–721, 1975.

17. B. Liskov, D. Curtis, P. Johnson, and R. Scheifler. Implementation of Argus. In *Proceedings of the Symposium on Operating Systems Principles*, pages 111–122, 1987.

18. D. B. Lomet. Process structuring, synchronization, and recovery using atomic actions. *Language Design for Reliable Software*, pages 128–137, 1977.

19. J. Misra. *A Discipline of Multiprogramming: Programming Theory for Distributed Applications*. Springer-Verlag, 2001.

20. C. Papadimitriou. *The theory of database concurrency control*. Computer Science Press, 1986.

21. D. Peled. Combining partial order reductions with on-the-fly model-checking. In D. Dill, editor, *Proceedings of the IEEE Conference on Computer Aided Verification*, Lecture Notes in Computer Science 818, pages 377–390. Springer-Verlag, 1994.

22. S. Qadeer and D. Wu. Debugging concurrent programs with sequential analysis. 2003. Submitted for publication.
23. L. Wang and S. D. Stoller. Run-time analysis for atomicity. In *Proceedings of the Workshop on Runtime Verification*, volume 89(2) of *Electronic Notes in Computer Science*. Elsevier, 2003.

Analysis of Distributed Spin Applied to Industrial-Scale Models[*]

Murali Rangarajan, Samar Dajani-Brown, Kirk Schloegel, and Darren Cofer

Honeywell Laboratories
3660, Technology Drive, Minneapolis, MN 55418, USA
{murali.rangarajan, samar.dajani-brown, kirk.schloegel,
darren.cofer}@honeywell.com

Abstract. As software systems become increasingly complex, there is growing interest in the use of formal techniques to obtain higher assurance in their correctness. The most commonly used tools involve model-checking, such as SMV and Spin. But modeling complex systems with a high degree of fidelity implies exceedingly large state spaces that must be analyzed. These state spaces are typically too large for single processing nodes, in spite of great advances in memory reduction techniques. Moreover, approximation techniques such as hash compaction are less well-received where safety-critical systems are concerned. Effective distribution of the problem over many processing nodes has the potential of supporting the huge state spaces. Since our primary interest is in safety-critical software, we have spent considerable time evaluating the performance of distributed implementations of Spin in this context. In this paper, we present our analysis of PSPIN, a distributed implementation of Spin. We identify key measures of effectiveness, and evaluate PSPIN with respect to these measures. We also present an alternative approach to partitioning that performs comparably with respect to all measures, and is up to orders of magnitude faster. Finally, we consider the question of which measures have the greatest impact on peak memory, a measure that is most critical to effective distribution.

1 Introduction

Software applications used to assist the flight of aircraft have long been considered safety-critical, and as such have been required to be developed using strict processes to maintain the high standards of the end products. These processes rely on reviews, simulations and testing to achieve those high standards. A number of factors have resulted in Formal Methods tools being seriously considered as part of this mix. The first of these reasons is the increasing functionality being demanded from the software, resulting in a steady increase in complexity. The second is the pressure to bring the product to market as quickly as possible. Third is the growing realization that existing processes are inadequate. It is not possible to test some requirements

---

[*] This material is based upon work supported in part by NASA under cooperative agreement NCC-1-399.

S. Graf and L. Mounier (Eds.): SPIN 2004, LNCS 2989, pp. 267–285, 2004.

explicitly (requirements such as all threads are guaranteed their budgets by the operating system). It is also not possible to identify and test all corner cases in complex systems – especially in systems that involve parallelism or distribution. Finally, there is growing data that early and effective use of formalisms in the development process reduces the chances of major rework late in the development process.

Among the formal analysis techniques available, we have found model checking, and in particular, Spin[7], to be the most amenable to integration with safety-critical software development processes. As with other model-checking tools, Spin's verifier can automatically analyze models against requirements. In addition, we have found Spin's modeling language, PROMELA, to be easiest to translate to from the C++ code being used in our studies. Finally, Spin has been used extensively and is highly trusted, and it can check for a wide range of properties.

We have successfully used Spin to analyze various embedded software in the past[4]. Our current work with the Deos™ real-time operating system[8] has pushed Spin to its limits. In particular, as features were added to the model, the memory requirements for full verification far exceeded the 4GB memory limit imposed by the 32-bit Spin implementation. This was in spite of using Spin's memory reduction techniques such as state-vector compression and partial order reduction, and also predicate abstractions.

One solution to deal with the memory problems is to look at distributing the problem over many processing nodes. In theory, parallelization should cut the computation time as well as the amount of memory per node. However, it is believed [12] that due to fine grained communication requirements, distributed model-checking is inherently unscalable. Therefore, parallelization actually results in significant performance slow down. Thus, distribution of Spin is most effective when the memory overhead of distribution is low, and the time overhead is not prohibitively large.

In this paper, we evaluate the performance of a distributed implementation of Spin, namely PSPIN[12]. This is particularly interesting as it is implemented as a wrapper around the traditional Spin, thereby reducing the probability of errors in the verification. In particular, we analyze the memory and time performance of this implementation. We identify measures of effectiveness for this category of distributed verifiers. We present an alternative scheme that partitions the state space according to the value of automatically selected elements of the state vector. We provide results that show that the new scheme performs comparably with respect to all these measures while over 25 times better with respect to verification time. Finally, we consider the issue of memory overhead for distribution and identify potential optimization measures that have the most effect on this.

This paper is organized as follows. In the next section, we provide an overview of the Deos real-time operating system, and discuss briefly our approach to modeling it. Next, we analyze the performance of PSPIN, and identify the key measures by which we can judge the effectiveness of distribution. Then, we present our approach to partitioning and compare it with PSPIN's partitioning schemes. We conclude the paper with related work and directions for further study.

2 The Deos RTOS and Its Modeling

The Deos real-time operating system was developed by Honeywell for use in the Primus Epic avionics suite for business, regional, and commuter jet aircraft. Deos hosts many safety-critical applications in these aircraft, including primary flight controls, autopilots, and displays.

Deos is a microkernel-based real-time operating system that supports flexible Integrated Modular Avionics applications by providing both space partitioning at the process level and time partitioning at the thread level. Space partitioning ensures that no process can modify the memory of another process without authorization, while time partitioning ensures that a thread's access to its CPU time budget cannot be impaired by the actions of any other thread. Deos supports many advanced features such as dynamic creation and deletion of processes and threads, reuse of unused thread budgets (also known as *slack time*), aperiodic interrupts, synchronization mechanisms such as mutexes, etc.

Deos is an interesting problem for this study for many reasons. First, analysis of source code is an unobtrusive way for formal analysis tools to gain acceptance within existing development processes. Second, Deos has a number of interesting properties that are well-suited for formal analysis. These include: (1) Time partitioning, which is a property that is practically impossible to test; and (2) Function pre-conditions, inserted in the code as comments that need to be checked at every invocation of the function. Finally, the Deos model has an atypical asymmetric model with one very large process and many smaller processes, which is a more challenging distribution problem.

One requirement for our approach was the ability to automatically generate verification models, since it was expected that engineers with minimal training in formal analysis techniques would be the users. Therefore, though our Deos model was constructed by hand, automated translation was a key consideration in creating the model. This resulted in a model with a direct mapping (almost line-to-line correspondence) to the source code, which had the added benefit of being easier to review by the developers.

The Deos model consists of three parts – the kernel, user threads and the environment. The kernel corresponds to the code translated from C++. It provides services to the user threads and interfaces with the hardware environment. It is the most complex part of the model. The user threads are very simple and just invoke various calls to the kernel and responds to messages (such as preemption) from the kernel. The environment provides the hardware services such as timers and interrupts. Though the environment is not as complex as the kernel, it is more difficult to model realistic hardware behavior in pure software. In our tests, we have found an event-based simulation-like approach to be the most suitable for modeling the environment. The Deos model initially consisted of the basic rate-monotonic scheduling algorithm with support for multiple threads and periods. Various features were incrementally added to the base model, including slack time, asynchronous interrupts, mutexes and overhead accounting.

The model incorporates a number of memory optimizations. These optimizations fall into two categories – those that reduce the size of the state vector, and those that reduce the number of distinct states seen by the verifier. State vector size is reduced by replacing all integers with bytes, reusing temporary variables, and by judicious use of hidden variables. The size of the state space is reduced by the use of predicate abstractions where possible, and judicious use of configurations (number of threads, their budgets, whether the threads are slack-enabled, etc.).

Our initial models could be exhaustively verified by Spin in 335 MB of memory. But by the time slack and interrupt threads were added, the state space became too large to be exhaustively verified in 4GB of memory. Though we continued to use Spin's approximation techniques such as bit-state hashing as debugging aids, these techniques are a harder sell for incorporation in the development processes of safety-critical systems. This led to our interest in other tools that can handle these large state spaces, and in particular, PSPIN.

3 PSPIN Overview

PSPIN is a wrapper around Spin that distributes the memory used for verification over many processing nodes (typically workstations in a network). The overall state space is partitioned into as many state sub-domains as the number of network nodes. Each node is assigned a different state sub-domain, and holds only the states that belong to that subset of the state space. During the verification run, each node computes the successors of the states it holds, and if it finds any successors belonging to other state sub-domains, it sends them to the nodes that are in charge of processing them. Since this is implemented as a wrapper around Spin, it is compatible with some of Spin's memory reduction techniques such as state compression. Its compatibility with partial order reduction is discussed later in this paper.

There are a number of challenges associated with partitioning vast and unknown state spaces:

1. It is not efficient to construct a structural model of the entire state space. Therefore, all schemes must utilize a predictive approach. The use of such an approach can impact guarantees of optimality that may characterize particular partitioning schemes. (Although it is still possible to provide guarantees of optimality for a sample of the state space.) Furthermore, it is often not possible to guarantee communications and load balance bounds for predictive schemes.

2. Since the partitioning function is called frequently (every time a child state is examined), processing nodes should be able to compute the owner node of a particular state quickly using purely local information. At the very least, the partitioning scheme must require non-local information infrequently.

3. As the state space is larger than the available memory of a single processing node, it is not feasible for each processing node to maintain an array that maps every state to its assigned node. (We refer to such an array as a *partition array*.) Instead, it is necessary to encode and decode the partitioning using some technique whose memory requirement is much less than the size of the state space and that is relatively fast. It is typically the case that not every possible partition array is representable by a particular encoding technique. Therefore, the reachable partitioning space is effectively reduced by such methods. This effect impacts optimality, as optimal partitionings may not reside within the reachable solution space.

PSPIN implements three partitioning functions: *Global Hash (GHP)*, *Local Hash (LHP)*, and a graph partitioning-based method that we refer to as *Source Code Partitioning (SCP)*. These address the above challenges in various ways. The Global Hash partitioning function maps states to processing nodes using a computation that involves the whole state vector. For example, the computation could be as simple as adding the values of all the variables in the state vector and computing its modulo with the number of processing nodes. Figure 1 illustrates this scheme as well as the Local Hash scheme. Here, a state vector v of size m is divided into n sub-vectors, one for each process in the model. Figure 1 shows the resulting processing node computation for this state vector using the Global Hash scheme. (Note that the computation is incomplete, as some of the state vector is not shown.) Global Hash requires only local information (i.e., the state vector). It can be shown to balance the load with high probability given a few reasonable assumptions about the distribution of the values of the state vector. However, this partitioning approach displays little or no locality with respect to how the states will be partitioned. That is, the probability that any two states that are adjacent in the state space will be mapped to the same processing node approaches zero as the number of nodes approaches infinity.

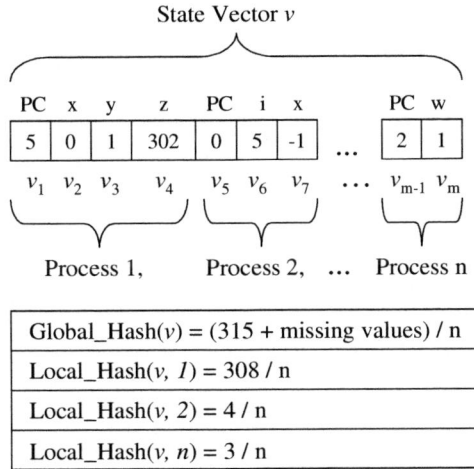

Fig. 1. Illustration of Global Hash and Local Hash partitioning schemes

Local Hash performs a similar computation to Global Hash, but utilizes only the values of a portion of the state vector belonging to a single Spin process, p. Figure 1 shows the resulting processing node computations for the state vector v when p is set to 1, 2, and n. Local Hash requires only local information. It increases locality compared to Global Hash, as any two adjacent states are guaranteed to be mapped to the same processing node if PSPIN is not currently executing the selected process p. So given a model consisting of processes of roughly equal sizes, the probability that any two adjacent states will be mapped to the same processing node approaches one as the number processes approaches infinity. However, as the portion of the state vector that is associated with process p is small compared to the entire state vector, the modulus scheme is less likely to result in good load balance. Furthermore, as the number of processes increases, the Local Hash scheme will tend to obtain worse load balancing results than the Global Hash scheme.

The third partitioning scheme available in PSPIN, Source Code Partitioning, is based on graph partitioning. In this scheme, the graph representing the source code for a selected process p is partitioned (and not a graph modeling the state space or a sample of the state space). Figures 2 and 3 illustrate this approach. Figure 2 shows a Promela model consisting of two processes, *init* and *P1*.

```
int sum;

    proctype P1()
    {
      int i = 0;
      int evensum = 0;
      do
1:      :: sum < 7 ->
          do
2:          :: i< 10 ->
3:             if
4:                :: (i % 2 == 0) -> evensum =evensum + i;
                  i++;
5:                :: i % 2 !=0  -> i++;
               fi
6:             :: else ->
               break;
            od;
7:          sum++;
8:       :: else ->
          break;
        od;
9:      printf("sum=%d\tsum= %d\n", sum, evensum);
10:   }

    init {
      sum = 0;
      run P1();
    }
```

Fig. 2. Sample code to illustrate Source Code Partitioning

Assume that the selected process is P1. (Note that using the init process would result in a partitioning with extremely poor load balance.) Figure 3(a) illustrates the source code graph for P1. This graph is constructed by PSPIN and models the possible control flows for the model. The circled numbers next to each vertex refer to the relevant line of source code from Figure 2. PSPIN can optionally weight the vertices and edges of this graph. It does so by performing a prerun of Spin. Each time a forward transition is taken, the weight of the associated edge on the graph is incremented. Similarly for vertices, each time a line of source code is executed by

Spin, the weight of the corresponding vertex is incremented. Figure 3(a) includes edge weights, but for the sake of clarity, vertex weights are not shown. A simple method for computing the vertex weights is to add up the weights of all outgoing or incoming arcs.

Figure 3(b) shows the abstract graph that is passed to the Metis Graph Partitioning Package [10]. Metis partitions this graph into a number of sub-domains equal to the number of processing nodes. (In this example, we have three processing nodes.) Metis returns a partition array similar to the one shown in Figure 3(b). This partition array is compiled into a lookup table for the PSPIN partition function. The input to this partition function is the value of the program counter (PC) element from the state vector for the selected process (P1). In Figure 3(b), when the value of the PC is 6, 7, 9, or 10, the state maps to node 0. When the value is 1, 2, or 8, the state maps to node 1. PC values of 3, 4, and 5 map to node 2.

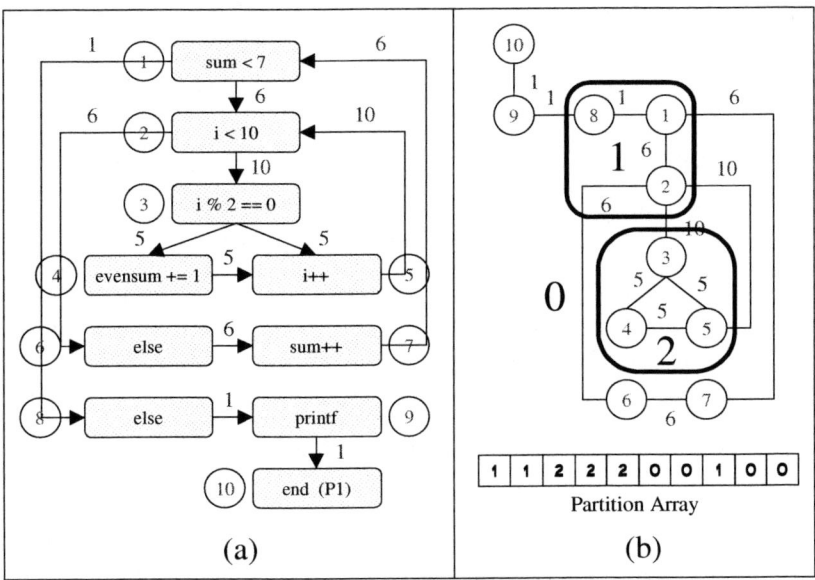

Fig. 3. (a) Source code graph for p1, and (b) the abstract graph that is passed to Metis

The key idea behind Source Code partitioning is that the structure of the state space can be predicted given the flow control structure of one of the processes. By partitioning the source code graph to minimize the total weight of the control flow edges that are cut by the partitioning (as Metis does), the resulting partitioning should demonstrate good locality. Furthermore, by applying vertex weights that correspond to the relative frequency that source code lines are executed, the state space can be load balanced. That is, source code lines that are likely to be executed frequently (for instance, the code within a nested loop), will be likely to result in proportionally more states in the state space than less frequently executed code. So taking this information into account when partitioning the source-code graph can result in good load balance for PSPIN. Finally, the mapping of a state to its owner node can be computed using purely local information if the Metis partition array is duplicated on every node. In this case, the value of the appropriate PC in the state vector is used as the index to this local copy of the partition array.

3.1 PSPIN Evaluation with Small Deos Model

The results from our initial evaluation of PSPIN's three partitioning schemes on a model of Deos over 2 and 4 processors is shown in Table 1. Note that GHP refers to Global Hash partitioning, LHP refers to Local Hash partitioning and SCP refers to Source Code partitioning schemes. Also note that the memory values are those reported by Spin at the end of the verification run, with the values in bold face being the aggregate sum from all the individual processing nodes. The time is the user time reported by the `time` command. Finally, all these results were obtained with partial order reduction disabled. The following points are evident from the results:

1. GHP results in even distribution of state space (memory) over all the processing nodes. But the verification time (run time) for GHP is much higher than the other two partitioning schemes, and also serial Spin. Moreover, the rate of increase in verification time with the increase in number of processing nodes is far too great for this approach to be practical. This is expected, as there is no locality in the partitioning scheme.

2. LHP on two nodes resulted in an approximately even distribution of states (memory) among the two nodes. The amount of memory used per node was less than half the memory used by serial Spin, and the run time was approximately the same as serial Spin. However, with 4 nodes, the results were more like running the test on two nodes, with one node not processing any states, and another node seeing very few states. Most of the work was done by two nodes.

3. SCP over two nodes provided results that were comparable to those using local hash partitioning. But, over four nodes, two of the nodes did not perform any work.

It is to be noted that the above results were obtained with partial order reduction (POR) turned off. This is significant, as we found in our tests that turning POR on results in inconsistent performance of distributed verification. With POR turned on, the sum total of states seen by all the nodes is typically larger than that seen by serial Spin. Traditional wisdom [12] has been that this is due to the fact that POR is less effective when distributed over many nodes. But when we compared the states seen by the distributed PSPIN with those seen by serial Spin, we found that while the distributed version saw some additional states, it also missed some states seen by serial Spin. This is a big problem, as it now becomes more difficult to validate the correctness of the distributed implementation. We are studying this issue further. For the purposes of this paper, all the results henceforth are with POR turned off.

It is clear that both local hash and source code partitioning have better time and memory performance as compared to global hash partitioning. But both techniques were not making effective uses of all available nodes. Repeated tests with increasing prerun times for source code partitioning did not result in better use of all available nodes. Further study indicated that the problem was with the choice of Spin process used by the partitioning algorithm, which must be specified by the user.

Table 1. Comparitive performance of PSPIN's partitioing schemes

	Partition Function	Memory	Messages Sent	States Stored	Computation Time
Serial	**none**	**24.077**		**477722**	**17 seconds**
2 Nodes	**SCP**	**20.703**	**17824**	**476577**	**13 seconds**
Node 1		10.607	13468	201431	
Node 2		10.095	4356	275146	
4 Nodes	**SCP**	**25.738**	**17824**	**476577**	**10 seconds**
Node 1		10.607	13468	201431	
Node 2		2.518	0	0	
Node 3		2.518	0	0	
Node 4		10.095	4356	275146	
2 Nodes	**LHP**	**20.703**	**17824**	**476577**	**14 seconds**
Node 1		10.607	13468	201431	
Node 2		10.095	4356	275146	
4 Nodes	**LHP**	**26.659**	**88368**	**476577**	**12 seconds**
Node 1		10.607	13468	201431	
Node 2		7.638	4356	169646	
Node 3		2.518	0	0	
Node 4		5.897	70544	105500	
2 Nodes	**GHP**	**48.864**	**3125460**	**1467660**	**251 seconds**
Node 1		24.432	1562940	733953	
Node 2		24.432	1562520	733712	
4 Nodes	**GHP**	**66.495**	**5139780**	**1665980**	**2835 seconds**
Node 1		16.649	1283630	416332	
Node 2		16.547	1283730	416197	
Node 3		16.649	1287480	417253	
Node 4		16.649	1284940	416202	

Our Promela model consists of one large process (corresponding to the Deos kernel) and a number of smaller processes. However, the default value for selecting the process whose source code graph is partitioned (variable NPROC in files `table.t` and `ppan.c`) corresponded to one of the smaller processes. We set the process selection variable (NPROC in SCP, HASHPROC in LHP) to correspond to the large Deos process (the Deos kernel) and the results were much better (as reflected in results shown later in this paper), with all the processors being well utilized.

3.2   PSPIN Evaluation with Large Deos Model

We next analyzed larger models, albeit models that could be verified using serial Spin within 4GB of memory, using PSPIN. We found that some of these runs did not complete, and had to be killed, for no apparent reason. Detailed analysis of reasons for PSPIN's behavior pointed to issues of memory usage. PSPIN code was then modified to incorporate counters that kept track of memory allocation and deallocation within the Spin and PSPIN parts of the code. In addition, the new code also kept track of the corresponding maximum values (*peak memory*) reached by the memory counters for both Spin and PSPIN during the verification runs. Experiments with this updated implementation indicated that actual memory usage, at some point in the verification run, far exceeded the amounts being reported by Spin, thus explaining why PSPIN failed on some large Deos models.

The results from one such experiment are presented in Table 2. Verification using serial Spin of the model used in this experiment consumed 1100.946 MB of memory. This experiment was performed on a four processor (P0, P1, P2, and P3) shared memory LINUX computer with 16GB of total physical memory. The total amount of memory used by all four processors to distribute the memory requirements of SPIN was 1414 Mbytes. The amounts of memory consumed by each processor as reported by PSPIN are listed in the column labeled *Total Memory Reported*, rows one through four. Note that the values in this column match the values of peak memory consumed by a processor for the SPIN verification (column *Peak Memory SPIN*). So we can conclude that the reported memory usage only consists of SPIN-allocated memory (and not PSPIN-allocated memory). The column labeled *Peak Memory PSPIN* is the peak memory consumed by a processor as a result of overhead from PSPIN memory allocations. It does not include SPIN memory.

Table 2. PSPIN on four processors, with detailed tracking of memory usage.

Proc-essors	Total Memory Reported (MB)	Peak Memory Spin (MB)	Peak Memory PSPIN (MB)	Script Results from Top
P0	302.19	302.19	50.44	~ 328 MB
P1	322.37	322.37	1,883.87	~ 3 GB
P2	407.15	407.15	115.48	~ 464 MB
P3	382.99	382.99	49.28	~ 400 MB

Table 2 shows that one processor (P1) requires approximately 30% more memory than serial SPIN. To confirm this observation, we wrote a simple UNIX shell scripts that recorded results from the UNIX system command "top" every 5 seconds while the above experiment was conducted. The results from the shell script, described in column 5, shows that processor one (P1) requires the largest amount of memory by far. The unreported PSPIN memory usage is due to communication buffers and explains why at times PSPIN does not complete on large DEOS models.

The notion of peak memory is a critical measure of effectiveness of any distributed verification scheme. If the actual memory consumed during a verification run is more than the available physical memory, it does not matter if the final consumption would be less than the physical memory, as verification would definitely fail. Our analyses show that the predominant component of this memory used by PSPIN is communication overhead.

4 State Space Partitioning

The Source Code Partitioning scheme tries to elicit the structure of the state space given the structure of the flow control graph as well as by weighting this graph by traversing a sample of the state space. A related approach is to elicit the structure of the state space by examining a sample of this space and constructing a graph, not of the flow control, but of the state space directly. That is, during a prerun, a graph can be constructed that represents states as vertices and the transitions between states as the edges of a graph. Then this graph can be partitioned directly by an off-the-shelf graph-partitioning package.

4.1 Weighting Vertices

Weights can be applied to vertices by a number of methods. Typically a single weight is assigned to each vertex. However, a single weight does not allow you to model both the memory and computation associated with a single state. You can only model one or the other. It is possible to model both memory and computation if each vertex is given two weights. That is, each vertex of the graph is assigned a weight vector of size two. The first element of this vector represents the memory requirement of the state and the second represents the work requirement of the state. Every vertex that corresponds to an examined state is given a weight vector of (1, 0) that indicates the state requires one unit of memory to store, but no further work is associated with this state. Every vertex that corresponds to an open state is given a weight vector of (1, 1) that indicates it has both memory and work requirements. A multi-constraint graph partitioner [11] can be used to partition such a graph. (Note that the Metis package also implements a number of multi-constraint graph partitioning algorithms.)

4.2 Generalized State Vector Element Partitioning

The Source Code Partitioning scheme essentially partitions the state space based upon the PC for a selected process p. We can automate this approach to some extent by computing a partitioning for each Spin process, and then automatically selecting the best partitioning to use. Hence, the user does not need to select a process manually. Indeed, in our experiments, we have found that it is often the case that certain processes can result in extremely bad partitionings.

We can further extend and generalize this scheme by allowing the state space to be partitioned based upon any element of the state vector -- and not just the various PCs. A simple algorithm is to compute a partitioning for every element of the state vector and to select the state vector element and partition array of the best partitioning seen. We have implemented an algorithm that does so and refer to it as State Vector Element Partitioning (SVEP).

The SVEP algorithm requires a prerun, during which the graph that models the state space is constructed. At this time, it is necessary to record not only the connectivity among the states in the state space, but also the state vector for each state visited. The prerun terminates after a pre-selected depth is reached. After the augmented state-space graph is constructed, SVEP applies the following algorithm in a recursive bisection manner [2] to result in a k-way partitioning.

For each element of the state vector:

1. The range of values r that has been seen for the element is determined.
2. If the r is less than or equal to a specified threshold t, then the graph is collapsed into r vertices. If r is greater than t, then the values are grouped together into t evenly sized sets, and the graph is collapsed into t vertices.
3. The graph is collapsed by creating a single *super vertex* for each distinct value (or set of values in the case in which r is greater than t) seen. The weight of each super vertex is equal to the sum of the weights of its component vertices.
4. For each edge e in the initial (i.e., uncollapsed) graph that connects two vertices that are mapped to different super vertices, either (i) a *super edge* is added to the collapsed graph, or (ii) if a super edge already exists between the two super vertices, then the weight of e is added to the weight of the super edge.
5. All edges of the initial graph that connect vertices that are mapped to the same super vertex are ignored.
6. The resulting collapsed graph is likely to be small. If it contains less than 15 vertices, a two-way partitioning is computed optimally by brute force. (That is, every possible partitioning is examined, and the best one is returned.) If the collapsed graph is larger than 15 vertices, Metis is called to partition it in half.

The best partitioning that is found by this process is returned along with identification information (e.g., the index of the associated element and its range information). The returned information is used to generate a partition function.

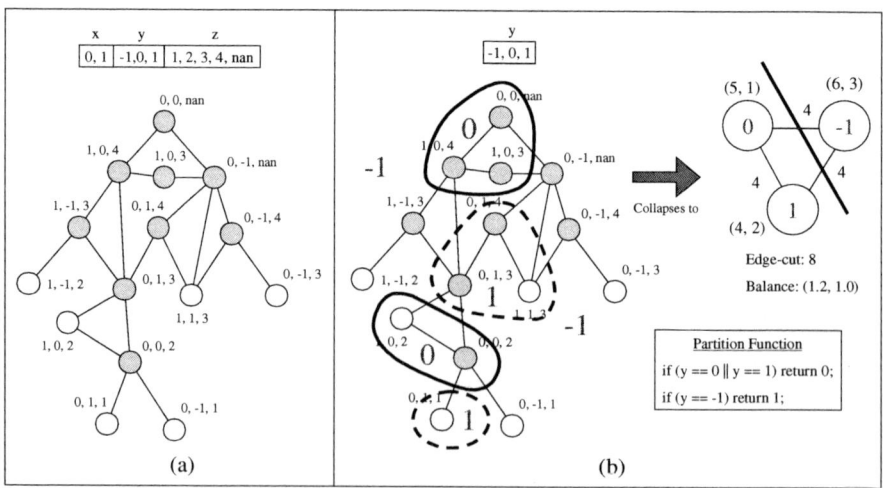

Fig. 4. (a) An example of an augmented state-space graph, and (b) the resulting collapsed graph with respect to the value of variable y

Figures 4 and 5 illustrate this process. Figure 4(a) shows an augmented state space graph. In this example, the state vector consists of three elements that correspond to Promela variables x, y, and z. (Note, that for purposes of this simple example we do not include process PCs in the state vector. However, any or all of these three variables could be PCs and the results would be the same.) Vertices are shaded if their corresponding states have been examined. White vertices correspond to open states. The range of seen values for each element is shown at the top of the figure. For example, variable z has taken the values 1, 2, 3, 4 and nan (i.e., undefined) in the sampled state space. The graph shows each state encountered along with its unique state vector and the connectivity among the states. For example, state (1, 0, 4) can reach or be reached by states (0, 0, nan), (1, 0, 3), and (1, -1, 3).

Figure 4(b) shows how the augmented graph is collapsed with respect to variable y. (Note that since only two values are seen for variable x, the resulting graph has only two vertices and the partitioning can be performed trivially.) In this case, the range of three values that are seen for y result in a collapsed graph with three vertices. The optimal partitioning of this graph is shown. This partitioning has an edge-cut of nine and state balances of 1.2 and 1.0. (Balances are computed by max sub-domain weight over average weight.) The partition function that is derived from this partition array is shown. In this case, the partitioning results in a better edge-cut and the same balance compared to the partitioning that was trivially computed for variable x. Hence, this partitioning is saved as the *current best*.

Figure 5 shows the graph collapsed with respect to variable z. A range of five values results in a collapsed graph with five nodes. The optimal partitioning is shown for the collapsed graph. This partitioning has an edge-cut of eight (same as the current best) and balances of 1.07 and 1.3. Depending on which vertex weight is favored, either of these partitionings could be selected as the current best. We give more weight to the balance that corresponds to the open vertices, as this approach will favor balancing the predicted work among the processing nodes to balancing the memory load. Therefore, the current best partitioning is that of variable y.

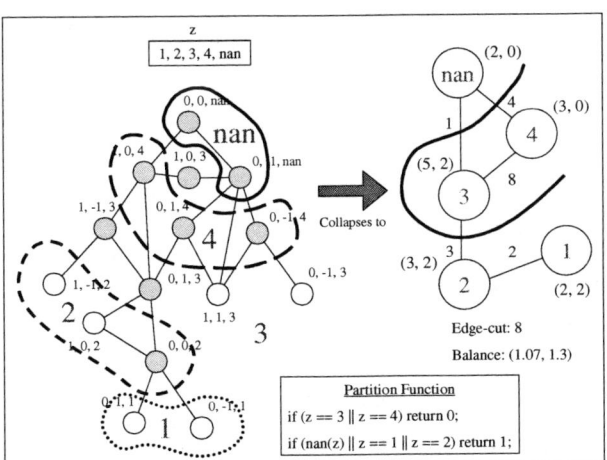

Fig. 5. The augmented state-space graph collapsed with respect to the value of variable z

This algorithm is applied in a general recursive bisection manner [2]. That is, for a k-way partitioning, after the initial bisector of the state space is determined, the augmented state-space graph is split into two graphs using this bisector. Then the algorithm is applied recursively to both sub-graphs. The automatically generated partition function then is structured as a set of nested if-then-else statements. This scheme can handle values of k that are not powers of two by splitting the graph, not exactly in half by weight, but into one-third and two-third weight regions. The one-third side is not split further, while the two-third side is split further.

Sometimes a variable might only take a single value throughout the entire sample space. In this case, it is not possible to compute a partition using this variable. Also, it is possible that more values might be eventually encountered in the full state space than are seen during the prerun. Therefore, the partition function must be generated to be complete. In our implementation, we cover these possible values by a simple scheme. (That is, all values less than those seen are mapped to node zero. All values higher than those seen are mapped to node one.)

4.3   Evaluation of SVEP

In this section, we compare the results from using SVEP against those obtained by PSPIN's SCP and LHP schemes. All experiments were conducted on a network of LINUX workstations at Michigan Technological University (MTU). The MTU cluster is a network of workstations that are all 2.0 GHz P4's with 2GB of memory. In all of the experiments, partial order reduction was disabled and compression was enabled. In addition, the amount of memory that a SPIN process can consume was set to 2GB. The maximum depth of the stack was set to 300,000 for experiments using LHP and SVEP schemes as they typically produced search depths in excess of the 10,000 default used by Spin. The maximum depth for the stack was left at 10,000 for experiments using SCP. The stack depths were not fine-tuned as specifying depths greater than the actual depths do not invalidate the results, and having the same depth for both LHP and SVEP eliminated the effects of stack depth on memory usage from consideration. The Deos model used for these tests was a medium sized one, with a depth of 267,386, memory of 1000.84MB, and a run time of 98 seconds when run serially. Note that peak memory is discussed separately, after the discussions regarding other performance measures.

Results from SVEP
As stated earlier, our scheme generates a partition function based on exploring a sample of the state space. Table 3 lists results obtained using our algorithm on three sets of experiments from between two and 16 processors. In the first set, a very small amount of the state space (0.04%) was explored during the prerun. In the second set, 0.16% of the state space was explored, and 0.24% of the state space was explored in the third set of experiments. The table is arranged such that results of all three sets are grouped together for easy comparison. The first criterion examined is computation time in seconds. The table shows both the time for the PSPIN computation, and the time for the prerun in the parentheses. We note that the computation time when four through sixteen processors are used is always less than the computation time required for 2 processors. This is a good result in the sense that we do not see a trend where the computation time increases as the number of processors is increased. The second criterion examined is the amount of memory in Mbytes reported by PSPIN. Recall that the results listed are strictly the amounts of memory required by the Spin part of the verification and do not reflect the overhead

memory required by a single PSPIN process. Our tables list the memory consumed by the node that consumed the highest memory. These results show that the maximum amount of memory required to perform the Spin verification decreases as the number of processor is increased for all three sets of experiments. The third and fourth criteria measure communication overhead. The third criterion is the total number of messages transmitted as a result of the distributed computation using PSPIN. The fourth criterion is the total information transmitted in a distributed computation of PSPIN. Note that all criteria examined are generated as output of PSPIN. There are no discernable trends that can be observed from the communications results. In general, when sampling between 0.04% and 0.24% of the state space, the results can vary significantly. This is not unexpected, as our partitioning scheme is both heuristic and predictive.

In order to make the following comparisons straightforward, we will use a single result from our experiments above (and not three results). For the remainder of the paper, when comparing the results from our algorithm versus results from partitioning by SCP and Local Hash partitioning, we will use the worst result selected from each criterion given in Table 3. For example, we use a PSPIN computation time of 3230 seconds for two processors, with the corresponding prerun time of 80, and a max memory of 170.768 for 16 processors. We feel that this is a fair way to compare the schemes as results from our algorithm can vary significantly. Note that performance comparisons with respect to peak memory is discussed later in this section.

SVEP versus SCP

Table 4 is similar in format to Table 3 with the exception that the column labeled "Algo" indicates the type of algorithm used for generating the results. The results from partitioning by SCP show that the maximum amount of memory needed for Spin on any given processor is higher than the corresponding amount of memory needed by our algorithm. Also, the total number of messages communicated with SCP is much higher than the corresponding number for SVEP. In addition, the computation time required by SCP is higher than the computation time with SVEP. Thus, the SVEP scheme requires less memory than SCP, less communication and also less computation time. Therefore, our method is an improvement over SCP. This result is reasonable as our scheme can be considered as a generalization of the SCP scheme.

SVEP versus LHP

As stated earlier, we have found that LHP yields the best results when we use the local process that corresponds to the DEOS kernel to generate the partition function. The results for LHP that are listed in Table 5 were obtained by using the local process corresponding to the DEOS kernel to generate the partition function.

When comparing LHP and SVEP schemes, we notice that our scheme is much faster across the board, and especially as the number of processors increases, than using PSPIN with LHP. This is explained because both the number of messages and the total amount of information communicated in LHP is much higher than with SVEP scheme. The max memory requirements are better for LHP than for our scheme. This is because the LHP balances the states better across the processors. However, it is important to note that both schemes are scalable with respect to maximum memory usage.   That is, the maximum memory requirements of both schemes decrease as the number of processors increase.

Though LHP outperforms our SVEP scheme in minimizing the amount of memory consumed by any given processor, the SVEP scheme reduces communication and computation time. The problem of minimizing the amount of memory on any given processor is not dependent on computation time. However, if the maximum amount of memory consumed by the SVEP scheme and all overhead memory needed are within the constraints of the driving environment, then our method can be used to partition a serial application on n processors and can outperform local hash by over an order of magnitude in runtime.

Table 3. SVEP performance when different amounts of state space are explored during prerun

	%State Space	2	4	8	12	16
Time (s)	0.04%	3062(80)	1133(107)	702(129)	1645(115)	2409(116)
	0.16%	3053(80)	1714(107)	2250(129)	1692(115)	2388(116)
	0.24%	3230(80)	2119(107)	1171(132)	1205(150)	2039(152)
mem (MB)	0.04%	508.911	358.793	208.981	185.225	170.786
	0.16%	508.911	364.117	235.298	199.765	138.837
	0.24%	747.81	381.73	233.557	234.786	128.29
Msgs	0.04%	1,800	951,847	1,662,040	4,594,660	4,685,420
	0.16%	1,800	332,484	704,782	3,372,180	3,430,090
	0.24%	276,300	400,659	1,496,420	1,872,560	2,088,260
Inf Trans	0.04%	6.24	1,511.57	3,526.98	9,974.27	9,962.32
	0.16%	6.24	793.156	1,820.6	6,916.97	85,363.06
	0.24%	741.01	1,318.75	3,641.21	4,959.62	5,590.97

Table 4. Comparison of SVEP and SCP partitioning schemes

	Algo	2	4	8	12	16
Time (s)	SVEP	3,230 (80)	2,119 (107)	2,250 (129)	1,692 (115)	2,388 (116)
	SCP	5,937(4)	4,815(5)	3,334(9)	4,078(12)	3,145(16)
mem (MB)	SVEP	747.81	381.73	235.30	234.79	138.84
	SCP	879.18	879.18	392.58	356.12	218.85
Msgs	SVEP	276,300	400,659	1,662,040	4,594,660	4,685,420
	SCP	3.97 M	3.97 M	9.44 M	10.274 M	14.617 M
Inf Trans	SVEP	741.02	1,511.57	3,641.21	9,974.27	85,363.06
	SCP	6,774.86	6,774.74	15,869.1	20,032.1	24,471.1

Analysis of peak memory
We have mentioned earlier that LHP requires less memory than our partitioning scheme to distribute Spin memory requirements. We have also mentioned that PSPIN overhead memory requirements for LHP can at times be much higher than the memory for serial Spin. Therefore, in analyzing our algorithm versus LHP, we need to look at PSPIN overhead memory requirements in both approaches.

Table 5. Comparison of SVEP and LHP partitioning schemes

	Algo	2	4	8	12	16
Time (s)	SVEP	3,230	2,119	2,250	1,692	2,388
	LHP	3,631	6,025	35,367	40,772	11,783
mem (MB)	SVEP	747.81	381.73	235.30	234.79	138.84
	LHP	532.053	281.89	154.709	104.943	87.842
Total Msgs	SVEP	276,300	400,659	1.662M	4.595 M	4.685 M
	LHP	11.685M	22.048M	28 M	27.925M	29.889M
Inf Trans	SVEP	741.02	1,511.57	3,641.21	9,974.27	85,363.06
	LHP	18,731.4	62,858.4	91,014.7	120,717.0	96,186.9

Table 6. Comparison of peak memory between LHP and SVEP

Peak Mem (MB)		2 procs	4 procs	8 procs	12 procs	16 procs
LHP		267.73	655.43	1144.22	2580.74	1242.11
SVEP	0.24%	849.74	1084.5	1460.49	1510.21	1466.92
SVEP	0.16%	19.12	415.01	582.56	2104.37	1684.53

Table 7. Comparison of max messages between LHP and SVEP

Max msg	2 procs	4 procs	8 procs	12 procs	16 procs
LHP	1.131E+11	3.703E+11	3.790E+11	3.044E+11	2.247E+11
SVEP 0.24%	163884	53172	390672	357636	357636
SVEP 0.16%	1800	104416	129312	505054	372574

As we can see from Table 6, there are times when our algorithm requires more overhead memory for PSPIN and other times when LHP requires more memory. Our initial thought is that reductions in total number of communications and total amount of information transferred will reduce overhead memory. However, further analysis is required. At the present, we are looking at the maximum number of messages that any processor sent and the maximum overhead of possibly a different processor in the same verification in an attempt to understand if there is a correlation between the two quantities. Table 7 compares the maximum number of messages (*max msg*) sent by a node with overhead.

In an attempt to further analyze trends for the increase in memory overhead, we resorted to statistical analysis of the maximum number of messages sent versus the memory overhead. When using SVEP, we noticed that maximum messages and overhead memory correlate positively (i.e. one increases as the other increases), with a correlation factor of 0.82. This strong correlation indicates that it might be a worthwhile direction for better understanding memory overhead.

5   Related Work

The work done by Lerda and Visser [13] on distributing JPF is most closely related to our work. The difference lies in their approach of starting from Java. In addition, they also explore various ways of optimizing the communication and verification time. We plan to implement such optimizations once we better understand the nature of the peak memory. There has also been work on various extensions to PSPIN [1] and Spin [5,9]. In addition, there has also been work in distributing other formal analysis tools such as Petri nets [3].

6   Conclusions and Future Directions

There is increasing interest in verifying large models in the context of safety-critical systems, and distributed verification is a promising approach for achieving this. In this paper, we evaluated a distributed implementation of Spin. Our analyses show that there is a penalty in terms of verification time for distribution, while the actual memory used for states (i.e. the PSPIN reported memory) reduces almost linearly with the number of processing nodes. We also presented another partitioning scheme that performs much better in terms of verification time, while not requiring the user to choose a specific Spin process in order to achieve good partitioning. But all the partitioning schemes suffer from high memory overhead. Our results point to a strong correlation between overhead and the maximum number of messages sent by a node. Exploration of this correlation and distribution of partial order reduction are aspects we will be pursuing in the future.

It is possible to generalize the SVEP scheme by considering partitionings that are combinations of the values seen from multiple variables. For example, the example graph shown in Figure 4(a) could be collapsed with respect to the values of both x and y. In this case, there are six possible permutations of the seen values ((0,-1),(0,0),(0,1),(1,-1),(1,0),(1,1)), and so the collapsed graph would have six vertices. This extension will increase the run time of the algorithm significantly, as many more partitionings need to be computed and compared. However, it is likely to come up with better results. Also, it is worth investigating extending the SVEP scheme to be used not only for static (i.e., a priori) load balancing, but also for dynamic load balancing. This extension would address the problem that the structural characteristics of the state space might change after a certain point in the execution. In the current, static load balancing approach, only a small portion of the state space is sampled and this space is early in the execution. Finally, we would like to develop a partitioning scheme that focuses on minimizing peak memory.

Acknowledgements. We would like to convey our thanks to Michigan Technological University for letting us use their cluster for our tests.

References

[1]   Barnat, J, Brim, L, and Stribrna, J, "Distributed LTL Model-Checking in SPIN, Technical Report FIMURS -2000-10, Faculty of Informatics, Masaryk University, 2000.

[2]   Berger, M and Bokhari, S.   "A Partitioning Strategy for Nonuniform Problems on Multiprocessors". IEEE Transactions on Computers, C-36(5), pages 570-580, May 1987.

[3]   Ciardo, G, German, R, and Lindemann, C, "A Characterization of the Stochastic Process Underlying a Stochastic Petri Net", Software Engineering, Vol. 20 No. 7, 1994.

[4]   Cofer, Darren and Rangarajan, Murali, "Formal Modeling and Analysis of Advanced Scheduling Features in an Avionics RTOS", in Proceedings of EMSOFT '02: Second International Workshop on Embedded Software, Springer-Verlag.

[5]   Demartini, C, Iosif, R, and Sisto, R, "dSpin: A Dynamic Extension of SPIN", Lecture Notes in Computer Science, Vol 1680, September 1999.

[6]   Giannakopoulou, D and Lerda, F, "From States to Transitions: Improving Translation of LTL Formulae to Buchi Automata", Proc. of 22nd {IFIP} International Conference on Formal Techniques for Networked and Distributed Systems, November, 2002.

[7]   Holzmann, G. J., "The Model Checker Spin", IEEE Trans. on Software Engineering, 23(5):279-295, May 1997.

[8]   Honeywell, 1999, "Design Description Document for the Digital Engine Operating System," Honeywell Specification no. PS7022409.

[9]   Iosif, R, and Sisto, R, "Using Garbage Collection in Model Checking", Proc. of the 7th International SPIN Workshop, Vol. 1885, Springer-Verlag, 2000.

[10] Karypis, G and Kumar, V. METIS: A Software Package for Partitioning Unstructured Graphs, Partitioning Meshes, and Computing Fill-Reducing Orderings of Sparse Matrices, Version 4.0. Technical Report, Dept. of Computer Science, University of Minnesota, 1998.

[11] Karypis, G and Kumar, V.   Multilevel Algorithms for Multi-Constraint Graph Partitioning. In Proceedings of Supercomputing 1998, 1998.

[12] Lerda, F, and Sisto, R, "Distributed-Memory Model Checking with Spin", in Proceedings of the 5th International Spin Workshop, Vol. 1680 of LNCS, Springer-Verlag, 1999.

[13] Lerda, F, and Visser, W, "Addressing Dynamic Issues of Program Model Checking", Proc. 8th SPIN Workshop, Lecture Notes in Computer Science, Vol. 2057, 2001.

Verification of MPI-Based Software for Scientific Computation

Stephen F. Siegel and George S. Avrunin

Laboratory for Advanced Software Engineering, Dept. of Computer Science,
University of Massachusetts, Amherst MA 01003, USA
{siegel,avrunin}@cs.umass.edu
http://laser.cs.umass.edu

Abstract. We explore issues related to the application of finite-state
verification techniques to scientific computation software employing the
widely-used Message-Passing Interface (MPI). Many of the features of
MPI that are important for programmers present significant difficulties
for model checking. In this paper, we examine a small parallel program
that computes the evolution in time of a discretized function u defined
on a 2-dimensional domain and governed by the diffusion equation. Although this example is simple, it makes use of many of the problematic
features of MPI. We discuss the modeling of these features and use SPIN
and INCA to verify several correctness properties for various configurations of this program. Finally, we describe some general theorems that
can be used to justify simplifications in finite-state models of MPI programs and that guarantee certain properties must hold for any program
using only a particular subset of MPI.

1 Introduction

The advent of relatively cheap clustered computers and infrastructure supporting parallel programs on them has made supercomputers much more accessible
and greatly expanded the range of application of scientific computing. Yet developers of parallel scientific software have encountered many problems that
are familiar to specialists in verification of concurrent software: programs deadlock; they display inappropriate nondeterministic behavior; bugs are difficult to
reproduce, let alone pinpoint and correct. Finite-state verification (FSV) techniques, such as model checking, can offer solutions to many of these problems, at
least in principle. But typical scientific parallel programs pose special challenges
for FSV techniques. For instance, in the widely used Message-Passing Interface
(MPI) [13], the memory available for buffering messages between two processes,
and thus the number of messages that can be buffered, can change dynamically
and unpredictably during execution.

In this paper, we describe some first attempts at applying FSV techniques
to a small, but realistic, example of a parallel scientific program that uses MPI.
This program computes the evolution in time on a 2-dimensional domain of a

S. Graf and L. Mounier (Eds.): SPIN 2004, LNCS 2989, pp. 286–303, 2004.

discretized function governed by the differential equation known as the "diffusion" (or "heat") equation. We discuss some of the issues in modeling such programs and present the results of verifying several data-independent properties of the communication skeletons of various configurations of this program, using SPIN [7] and INCA [3,15]. Finally, we describe some theorems that can be used to justify simplifications in models of MPI programs, and that guarantee certain properties must hold for programs using only a particular subset of MPI.

In the next section, we briefly discuss the basic MPI constructs and introduce our example program, Diffusion2d. In section 3, we explain how we modeled this program for SPIN and present the results of our initial attempts to verify properties with SPIN. We then discuss modeling and verification with INCA. In section 5, we present the theorems. In section 6, we briefly describe some related work, and we discuss our conclusions and plans for future work in section 7.

2   The Message-Passing Interface and an Example Program

Most parallel scientific programs rely on *message-passing* for inter-process communication. The basic ideas of this paradigm have been around since the late 1960s, and by the early 1990s, several different and incompatible message-passing systems were being used to develop significant applications. The desire for portability and a recognized standard led to the creation of the *Message-Passing Interface*, which defines the precise syntax and semantics for a library of functions for writing message-passing programs in a language such as C or Fortran. Since that time, a number of high-quality proprietary and open-source MPI implementations have become available on almost any platform, and MPI has become the *de facto* standard for parallel scientific software.

2.1   MPI Basics

An MPI program consists of autonomous processes executing their own code in an MIMD style, although in practice the code executed by the different processes is often identical. The processes communicate by calls to functions implementing the MPI communication primitives. There are more than 140 such functions in the MPI-1 Standard. In this section, we briefly describe a few of the most basic ones, those used in our Diffusion2d example.

Each of the MPI functions described here takes, as one of its arguments, an MPI *communicator*. A communicator specifies a set of processes which may communicate with each other through MPI functions. Given a communicator with n processes, the processes are numbered 0 to $n-1$; this number is referred to as the *rank* of the process in the communicator. MPI provides a pre-defined communicator, MPI_COMM_WORLD, which represents the set of all processes.

The simplest function for sending a message from one process to another is the *standard mode, blocking send* function, with the form

MPI_SEND(buf, count, datatype, dest, tag, comm),

where buf is the address of the first element in the sequence of data to be sent; count is the number of elements in the sequence, datatype indicates the type of each element in the sequence; dest is the rank of the process to which the data is to be sent; tag is an integer that may be used to distinguish the message; and comm is a handle representing the communicator in which this communication is to take place.

The simplest function for receiving a message is the *blocking receive* function, with the form

MPI_RECV(buf, count, datatype, source, tag, comm, status).

Here, buf is the address for the beginning of the segment of memory into which the incoming message is to be stored. The integer count specifies an upper bound on the number of elements of type datatype to be received. The integer source is the rank of the sending process and the integer tag is the tag identifier. However, unlike the case of MPI_SEND, these last two parameters may take the *wildcard* values MPI_ANY_SOURCE and MPI_ANY_TAG, respectively. The parameter comm represents the communicator, while status is an "out" parameter used by the function to return information about the message that has been received. An MPI receive operation will only select a message for reception if the source, tag, and communicator of the message match the corresponding receive parameters appropriately.

The MPI implementation may decide to buffer an outgoing message. On the other hand, the implementation may decide to block the sending process, perhaps until the size of the system buffer becomes sufficiently small, before sending out the message. Finally, the system may decide to block the sending process until the receiving process is at a matching receive, and there is no pending message in the system buffer that also matches that receive. If the implementation chooses this last option, we say that it forces this particular send to be *synchronous*.

The MPI Standard requires that messages be nonovertaking, in the sense that two messages from a single sender to single destination, both matching the same receive, can only be received in the order in which they were sent. But this is the only guarantee concerning the order in which messages are received—if two different processes send messages to the same process, the messages may be received in the order opposite to that in which they were sent.

MPI also provides *non-blocking* send and receive operations in which, for example, a sending process can continue execution even before the system has finished copying the message from the send buffer. In addition, both the blocking and non-blocking sends come in several *modes*. We have described the *standard* mode, but there are also the *synchronous, buffered,* and *ready* modes.

It is common in MPI programs to have processes exchange data, either directly, when two processes send to and receive from each other, or more generally, as when each process in a grid sends to one neighbor and receives from another neighbor. In such cases, each process must execute one send and one receive, but if the program is coded so that each process first sends and then receives, the program will deadlock if, for example, the MPI implementation chooses to synchronize all the sends. The situation occurs frequently enough that MPI provides a special function that executes a send and a receive in one invocation, as if the process forks off two independent threads—one executing the send, the other the receive—and returns when both have completed. This function has the form

MPI_SENDRECV(sendbuf, sendcount, sendtype, dest, sendtag, recvbuf, recvcount, recvcount, recvtype, source, recvtag, comm, status).

The first 5 parameters are the usual ones for send, the next 5 together with status are the usual ones for receive, and comm specifies the communicator for both the send and receive.

Finally, MPI provides a function MPI_BARRIER(comm) that is used to force all processes in the communicator comm to synchronize at a certain point.

2.2   Diffusion2d

Diffusion2d is a parallel program that computes the evolution in time of a discretized function u defined on a 2-dimensional domain and governed by the diffusion equation. It is the "teacher's solution" to a programming project for a course in Parallel Programming (taught by Andrew Siegel) at the University of Chicago. Though quite simple, it has many features common in scientific programs: the physical domain is divided into a "grid" in which one process is responsible for each section; each process also maintains a number of "ghostcells" that mirror the contents of cells on neighboring processes. The program is written mostly in C, with some Fortran, and consists of 1036 lines spread out over six files. Slightly more than half this total consists of a generic package for dealing with grid structures; this package includes the exchangeGhostCells and grid_write functions defined below.

Our first task was to create a more compact and abstract representation of the code which captured the essential communication infrastructure. We follow the convention of [17, 6] in using uppercase sans serif type for the general functions, and mixed-case typewriter font for their C bindings. We also abbreviate the parameter lists by including only the send buffer and destination for a send, and the receive buffer and source for a receive, resulting in the following pseudo-code:

```
int nprocsx, nprocsy, nxl, nyl, nprint, nsteps;
int myproc, mycoord0, mycoord1;
int upperNabe, lowerNabe, leftNabe, rightNabe;
int[,] u;
int[] send_buf, recv_buf, buf;

void main() {
  int iter = 0;
  // read nprocsx, nprocsy, nxl, nyl, nprint, nsteps
  MPI_Init();
  myproc = MPI_Comm_Rank();
  mycoord0 = myproc % nprocsx; mycoord1 = myproc / nprocsx;
```

```
  upperNabe = mycoord0 + nprocsx*((mycoord1 + 1)%nprocsy);
  lowerNabe = mycoord0 + nprocsx*((mycoord1 + nprocsy - 1)%nprocsy);
  leftNabe = (mycoord0 + nprocsx - 1)%nprocsx + nprocsx*mycoord1;
  rightNabe = (mycoord0 + 1)%nprocsx + nprocsx*mycoord1;
  send_buf = new int[nxl]; recv_buf = new int[nxl]; buf = new int[nxl];
  u = new int[nxl+2,nyl+2];
  setInitialValues();
  exchangeGhostCells();
  MPI_Barrier();
  for (iter = 1; iter <= nsteps; ++iter) {
    update(u);
    exchangeGhostCells();
    if ((iter % nprint) == 0) grid_write();
  }
  MPI_Barrier();
  MPI_Finalize();
}
void exchangeGhostCells() {
  for (int i = 1; i <= nxl; ++i) send_buf[i-1] = u[i,1];
  MPI_Sendrecv(send_buf, lowerNabe, recv_buf, upperNabe);
  for (int i = 1; i <= nxl; ++i) u[i,nyl+1] = recv_buf[i-1];
  for (int i = 1; i <= nxl; ++i) send_buf[i-1] = u[i,nyl];
  MPI_Sendrecv(send_buf, upperNabe, recv_buf, lowerNabe);
  for (int i = 1; i <= nxl; ++i) u[i,0] = recv_buf[i-1];
  for (int j = 1; j <= nyl; ++j) send_buf[j-1] = u[1,j];
  MPI_Sendrecv(send_buf, leftNabe, recv_buf, rightNabe);
  for (int j = 1; j <= nyl; ++j) u[nxl+1,j] = recv_buf[j-1];
  for (int j = 1; j <= nyl; ++j) send_buf[j-1] = u[nxl,j];
  MPI_Sendrecv(send_buf, rightNabe, recv_buf, leftNabe);
  for (int j = 1; j <= nyl; ++j) u[0,j] = recv_buf[j-1];
}
void grid_write() {
  if (myproc != 0) {
    for (int n = 0; n < nprocsy; ++n)
      if (mycoord1 == n)
        for (int j = 1; j <= nyl; ++j)
          for (int m = 0; m < nprocsx; ++m)
            if (mycoord0 == m) MPI_Send(u[1..nxl,j], 0);
  } else {
    for (int n = 0; n < nprocsy; ++n)
      for (int j = 1; j <= nyl; ++j)
        for (int m = 0; m < nprocsx; ++m) {
          int from_proc = m + nprocsx*n;
          if (from_proc != 0) MPI_Recv(buf, from_proc);
          else for (int i = 0; i < nxl; ++i) buf[i] = u[i+1,j];
          disk_write(buf);
        }
  }
  MPI_Barrier();
}
```

Each process executes its own copy of this code, and all of the variables are local to this process. One process may take a different execution path through the code than another by branching on its rank. The total number of processes is specified by a flag to the MPI implementation when the program is executed.

The first six variables in the code are read from a file at the beginning of program execution; they act essentially as the parameters which define the geometry of the grid, the number of loop iterations, and the frequency with which the data are to be written to disk. (Actually, the original source code implicitly requires that nxl = nyl, so there are really only 5 parameters.) The processes themselves may be thought of as being arranged in a global $M \times N$ grid, where $M =$ nprocsx and $N =$ nprocsy. The variable myproc is set to the rank r of this process; it is obtained from the MPI infrastructure via the function MPI_COMM_RANK. The position of this process on the global grid is $(m, n) =$ (mycoord0, mycoord1), where $0 \leq m < M$, $0 \leq n < N$, and $r = m + nM$.

The next four variables are used to store the ranks of the neighboring processes. The grid "wraps" around in both the x- and y-directions, so every process has an upper, lower, left, and right neighbor. The four neighbors are not necessarily distinct. In fact, if nprocsx = 1 then this process will be its own left and right neighbor, and if nprocsy = 1 this process will be its own lower and upper neighbor. In these cases some of the MPI calls will actually send messages from a process to itself; this is allowed by MPI.

The variable u is used to store the values of the function that is evolving with time. It stores the values of this function for the coordinates that lie within the portion of the grid corresponding to this process. The dimensions of u are (nxl + 2) × (nyl + 2) because the top and bottom rows, and the left and right columns, are used to store the ghost cells—these are the cells that mirror the corresponding cells in the neighboring processes. (The four "corner" positions are not used.) The next three variables are used as temporary buffers for the MPI communication carried out in exchangeGhostCells and grid_write.

After initializing the variables, the basic structure of execution is relatively simple. First, a ghost-cell exchange is carried out. This updates the ghost cells by sending out the current values of the boundary cells to the appropriate neighbors and in turn receiving the values of their boundary cells, and storing the received values into the ghost-cell positions of u.

Next, a barrier is called, and then the main loop begins. In each iteration, first the values of u[1..nxl,1..nyl] are updated according to a formula derived from the discretization of the diffusion equation. This is purely a local function—it does not involve any MPI communication. Then a ghost-cell exchange takes place, and, if iter is divisible by nprint, grid_write is called.

The function grid_write is somewhat complicated. The goal is to write the cells to disk in the proper order: first, the entire global row 0 must be written, from left to right, then the same for global row 1, etc. To control the order, the data are sent, one local row at a time, from all of the processes of positive rank to the process of rank 0, which then writes to the disk. The nested loops encode a common MPI idiom for dealing with grid structures: n runs through global

y-coordinates of the processes; for each **n**, **j** runs through the local rows, and then **m** runs through the global x-coordinates of the processes. For a process of positive rank, action is taken only when (**n**,**m**) matches the global coordinates of this process.

Through discussions with the programmer, we arrived at several correctness properties for Diffusion2d. We describe three of these here: **Deadlock-Free**, **GlobalLockstep**, and **LocalLockstep**. The first says that the program can never deadlock. The second says that, for all $n > 0$, no process will call update(u) at step n unless every process has already completed update(u) at step $n - 1$. The programmer pointed out that though he expected this property to hold, all that was actually required for correctness was the weaker property **LocalLockstep**—this says the same thing, but only for the four neighbors of a process.

In addition to these correctness properties, there were several questions concerning Diffusion2d that arose in our discussions with the programmer. One is **Q1**: *Could the removal of the* MPI_Barrier *statements from the code lead to a calculation that would not have occurred with the barriers, or could their removal lead to deadlocks if there were none before?* The ability to answer questions of this sort could be very valuable to scientific programmers: barriers can take a huge toll on the performance of a parallel program, but it is often difficult to reason about them informally. Another is **Q2**: *Are the final values written to disk independent of the interleaving or buffering choices made by the MPI implementation?* The expectation is certainly that this should be so, but it is not obvious, a priori, why that must be.

3   Applying SPIN

3.1   Modeling the MPI Communication Primitives

Our first task was to model precisely the MPI communication functions. This task was simplified somewhat by the fact that Diffusion2d uses only one tag, and never makes use of the wildcards MPI_ANY_SOURCE or MPI_ANY_TAG. For these reasons, we could simply use one SPIN channel chan_i_j, for every ordered pair of processes (i, j), to transfer messages from process i to process j.

Of course we must place a bound on the size of the channels. We call this chan_size. A priori, this means that our model fails to be conservative, in that the number of pending messages sent from one process to another can never exceed chan_size in the model, whereas MPI imposes no such bound. However, we will see that in certain cases we can justify a particular choice for chan_size.

We allow for the possibility that chan_size = 0, i.e., for the case where all communication is forced to take place synchronously. In this case the definitions of send and receive coincide exactly with those of SPIN:

```
inline MPI_Send(schan, msg) { schan!msg }   /* chan_size = 0 */
inline MPI_Recv(rchan, rbuf) { rchan?rbuf }
```

A process i wishing to send a message `msg` to process j calls `MPI_Send` with `schan = chan_i_j`. The receive is used in a similar way, and there `rbuf` is a variable, representing the receive buffer, into which the incoming message will be stored.

If `chan_size > 0` the situation is a little more complicated. The semantics of SPIN channels guarantees that each channel will maintain the messages in FIFO order. However, recall that the MPI Standard allows for the MPI implementation to choose, at any time, to force a particular communication to synchronize. To capture this behavior in our model, we leave the receive procedure as is, but we modify the send procedure by inserting a statement that may block until the channel is empty:

```
inline MPI_Send(schan, msg) {  /* chan_size > 0 */
  schan!msg; if :: 1 -> empty(schan) :: 1 fi }
```

We represent MPI_SENDRECV by allowing the send and receive to happen in either order. Again, we must also allow for the possibility that the send is synchronized. For `chan_size > 0` we hence arrive at the following:

```
inline MPI_Sendrecv(schan, msg, rchan, rbuf) { /* chan_size > 0 */
  if :: schan!msg -> rchan?rbuf :: rchan?rbuf -> schan!msg fi;
  if :: 1 -> empty(schan) :: 1  fi }
```

The case `chan_size = 0` must be dealt with separately because of the possibility that `schan = rchan`, i.e., the case where process i attempts to send/receive a message to/from itself. The MPI Standard guarantees that the send and receive must be able to take place synchronously if there are no pending messages (sent from i to i). This situation requires no special handling in the positive `chan_size` case because, if there are no pending messages, the channel will be empty, and so the message can first be placed in the channel and then received. However, for `chan_size = 0`, the procedure defined above would always block, when in fact it should always be able to complete without blocking. Hence we modify the definition in this case so that the message is just placed directly into the receive buffer:

```
inline MPI_Sendrecv(schan, msg, rchan, rbuf) { /* chan_size = 0 */
  if :: (schan == rchan) -> rbuf = msg :: else ->
    if :: schan!msg -> rchan?rbuf :: rchan?rbuf -> schan!msg fi
  fi }
```

For `chan_size > 0`, we will refer to the procedures above as the *complex communication model*. We will also consider the *simple communication model*, in which we just remove the potentially blocking statement from the send and send-receive procedures. The effect of this will be that some statements in the simple model will not block whereas they might when the actual MPI program is executed. However, we will see that in some cases, the simple model will suffice for verifying certain properties, and can also improve the performance of SPIN.

Finally, we turn to MPI_BARRIER. There are many standard ways to model a barrier; we chose a simple "coordinator barrier" approach. This entailed introducing an extra process with which an ordinary process interacts when it wishes to enter and exit a barrier. A special synchronous channel is used exclusively for this purpose. A 0 is sent on this channel when the process enters the barrier, and then a 1 is sent when the process attempts to exit the barrier. The barrier function waits to receive one 0 for each original process before accepting any 1s:

```
chan barrier_chan = [0] of {bit};
inline MPI_Barrier() { barrier_chan!0; barrier_chan!1 }
active proctype Barrier() {
end_b: do :: barrier_chan?0; ...; barrier_chan?0;
             barrier_chan?1; ...; barrier_chan?1 od }
```

The label end_b is used to indicate to SPIN that an execution in which all other processes have terminated and the barrier is at position end_b should not be considered deadlocked.

3.2   Modeling Diffusion2d and Properties in SPIN

Having dealt with the model of the MPI infrastructure, we turned to the Diffusion2d program itself. The first question was how to represent the floating point data. However, we observed that none of the properties discussed here depend in any way on the actual values of the data. This fact reflects the simplicity of the program we have chosen as our example. Had our program contained, for example, a conditional statement that branched on an expression involving some of the data, we would have had to think carefully about the appropriate abstractions. Indeed, we plan on looking at such an example in future work. But for this example, we could simply abstract away the data altogether, and we sent only the bit 1, representing any message, on the channels. The upshot is that the channels in our model keep track only of the number of pending messages sent from one process to another.

We made a few other simple optimizations (for example, leaving out channels that would never be used). Otherwise, the Promela code for each process looks very much like the pseudo-code for Diffusion2d given above. To make it easy to experiment with different choices of the parameters and other options, we wrote a simple Java program that takes as input those choices, and outputs the corresponding SPIN model. The 5 parameters that come from the program itself are nprocsx, nprocsy, nxl, nsteps, and nprint. The additional choices affecting the model include chan_size, the choice between the simple or complex communication model (if chan_size > 0), and the choice of whether or not to include the barriers.

We now explain how we expressed the lockstep properties. (SPIN already has a built-in capacity to check for deadlock.) Let $far(i, j)$ be the predicate which is true precisely when process i is at the position just before the call to update(u) and the value of iter in process i minus the value of iter in process j is greater than 1. This can be expressed in SPIN by making the two `iter` variables global, inserting a label (`Calculate`) at the appropriate positions in the code, and adding the following:

```
#define far_i_j (proc_i@Calculate && (iter_i - iter_j > 1))
```

This predicate represents the undesirable behavior; let **Lockstep**(i,j) be the claim that $\mathsf{far}(i,j)$ is always false. We can use SPIN to check this property by including the never claim generated from the LTL formula `<>far_i_j`.

Now, **GlobalLockstep** is equivalent to the conjunction of the **Lockstep**(i,j) over all (i,j) for which $i \neq j$. To check this property, we could either verify the **Lockstep**(i,j) individually, or we could define p to be the disjunction of the $\mathsf{far}(i,j)$ and check the single never claim generated from `<>p`. The first approach may allow SPIN to scale further, though the second is probably more efficient for small configurations. Similar comments apply to **LocalLockstep**, which is the conjunction over all (i,j) for which i and j are neighbors and $i \neq j$.

There is another approach which is more specific but could help the model checker further by reducing the number of states that need to be explored. Let $\mathsf{calc}(i,n)$ be the predicate which is true precisely when process i is at the position just before the call to `update(u)` and the value of `iter` in process i is n:

```
#define calc_i_n (proc_i@Calculate && (iter_i == n))
```

For $n \geq 1$, let **Lockstep**$(i,j;n)$ be the claim that, on any execution, $\mathsf{calc}(i,n)$ must be preceded by $\mathsf{calc}(j,n-1)$. Hence **Lockstep**(i,j) is equivalent to the conjunction, over all n, of the **Lockstep**$(i,j;n)$. To check this property with SPIN, we use the never claim generated from the LTL formula `(!q)Up`, where $p = \mathsf{calc}(i,n)$ and $q = \mathsf{calc}(j,n-1)$. The potential advantage arises from the fact that the search can be truncated as soon as q becomes true when p is false.

3.3   Verification with SPIN

We instantiated a large number of models for various choices of the parameters and model options, and checked various versions of the properties. We used Spin version 4.0.0 of 1 January 2003, running on a Linux box with a 2.2 GHz Xeon processor and 4 GB of memory. In all cases we used the SPIN options `-DSAFETY` (as ours are all safety properties), `-DNOFAIR` (as no fairness assumptions were needed), `-DCOLLAPSE` (for better compression), and `-DMEMLIM=3000` (to utilize all 3 GB of memory available to a single process). To simplify the discussion that follows, we will use the term "$n \times m$ configuration" to refer to the configuration with `nprocsx` $= n$, `nprocsy` $= m$, and, unless explicitly stated otherwise, `nxl` $= 1$ and `nprint` $=$ `nsteps` $= 2$. (All inputs and results are available at `http://laser.cs.umass.edu/~siegel/projects`.)

We were able to verify **DeadlockFree** and **LocalLockstep** in all cases where SPIN did not run out of memory. But in verifying **GlobalLockstep**, a surprising thing occurred: for certain configurations, SPIN found a counterexample. In general, the existence of a counterexample required `nprocsx` or `nprocsy` to be at least 4, `chan_size` ≥ 1, and `nsteps` ≥ 2. In such circumstances, it is possible for one process to begin its calculation of u^2 (the value of u at time step 2) before another has begun its calculation of u^1.

To see how this can happen, we outline the trace produced by SPIN for the 4×1 configuration. We may ignore the vertical exchanges of ghost cells as these just involve a process communicating with itself. Say all processes have just exited the first barrier and are about to enter the `for` loop. At this point `iter` is 0 in each process. Now process 3 may proceed to call `exchangeGhostCells` and send a message to process 2 as part of its first `Sendrecv`. Process 2 may also proceed to this point, receive this message, and send a message to process 1. At this point, process 2 may proceed to its second `Sendrecv` statement and send a message to process 3. Now process 1 may proceed to send a message to process 0, receive the message from process 2, proceed to its second `Sendrecv` and send a message to process 2. Process 2 can then receive that message, completing its participation in the `exchangeGhostCells` routine, return to the top of the loop, and then begin its calculation of u^2. Process 0 has still not entered the loop. Notice that at this point there will be two pending messages: one sent from process 2 to process 3, the other sent from process 1 to process 0.

As remarked earlier, the correctness of Diffusion2d does not depend on this property. However, the violation was a surprise to the programmer, who thought the synchronization enforced by the sends and receives would force all the processes to stay "close". In fact, once we have understood this counterexample, it is not hard to see that in a strip of $2n$ processes, processes 0 and n can become n time steps apart, if `chan_size` ≥ 1. It appears, however, that for `chan_size` $= 0$, **GlobalLockstep** holds.

We did run out of memory for relatively small configurations—for example, 4×4 for **DeadlockFree**, even with `chan_size` $= 0$. We were able to verify the 4×3 case with `chan_size` $= 0$ and with barriers. In this case there were 3.8×10^6 states stored, SPIN used 153 MB of memory, and it took slightly over 3 minutes to execute `spin -a` and compile and execute the analyzer. Without barriers, the performance was 1.5×10^6 states, 60 MB, and just over 1 minute.

For positive `chan_size`, the choice of simple or complex communication model made a big difference in the size of the state space. Consider, for example, the 4×2 configuration without barriers and with `chan_size` $= 1$. Using the complex model, there were 2.8×10^7 states stored in verifying **DeadlockFree**; with the simple model this number was reduced to 9.6×10^4.

As we suspected, verification of **Lockstep**$(0, 1; 2)$ required fewer states than for the stronger **Lockstep**$(0, 1)$. For example, verification in the 3×3 configuration with `chan_size` $= 1$, no barriers, and the simple communication model, required storing $89,838$ states for the former property, and $400,482$ states for the latter. This allowed us to scale **Lockstep**$(0, 1; 2)$ as far as the 4×4 configuration (2.5×10^7 states, 1655 MB, 29 minutes). SPIN was able to find the counterexample to **Lockstep**$(0, 2; 2)$ in quite large configurations—at least 7×7 (beyond this point, SPIN complains that there are too many channel types).

The lockstep properties provide an example for which the simple communication model is conservative. For, if we ignore what goes on within a call to an MPI function, the set of all execution prefixes is the same whether one uses the simple or complex model; the difference lies in the fact that some of those finite prefixes may be considered deadlocked in the complex model, but not in the simple one. Since a lockstep property does not depend on this distinction, it will hold under the simple model if, and only if, it holds under the complex one.

All of the results were the same with and without the barriers. At the very least, this provided some evidence that the barriers might not be necessary.

4   Applying INCA

INCA takes as input a description of a concurrent program in the S-Expression Design Language (SEDL) together with a property expressed in the INCA query language [14]. (The query actually describes a violation of the property, much like the never claims in SPIN.) From these it produces an Integer Linear Programming (ILP) problem which can be analyzed by standard linear programming tools such as CPLEX. If the ILP problem has no solution, the property is guaranteed to hold on all executions of the program. On the other hand, a solution to the ILP problem may or may not correspond to an actual counterexample to the property; if not, then there are ways to augment the ILP problem to increase the precision of the model. A constrained search using the values in a solution to the ILP problem as the counts of events in an execution can be used to determine whether a solution corresponds to a counterexample.

SEDL resembles a subset of Ada in a Lisp-like syntax. One defines tasks, which have their own local variables, execute concurrently, and communicate via rendezvous. SEDL does not explicitly provide for buffered communication, nor for shared variables (which is essentially what the SPIN channels are). For these reasons, for our initial experiments with INCA we restricted ourselves to the case `chan_size = 0`.

As with SPIN, our first task was to model the MPI primitives. To do this, each task j declares entries `chan_i_j`. Process i sends a message to process j by calling that entry; process j receives from i by issuing an accept on that entry. The MPI_SENDRECV is modeled using the SEDL `select` statement, which is like the SPIN if statement. For example, an MPI_SENDRECV issued in process 0, sending to process 6 and receiving from 3, would be represented as follows:

```
(select (when t (call proc_6 chan_0_6) (accept chan_3_0))
        (when t (accept chan_3_0)  (call proc_6 chan_0_6)))
```

This even works in the case where a process send-receives itself as INCA allows a task to call one of its own entries. The barrier was modeled exactly as with SPIN, and again, we abstracted away the floating point data to produce a model much like the one used for SPIN.

There is a standard INCA deadlock query, and the queries for **Lockstep**(i, j) and **Lockstep**$(i, j; n)$ are just like the corresponding never claims in SPIN. There is no easy way to represent the conjunction of two properties as a single property in INCA (this is because one cannot easily represent the disjunction of two ILP problems as a single ILP problem) and so, unlike the case for SPIN, we could not check all parts of **GlobalLockstep** or **LocalLockstep** all at once.

We instantiated models for the same configurations that we had used for SPIN, and used INCA version 3.5 and CPLEX Optimizer 8.1.0 on the same hardware. For INCA, the limiting factor is more often time than memory: the ILP problems generated by INCA can often be solved by CPLEX very quickly, but sometimes CPLEX will run for hours without reaching a conclusion; in these cases we say we "ran out of time."

We were able to verify all of the properties whenever we did not run out of time. (Recall that the violation to **GlobalLockstep** requires a positive value for `chan_size`.) For **DeadlockFree**, the choice of whether or not to include the barriers made a big difference in how far we could scale. With the barriers we ran out of time on the 3×3 grid. Without them we could scale as far as 8×8, and the time required (which includes the time to run INCA and CPLEX) grew roughly exponentially in the number of processes: 33 seconds for the 5×5 grid, 5 minutes for 6×6, 54 minutes for 7×7, $2,577$ minutes for 8×8.

We were able to verify **Lockstep**$(0, 1; 2)$ and **Lockstep**$(0, 2; 2)$ for very large grids as well (at least 12×12), with and without barriers. For even the largest of these, the analysis time is under one minute.

4.1   Using INCA for Buffered Communication

In order to incorporate buffers into our INCA model, we created a separate channel task `chan_`i`_`j for each pair of processes. Since we are only keeping track of the number of messages in a channel, each channel task contains one integer variable (`len`) which is incremented or decremented as messages are deposited or removed. The sending task calls an entry `send` in the channel task to deposit a message; the receive task calls an entry `receive` to pick up a message.

As with SPIN we had two channel models: the simple one, in which a send blocks only if the channel is full, and the complex one, which might block the sender until the message can be received. For the simple model, the definition of `chan_0_1` appears as follows:

```
(task chan_0_1
 ((entry send) (entry receive) (variable len chan_range 0))
 ((loop (select
   (when (< len chan_size) (accept send) (assign len (+ len 1)))
   (when (> len 0) (accept receive) (assign len (- len 1)))))))
```

Now an MPI_SEND from process 0 to 1 becomes simply (`call chan_0_1 send`), while the corresponding receive is (`call chan_0_1 receive`). The send-receive statement is modeled using the `select` construct as before.

For the complex channel model, we modified the channel task by requiring the sender to make two calls: the first to an entry `send` as before, the second to an entry `complete`. The latter has the possibility of blocking until the channel becomes empty, i.e., until the message has been received. The definition of MPI_SENDRECV must also be modified as follows:

```
(select
  (when t (call chan_0_6 send)
    (select
      (when t (call chan_0_6 complete) (call chan_3_0 receive))
      (when t (call chan_3_0 receive) (call chan_0_6 complete))))
  (when t (call chan_3_0 receive)
    (call chan_0_6 send) (call chan_0_6 complete)))
```

In our first attempts applying this approach to the lockstep properties, we obtained many spurious solutions with disconnected cycles in the channel tasks. However, we were able to take advantage of the special structure of the channel tasks to create a very efficient form of the cycle-elimination procedure described in [15], and this provided enough precision for a conclusive result in all cases.

Using the simple communication model with `chan_size` $= 1$, we were able to verify **Lockstep**$(0, 1; 2)$ and find the counterexamples to **Lockstep**$(0, 2; 2)$, each in configurations up to size 12×12. The times for the 12×12 grid were 2 and 43 minutes, respectively. We were even able to use INCA to find an execution prefix, for a 12×12 grid, in which two processes become 6 time steps apart.

5   Theoretical Results

Our experience analyzing Diffusion2d led us to begin a more general investigation of the properties of MPI programs. Here we give a brief summary of our inquiry; the details and proofs appear in [16]. To simplify matters, we focused on programs that use only the subset of MPI that occurs in Diffusion2d. While these functions represent only a small subset of the MPI library, they are among the most fundamental and commonly used MPI functions, and many interesting and complex parallel programs can be written using only them. Furthermore, we expect that the techniques we have developed to deal with this subset can be extended to a much larger portion of MPI, including the collective functions such as MPI_BROADCAST and MPI_GATHER.

In order to reason about such programs, we defined a precise notion of a model $\mathcal{M}$ of an MPI program. In essence $\mathcal{M}$ consists of an automaton for each process, and a set of channels (each with a fixed sending and receiving process). The transitions may be labeled by either local events, or by communication events. The latter have the form $c!a$ and $c?a$, where a is a constant. Each state is either a *terminal state* (a state with no outgoing transitions, representing process termination), a *local-event state* (all transitions departing from that state are local), a *sending state* (there is only one departing transition and it is labeled by a send event), a *receiving state* (all the departing transitions are labeled by receive events), or a *send-receive state*—a state from which first a send can happen and then a receive, or first a receive then the send.

An *execution prefix* of $\mathcal{M}$ is a sequence of transitions from the various automata such that (i) the projection onto each automaton is a path starting from the initial state, and (ii) for each channel, the sequence of sends and receives on the channel obey FIFO ordering. A *synchronous* prefix is one in which every send is immediately followed by its matching receive. All of the theorems here also require that $\mathcal{M}$ have no wildcard receives—this means that for any state s, there exists a channel c such that every receive transition departing from s has a label of the form $c?a$ for some a. This corresponds to a program that uses neither MPI_ANY_TAG nor MPI_ANY_SOURCE.

An execution prefix results in a *potential deadlock* if (i) at least one process is not at a terminal state, (ii) no process is at a local state, and (iii) if a process p is at a receiving or send-receive state, then for all channels c for which there is a receive transition leaving that state, there are no pending messages on c and no process is at a state from which it can execute a send on c. We say "potential" because it is not necessarily the case that a program that has followed such a path will deadlock. It is only a possibility—whether or not an actual deadlock occurs depends on the buffering choices made by the MPI implementation at the point just after the end of this prefix: if the implementation decides to force all sends to synchronize at this point, the program will deadlock; if it decides to buffer one or more sends, the program may not deadlock. Hence the potentially deadlocked prefixes are precisely the ones for which some choice by a legal MPI implementation would lead to deadlock. Since this is precisely the kind of behavior we wish to avoid, we say that $\mathcal{M}$ is *deadlock-free* if it has no execution prefix of this form. We say that it is *synchronously deadlock-free* if it has no synchronous execution prefix of this form. We can prove the following:

Theorem 1. *Let $\mathcal{M}$ be a model of an MPI program with no wildcard receives. Then $\mathcal{M}$ is deadlock-free if, and only if, $\mathcal{M}$ is synchronously deadlock-free.*

The consequence is that, for such a model, it suffices to check deadlock-free with chan_size $= 0$.

The next theorem concerns the question of barriers. It states that if a model is deadlock-free, it must remain deadlock-free after removing all barrier statements. Barriers can be represented in our formalism by adding a coordinator process as we did with our SPIN and INCA models. If $\mathcal{M}$ is a model and B is an appropriate set of states from the automata in $\mathcal{M}$, we let $\mathcal{M}^B$ denote the model with the new barrier process and with barriers added just after the states in B. We have

Theorem 2. *Assume $\mathcal{M}$ has no wildcard receives. If $\mathcal{M}^B$ is deadlock-free then $\mathcal{M}$ is deadlock-free.*

We say that $\mathcal{M}$ is *locally deterministic* if it has no wildcard receives and every local-event state has exactly one outgoing transition.

Theorem 3. *Suppose $\mathcal{M}$ is a locally deterministic model of an MPI program. Then there exists an execution prefix S for $\mathcal{M}$ with the following property: if T is any execution prefix of $\mathcal{M}$, then for all processes p, the projection of T onto p is a subsequence of the projection of S onto p, up to possible reordering of the send and receive parts of send-receive statements.*

Corollary 1. *Suppose $\mathcal{M}$ is a locally deterministic model of an MPI program. Then M is deadlock-free if, and only if, there exists a synchronous execution prefix T such that either T is infinite or T is finite and ends with each process in a terminal state.*

Now suppose we are given values of the parameters for Diffusion2d, and also a choice of platform for which the numeric operations are deterministic functions. Then the "full-precision" model $\mathcal{M}$ of the program is locally deterministic. Therefore Theorem 3 provides an affirmative answer to **Q2**. As for **Q1**, Theorem 2 shows that if Diffusion2d was deadlock-free with the barriers, it will be deadlock-free after the barriers are removed; it must necessarily result in the same computation by Theorem 3. Hence the barriers really are unnecessary for the correctness of the program. Moreover, to check that Diffusion2d (with the given parameters) is deadlock-free, Corollary 1 shows that it suffices to check *a single execution* of $\mathcal{M}$ and observe that it terminates normally. So verifying **DeadlockFree** does not really require any model checking at all (though the lockstep properties are a different matter).

6   Related Work

Finite-state verification techniques have been applied to various message-passing systems almost from the beginning and SPIN, of course, provides built-in support for a number of message-passing features. Various models and logics for describing message-passing systems (e.g., [12, 1]) are an active area of research. But only a few investigators have looked specifically at the MPI communication mechanisms. Georgelin et al. [5] have described some of the MPI primitives in LOTOS, and have used simulation and some model checking to study the LOTOS descriptions. Matlin et al. [10] used SPIN to verify part of the MPI infrastructure.

Our theorems about MPI programs depend on results about the equivalence of different interleavings of events in the execution of a concurrent program. Our results are related to the large literature on reduction and atomicity (e.g., [8,2,4]) and traces [11]. Most of the work on reduction and atomicity has been concerned with reducing sequences of statements in a single process, although Cohen and Lamport [2] consider statements from different processes and describe, for example, a producer and consumer connected by a FIFO channel in which their results although them to assume that messages are consumed as soon as they are produced. We do not yet fully understand, however, the extent to which our results in the MPI setting correspond to their results for TLA.

Manohar and Martin [9] introduce a notion of *slack elasticity* for a variant of CSP. Essentially, a system is slack elastic if increasing the number of messages that can be buffered in its communication channels does not change the behavior of the system. Their goal is to obtain information about pipelining for hardware design and the nondeterminism and communication constructs in their formalism are somewhat different from ours. The theorems they prove, however, are similar in many respects to ones we describe for MPI programs.

7   Conclusions

MPI-based software for scientific computation represents an important and grow-ing domain of concurrent software, with all the standard problems introduced by concurrency. Although FSV techniques can offer solutions to many of these problems, various aspects of the MPI framework, such as dynamic changes in message buffer size, and the scale of typical MPI programs present substantial obstacles to the successful application of FSV methods. In this paper, we have applied FSV techniques to a small, but realistic, example of a parallel scientific program using MPI in order to check some properties of interest to the program-mer. We have shown how to model some of the problematic MPI communication constructs, and we have described some theoretical results that simplify the ver-ification process.

For small configurations of the MPI program, both SPIN and INCA could verify the two properties that hold and found counterexamples for the one that did not. The programmer was surprised that **GlobalLockstep** was violated, but the violation can occur only when at least one dimension of the grid is greater than three and messages are buffered, making the system big enough to be hard to reason about informally (although certainly tiny by MPI standards). We do not attach much significance to the fact that INCA could do larger configurations than SPIN. Although we regard ourselves as reasonably skilled SPIN users, we are certainly more expert in applying INCA. It may well be that there are more efficient ways to model the MPI constructs in Promela, or that different settings would significantly improve the performance of SPIN. In any case, it would be foolish to generalize very far on the basis of analysis of a single program.

Although MPI programs like the examples described here exhibit significant symmetry, we do not expect substantial gains from applying standard symmetry methods in model checking. The problem is that these methods cannot reduce the state space by a factor of more than the order of the symmetry group, and the growth of the symmetry group does not keep pace with the growth of the state space as the systems are scaled up. Compositional methods, on the other hand, might very well allow for collapsing the system to some minimal config-uration, depending on the property being checked, and we hope to investigate this approach in the future.

Our theoretical results help simplify the verification and suggest that other results tailored to the MPI domain may increase the range of MPI programs to which FSV techniques may be effectively applied. We plan to extend our investigation to the more general cases of programs making use of wildcard receives, non-blocking sends and receives, and the MPI collective operations. It will also be important to find appropriate abstractions for programs where the values of floating point data affect the flow of control.

We thank Andrew Siegel for supplying the Diffusion2d example and for many discussions of the problems of developing MPI-based scientific software. We are also grateful to Ewing Lusk for clarifying some of the more complicated parts of the MPI Standard and for encouraging this work. This research was partially supported by the U. S. Army Research Laboratory and the U. S. Army Research Office under agreement number DAAD190110564.

References

1. Bollig, B., Leucker, M.: Modelling, specifying, and verifying message passing systems. In Bettini, C., Montanari, A., eds.: Proceedings of the Symposium on Temporal Representation and Reasoning (TIME'01), IEEE Computer Society Press (2001) 240–248
2. Cohen, E., Lamport, L.: Reduction in TLA. In Sangiorgi, D., de Simone, R., eds.: CONCUR '98. Volume 1466 of LNCS., Nice, Springer-Verlag (1998) 317–331
3. Corbett, J.C., Avrunin, G.S.: Using integer programming to verify general safety and liveness properties. Formal Methods in System Design **6** (1995) 97–123
4. Flanagan, C., Qadeer, S.: A type and effect system for atomicity. In Cytron, R., Gupta, R., eds.: Proceedings of the ACM SIGPLAN 2003 Conference on Programming Language Design and Implementation, San Diego, ACM Press (2003) 338–349
5. Georgelin, P., Pierre, L., Nguyen, T.: A formal specification of the MPI primitives and communication mechanisms. Technical Report 1999-337, LIM (1999)
6. Gropp, W., Huss-Lederman, S., Lumsdaine, A., Lusk, E., Nitzberg, B., Saphir, W., Snir, M.: MPI—The Complete Reference: Volume 2, the MPI Extensions. MIT Press, Cambridge, MA (1998)
7. Holzmann, G.J.: The SPIN Model Checker. Addison-Wesley, Boston (2004)
8. Lipton, R.J.: Reduction: A method of proving properties of parallel programs. Communications of the ACM **18** (1975) 717–721
9. Manohar, R., Martin, A.J.: Slack elasticity in concurrent computing. In Jeuring, J., ed.: Proceedings of the Fourth International Conference on the Mathematics of Program Construction. Volume 1422 of LNCS., Marstrand, Sweden, Springer-Verlag (1998) 272–285
10. Matlin, O.S., Lusk, E., McCune, W.: SPINning parallel systems software. In Bonaki, D., Leue, S., eds.: Model Checking of Software: 9th International SPIN Workshop. Volume 2318 of LNCS., Grenoble, Springer-Verlag (2002) 213–220
11. Mazurkiewicz, A.: Trace theory. In Brauer, W., Reisig, W., Rozenberg, G., eds.: Petri Nets: Applications and Relationships to Other Models of Concurrency. Volume 255 of LNCS., Berlin, Springer-Verlag (1987) 279–324
12. Meenakshi, B., Ramanujam, R.: Reasoning about message passing in finite state environments. In Montanari, U., Rolim, J.D.P., Welzl, E., eds.: Automata, Languages and Programming, 27th International Colloquium, ICALP 2000. Volume 1853 of LNCS., Geneva, Springer-Verlag (2000) 487–498
13. Message-Passing Interface Standard 2.0. http://www.mpi-forum.org/docs (1997)
14. Siegel, S.F.: The INCA query language. Technical Report UM-CS-2002-18, Department of Computer Science, University of Massachusetts (2002)
15. Siegel, S.F., Avrunin, G.S.: Improving the precision of INCA by eliminating solutions with spurious cycles. IEEE Transactions on Software Engineering **28** (2002) 115–128
16. Siegel, S.F., Avrunin, G.S.: Analysis of MPI programs. Technical Report UM-CS-2003-036, Department of Computer Science, University of Massachusetts (2003)
17. Snir, M., Otto, S., Huss-Lederman, S., Walker, D., Dongarra, J.: MPI—The Complete Reference: Volume 1, The MPI Core. 2 edn. MIT Press, Cambridge, MA (1998)

Advanced SPIN Tutorial

Theo C. Ruys[1] and Gerard J. Holzmann[2]

[1] Department of Computer Science, University of Twente.
P.O. Box 217, 7500 AE Enschede, The Netherlands.
http://www.cs.utwente.nl/~ruys/
[2] NASA/JPL, Laboratory for Reliable Software.
4800 Oak Grove Drive, Pasadena, CA 91109, USA.
http://spinroot.com/gerard/

Abstract. SPIN [9] is a model checker for the verification of distributed systems software. The tool is freely distributed, and often described as one of the most widely used verification systems. The Advanced SPIN Tutorial is a *sequel* to [7] and is targeted towards intermediate to advanced SPIN users.

1 Introduction

SPIN [2,3,4,5,9] supports the formal verification of distributed systems code. The software was developed at Bell Labs in the formal methods and verification group starting in 1980. SPIN is freely distributed, and often described as one of the most widely used verification systems. It is estimated that between 5,000 and 10,000 people routinely use SPIN. SPIN was awarded the ACM Software System Award for 2001 [1].

The automata-theoretic foundation for SPIN is laid by [10]. The very recent [5] describes SPIN 4.0, the latest version of the tool.

The SPIN software is written in standard ANSI C, and is portable across all versions of the UNIX operating system, including Mac OS X. It can also be compiled to run on any standard PC running Linux or Microsoft Windows.

2 Tutorial

The Advanced SPIN Tutorial is a *sequel* to [7] and is targeted towards intermediate to advanced SPIN users. The objective of the Advanced SPIN Tutorial is to (further) educate the SPIN 2004 attendees on model checking technology in general and SPIN in particular.

The tutorial starts with a brief overview of the latest additions to PROMELA, the specification language of SPIN. General patterns are discussed to contruct efficient PROMELA models and how to use SPIN in the most effective way [6]. Topics to be discussed include: SPIN's optimisation algorithms, directives and options to tune verification runs with SPIN and guidelines for effective PROMELA modelling, e.g. invariance, atomicity, modelling time, lossy channels, fairness, optimisation problems [8].

S. Graf and L. Mounier (Eds.): SPIN 2004, LNCS 2989, pp. 304–305, 2004.

The second part of the tutorial looks in more detail at the theoretical underpinnings of SPIN, and discusses some of its more recent applications to the verification of implementation level systems code, using model extraction techniques. Also basic and more advanced abstraction techniques for building SPIN models will be presented, and some examples of large applications of SPIN based logic model checking. Topics to be discussed include: automata theoretic verification, model construction, abstraction and extraction, and application studies.

After the tutorial, attendees should:

- be able to construct (more) efficient and effective PROMELA models;
- be able to formulate effective properties that can be checked with SPIN;
- have a basic understanding of the theory and algorithms that make SPIN work efficiently;
- have a good understanding of the importance of abstraction in model construction;
- understand how and when verification models can be extracted from implementation level source code.

References

1. ACM Software Systems Awards. URL: http://www.acm.org/awards/ssaward.html.
2. G. J. Holzmann. *Design and Validation of Computer Protocols*. Prentice Hall, Englewood Cliffs, New Jersey, USA, 1991.
3. G. J. Holzmann. SPIN Model Checking - Reliable Design of Concurrent Software. *Dr. Dobb's Journal*, pages 92–97, October 1997.
4. G. J. Holzmann. The Model Checker SPIN. *IEEE Transactions on Software Engineering*, 23(5):279–295, May 1997.
5. G. J. Holzmann. *The SPIN Model Checker – Primer and Reference Manual*. Addison-Wesley, Boston, Massachusetts, USA, 2004.
6. T. C. Ruys. *Towards Effective Model Checking*. PhD thesis, University of Twente, Enschede, The Netherlands, March 2001. *Available from the author's homepage*.
7. T. C. Ruys. SPIN Tutorial: How to become a SPIN Doctor. In D. Bosnacki and S. Leue, editors, *Model Checking of Software, Proc. of the 9th Int. SPIN Workshop (SPIN 2002)*, volume 2318 of *LNCS*, pages 6–13, Grenoble, France, April 2002.
8. T. C. Ruys. Optimal Scheduling Using Branch and Bound with SPIN 4.0. In T. Ball and S. K. Rajamani, editors, *Model Checking of Software, Proc. of the 10th Int. SPIN Workshop (SPIN 2003)*, volume 2648 of *LNCS*, pages 1–17, Portland, Oregon, USA, May 2003.
9. SPIN Homepage. URL: http://spinroot.com/spin/.
10. M. Y. Vardi and P. Wolper. An Automatic-Theoretic Approach to Automatic Program Verification. In *Proc. of the First IEEE Symposium on Logic In Computer Science (LICS'86)*, pages 322–331, Cambridge, UK, June 1986.

IF Validation Environment Tutorial

Marius Bozga, Susanne Graf, Laurent Mounier, and Iulian Ober

VERIMAG, Centre Equation, 2 avenue de Vignate, F-38610 Gières
http://www-verimag.imag.fr/~async/IF

1 Introduction

IF[3,7] is an open validation platform for asynchronous timed systems developed at Verimag during the last 5 years.

The toolbox is built upon a specification language based on communicating extended timed automata supporting various communication primitives and dynamic process creation and destruction. This language is expressive enough to represent most useful concepts of modeling and programming languages for distributed systems (like SDL, UML, Java, ...)

The core of the toolbox consists of a set of model-based validation components including exhaustive/interactive simulation, on-the-fly temporal logic model-checking, test case generation and optimal path extraction. In order to control state explosion, the toolbox provides several static analysis tools operating at the source level such as live variable analysis, dead-code elimination and slicing. Finally, the toolbox is connected to commercial environments (such as Rational Rose, Rhapsody, Objecteering, Object Geode) and may be used for validating SDL and UML specifications [1,6].

The toolbox has been successfully applied on several case studies including telecommunication protocols, distributed algorithms, real-time controllers, manufacturing, asynchronous circuits [2,5,4].

2 Objectives

The objectives of this tutorial are first, to give a complete presentation of the main functionalities of the IF validation environment, and second, to show how this environment can be used to experiment on new model-checking techniques.

Expected attendees are people interested in model-checking techniques, either from an (experienced) user or from a tool designer or researcher point of view.

3 Summary of Material

In this tutorial, we will guide participants trough the concepts and the use of the IF language and the associated tools. More precisely, we will focus on the following items:

S. Graf and L. Mounier (Eds.): SPIN 2004, LNCS 2989, pp. 306–307, 2004.
© Springer-Verlag Berlin Heidelberg 2004

Language: In the first part we will provide a survey of the main concepts of the IF language. We will focus on both functional features (structure, communication, dynamic creation, external code integration) and non-functional ones (real-time primitives, resource management, priorities). Moreover, we will show how to express properties on IF specifications by means of dedicated observers.

Core tools: In this second part we will introduce the toolbox architecture and its main components. We will describe the two main APIs: the syntax level API (abstract syntax tree) and the semantic level API (state graph). Among the tools, we will focus on the static analyser and some of the model based tools (e.g, model checker, test generator, optimal path extractor).

Front-ends and applications: Finally, the third part will be dedicated to existing front-ends to SDL and UML. It will also give an overview of the most relevant case studies handled with the IF toolbox.

The tutorial will be illustrated with examples, on-line demos and comparisons with other related tool environments (Spin, CADP, Kronos, Uppaal, etc). Participants will receive CDs with the latest version of the IF toolbox and an example repository including the examples used in the tutorial.

References

1. M. Bozga, J.Cl. Fernandez, L. Ghirvu, S. Graf, J.P. Krimm, L. Mounier, and J. Sifakis. IF: An Intermediate Representation for SDL and its Applications. In R. Dssouli, G. Bochmann, and Y. Lahav, editors, *Proceedings of SDL FORUM'99 (Montreal, Canada)*, pages 423–440. Elsevier, June 1999.
2. M. Bozga, S. Graf, and L. Mounier. Automated Validation of Distributed Software using the IF Environment. In *Workshop on Software Model-Checking*, volume 55. TCS, July 2001.
3. M. Bozga, S. Graf, and L. Mounier. If-2.0: A validation environment for component-based real-time systems. In K.G. Larsen Ed Brinksma, editor, *Proceedings of CAV'02 (Copenhagen, Denmark)*, volume 2404 of *LNCS*, pages 343–348. Springer, July 2002.
4. M. Bozga, D. Lesens, and L. Mounier. Model-Checking Ariane-5 Flight Program. In *Proceedings of FMICS'01 (Paris, France)*, pages 211–227. INRIA, 2001.
5. S. Graf and G. Jia. Verification Experiments on the Mascara Protocol. In *Proceedings of the SPIN'01 Workshop (Toronto, Canada)*, volume 2057 of *LNCS*. Springer, 2001. ISBN 3-540-42124-6.
6. Iulian Ober, Susanne Graf, and Ileana Ober. Validating timed uml models by simulation and verification. In *Proceedings of the SVERTS'03 Workshop (satellite of UML'03 Conference), San Francisco, California*, 2003.
7. VERIMAG/DCS. If web page. http://www.verimag.imag.fr/~async/IF.

Author Index

Lecture Notes in Computer Science

For information about Vols. 1–2876

please contact your bookseller or Springer-Verlag

Vol. 2934: G. Lindemann, D. Moldt, M. Paolucci (Eds.), Regulated Agent-Based Social Systems. X, 301 pages. 2004. (Subseries LNAI).

Vol. 2930: F. Winkler (Ed.), Automated Deduction in Geometry. VII, 231 pages. 2004. (Subseries LNAI).

Vol. 2926: L. van Elst, V. Dignum, A. Abecker (Eds.), Agent-Mediated Knowledge Management. XI, 428 pages. 2004. (Subseries LNAI).

Vol. 2923: V. Lifschitz, I. Niemelä (Eds.), Logic Programming and Nonmonotonic Reasoning. IX, 365 pages. 2004. (Subseries LNAI).

Vol. 2919: E. Giunchiglia, A. Tacchella (Eds.), Theory and Applications of Satisfiability Testing. XI, 530 pages. 2004.

Vol. 2917: E. Quintarelli, Model-Checking Based Data Retrieval. XVI, 134 pages. 2004.

Vol. 2916: C. Palamidessi (Ed.), Logic Programming. XII, 520 pages. 2003.

Vol. 2915: A. Camurri, G. Volpe (Eds.), Gesture-Based Communication in Human-Computer Interaction. XIII, 558 pages. 2004. (Subseries LNAI).

Vol. 2914: P.K. Pandya, J. Radhakrishnan (Eds.), FST TCS 2003: Foundations of Software Technology and Theoretical Computer Science. XIII, 446 pages. 2003.

Vol. 2913: T.M. Pinkston, V.K. Prasanna (Eds.), High Performance Computing - HiPC 2003. XX, 512 pages. 2003. (Subseries LNAI).

Vol. 2911: T.M.T. Sembok, H.B. Zaman, H. Chen, S.R. Urs, S.H. Myaeng (Eds.), Digital Libraries: Technology and Management of Indigenous Knowledge for Global Access. XX, 703 pages. 2003.

Vol. 2910: M.E. Orlowska, S. Weerawarana, M.M.P. Papazoglou, J. Yang (Eds.), Service-Oriented Computing - ICSOC 2003. XIV, 576 pages. 2003.

Vol. 2909: R. Solis-Oba, K. Jansen (Eds.), Approximation and Online Algorithms. VIII, 269 pages. 2004.

Vol. 2909: K. Jansen, R. Solis-Oba (Eds.), Approximation and Online Algorithms. VIII, 269 pages. 2004.

Vol. 2908: K. Chae, M. Yung (Eds.), Information Security Applications. XII, 506 pages. 2004.

Vol. 2907: I. Lirkov, S. Margenov, J. Wasniewski, P. Yalamov (Eds.), Large-Scale Scientific Computing. XI, 490 pages. 2004.

Vol. 2906: T. Ibaraki, N. Katoh, H. Ono (Eds.), Algorithms and Computation. XVII, 748 pages. 2003.

Vol. 2905: A. Sanfeliu, J. Ruiz-Shulcloper (Eds.), Progress in Pattern Recognition, Speech and Image Analysis. XVII, 693 pages. 2003.

Vol. 2904: T. Johansson, S. Maitra (Eds.), Progress in Cryptology - INDOCRYPT 2003. XI, 431 pages. 2003.

Vol. 2903: T.D. Gedeon, L.C.C. Fung (Eds.), AI 2003: Advances in Artificial Intelligence. XVI, 1075 pages. 2003. (Subseries LNAI).

Vol. 2902: F.M. Pires, S.P. Abreu (Eds.), Progress in Artificial Intelligence. XV, 504 pages. 2003. (Subseries LNAI).

Vol. 2901: F. Bry, N. Henze, J. Ma luszyński (Eds.), Principles and Practice of Semantic Web Reasoning. X, 209 pages. 2003.

Vol. 2900: M. Bidoit, P.D. Mosses (Eds.), Casl User Manual. XIII, 240 pages. 2004.

Vol. 2899: G. Ventre, R. Canonico (Eds.), Interactive Multimedia on Next Generation Networks. XIV, 420 pages. 2003.

Vol. 2898: K.G. Paterson (Ed.), Cryptography and Coding. IX, 385 pages. 2003.

Vol. 2897: O. Balet, G. Subsol, P. Torguet (Eds.), Virtual Storytelling. XI, 240 pages. 2003.

Vol. 2896: V.A. Saraswat (Ed.), Advances in Computing Science - ASIAN 2003. VIII, 305 pages. 2003.

Vol. 2895: A. Ohori (Ed.), Programming Languages and Systems. XIII, 427 pages. 2003.

Vol. 2894: C.S. Laih (Ed.), Advances in Cryptology - ASIACRYPT 2003. XIII, 543 pages. 2003.

Vol. 2893: J.-B. Stefani, I. Demeure, D. Hagimont (Eds.), Distributed Applications and Interoperable Systems. XIII, 311 pages. 2003.

Vol. 2892: F. Dau, The Logic System of Concept Graphs with Negation. XI, 213 pages. 2003. (Subseries LNAI).

Vol. 2891: J. Lee, M. Barley (Eds.), Intelligent Agents and Multi-Agent Systems. X, 215 pages. 2003. (Subseries LNAI).

Vol. 2890: M. Broy, A.V. Zamulin (Eds.), Perspectives of System Informatics. XV, 572 pages. 2003.

Vol. 2889: R. Meersman, Z. Tari (Eds.), On The Move to Meaningful Internet Systems 2003: OTM 2003 Workshops. XIX, 1071 pages. 2003.

Vol. 2888: R. Meersman, Z. Tari, D.C. Schmidt (Eds.), On The Move to Meaningful Internet Systems 2003: CoopIS, DOA, and ODBASE. XXI, 1546 pages. 2003.

Vol. 2887: T. Johansson (Ed.), Fast Software Encryption. IX, 397 pages. 2003.

Vol. 2886: I. Nyström, G. Sanniti di Baja, S. Svensson (Eds.), Discrete Geometry for Computer Imagery. XII, 556 pages. 2003.

Vol. 2885: J.S. Dong, J. Woodcock (Eds.), Formal Methods and Software Engineering. XI, 683 pages. 2003.

Vol. 2884: E. Najm, U. Nestmann, P. Stevens (Eds.), Formal Methods for Open Object-Based Distributed Systems. X, 293 pages. 2003.

Vol. 2883: J. Schaeffer, M. Müller, Y. Björnsson (Eds.), Computers and Games. XI, 431 pages. 2003.

Vol. 2882: D. Veit, Matchmaking in Electronic Markets. XV, 180 pages. 2003. (Subseries LNAI).

Vol. 2881: E. Horlait, T. Magedanz, R.H. Glitho (Eds.), Mobile Agents for Telecommunication Applications. IX, 297 pages. 2003.

Vol. 2880: H.L. Bodlaender (Ed.), Graph-Theoretic Concepts in Computer Science. XI, 386 pages. 2003.

Vol. 2879: R.E. Ellis, T.M. Peters (Eds.), Medical Image Computing and Computer-Assisted Intervention - MICCAI 2003. XXXIV, 1003 pages. 2003.

Vol. 2878: R.E. Ellis, T.M. Peters (Eds.), Medical Image Computing and Computer-Assisted Intervention - MICCAI 2003. XXXIII, 819 pages. 2003.

Vol. 2877: T. Böhme, G. Heyer, H. Unger (Eds.), Innovative Internet Community Systems. VIII, 263 pages. 2003.